The Next Wave of Technologies

Opportunities from Chaos

PHIL SIMON

WILEY

John Wiley & Sons, Inc.

Published by John Wiley & Sons, Inc., Hoboken, New Jersey.
Published simultaneously in Canada.

For general information on our other products and services or for technical support, please contact our Customer Care Department within the United States at (800) 762-2974, outside the United States at (317) 572-3993 or fax (317) 572-4002.

Wiley also publishes its books in a variety of electronic formats. Some content that appears in print may not be available in electronic books. For more information about Wiley products, visit our web site at www.wiley.com.

Library of Congress Cataloging-in-Publication Data:

Simon, Phil.
   The next wave of technologies : opportunities from chaos / Phil Simon.
      p. cm.
   Includes bibliographical references and index.
   ISBN 978-0-470-58750-8 (cloth)
1. Information technology–Management. 2. Technological innovation–Management.
3. Computer systems–Management. 4. Cloud computing. I.   Title.
   HD30.2.S577 2010
   004.068–dc22   2009046294

Printed in the United States of America

10 9 8 7 6 5 4 3 2 1

Contents

Foreword

A primary lesson of history is that periodically, and often at the most inconvenient times, society needs to make a sharp break with old habits and deliberately learn new ways of behaving.

Nicholas Imparato and Oren Harari, *Jumping the Curve*

In his May 2003 *Harvard Business Review* article, "Why IT Doesn't Matter," editor-at-large Nicholas Carr proclaimed that information systems had become a commodity. You could almost hear the teeth of chief information officers (CIOs) grinding en masse as they read Carr's assertion that "the most lavish spenders on IT rarely post the best results." Carr went on to quote Oracle founder Larry Ellison, who in a rare moment of circumspection admitted that "most companies spend too much [on information technology] and get very little return."

That same year Nucleus Research, a small Massachusetts market research firm, contacted 66 reference customers of Siebel Systems to discover the true business benefits of Customer Relationship Management (CRM) software. These customers had been quoted in various Siebel marketing testimonials as satisfied reference customers. But when Nucleus contacted them, 61 percent admitted that they had yet to realize any significant return on investment from CRM.

Fast forward to 2009, and you would think that the glory days of information technology would be a distant memory. But think again. Corporate boards continue to pressure executive teams to drive revenues and contain costs. Executives are up at night dreaming of new ways to innovate. Business people are being asked to do more with less. And IT people know in their gut that there are better ways of working and that there are emerging technologies that can help.

In my work as a management consultant for Global 2000 firms, I listen to business and IT executives wring their hands and bemoan shrinking budgets and increased expectations. Here are some examples that might sound familiar:

- 'I've got too many balls in the air. I'm trying to get more organized and get my arms around some of these new technologies that will supposedly show me how to work smarter. But I haven't even had time to load new music onto my iPod. So how am I supposed to have time to research emerging technologies?"

- "The CEO (chief executive officer) keeps telling me that marketing should lead the firm's innovation initiatives. He says that as the CMO (chief marketing officer) I need to keep differentiating the company through new ways of doing business. But I'm being measured on my P&L (profit and loss), not on my Big Ideas—which, by the way, haven't really been rolling up to my doorstep."

- "Between you and me, I'm afraid for my job. Our two largest competitors have just cut their IT budgets by sending key functions 'into the cloud,' and my boss has asked me twice about my SaaS software as a service strategy. I'm not even completely sure what the cloud is, let alone what to send to it. Where do I start?"

- "I've begun quantifying the value of business intelligence for my company. It could save us thousands of staff hours of data collection. It could get our line managers the reports they've been begging for. And it could actually help us collect more information about our best customers. But if I can't show how it directly drives revenues, no one wants to hear about it. I'm not going to bother."

- "At every executive team meeting someone's talking about social networking. If I had a dime for every time the word 'community' was used around here I could just quit right now. The irony about all the social media buzzwords is how political this company is. Half the executives won't even speak to the other half. Communities? Give me a break! Trying to adopt social media in this place would be hypocrisy!"

- "You're going to think I'm crazy, but could you just get me someone who will come in once a week and talk to me about what other companies are working on?"

Each of these is a true story. And each story reflects the desperation for time and knowledge that's confronting managers across geographies, industries, and corporate cultures. We not only have to do more with less. We have to find the time to innovate new ways of doing more with less. The paradox is almost palpable.

It turns out that rumors of IT's demise might have been greatly exaggerated. Nicholas Carr's argument, with its focus on commodity hardware and keep-the-lights-on infrastructure, was that IT was just table stakes. As soon as one company adopted a new technology, its competitors would follow suit, in effect continuing an environment of functional parity. Cynical? By half. Subversive? Perhaps. Accurate? It depends.

In the preface to his subsequent book, *Does IT Matter?* Carr does nod his head to the fact that how technology is actually used does make a difference. "Indeed," he says, "as the strategic value of the technology fades, the skill with which it is used on a day-to-day basis may well become even more important to a company's success." Carr is in fact making what should have been his central point: that while IT in a vacuum is indeed inconsequential, it's the application of the technology that provides the edge.

True, sometimes the best CRM is a friendly greeting when the shopper enters the store. But sometimes it's the fact that the coupons she carries in her recyclable tote are the result of her propensity to buy a certain set of high-margin products and fill her basket with profitable merchandise mix. Maybe we sent her a link to download those coupons via social media, and maybe we keep information about her preferences and purchase behaviors as part of our business intelligence program. The essence of our customer retention strategy is to get the customer back into the store (or to the casino, the branch, the hotel, the airplane, the web site, the catalog, or the agent's office). We don't need technology to greet our customer with a warm hello. But we do need it to beat our competitors to the punch.

Indeed, any strategic value from IT will blossom as it's used to enable unique and innovative business initiatives. In a rebuttal to Carr's article in the *Harvard Business Review*, authors John Seely Brown and John Hagel III wrote, "In short, many executives have started to view IT as a commodity because they have not thought aggressively enough about how IT can bring about new business practices. The differentiation is not in IT itself but in the new practices it enables."

To that end, Phil Simon and his contributors have written a timely and important book. *The Next Wave in Technologies: Opportunities from Chaos* is a veritable toolbox of the solutions our companies will be using to enable the next set of competitive and strategic business practices.

The voices in these pages are no less authoritative than their messages. Indeed, Phil has assembled a virtual panel of the best experts on the hottest IT topics, and they weigh in with practical, real-world advice about adoption and execution. Experts like Dalton Cervo (Chapter 12), established in my field of data integration and business intelligence, is an old friend. And I'm a recent convert to Michael Krigsman's blog and a fan of his writing on project failures (Chapter 19). Because of Phil, though, there are now some fresh points of view in my field of vision, like Heather Meeker's trenchant take on open source (Chapter 5) and Jay Miletsky's fresh perspective on the piping-hot topic of social media (Chapter 10).

They'll take your hand and guide you toward a fuller understanding their technical specialties, often with a refreshing and eminently readable irreverence. (Phil's own sections are ripe with fun references, and I love the title of one Amy Wohl section, "A Cloud of One's Own.") Ultimately, Phil and his contributors will help you make the pitch, secure the commitment, and move forward with a solution that's not only useful but transcends the buzzwords, the noise, and yes, the chaos to drive business value.

As with local branch banking, insurance agents, the family farm, and doctors who make house calls (aka home health care), IT is being taken seriously once again. Maybe, just maybe, it matters after all.

Jill Dyche
October 2009

Preface

Any sufficiently advanced technology is indistinguishable from magic.
> Arthur C. Clarke (1917–2008), *Profiles of the Future*,
> 1961 (Clarke's third law)

In February 2009, I published my first book, *Why New Systems Fail*. For a variety of reasons, I felt that the time was right for the book. Having worked on so many poorly conceived and terribly run projects in my career, it was painfully clear to me that there was something fundamentally wrong with most organizations' attempts to implement enterprise systems. My 11 years working on different information technology (IT) projects in different countries and industries almost invariably resulted in the same outcome each time: some type of failure.

However, in a way the title was a bit of a misnomer. The book referenced systems that were, for the most part, actually very mature; they were only new to the organizations implementing them. *Why New Systems Fail* addressed systems, software vendors, consultancies, and implementation methodologies that have, in large part, been in existence for over 20 years. Indeed, nascent Enterprise Resource Planning (ERP) organizations such as SAP and PeopleSoft were founded in 1972 and 1987, respectively, although Gartner Research is credited with introducing the term *ERP* in 1990.

Twenty years is an eternity in the world of technology. Still, many enterprise system implementations failed. I found this vexing. There are many attributes conducive to success: generous IT budgets, relatively mature applications, consulting firms with significant expertise, and thousands of previous projects to serve as examples and cautionary tales.

Against this backdrop, I could no longer claim that I just had a string of bad luck as a consultant. Something was broken, and I wanted to see if I could write a jargon-free, generally well-received book demystifying a process plagued by a 60 percent failure rate. While the first edition of the book was certainly not perfect, I believe that I succeeded in that regard.

Reviews for the book were largely positive. On his well-regarded Deal Architect blog,[1] Vinnie Mirchandani agreed with the general tenets of the book but asked a number of completely valid questions: "Where are the newer issues with mobile interfaces? Where are RSS feeds? How will clouds affect ERP infrastructure planning?"

Admittedly, *Why New Systems Fail* largely ignored these newer technologies. Without being defensive, the book focused for the most part on enterprise systems. I told Vinnie that it is hard to imagine a book of any reasonable length that addresses every conceivable type of technology.

I started thinking about why organizations have been so reluctant to embrace these technologies. (I had a decent amount of time, as consulting work in 2009 had dropped off.) Yes, many organizations had reduced their IT budgets and head counts as a result of the Great Recession. Still, I suspected that something else was going on. I didn't see the economy as the major factor in explaining why so many organizations have dragged their feet on clearly beneficial technologies. Many of these technologies were readily available and relatively mature well *before* the meltdown.

While exceptions abound, the answer was that the burnt hand teaches best. In other words, many organizations' attempts to implement and utilize new technologies have failed—and spectacularly at that. As a result, they are hesitant to adopt new ones—even when the benefits of these new technologies are so significant.

Technologies such as software as a service (SaaS), social networking, open source (OS), and cloud computing are relatively recent phenomena. Most suffer from a dearth of implementation methodologies and (successful) examples from which to learn. A high failure rate on these types of projects can be understood, if not expected, at least for the near future. Against this backdrop, what does this say about the ability of most organizations to successfully implement newer, much less understood technologies? In many ways, these technologies are the antitheses of the ones discussed in *Why New Systems Fail*. It shouldn't be surprising that many organizations aren't exactly waiting in line to fall on their faces.

I started thinking about the need for a book that would address the essentials, best practices, and pitfalls of these exciting new technologies. Wouldn't a book like this be beneficial to C-level executives unsure about what to do and how to do it? A busy chief information officer (CIO) could read this book and walk away with a much deeper, practical understanding of these new concepts. That same CIO might walk into work the next day and ask, "Why aren't we doing this?"

---

[1] See http://dealarchitect.typepad.com/deal_architect/2009/05/deja-vu—all-over-again .html.

It sounded great, but I could not write such a book alone—and I consider myself a pretty smart guy. (With age comes wisdom, I suppose.) It would take me at least a solid year to research each one of these topics and write a succinct and penetrating chapter on each. Writing for C-level executives, this wouldn't be an easy task. Technology changes so quickly these days that what I wrote one day would, in all likelihood, be very different in a few years.

Time wasn't the only factor, though. I put myself in the shoes of a CIO hesitant about using OS applications, for instance. It was entirely reasonable for that CIO to want to know my OS credentials before reading what I had to write, much less trusting my recommendations and making key business decisions based on them. If I were going to do this book the right way, I would need help and lots of it. Why not surround myself with really smart people?

I started contacting friends who had expertise in these very technologies. Not all of my friends work in the technology world, so I started networking online. God bless LinkedIn. Most people thought that I had a good idea for a book and signed on, some within a few minutes. More than a few were willing to contribute, but they had other commitments and my time frame was a deal breaker. By June 2009, though, I realized that this book was going to become a reality.

My primary challenge on this book would be much different than that of its predecessor—mainly writing thousands of words and organizing them in a logical fashion. Prolific author Bob Charette (who wrote Chapter 15 on enterprise risk management) told me that survey books like this tended to suffer from a number of problems. (Always stubborn, I was convinced that I could avoid or at least minimize them.) First, the messages and writing styles of each contributor are usually very different. I have taken great pains to ensure that there is a good deal of flow and consistency throughout the book, even though the contributors' backgrounds, native languages, and areas of expertise are hardly identical.

Second, many compilation books lack integration. Make no mistake here: Because many of the book's technologies are completely independent of one other, each chapter certainly does *not* overlap with all of the others. By the same token, however, themes such as IT management, data integrity, enterprise architecture, and the like are not confined to any one chapter; they permeate the book. As such, the book's chapters are anything but islands.

More than content overlap, however, I felt the need to ensure a generally consistent message throughout the book. In selecting the contributors for this project, I ensured that everyone was on the same page with regard to the book's overall philosophy. Everyone understood that this is a management book first and an IT book second. Cool technology is fine and dandy, but I did not want chapters rife with unrealistic, pie-in-the-sky recommendations.

The material had to be rooted in the day-to-day realities of the current business world. This book is a practitioner's guide, not an academic text.

Third, many survey books leave readers wondering, "Now what do I do?" In that vein, the end of each chapter provides "next steps." These are key points and questions designed to help the reader ask the right questions within the organization.

Finally, this book knows its limitations. It does not aim to be a how-to guide for implementing any specific technology, much less every one. Rather, because each subject is written by a very knowledgeable practitioner, the book distills the best practices and identifies the pitfalls and land mines of each topic. Those looking for more detail can pick up more comprehensive texts, often written by the very same people who wrote that chapter.

Objectives of This Book

The goal of the book is to help organizations understand the intersection of people, business, and these new technologies in a concise manner. It collates a number of independent points of view on emerging technologies from prominent senior executives, authors, IT practitioners, journalists, thought leaders, and pundits. Specific technologies and topics include:

- Agile software development (SD)
- Business intelligence (BI)
- Cloud computing
- Enterprise 2.0 project failure
- Enterprise risk management (ERM)
- Enterprise search and retrieval (ESR)
- Green IT
- Master data management (MDM)
- Mobile applications
- Open source (OS) software
- Procure-to-pay (P2P)
- Service-oriented architecture (SOA)
- Social networking
- Software as a service (SaaS)

The book endeavors to provide extensive insights, advice, and best practices regarding promising technologies that have yet to be fully understood—much less utilized—in most organizations. More than a theoretical text, it examines how organizations can and should introduce these new technologies, with specific emphases on lessons learned and people and management issues.

Book Layout

The chapters in this book are grouped into five parts.

Part I: Introduction, Background, and Definitions

The first few chapters lay the foundation for the rest of the book, providing a background against which these massive changes can be viewed. This part provides a framework in which organizations can assess the threats and opportunities created by these disruptive technologies.

Part II: Architecture, Software Development, and Frameworks

The second part of the book deals with the vast changes taking place in the way in which organizations develop, run, and integrate their core applications. This is hardly the first tectonic shift in technology, nor will it be the last.

Twenty years ago, client-server applications gradually began to replace bulky mainframes, allowing for distributing computing. In the late 1990s, the Internet and virtual private networks (VPNs) allowed end users to access corporate information from a browser, whether they were in the office or not. Now seismic shifts in system architecture and application developments are taking place with the advent and increasing adoption of SOA, cloud computing, mobile computing, SaaS, and the like.

Part III: Data, Information, and Knowledge

Corporate applications, databases, and systems have always existed—in large part—to create, store, and retrieve data information. While this raison d'être has not changed in recent years, there have been sea changes in the past five years with regard to the information stored in these systems.

The types of information generated today no longer exclusively fit neatly into orderly databases (if they ever did). The massive growth of the Internet, mobile phones and applications, blogs, social networks, wikis, mashups, videocentric sites such as YouTube, and email have led to a vast increase in the amount of unstructured data. In fact, an estimated 80 percent of all business data is unstructured.[2] These new types of data (along with cheap storage) have resulted in an absolute explosion in the sheer quantity of data available.

---

[2]See http://clarabridge.com/default.aspx?tabid=137&ModuleID=635&ArticleID=551.

Structured data is much easier to store, interpret, and retrieve than unstructured data. Think about the following two questions:

- "How much in travel expenses have we paid this year?"
- "Are our customers satisfied with the quality of our products?"

The first question typically can be answered with a simple report or database query. The second is a much different story. Surveys are helpful, but insightful comments and feedback are typically difficult to analyze. Adding social media and blogging to the mix only complicates matters further.

To the extent that web services create massive amounts of unstructured data, organizations need to employ powerful tools to turn raw data—structured and unstructured—first into information and then, ideally, into knowledge.[3] Unfortunately, few companies have deployed effective tools to organize, interpret, and act upon this surfeit of data. This part of the book addresses the challenges, best practices, and tools available with respect to managing enterprise data.

Part IV: Management and Deployment

Faced with new, powerful, and malleable technologies and a seemingly insurmountable array of data, what is an organization to do? The fourth part of the book focuses on organizations' efforts to make these immense technological changes operational, on seizing opportunity in chaos. While "moving the rock" is important, this part also addresses avoiding undesirable yet common outcomes on IT projects. Insights and best practices are provided for averting IT project failures, minimizing enterprise risk, adopting agile and green IT methods, and overcoming the challenges associated with implementing different types of Enterprise 2.0 technologies.

Part V: Conclusion

The final part briefly summarizes the major themes of the book with an eye on successful adoption of these new technologies. It does not provide all of the answers to any one technology, but summarizes the questions that readers should be asking themselves.

---

[3]Jeff Papows's book *Enterprise.Com: Market Leadership in the Information Age* emphasizes the importance of turning data into knowledge.

Who Should Read This Book?

I have yet to read an IT management book that can be everything to everybody (and I read quite a bit). This book certainly is no exception. While this book has no one intended audience, I have written it with three in mind.

First, this is a book aimed at IT professionals of all levels. CIOs and chief technology officers (CTOs) thinking about utilizing an Enterprise 2.0 technology would be wise to read the corresponding chapter before making the commitment and investment. Below the C-level, IT directors, project managers, and analysts would benefit from the material. Organizations cannot efficiently utilize these technologies without IT staff members effectuating executive decisions.

Second, this is a book many types of students. Specifically, those in MBA and MIS programs will learn a great deal about emerging technologies that they will soon need to learn and use in the workplace.

Finally, management consulting firms and systems integrators can use the insights in this book to assist their clients in optimizing Enterprise 2.0 technologies.

I expect and even encourage readers to read what they like, to use the *New York Times*'s motto. Readers not interested in a particular topic can skip or skim a chapter without fear of missing out. I wrote this book specifically to allow the busy reader to jump around as needed.

—Phil Simon
Caldwell, New Jersey
November 2009

Acknowledgments

This book could not have become a reality without the dedicated efforts of the contributors. Not only did I learn a great deal writing this book, I am pleased to have made new friends as well. In particular, Amy Wohl, Bob Charette, and Heather Meeker served as mentors during the project, saving me a great deal of money on psychiatrists. Tim Burgard, Dexter Gasque, and Stacey Rivera at John Wiley & Sons provided essential guidance. Kim Leonard, David Riccardi and Mitzi Koontz, and David Fugate helped me formulate the book's proposal and navigate the publishing waters.

I also would like to thank my longtime Carnegie Mellon friends Scott Berkun, David Sandberg, Michael Viola, Joe Mirza, and Chris McGee. A tip of the hat to Brian Morgan, Craig Heyrman, Scott Erichsen, Greg Dolecki, Thor Sandell, Michael West, Michael DeAngelo, Jason Horowitz, Andrew Botwin Rob Metting, Rosalinda Cifuentes, MJ Stabinski-Heckman, Jeremy Rothschild, Ellen French, Alex Saint-Victor, Marc Paolella, Jenifer Simon, Naynish Jhaveri, Tom Bardzell, Steve Katz, Mark Hayes, John Henley, Shiri Amram, Ben Lewis, Teri Watkins, Wayne McDermott, Bruce F. Webster, Rose Aulik, Jim Harris, Phil Brown, David Cotter, David Clinart, and Jake Wyant.

My heroes from Dream Theater (Jordan, John, John, Mike, and James) and Rush (Geddy, Alex, and Neil) have given me many years of creative inspiration through their music. Keep on keeping on.

Special thanks go to my parents, Linda and Sandy Simon.

Finally, I would like to thank you, the reader, for buying this book. I'm an independent author and consultant without a marketing team getting my name out there. I rely on people like you to make a living. If you enjoy the book, please recommend it to a friend, post your thoughts on Facebook, LinkedIn, Digg, or Twitter, or contact me at www.philsimonsystems.com/contact.

About the Contributors

Charlie Bess is an HP Fellow who has performed various technical and formal leadership roles throughout his career. Currently, Charlie is the owner of the global architecture capability that aligns EDS's architecture activities for clients with industry standards and methods. He has been the chief technologist for the EDS relationship with a number of large clients, including most recently Kraft Foods. He has also been the chief technologist of EDS's global application delivery organization and started the application portfolio. He has numerous patents pending related to the software development process, knowledge management, and information recovery. Charlie received a BS degree in electrical engineering from Purdue University and a master's degree in business administration from Southern Methodist University. He is currently licensed as a professional engineer in the state of Texas. He is active on Southern Methodist University's MBA associate board, where he acts as mentor and coach for MBA candidates and interfaces regularly with Purdue University's Electrical Engineering school on technology direction. He is also on the executive board of the US-FIRST robotics competition in North Texas and is a senior IEEE member.

Dalton Cervo is the customer data quality lead at Sun Microsystems. He is part of Customer Data Steward and a member of the Customer Data Governance team responsible for defining policies and procedures governing the oversight of master customer data. Dalton has worked at Sun for over eight years. He started as an information technology (IT) software engineer developing Web applications, then moved into IT project management and eventually into the business area as part of the Market and Business Intelligence team. In the past three years, Dalton has led several customer data management efforts, including data collection, cleansing, standardization, enrichment, and hierarchy classification; master data management conversion, consolidation, standardization, and cleansing; and data quality standards, policies, metrics, and monitors. Dalton is a member of the Customer Advisory Board for DataFlux and spoke at the IDEAS conference in 2008 on the topic of customer data metrics. He is an expert panelist and a featured blogger for Data Quality PRO. Prior to Sun, Dalton worked for almost ten years as a software and systems engineer in the aerospace industry in multiple international projects. Dalton is PM certified and has a BS in computer science and an MBA.

Robert N. Charette is a frequent international lecturer and author with nearly 35 years' experience in a wide variety of software, systems, and management positions. He is an internationally acknowledged authority and pioneer in risk management and its use to increase corporate innovation and risk taking. He serves as a senior adviser to a wide variety of international organizations, high-tech consortiums, as well as government departments on the effectiveness, impacts, and rewards/risks of their high-technology programs and policies. He also acts as chief risk consultant to financial organizations and organizations when investments, mergers, or takeovers are considered. Over his career, Robert has been involved in dozens of risk assessments on projects and programs ranging in cost from several million to several billion dollars each. He co-founded the Decision Empowerment Institute with Dr. Brian Hagen in 2007, and founded the ITABHI Corporation, a risk management consultancy, in 1987. He is also on the advisory board of Foundation Ventures, a New York City–based investment firm. He is a Fellow and director of the Enterprise Risk Management and Governance practice for the Cutter Consortium, a Boston-based IT information and research company. He is also a national award-winning contributing editor to IEEE's *Spectrum* magazine, the flagship magazine of the world's largest professional technical society. In 2009, Robert received the IEEE Computer Society's coveted Golden Core Award, which recognizes IEEE Computer Society members for their long-standing membership and outstanding service to the IT community.

Roland Cuellar is vice president at LitheSpeed LLC, a consultancy focused on helping organizations successfully adopt agile and lean methods at the enterprise scale. He has worked with a number of Fortune 500 firms in the deployment of agile methods. He regularly speaks and publishes in a variety of journals and conferences on the topics of enterprise lean and agile, software metrics, and IT portfolio management. Roland has also worked for such organizations as IBM, Lockheed Martin, DHL, and the Baylor College of Medicine. He has a BS in computer science from the University of Houston and an MBA from UCLA, and is a Lean-Six-Sigma Green Belt.

Tushar K. Hazra, PhD, is the president, founder, and CTO of EpitomiOne, a strategic consulting company specializing in enterprise architecture, service-oriented architecture (SOA) deployment, portals, Web services development, model-driven solution delivery, IT governance and service delivery management, and global sourcing strategy facilitation. He is an educator and recognized speaker with 16 years of experience in developing and integrating service-oriented enterprise (SOE) and strategic component–based systems. Before founding EpitomiOne, he served as CTO and vice president of several Fortune 100 companies.

Jason Horowitz is a New York City–based business consultant working with organizations in IT and green technology in areas including global operations, product management, and social media. He also serves on the board of directors for Cultural Heritage Imaging, a nonprofit engaged in development and adoption of practical digital imaging and preservation solutions to save humanity's cultural treasures. From 1997 to 2008, he played a key role in expanding Sun Microsystems, Inc.'s global product development activities: as director of business operations for a California-based division with product development at more than a dozen locations spread across four continents, as founder and director of the organization's St. Petersburg (Russia) software development center, managing Sun's Prague operation, and running an outsourced global engineering program. Prior to joining Sun, Jason worked for the U.S. State Department as a career member of the U.S. Foreign Service. Jason has bachelor's and master's degrees from Columbia University and UCLA, respectively.

Steve King is the head of consulting and architecture for the DMSBT Group. He leads a team of enterprise and solutions architects to provide design, integration, and consulting services to numerous Global 500 organizations and government organizations. Steve has had a lifelong interest in computer systems and began his career as an application programmer. Since then, he has been responsible for the design, development, and management of multimillion-dollar technology projects across the globe. Steve is considered by many to be one of the foremost experts in the Asia-Pacific region on Google Enterprise technologies and is an active contributor to both the Google Developer Community and Google Support Community. Throughout his career, he has been a regular contributor to a variety of open source (OS) projects, and has been an advocate and pioneer in the delivery of business applications through the browser. Steve collaborates regularly with industry leaders from all over the world, keeping them abreast of the latest trends and developments.

Michael Krigsman is the CEO of Asuret, Inc., a consultancy that optimizes organizations' use of technologies. He is a recognized authority on the causes and prevention of IT failures and is frequently quoted in the press on IT project and related CIO issues. He writes a respected and popular blog called IT Project Failures for ZDNet, a unit of CBS News. He is considered an enterprise software industry influencer and provides advice to technology buyers, vendors, and services firms. Previously, Michael served as CEO of Cambridge Publications, which develops tools and processes for software implementations and related business practice automation projects. He has been involved with hundreds of software development projects, for organizations ranging from small start-ups to Fortune 500 organizations. Michael graduated with an MBA from Boston University and a BA from Bard College. He is a board member of the America's Cup Hall of Fame and the Herreshoff Marine Museum in Bristol, Rhode Island.

Heather Meeker is the chair of the IP/IT licensing and transactions group at Greenberg Traurig, LLP. She is one of the leading authorities on legal issues in open source licensing and is a frequent commentator and lecturer on the subject. She is involved in many organizations helping to educate lawyers and set policy in this area: former chair of the Open Source Committee of the SciTech Section of the ABA, Advisory Board Member of Open Bar, and pro bono counsel to Mozilla Foundation. Heather has provided open source counseling to clients ranging from technology start-ups using open source in product development, to public technology organizations conducting open source code releases, to venture capitalists assessing new business models in the software industry. She also served as an adjunct professor at the University of California at Berkeley School of Law and Hastings School of the Law, is a member of the American Law Institute, and in 2005 was selected by the *Daily Journal* as one of the top 30 intellectual property lawyers in California. She is listed in the *Chambers 2008* guide as a leading business lawyer in California. She also worked for many years in the entertainment and computer industries prior to her work as an attorney. Her book *The Open Source Alternative: Understanding Risks and Leveraging Opportunities* was published by John Wiley & Sons in February 2008.

Jay Miletsky is CEO and executive creative director at PFS Marketwyse, a leading New Jersey agency specializing in helping midsize to large companies bridge the gap between traditional and Internet marketing. An industry veteran, he heads up a creative team of marketing professionals focused on developing brands and generating awareness through traditional, online, and integrated efforts. His marketing work has included successful consultations and campaigns for companies such as Hershey's, Amerisource-Bergen, Emerson Electric, JVC, and the Michael C. Fina Company. He is the author of ten books, including *Perspectives on Marketing* and *Perspectives on Branding*, as well as his new college textbook, *Principles of Internet Marketing*.

Brian P. Morgan works as an assistant vice president at a large asset management firm in New York City, where he has spent over seven years implementing business intelligence (BI) systems, starting a business intelligence competency center (BICC), and managing application development in finance. He is a leader in his field, and others look to him for ways to help streamline company solutions. He spent two years at Merck & Company, doing BI/OLAP development on projects around the world. He then worked as an independent consultant implementing BI solutions at organizations in and around the New York tristate area. He graduated from the College of New Jersey (formerly Trenton State College) with a BS in computer science.

Brian G. Rosenberg has worked with the implementation and optimization of Enterprise Resource Planning (ERP) software for nearly 18 years. In 1999, after leading multiple ERP and accounting software implementations, he founded RPI Consultants in order to provide cost-efficient solutions that focused on addressing customer-specific business needs. His extensive work on needs analysis, business process redesign, work flow, and custom application development allows a unique perspective on how information technology can be leveraged to increase operational efficiencies and deliver bottom-line results. As an industry leader in procure-to-pay best practices, he has served on executive steering committees for multiple ERP implementations and assisted numerous billion-dollar organizations in moving toward shared services environments. He regularly presents at conferences on topics such as accounts payable (AP) optimization and ERP improvement. He is an active member of International Accounts Payable Professionals (IAPP) and the Association for Healthcare Resource and Materials Management (AHRMM). In addition, he has supported charitable efforts as the founding treasurer of the Baltimore Waterfront Rotary Club.

Damien Santer is chief executive officer and chairman of the DMSBT Group, an international business and technology consulting firm operating across the Asia-Pacific region, specializing in Enterprise 2.0 solutions, enterprise search and retrieval, geospatial portals, and software as a service solutions. Damien is a 15-year veteran of the industry, with experience across software development, applications, platforms, network infrastructure, project management, and consulting with Fortune 500 organizations and government departments across the region. Damien began his career as a systems engineer specializing in Novell Netware but more recently has specialized in consulting on the creation of competitive advantage through the application of Web 2.0 technologies within the enterprise (Enterprise 2.0) and the associated organizational change required to implement them. Damien serves as a director and business and technology adviser to numerous organizations and is a recognized industry expert and speaker, having presented at Singapore Institute of Management, Broadcast Asia, and various CIO, government, and defense seminars and symposia.

Bhuvan Unhelkar, BE, MDBA, MSc, PhD, FACS, has 26 years of strategic as well as hands-on professional experience in information and communication technologies (ICT) and their application to business and management. He is the founding principal of MethodScience.com and has notable consulting and training expertise in software engineering (modeling, processes, and quality), as well as in enterprise architecture, project management, collaborative Web services, and mobile business. He earned his doctorate in the area of object orientation from the University of Technology, Sydney, in 1997. Subsequently he designed and delivered course units like global information systems, object-oriented analysis and design, business process reengineering, and IT project management in various universities in Australia, China, and India. He leads the Mobile Internet Research and Applications Group (MIRAG) at the University of Western Sydney, where he is also an adjunct associate professor. He has authored/edited 14 books in the areas of globalization, mobile business, software quality, business analysis, business processes, and the unified modeling language (UML), and has extensively presented and published research papers and case studies. His current research interests include composite software development processes for mobile applications and application of mobile technologies in helping organizations with their environmentally responsible business strategies (ERBS). Dr. Unhelkar is a Fellow of the Australian Computer Society, life member of the Computer Society of India, Rotarian at St. Ives, Discovery volunteer at New South Wales parks and wildlife, and a previous TiE Mentor.

Amy Wohl is a noted expert on the computer market, its products, and its dynamics. She has been observing, analyzing, commenting on, speaking and writing about, and consulting to the information industry for nearly 30 years. She is the author of the book *Succeeding at SaaS: Computing in the Cloud*. The focus of her expertise and interest is the commercialization of new technology and the creation of new markets and business models. She has provided guidance to clients seeking to invest in or create and market products in areas ranging from word processing, desktop publishing, and office automation to voice processing, development tools, digital rights management, new operating systems (and their platforms and interfaces), Linux, Java, and Web services. Her current interests include SaaS, SOA, and Web 2.0. Wohl is president of Wohl Associates, a consulting firm established in 1984, whose clients include every major systems and software vendor. She has also consulted to the U.S., state, and foreign governments; to major corporations; and to a number of universities and major hospitals. She is editor and publisher of the blogs Amy D. Wohl's Opinions and Amy Wohl's

Opinions on SaaS. She is a frequent contributor to the trade and general business press on the Internet, software, computing, computer trends, and technology. She has served as an expert witness and legal consultant on many occasions, as a board member and adviser to start-up organizations, and as lecturer on the commercialization of new technology at the University of Pennsylvania. Amy received a BA in economics from LaSalle College and an MA in economics from Temple University, where she was an NDEA doctoral fellow.

PART I

Introduction, Background, and Definitions

CHAPTER 1

The Changing Landscapes of Business and Technology

Phil Simon

Ex chaos facultas.
Latin, "From chaos comes opportunity."

Introduction

The worlds of technology and business are colliding faster and more intensely than ever. Organizations today are facing increasing pressures with respect to innovation, operational excellence, and financial performance while concurrently keeping costs at an absolute minimum. Relatively recent technologies provide enormous possibilities for organizations to confront everyday and long-term business challenges. The need for organizations to understand how to use these new technologies—and then actually utilize them effectively—has never been greater.

At best, organizations slow to embrace these opportunities often cost themselves money, via reduced revenue, profits, and market share or via higher expenses. First-mover advantage has arguably never been more pronounced, as organizations such as Google, Twitter, and Facebook can go from anonymous to ubiquitous almost overnight. At worst, technological laggards may no longer be around to eventually get with the program. Along these lines, Jim Collins's latest book, *How the Mighty Fall: And Why Some Companies Never Give In*, addresses the five stages of organizational decline. This prompts the question: What, if anything, can information technology (IT) do to stop an organization's demise? (Chapter 3 addresses this topic.)

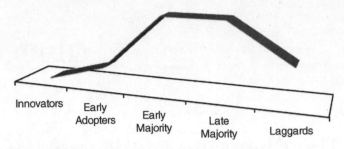

Innovators   Early   Early   Late
              Adopters   Majority   Majority   Laggards

FIGURE 1.1 The Technology Adoption Life Cycle (TALC)

Of course, not every organization embraces new technologies as quickly as others. This concept is known as the Technology Adoption Life Cycle (TALC).[1] TALC is used to describe the adoption of new technologies, typically including the stages of innovators, early adopters, early majority, late majority, and technology laggards. In a nutshell, very few organizations implement new technologies right after their introduction; graphically represented in Figure 1.1.

In his well-researched book *Does IT Matter?: Information Technology and the Corrosion of Competitive Advantage*, Nicholas Carr makes the case that most organizations should learn from the competition; they should wait for other organizations to make IT-related mistakes. He deftly points out examples such as United Parcel Service (UPS) successfully adopting a "follow, don't lead" IT approach. Carr writes that "UPS was often attacked through the 1980s and 1990s for being a technological slowpoke. All the while, though, UPS was carefully following in FedEx's tracks, learning not just how to copy its rival's systems but often how to make them better and cheaper. When UPS rolled out its own logistics-management software, for instance, it went with a more open system than FedEx's, making it easier for customers to incorporate UPS's technology into their existing systems."

A thorough discussion on how, why, and when organizations should implement technologies is not warranted here. For now, suffice it to say that the vast majority of organizations echoes Carr's sentiment; they wait until a new technology has become pervasive and mature before deciding to use it, if at all. In other words, very few tend to be "on the left side of the curve."

Enterprise 2.0: What's in a Name, Anyway?

Some of the topics in this book have been collectively dubbed "Enterprise 2.0," a term originally coined by Harvard Business School associate

---

[1]See http://dictionary.bnet.com/definition/technology+adoption+life+cycle.html.

professor Andrew McAfee in a 2006 *Sloan Management Review* article. McAfee defined Enterprise 2.0 as "the use of emergent social software platforms within organizations, or between organizations and their partners or customers."

Along those lines, in a 2008 report for the Association for Information and Image Management (AIIM), Carl Frappaolo and Dan Keldsen defined Enterprise 2.0 as "a system of web-based technologies that provide rapid and agile collaboration, information sharing, emergence and integration capabilities in the extended enterprise."

This book intentionally uses the term *Enterprise 2.0* more broadly than those definitions. I admit that it is quite difficult to succinctly distill all of the aspects of the next wave of technologies into a few sentences. Because of this, perhaps Enterprise 2.0 is best defined in the negative against "Enterprise 1.0."

Now, I'm no revisionist. I know that the term *Enterprise 1.0* never formally existed back in the 1990s and early 2000s. I was there. With the benefit of hindsight, however, what I'm calling Enterprise 1.0 ultimately represented organizations' initial efforts to democratize computing in the workplace. They replaced their clunky mainframes and ugly boxes previously confined to hard-core programmers with more user-friendly personal computers (PCs) that the everyday employee could use. Enterprise systems replaced paper-driven and manual processes. The PC became part and parcel of almost every corporate white-collar job as organizations moved from memos to emails. Examples of 1.0 technologies included Enterprise Resource Planning (ERP) systems, relational databases such as Oracle and SQL Server, client-server applications, email (arguably the era's killer app), and corporate web sites and intranets.

In short, Enterprise 1.0 represented the first technological wave that allowed organizations to do the following:

- Increase the level of enterprise integration.
- Allow employees to access information away from traditional mainframes.
- Begin to knock down organizations' information silos.
- Embrace email and the Internet.
- Dabble with different communication and collaboration tools.

Conversely, Enterprise 2.0 represents the next wave of technologies. In this book, I define Enterprise 2.0 as organizations' efforts to deploy and utilize emerging technologies, systems, applications, platforms, social media, and software development methodologies. Examples of these technologies include: cloud computing, social networking, business intelligence (BI), software as a service (SaaS), enterprise search and retrieval (ESR), and open source (OS) applications.

In other words, for the purposes of this book, Enterprise 2.0 means going beyond the basics. It assumes that organizations can already accurately run financial reports, pay employees, communicate with customers and employees, track inventory, and the like. (At a high level, this was the entire point of Enterprise 1.0.) Note, however, that there is almost always room for improvement, as many organizations may not be performing these activities in an optimal manner.

Enterprise 2.0 consists of three general and intertwined principles:

1. Managing systems and data in a better, more integrated fashion.
2. Interpreting data to allow for higher-level analytics.
3. Enhancing communication among organizations, vendors, suppliers, employees, and customers.

Enterprise 2.0 versus Web 2.0

Enterprise 2.0 should not be confused with Web 2.0. The latter presently consists largely of social networking sites such as Twitter and Facebook, wikis, and mashups that people use for entertainment or personal reasons. Families, friends, and strangers can communicate online and share information outside of organizational walls.

For their part, Enterprise 2.0 technologies exist *inside* organizations—though this is a far cry from being closed off from the rest of the world. The primary objective of Enterprise 2.0 technologies is *not* to connect family, friends, or strangers. Rather, these technologies aim to improve productivity and enhance communication and collaboration among vendors, suppliers, customers, and employees. As such, emerging technologies need to provide greater security than Web 2.0 technologies. What's more, they should enforce business rules, provide for audit capability, and improve end users' access to key organizational information.

Caveats

I use the term *Enterprise 2.0* a bit sheepishly and with two caveats. First, I am very aware that the term smacks of consultant-speak. I am not a fan of jargon and favor a constitutional amendment outlawing the abuse of words such as "synergy" and phrases like "thinking outside the box." However, it's simply easier for this book to refer to these concepts by one umbrella term.

Second, I am very well aware that many of these emergent technologies are in reality hardly new. Examples include SaaS, BI, and ESR. Think of them as children. While many may not have been born recently, they are only now hitting puberty. In other words, as of mid-2009, most organizations had yet to implement most of these technologies—much less utilize them effectively. This is certainly not to imply that every organization needs to use every technology. In some cases, individual systems or applications may not make sense for different companies or industries. Still, foolish is the organization that believes that social networking or BI would offer no benefits.

Displacing the Displacers

Technology giveth and technology taketh away, a concept for which Joseph Schumpeter aptly coined the term *creative destruction* in his 1942 book *Capitalism, Socialism, and Democracy.* The term has had enormous staying power. How many economics texts are referenced almost 70 years after their publication date?

While Schumpeter wasn't writing about Enterprise 1.0 or 2.0, his central thesis still holds a great deal of water: All organizations are at risk of displacement at the hands of technology.

Creative destruction seemed to be all the rage during the dot-com boom of the 1990s. While that era seems quaint today, the few remaining and successful dot-coms are facing increasing pressure from nimble and hungry start-ups.

Consider LinkedIn, the six-year-old social networking site geared toward professionals, which has been making significant inroads against traditional job boards. In a recent *BusinessWeek* article, Matthew Boyle writes that Monster.com CEO Sal Iannuzzi recently acknowledged as much, saying, "We are not done," hinting that acquisitions could be forthcoming. But even Monster's architects see the writing on the wall. Bill Warren, the founder of an early job board that morphed into Monster, is now executive director of the Direct Employers Association, a consortium of corporate employers. He's partnering with the owner of the ".jobs" domain and will launch job sites under that domain later this year. Says Warren: The days of the big, expensive job boards are over.[2]

It seems like that just yesterday, online job boards replaced newspapers' classified ads. To paraphrase Jim Collins, it doesn't take time for the mighty to fall.

Particularly interesting is LinkedIn's use of push technology. As it relates to job searches, push technology allows recruiters and hiring managers to receive the profiles of candidates without having to actively pull them via searches. For example, a recruiter (Roger) is trying to fill an IT manager position at his company. LinkedIn will find and send Roger the profiles of qualified candidates without his having to wade through the backgrounds of hundreds of potentially underqualified applicants. This saves Roger time

---

[2]See www.businessweek.com/magazine/content/09_27 /b4138043180664.htm.

and makes the entire process less costly and cumbersome. While LinkedIn cannot guarantee a good hire, perhaps the company can use business intelligence tools to answer that very question.

The LinkedIn example underscores two main points:

1. Every technology is potentially ephemeral. Eventually something may very well replace LinkedIn and social networking sites.
2. No organization can rest on its laurels. New technologies can be used quickly to displace industry leaders.

Understanding the Caution

The potential of these new technologies is hardly unproven. OS software SaaS, cloud computing, social networking, service-oriented architecture (SOA), BI, and other exciting new technologies are enabling organizations to do amazing things *right now*. Beyond merely reducing costs, they are already doing the following:

- Reducing product development times.
- Allowing organizations to better understand their customers.
- Expediting innovation and new product development.
- Enhancing employee communications and productivity.

For more on how organizations have harnessed the power of Web 2.0 technologies in often-unexpected ways, see Don Tapscott's excellent book *Wikinomics*. My favorite anecdote is of Goldcorp essentially allowing netizens to become virtual treasure hunters.

Nor are these technologies being deployed exclusively by nimble start-ups such as LinkedIn. Old-school corporations such as IBM and Wal-Mart are classic examples. The former got religion in the 1990s' on collaboration and OS software. Indeed, it is hard to imagine IBM as a shell of its current self if then-CEO Lou Gerstner had not fundamentally changed the organization's thinking and culture.

The story of Wal-Mart's use of customer data is both well documented and simply astonishing. For years, Wal-Mart has used data mining technology to unearth remarkable customer insights. A *New York Times* article[3] written one week before Hurricane Frances in 2004 summarizes one fascinating discovery with respect to expected weather and consumer purchasing behavior. Reporter Constance L. Hays writes that "experts mined the data and found that the stores would indeed need certain products—and not just the usual

---

[3]http://www.nytimes.com/2004/11/14/business/yourmoney/14wal.html?pagewanted=1

flashlights. We didn't know in the past that strawberry Pop-Tarts increase in sales, like seven times their normal sales rate, ahead of a hurricane, then-CIO Linda Dillman said in a recent interview. And the pre-hurricane top-selling item was beer."

IBM and Wal-Mart are merely two examples of organizations that are simply doing amazing things with Enterprise 2.0 technologies. As they say, however, the exception proves the rule.

So, let's return to the original question: What is stopping so many organizations from jumping into these largely uncharted waters with both feet? Four things spring to mind:

1. Financial considerations
2. IT project failure rates
3. Uncertainty over the future
4. The Software Establishment

Financial Considerations

The meltdown of the financial system—and the subsequent pronounced recession—is a significant but not exclusive factor in explaining many organizations' resistance to numerous new technologies. Organizations' IT budgets were expected to grow between zero and 2.3 percent in 2009, according to Peter Sondergaard, senior vice president of research at Gartner Research.[4] This range is considerably below recent norms. Another study by research firm Computer Economics found that one-third of organizations cut their IT budgets for 2009.[5]

In an effort to reduce costs, many organizations have gone way beyond trimming the fat; some have cut down to the bone, shredding essential IT personnel, canceling current projects, and putting the kibosh on future ones. However, simple economics and budgetary realities alone do not tell the whole story. We have to dig deeper.

IT Project Failure Rates

The failure rate for IT projects is conservatively estimated to be 60 percent.[6] Particularly in the ERP sphere, these systems and their technologies have been relatively well understood for at least the past decade. This is not to say that ERP is a completely static technology. However, the basic precepts

---

[4]See Larry Dignan's ZDNet blog at http://blogs.zdnet.com/BTL/?p=10403.
[5]www.computereconomics.com/article.cfm?id=1409.
[6]See http://advice.cio.com/remi/two_reasons_why_it_projects_continue_to_fail.

of paying employees, running financial reports, and tracking inventory have not fundamentally changed over the past ten years.

The political and financial costs of a failed IT endeavor are enough to deter many senior executives from improving their organizations' applications, systems, and architectures. New technologies such as enterprise search and retrieval (ESR) offer enormous promise. Until these new toys become mainstream and mature, many organizations will remain reluctant to adopt them—and may pass altogether.

Uncertainty over the Future

Aside from—and related to—fear of failure, many organizations and their decision makers simply do not know enough about these new technologies to implement them in an effective manner. New software, platforms, and services can do many powerful and transformative things. However, absent a clear business purpose, properly defined business requirements, sufficient resources, and the like, these technologies will likely not achieve their intended goals.

What's more, many senior executives are not familiar with new technologies. As a result, they are justifiably risk-averse about adopting them. For example, consider a chief information officer (CIO) who uses a social networking site such as Facebook to connect with friends. It is not difficult to sign up and add friends; one can be up and running in no time. The same CIO knows that this process is fundamentally different from implementing a new—and untested—social networking tool designed to promote collaboration, communication, innovation, and improved employee productivity inside the organization.

Even assuming a successful new IT endeavor, there are no guarantees that the technology will have staying power. No chief technology officer (CTO) wants to spend millions of dollars on an IT initiative that turns out to be antiquated after a mere two years.

Historically, two types of organizations have helped organizations make sense of new technologies (or at least tried): large consulting firms and software vendors. Let's ponder the biases of each group. Consultants like me can offer guidance, but perhaps many organizations have viewed us suspiciously in the past. After all, we have a strong incentive to advocate all types of far-reaching (read: expensive) technological changes for our clients. For their part, traditional software vendors have always encouraged their clients to go in specific directions, again with a vested interest.

During the Great Recession, clients did not listen to either group to the same extent, as the financial results of each group reflected. With signs of the recession abating and the number of technological choices on the rise, the best advice for organizations on how to navigate these waters may *not* stem from traditional sources.[7]

The Software Establishment

The late 1990s and early 2000s represented the halcyon days for many large software companies and consulting firms. ERP vendors such as SAP, PeopleSoft, Baan, and Oracle thrived as many organizations finally realized that their internal applications were antiquated and needed to be replaced by a single, integrated solution. The 1990s also represented the acme of Microsoft's hegemony. For their part, many systems integrators (SIs) such as IBM, CSC, D&T, Accenture, and PricewaterhouseCoopers (PwC) saw revenues and profits climb as their clients needed partners to help them implement new technologies.

Today, however, two things are certain. First, the heyday for many traditional technology heavyweights has long passed. Second, beyond their clients' shrinking IT budgets, many "old guard" technology vendors today are facing a number of significant threats to their revenue streams:

- SaaS
- OS software
- A new breed of independent software vendors (ISVs)

Note that neither this section nor book intends to demonize traditional software vendors. Emerging technologies pose major threats to many firms that were (and in some cases remain) powerful players.[8] If history teaches us anything, it's that current stalwarts rarely embrace new technologies that will cannibalize their existing business models, especially early on. Displacement at the hands of new technologies has affected many industries and organizations with vested interests in maintaining the status quo. Looking back at the past 15 years provides a veritable litany of examples, including:

- Kodak's dismissal of digital photography until very late in the game
- Microsoft's longtime resistance to open source
- The reluctance of the music industry to accept digital music and the Internet as a platform for commerce
- The opposition of the telecommunications industry to accept voice over Internet protocol (VOIP)

---

[7]During the writing process, this struck me as one of the most important reasons for writing this book.
[8]I'm hardly the first to notice this.

This ethos is best exemplified in the words of Upton Sinclair: "It's difficult to get a man to understand something if his salary depends upon his not understanding it."[9]

Many of the aforementioned examples have been well documented. The next section uses the example of Lawson Software, an established mid-market ERP software vendor facing significant threats from new technologies.

SOFTWARE AS A SERVICE (SaaS)   In recent years, few developments in the technology world have scared on-premises software vendors as much as SaaS. Salesforce.com founder and marketing whiz Marc Benioff has stirred up a great deal of controversy by openly talking about the "death of software." Talk like that is not likely to go unnoticed, and Benioff is very aware of this.

Benioff is throwing down the gauntlet. He knows that on-premises software vendors have historically relied upon the following revenue streams:

- Costly software licenses, often on products purchased but not used (Aka "shelfware")
- Annual support fees to the tune of roughly 20 percent of the initial license fee
- Consulting services
- Routine upgrades

For traditional vendors, SaaS is the very definition of a disruptive technology; if adopted en masse, it would eradicate a significant portion of their revenue and profits. It should be no surprise that many executives have viewed Beinoff's remarks as fighting words.

A jarring rebuke to Benioff's comments recently came from Lawson Software CEO Harry Debes. Debes gave an interview on August 28, 2008, in which he dismissed the long-term viability of SaaS, arguing that it is essentially the application service provider (ASP) model revisited. Nor is SaaS an alternative to a license-and-support model at the very heart of his organization's business model. Debes said, "SaaS is not God's gift to the software industry or customer community. The hype is based on one company in the software industry having modest success. Salesforce.com just has average to below-average profitability. People will realize the hype about SaaS organizations has been overblown within the next two years. An industry has to have more than just one poster child to overhaul the system. One day Salesforce.com (CRM) will not deliver its growth projections, and its stock

---

[9]Upton. Sinclair, *I, Candidate for Governor: And How I Got Licked* (1935), repr. University of California Press, 1994, p. 109.

price will tumble in a big hurry. Then, the rest of the [SaaS] industry will collapse."[10]

The natural question becomes "Is Debes right about SaaS?" At this point, it's doubtful. SaaS has moved way beyond theory and into practice, as we will see in Chapter 6. I will, however, agree with Debes on the following point: For a variety of reasons, it's unlikely that every on-premises client will supplant its core applications with SaaS equivalents. Some organizations will always want to control their applications and their data, refusing to cede control to a SaaS vendor even if they can reduce IT expenditures in the process.

OPEN SOURCE SOFTWARE OS has made inroads in many areas. As we will see in Chapters 5 and 16, OS alternatives have emerged to operating systems (Linux), productivity suites (OpenOffice), web servers (Apache), and many other applications. ERP may well be next.

Organizations such as Compiere sell customizable OS applications that their clients not only own but *control*. This is an important distinction. Clients of traditional ERP vendors purchase licenses but are in many ways at the mercy of their vendors' upgrade and customization policies.

OS applications are fundamentally different than their commercial, off-the-shelf (COTS) brethren. Much like SaaS, OS circumvents a number of major complaints among clients of traditional vendors: forced upgrades, dangerous customizations to the plain-vanilla products, and unnecessary functionality.

An organization that wants to run an antiquated version of a finance and accounting system can do just that—sans the vendor's pressure or requirement to upgrade. The organization can simply pay the vendor annual support fees without fear that its system will eventually be unsupported and risk potential system failure. I firmly expect the adoption of OS applications to continue rising in the next few years, further penetrating largely untapped markets such as ERP.

A NEW BREED OF INDEPENDENT SOFTWARE VENDORS Two recent and seemingly unrelated events have coalesced, resulting in more efficient software development. The first is the rise in the use of service-oriented architecture (SOA). In *Service Oriented Architecture for Dummies*, Judith Hurwitz, Carol Baroudi, Robin Bloor, and Marcia Kaufman describe the SOA world as one in which "business applications are assembled by using a set of building blocks known as components—some of which may be available 'off the shelf,' and some of which may have to be built from scratch."

---

[10]See http://seekingalpha.com/article/93066-lawson-s-harry-debes-saas-industry-will-collapse-in-two-years.

In other words, SOA provides greatly enhanced methods for systems development and integration. Individual systems and components give way to business processes and interoperable services. SOA allows different applications to exchange data with one another as they participate in business processes. Service orientation stitches together ostensibly different services with operating systems, programming languages, and other technologies underlying applications.

Second, the passage of the Sarbanes-Oxley Act[11] (SOX) has resulted in many organizations abandoning efforts to build their own internal systems. Faced with SOX's increased audit requirements, many are now opting to use independent software vendors (ISVs) to build proprietary systems. As organizations have increasingly sought the external expertise of ISVs in creating applications, it should not be surprising that organizations such as Infosys have prospered. (From its initial public offering in 1993 to 2007, the company's stock grew 3,000 percent, absent dividends.)

The end result is that successful IT projects are not uncommon these days—even if well-documented failures still persist. (Infosys's stock would not have climbed so high without high client reference and retention rates.) Unlike the 1980s, few organizations these days want to reinvent the wheel, finally accepting that they should stick to their knitting and not build applications from scratch. More organizations are using ISVs to build custom applications that address specific business needs, especially when those apps can be relatively easily integrated into existing system infrastructures. No longer are they forced to choose among a small number of viable alternatives.

REACTIONS TO DISRUPTIVE TECHNOLOGIES   For traditional software vendors, SaaS, open source, and the new breed of ISVs have collectively prompted an important question: Given potential challenges to their business models, how can these firms respond to such highly disruptive technologies?

Predictably, the reactions have fallen into three general categories:

- Denial of all threats
- Wait and see
- Acceptance the lesser evil

Denial of All Threats   Lawson clearly falls into this camp, as evinced by what Debes is asking his clients to do:

---

[11] In *Sarbanes-Oxley and the New Internal Auditing Rules*, Robert Moeller calls the 2002 passage of Sarbanes-Oxley "the most major and radical set of financial auditing changes in the United States since the 1930s[.] SOX has caused radical changes and strong new rules for public accounting, corporate governance, and others."

- Embrace certain Enterprise 2.0 technologies such as BI and enterprise search and retrieval (ESR). Naturally, Lawson makes products in these areas.
- Ignore a major and potentially game-changing technology, hoping that it will ultimately fail.
- Cling to existing on-premises applications, presumably with his company.

Reading between the lines, Debes's comments suggest that SaaS and open source frighten him. I for one find it curious that he is so effusive about certain technologies and so dismissive about others.

Wait and See   Many software vendors are waiting for certain dominoes to tumble. Software companies know that their clients aren't fond of them pushing new wares and changing "strategic" directions every year. If not executed properly, these pushes can have dire consequences, primarily driving their clients toward increasingly viable alternatives, such as SaaS and OS. What's more, it takes a great deal of time and money for vendors to rewrite their apps for different platforms. It's certainly reasonable for them to exercise prudence.

Acceptance of the Lesser Evil   Some software vendors see the writing on the wall and are effectively asking themselves, "How can we find opportunity in this chaos?" In other words, they understand that, as technology changes, so do their clients' needs. For example, consider two 800-pound gorillas in the software world:

1. SAP, which finally got SaaS religion in early 2009[12]
2. Oracle, whose CEO, Larry Ellison, has embraced the SaaS model for many of his organization's myriad applications

These two companies have recognized the immediate threats that these disruptive technologies are posting to their respective client bases. They realize that their clients may jump ship if they tire of on-premises software, preferring to use a different model altogether. SAP and Oracle know that clients dissatisfied with their offerings are now able to:

- Move to a SaaS vendor.
- Build a new software solution with an upstart ISV.
- Go the OS route.

---

[12]See www.informationweek.com/news/services/saas/showArticle.jhtml?articleID= 217800410.

With respect to the above, SaaS is probably the lesser of the three evils. Oracle and SAP seem to be abiding by the US Marines motto, "Follow, lead, or get out of the way."

THE END RESULT: GREATER ORGANIZATIONAL CHOICE   The threats facing established software vendors are already changing the dynamics of the traditional vendor-client relationship. Unlike a few years ago, organizations running mature applications with varying degrees of success now have much greater choice in the marketplace.

Many organizations have long waited for this day for a number of reasons. First, for years they have resisted their vendors' mandates that they routinely upgrade to more mature versions of applications, lest those applications be decommissioned and unsupported. Second, many organizations have been regularly paying their vendors annual support on unused applications, in effect wasting thousands of dollars per year. Third, IT departments must devote often considerable time, personnel, and expense to system maintenance, such as applying application patches and creating data areas to test upgrades.

To be sure, the increase in the number of different viable technologies for organizations is a largely positive event. Greater choice means lower prices for organizations, greater product innovation, more features, and an overall more efficient marketplace.

As just one of many possible examples, an organization in the mid-1990s was essentially forced to use Microsoft Windows as its operating system (OS) and Office as its productivity suite. Fast forward to 2009. Organizations unwilling to purchase and use Microsoft products have many alternatives. A bevy of options now exists for enterprises with respect to different types of systems, applications, databases, and technologies. Tool such as Google Docs and OpenOffice are arguably valid alternatives to MS Office. While its hegemony on the desktop OS front remains largely intact, Microsoft cannot ignore potentially legitimate alternatives to Windows such as Linux, Apple's Mac OS X, and Google's Chrome OS.

Against this backdrop, the question remains: How can organizations manage the chaos caused by all of these new technological options? A dizzying array of choices can cause confusion. Say what you will about monopolies; at least they remove the opportunity for an individual or enterprise to make the wrong choice. A similar logic exists among those who believe that the world was a safer place during the Cold War. The rationale is that the United States knew its enemies in those days: the USSR and Communism. According to this argument, the fall of the Soviet empire created a murkier world.

Electronic Health Records: A Case in Point

Given the financial crisis over the past two years, few mainstream economists embrace a laissez-faire mentality these days. On a general level, most mainstream practitioners of "the dismal science" call for some degree of government intervention to prevent future disasters and certainly when markets have failed to act efficiently.

One could argue that there has been no greater market failure over the past 50 years than the U.S. health care system. This is the elephant in the room, as the following figures from the National Coalition on Health Care suggest:

- In 2008, total national health expenditures were expected to rise 6.9 percent—two times the rate of inflation.
- Total spending was $2.4 trillion in 2007, or $7,900 per person.
- Total health care spending represented 17 percent of the gross domestic product (GDP) in 2007.
- U.S. health care spending is expected to increase at similar levels for the next decade, reaching $4.3 trillion in 2017, or 20 percent of GDP.[13]

Health care reformers have been advocating change for years. For starters, many have asked the question: Would the U.S. health care system benefit from electronic health records (EHRs)?

The answer is an unequivocal "yes." Karen Bell, director of the Office of Health IT Adoption at the U.S. Department of Health and Human Services, said as much in an interview in September 2008. She noted that many "health care . . . problem(s) could be solved, or at least drastically reduced, by electronic health records, which allow data to be easily shared among physicians, pharmacies, and hospitals. Such systems help coordinate a patient's care, eliminating duplicate testing and conflicting prescriptions, and ultimately cutting costs. But despite the benefits, only 15 to 18 percent of U.S. physicians have adopted electronic health records."[14]

In other words, nowhere is the technological chasm between the possible and the status quo arguably more pronounced than in EHR, an area in which the United States has been sorely lacking for years. But is EHR a reality? What can we learn from successful case studies?

Let's look at the Frederiksberg University Hospital in Copenhagen, Denmark, recently featured in a *Time* magazine article by Eben Harrell. It is an example of a health care institution that has successfully gone digital.

---

[13] See www.nchc.org/facts/cost.shtml.
[14] See www.technologyreview.com/biotech/21428/#afteradbody.

Harrell writes that "in the hospital's Department of Acute Medicine—where patients often arrive unconscious or disorientated—Klaus Phanareth's PDA prevents him from prescribing dangerous medications 'on a weekly basis,' he says. 'There's no doubt that it (EHR) saves lives.' "[15] It's interesting to note, however, that even digital hospitals in Denmark do not share electronic information with one other—i.e., they are not "interoperable" as of this writing.

Frederiksberg has managed to find opportunity in chaos. While other examples abound, the alarming fact remains: Despite incontrovertible financial benefits, fewer than one in five U.S. health records had been digitized as of 2008.

What are the possible reasons that so many U.S. heath care organizations have resisted EHR? Some possibilities include:

- Technological limitations.
- Unclear guidelines.
- Economic incentives.
- Institutional barriers.

TECHNOLOGICAL LIMITATIONS One cannot credibly cite technology limitations as a culprit for EHR's general lack of adoption in the United States. For years, the systems, applications, specific technologies (such as OCR[16]), and security have existed for hospitals and doctors' offices to go from paper to computer—if they chose to do so. The Frederiksberg University Hospital is a hardly a unique case in point.

UNCLEAR GUIDELINES The importance of clearly defined terms on a project as complex and important as EHR cannot be overstated. As a result, many health care organizations can hardly be faulted for not giving the green light to EHR initiatives when fundamental precepts have not been defined. Such is the case here. Only in April 2009 did the Healthcare Information and Management Systems Society (HIMSS) publish two definitions of *meaningful use* as it applies to certified EHR technologies and hospitals' use.[17]

---

[15]See www.time.com/time/health/article/0,8599,1891209,00.html.

[16]In his book *Adaptive Technologies for Learning & Work Environments*, Joseph J. Lazzaro writes that optical character recognition (OCR) "systems transmit printed material into your personal computer, allowing you to read the material in the mode you find most comfortable and appropriate. Once you have scanned a book into your computer, you can read the text using speech, Braille, or magnified output. You can also transmit the text to a note taker for use on the road."

[17]See www.healthcareitnews.com/news/himss-publishes-meaningful-use-definitions.

Without such definitions, hospitals may find themselves in court over misuse of confidential patient information.

According to its web site, "The Healthcare Information and Management Systems Society (HIMSS) is the healthcare industry's membership organization exclusively focused on providing global leadership for the optimal use of healthcare information technology (IT) and management systems for the betterment of healthcare. ... HIMSS frames and leads healthcare public policy and industry practices through its advocacy, educational and professional development initiatives designed to promote information and management systems' contributions to ensuring quality patient care."

Still, it is very difficult to believe that the lack of clear guidelines has served as the sole barrier to many organizations' desire to go digital. If that were the case, then it is unlikely that HIMSS would have waited until nearly 2010 to step up to the plate. Along with technological limitations, this factor seems minor in explaining the status quo of EHR in the United States.

ECONOMIC INCENTIVES AND INSTITUTIONAL BARRIERS Let's address the financial and institutional causes together, as they are essentially impossible to separate. Is there a marked financial incentive for health care institutions to go digital? The answer is a qualified "yes."

In the same *Time* article, Jeff Harris of the American College of Physicians points out that U.S. family physicians have the highest administration costs in the developed world and "are already under strain from all the paperwork required to run an office."

The economics of health care are more nuanced, however. While significant financial incentives exist for organizations to adopt EHR, many have not because of the industry's unique economics. Private insurance, government programs such as Medicare and Medicaid, and the relative inelasticity of demand[18] for health care have long lessened many institutions' perceived need to change in general—and adopt EHR specifically.

Moreover, the lack of successful U.S. deployments of EHR makes many executives wary. Aside from the cost of adopting EHR, breach of confidential personal health records seems like a perfectly reasonable reason to postpone its adoption. To this end, President Obama's $19 billion earmark in the 2009 stimulus plan for health information technology (HIT)[19] attempts to address the widespread institutional reluctance of organizations to adopt EHR.

---

[18]In simple English, elastic demand is very sensitive to price. If Big Macs become too expensive, then customers will flock to Burger King. Conversely, gas has a relatively inelastic demand and always will have until electric cars become more prevalent.
[19]See http://ces2010.digitalhealthsummit.com/index.php?option=com_myblog&show=Stimulus-Package-Contains-19-Billion-for-Health-Information-Technology-Telehealth.html&Itemid=5.

Perhaps Obama's carrot along with public pressure to reduce health care expenditures (the stick) will help attack institutional resistance to change in health care. One thing, however, is certain: Hospitals and doctors that embrace EHR will realize enormous benefits from going digital—increased profits and efficiencies, reduced costs and errors, saved lives, and so forth. Many currently don't understand how to successfully adopt these technologies. They don't know how to find opportunities in the chaos.

In a nutshell, that is the objective of this book.

Summary

As a general rule, senior managers in risk-averse organizations believe that "if it ain't broke, don't fix it." Even before the Great Recession, these decision makers were likely to maintain their organizations' legacy systems, traditional software architectures, and often-antiquated applications for the foreseeable future. These laggards avoid—or, at the very least, postpone—change increasingly at their own peril.

As SaaS, BI, agile development, cloud computing, and the like mature and business pressures intensify, most organizations will no longer have the luxury of maintaining a wait-and-see approach with regard to upping their IT ante. There are a number of reasons for this eventual shift:

- Senior managers will not be able to dismiss the carrots offered by these new technologies: increased revenue, innovation, and cost savings.
- The sticks of not using them will be too significant to ignore: organizational decline, loss of market share and profits, and possible extinction.
- The ease of adopting them will negate naysayers' main argument: "No one else is doing it."

Together, these three realities are already sparking the question in many progressive organizations: "Should we consider using these new technologies?" Increasingly, this query will be replaced by a different set of questions:

- What are the costs and benefits of using them?
- What can they do for our organization?
- How can we effectively use them?
- How can we avoid making the mistakes that others have made?

This book endeavors to answer this latter set of questions.

CHAPTER 2

How the Game Has Changed
Phil Simon

Those who cannot remember the past are condemned to repeat it.
—George Santayana

Introduction

As stated in Chapter 1, the central thesis of this book is that organizations have a unique opportunity to use newer technologies to thrive. Those unwilling or unable to exploit Enterprise 2.0 opportunities risk irrelevance or even extinction. If recent history is any indication, many organizations will not be terribly successful in their information technology (IT) endeavors.

To survive (much less thrive), many organizations need to vastly improve their batting averages with regard to adopting new technologies. Doing so requires more than purchasing software and hiring systems integrators (SIs) for long, expensive engagements. Organizations need to better understand the technologies themselves, explore the possibilities, and collaborate with their partners. In that vein, this chapter provides a deeper understanding of the following:

- The dynamics of Enterprise 1.0 projects.
- The reasons that so many Enterprise 1.0 projects missed their marks.
- How Enterprise 1.0 projects are different from their 2.0 brethren.

Understanding the shortcomings of many IT projects of the past 15 years is imperative if organizations are to avoid making the same mistakes again. Rather than cite a score of statistics, this chapter looks at several projects through the lens of a fictitious company, Lee Entertainment. Toward the end of the chapter, the Enterprise 2.0 challenges facing upstart Twitter will be examined.

TABLE 2.1 Groups Involved in a Typical Enterprise 1.0 Project

Organization	Description	Groups
Lee	Client	Steering committee/project management office (PMO)
		Implementation team
		Functional end users
		Technical end users
Peart	Vendor	Presales
		Sales
		Implementation and postproduction support
Lifeson	Systems integrator	Project manager (PM)
		Functional consultants
		Technical consultants

The Typical Enterprise 1.0 Project

Founded in 1970, Lee Entertainment had reached a technological crossroads. Its internal systems were stitched together by a series of computerized Band-Aids. Its legacy system was created well before the advents of the Internet, email, and self-service.[1] Looking at its system's architecture was similar to taking an eye exam.

In early 1998, Lee sought to replace its legacy system with an integrated Enterprise Resource Planning (ERP) system. The company dutifully sent out requests for information (RFIs) and requests for proposals (RFPs) to different software vendors, which, in turn, sent in their presales teams. These teams tried to turn contacts into leads, prospects, and ultimately customers.

Lee eventually selected Peart Software in 1999 after an extensive evaluation process. Once Lee management signed the papers with Peart, they needed to find a systems integrator (SI). Lee followed the same RFI and RFP process and ultimately selected Lifeson Consultants in 2000. Lifeson then assigned a different group of individuals (typically called "delivery" folks) to actually implement the system.

The typical Enterprise 1.0 project during the 1990s and early 2000s involved many different groups and individuals. Table 2.1 summarizes the organizations and different groups involved in the Lee project.

---

[1]Self-service applications allow nonusers to "touch" back-office systems themselves. For example, in a hospital, nurses can enroll in benefits online and change personal information without submitting forms to human resources (HR). Not surprisingly, these applications have significantly reduced the amount of paper required to conduct administrative transactions in many organizations.

To be sure, not every group in this table was involved throughout the duration of an Enterprise 1.0 project, and Lee was no exception. For example, presales folks usually stepped aside after leads were qualified. Also, vendor support needed to be involved only in the event that the implementation team found an issue.

However, the fact remains that on many Enterprise 1.0 projects, the sheer number of individuals and groups involved at different points created an enormous opportunity for fumbled handoffs and miscommunication within organizations and across them.

Michael Krigsman has called the relationship among vendors, organizations, and SIs "the Devil's Triangle."[2] To paraphrase, each entity has its own agenda and goals during an IT project; often the goals of each do not overlap sufficiently, increasing the risk of finger-pointing and ultimately a failed project.

Lifeson staffed the Lee project with consultants who specialized in particular areas of the Peart applications:

- One technical consultant to do the installation and set up security.
- One human resources (HR)/payroll functional consultant (James).
- One financial consultant (Jordan).
- One procurement consultant (Mike).

Why so many consultants? For one, ERP systems are complex animals. As such, no consultant could possibly know everything about Peart Software. These systems change far too frequently and there's simply too much to know.

Rarely would the skill sets of these consultants overlap a great deal. This fact, in turn, minimized the extent to which they could collaborate with one another—or really needed to do so. Rare is the functional HR/payroll consultant who could write SQL server code, do advanced data analysis, and the like. On Enterprise 1.0 projects, consultants had their clearly defined roles, typically sacrificing breadth for depth.

Common Issues on Enterprise 1.0 Projects

Continuing with the Lee example, the project encountered a variety of problems common to many Enterprise 1.0 projects, including:

- Often-incomplete documentation of existing processes and interfaces.
- Data issues.
- End user or consultant turnover.
- Resource availability issues.

---

[2]See Michael's blog: http://blogs.zdnet.com/projectfailures/?p=433.

The list could continue, but this last point is essential: Key Lee end users were at times pulled away from their implementation responsibilities because of different fire alarms. These intrusions resulted in the following challenges for two of the consultants on the project.

- Toward the end of the project, James could not complete a scheduled parallel payroll test for a few weeks because Lee's payroll manager had not provided a comprehensive set of required pay codes. After making this known to her project manager (PM), she began work on configuring Lee's benefit and vacation plans.
- Midway through the project, Jordan still could not produce a valid profit and loss (P&L) statement, because Lee's chief financial officer had not signed off on the complete list of accounts and accounting units. He then turned his attention to setting up Lee's vendors and training the end users in fixed asset management.

Why did Jordan and James have to insert fillers and reroute their work? Why did they start at point A, move to point B, divert to point C, and need to return to point B? The answer to these questions lies in one word: focus.

During Enterprise 1.0 projects, consultant focus was typically singular. Whether engaged to implement a new system, write reports, gather requirements, or perform gap analysis, consultants had no day jobs while on engagements. On the Lee project, Jordan and James only had implementation responsibilities; they were not required (or even qualified) to work on Lee's legacy system. Lee certainly did not expect James to run legacy payroll and Jordan certainly was not going to be keying journal entries. Nothing should have diverted their attention from their jobs at hand. Of course, *should* is a normative word.

Lee's employees, however, had a bifurcated focus during the project. They had to constantly balance (or at least try to balance) their present and future priorities during the implementation. The former almost always defeated the latter, an issue that caused the following:

- Project delays (the initial go-live date had to be moved from 2001 to early 2002).
- Cost overruns.
- Critical oversights.
- Minimized knowledge transfer between client and consultant.

Despite lack of resource availability, Jordan and James were able to make giants leaps of faith and continue to work productively—if not optimally—because they ultimately knew what their client needed to accomplish. When it comes to building enterprise systems, I always like to use house analogy. In this instance, both Jordan and James were able to come

TABLE 2.2 Lee Project Time Line

Task	Year
Lee decides to replace its legacy system	1998
Vendor evaluation begins	1998
Peart selected as vendor	1999
Lifeson selected as SI	2000
Initial go-live date	2001
Final go-live date	2002

back to the kitchen and work on other rooms; the foundation and the floors of the house had already been built.

Specifically, James needed the payroll application to remunerate Lee employees in accordance with state and federal labor laws. For his part, Jordan knew that all accounting setups and reports need to comply with generally accepted accounting principles (GAAP).[3]

Without question, Enterprise 1.0 projects would eventually reach points at which client input was essential and further work could not be completed. However, major project phases, such as requirements gathering, end-user training, application exploration, and even limited system testing, could take place with so-called placeholders. Very rarely and only under unusual circumstances would all work on a project cease.

After a few delays and postponed go-live dates, Lee successfully activated the Peart system in 2002. The project went about 30 percent over budget. Table 2.2 summarizes the time line of Lee's ERP project.

The major point here is that this project took almost four years for Lee to complete from soup to nuts. This time frame was not uncommon on Enterprise 1.0 projects.

Comparing Enterprise 1.0 and 2.0 Projects

It's hard to imagine any IT project these days taking four years. Will many Enterprise 2.0 projects take as long as their predecessors? For many reasons, most will not—or at least should not. Length of time aside, the better question is: Are Enterprise 1.0 and Enterprise 2.0 projects apples and coconuts?

Of course not. Certain truisms apply to all IT projects, irrespective of moniker. Still, there are major differences between the two with respect to

---

[3]GAAP is a widely accepted set of rules, conventions, standards, and procedures for reporting financial information, as established by the Financial Accounting Standards Board. Source: www.investorwords.com/2141/GAAP.html.

the following:

- Overriding objectives
- Customizations
- Design decisions
- Integration
- Technologies
- Activation

Overriding Objectives

Enterprise 1.0 projects focused on implementing systems and technologies that enforced hundreds of business rules (e.g., we need the system to do X, Y, and Z). On Enterprise 2.0 projects, organizations often start with a technological blank slate and a general business goal or a question. For example, we need a better way to communicate with our customers. How can we best accomplish this?

Customizations

On Enterprise 1.0 projects, systems and applications were difficult and expensive to customize. A modification to an application's underlying code could easily and unexpectedly break other parts of a system, wreaking havoc across the organization. On Enterprise 2.0 projects, tools such as application programming interfaces (APIs) and software development kits (SDKs) are just a few of the toys that developers have at their disposal. In many instances, the power and uses of these tools are only limited by the imaginations of their developers and the business users themselves.

Design Decisions

On many Enterprise 1.0 projects, software vendors already made—and delivered—key design decisions. For instance, organizations that purchased Oracle 11i received a great deal of out-of-the-box functionality. At the same time, however, they had limited flexibility to address gaps when the application could not address a business need. One typical solution was to customize the application. On Enterprise 2.0 projects, organizations have much greater flexibility to plug and play—that is, to configure systems and use technologies in conjunction with one another. Service such as service-oriented architecture (SOA) is invaluable in this regard.

Integration

On Enterprise 1.0 projects, integration was time-consuming, difficult, and expensive. On Enterprise 2.0 projects, integration among applications can be deeper and much easier to obtain; systems can much more easily talk to each other. Again, APIs, SDKs, and SOA can be very useful here.

Technologies

On Enterprise 1.0 projects, organizations often had to use disparate platforms, operating systems, and/or tools to run different applications. Band-Aids and work-arounds were common. On Enterprise 2.0 projects, organizations can use one platform, operating system, architecture, or development methodology throughout the enterprise.

Activation

On Enterprise 1.0 projects, systems were typically activated as a binary: all or nothing. Go-live dates were sacred, as major events such as cutting employee checks, producing financial statements, and the like all hinged upon hitting these dates. On Enterprise 2.0 projects, organizations can activate features of applications and systems in a piecemeal fashion—particularly if they opt for an agile approach to software development (SD). Versions of applications are released with documented issues and limitations to be fixed in future releases.

Given that Enterprise 2.0 projects are fundamentally different from their predecessors, the next logical question is: Which projects are harder and why?

That's not an easy question to answer. On some levels, Enterprise 1.0 projects were easier. For instance, compared to today, organizations' IT budgets were typically larger eight to ten years ago. What's more, organizations inarguably faced fewer regulatory hurdles than they do today. Additional regulation may be forthcoming. Senator Thomas Carper (D-DE) has proposed IT oversight legislation. S.920 is a bill to amend Section 11317 of Title 40, United States Code, to improve the transparency of the status of information technology investments, to require greater accountability for cost overruns on federal information technology investment projects, to improve the processes agencies implement to manage information technology investments, to reward excellence in information technology acquisition, and for other purposes.[4]

On other levels, Enterprise 2.0 projects are arguably easier from technology, implementation, and integration perspectives. Table 2.3 compares, at a very high level, the relative difficulty of different aspects of each type of project.

Ultimately, the question of whether Enterprise 2.0 projects are easier than 1.0 projects misses the point. Some are and some are not. In order

---

[4]Source: GovTrack.us

TABLE 2.3 Relative Difficulty of Enterprise 1.0 and 2.0 Project Attributes

Challenge	Enterprise 1.0	Enterprise 2.0	Notes
Financial/ budgetary	Easier	Harder	Many IT budgets have shrunk.
Implementation	Harder	Easier	Enterprise 1.0 projects with massive requirements often resulted in failures; many 2.0 projects have smaller scopes, often making implementation easier.
Integration	Harder	Easier	SOA and other technologies allow disparate applications and systems to talk to each other more easily and better.
Regulatory	Easier	Harder	SOX, accounting scandals, and the financial meltdown have increased government scrutiny of IT projects.
Technology	Harder	Easier	Many organizations have embraced open source (OS) applications and collaboration; fewer organizations are keeping their technological secrets under wraps.

to successfully deploy and utilize Enterprise 2.0 technologies, organizations must overcome different regulatory, workplace, and financial hurdles than ten years ago.

Three Requirements for Successful Enterprise 2.0 Projects

Note that these three requirements will not guarantee a successful project today any more than they would have 15 years ago. Many projects have died a painful death because of internal politics, poor data, end-user resistance to change, and a bevy of other reasons. For this reason, this section is not titled "*The* Three Requirements to Successful Enterprise 2.0 Projects."

Let's return to Lee in 2009. Up and running with its ERP, its management now wants to better understand its customer base through business intelligence (BI) and the use of dashboards. Lee management has seen some of its competitors successfully use key performance indicators (KPIs)—quantifiable metrics that reflect the performance of an organization in achieving its goals and objectives.[5] Management wants to give its end users the ability to drill down on the data, uncovering valuable knowledge and trends. Management believes that these tools will help Lee improve its customer satisfaction and retention, ultimately impacting the bottom line.

More Organic Questions and Objectives

Lee management is wiser than it was in 1998; it has learned from the mistakes of its ERP project and understands the aforementioned differences between Enterprise 1.0 and 2.0 projects. Rather than submitting hundreds of detailed requirements to different software vendors, including independent software vendors (ISVs), and to SIs, it takes a more organic approach this time. Lee asks itself the following fundamental questions:

- At a high level, what are we trying to accomplish?
- How are we going to accomplish this?
- How will we measure whether the project has met its goals?
- Is this the best measure?

These are much broader questions than those of Lee's previous project. This is not in and of itself an indictment of either Lee or Enterprise 1.0 projects in general. Remember that many of these projects—such as implementing back-office systems—existed to fulfill a number of very specific requirements and functions.

The Right Tools and Partner

Asking profound and dynamic questions is not the only sine qua non, however. Organizations need the right tools and experts to help answer them. The right tools and partners are collectively the second requirement for a successful Enterprise 2.0 project.

To its credit, Lee understands this. Showing that it will walk the talk, the company purchases Cognos Business Intelligence,[6] a very powerful set of data mining tools that should help Lee achieve its goals. Lee again contracts Lifeson because of its vast experience on these types of projects.

This should not represent an endorsement of Cognos's products. I actually like them quite a bit, but this book is vendor-agnostic. In truth, Lee could have easily chosen a BI product from Microsoft, Oracle, or SAP.

---

[5]See www.information-management.com/issues/20040901/1009207-1.html.
[6]Cognos was recently acquired by IBM. (*Source*: GovTrack.us)

Access and Collaboration

Successfully implementing Enterprise 2.0 projects (read: on time and on budget) involves more than merely asking fundamental business questions and purchasing software to answer them. Each of which is a necessary but not sufficient condition to ensure project success. Consultants need routine access to clients throughout projects—not simply at key points and milestones.

In other words, measuring customer satisfaction is inherently more subjective than paying employees correctly or tracking inventory (typical objectives of Enterprise 1.0 projects). Nor is such a measure definitive and permanent. Changes in consumer behavior might necessitate organizations' refining their metrics or changing them altogether.

Software vendors and SIs know this. Because of the lack of standards across their clients with respect to many KPIs, each organization embraces some degree of uncertainty. They would not win much business if they attempted to force a cookie-cutter application or solution down their clients' throats. In short, applications and services matter.

From the client's perspective, different BI products may ship with predelivered or "canned" dashboards and KPIs. These tools automatically link to databases, in a sense working out of the box. For example, earlier versions of some Cognos applications once shipped with delivered KPIs that, in theory, could provide immediate metrics.[7] In a way, this was a moot point, as many organizations felt—and still feel—the need to customize these default measures.

In that way, Enterprise 2.0 applications are fundamentally different from many of the commercial, off-the-shelf (COTS) applications so prevalent during the mid-1990s and early 2000s. Returning to the house analogy from before, Lee needs to work with Lifeson consultants to determine the following:

- The specific house that it wants to build (colonial, duplex, ranch, or hut).
- The materials available to it (wood, brick, cinderblocks, or straw).
- The type of land available.
- The *purpose* of the house (e.g., a bare-bones house for mere shelter or an opulent home to impress neighbors).
- What to do if problems arise during the building process.

Returning to Lee's BI project, online analytical processing (OLAP) tools mean different things to different people. For now, suffice it to say that they

---

[7]In November 2007, IBM acquired Cognos in a deal north of $4 billion.

allow end users to observe trends likely to be hidden in a sea of transactional data. OLAP tools typically require dimensions. For example, building an OLAP "cube" of data allowing detailed analysis may necessitate breakdowns by region, product category, quarter, year, and even salesperson.

Only through collaboration can Lifeson consultants effectively build the reports, dashboards, and OLAP cubes that would allow Lee to achieve its goals. Lee needs to understand that this entails much more than a one-time conversation with its partner; it's an ongoing dialogue. If they are worth their salt, Lifeson consultants will return with refined questions based on Lee data, initial findings, end-user suggestions, and the like.

In other words, the flexibility of Enterprise 2.0 applications is a two-way street. While it is certainly a net positive for all involved, with that flexibility comes a requirement: If Lee wants to realize the benefits of its new BI tools, it cannot expect Lifeson consultants to make fundamental design and measurement decisions for it. Telling Lifeson consultants to "just do it" is shortsighted and will most likely result in a suboptimal outcome. What are the odds that Lifeson precisely builds the house that Lee wanted?

Regular access and collaboration also address other common issues:

- Unlike Enterprise 1.0 projects, Enterprise 2.0 endeavors often will not allow for placeholders on key design decisions similar to the ones that Jordan and James used on the ERP project. To continue with the house analogy, what if Lifeson's consultants have to make assumptions on the number of bedrooms? This might temporarily allow progress to continue on other parts of the house, such as the kitchen or bathrooms. However, in the likely event that this assumption is inaccurate, then a great deal of rework will have to take place on the house. This will compromise the project's budget and dates.
- Enterprise 2.0 projects do not need to follow a one-size-fits-all model. Customizations tend to be easier. In this case, the Cognos applications can display customer-related information in many meaningful formats to meet the needs of Lee's different end users. For example, senior executives need to see different information than midlevel managers. Even those who need to see the same information need not view it in the same ways.
- With increased collaboration, the likelihood for miscommunication and fumbled handoffs drops significantly.

Scopes, Scales, and Reaches

Another major and fundamental difference between Enterprise 1.0 and 2.0 projects is that the former tended to have fairly well-defined scopes, scales, and reaches. Note that "fairly well-defined" hardly equates to perfect. Many Enterprise 1.0 projects suffered from omissions and ambiguities that caused project managers, consultants, and end users severe headaches. Lawsuits were not unheard of.

Consider the following hypothetical but typical examples of Enterprise 1.0 projects:

- A mid-1990s project to implement SAP in a manufacturing company (fictitiously called Petrucci) required 100 concurrent users. At the end of the project, SAP would need to cut a check for each of the organization's 4,000 employees.
- A paper company (fictitiously called Portnoy) created an intranet in early 2001. The intranet would allow the firm's 3,000 employees to view company policies, apply to internal job postings, and find out basic contact information on other employees. This project required the support of five IT help desk personnel.

In other words, Petrucci did *not* discover upon system activation that it needed licenses for 1,000 concurrent users to cut 40,000 checks. Nor did Portnoy find out that it actually had 30,000 employees and a whole host of other requirements and uses for the organization's intranet.

We are now in a whole new world. Enterprise 2.0 projects often *cannot* be defined from their onset with nearly such precision. In some cases, these projects' early expectations, estimates, and requirements can be wildly inaccurate, causing unforeseen issues. Microblogging site Twitter is an instructive example of Enterprise 2.0 technologies attempting to meet dynamic business requirements.

Company Background: Twitter

Jack Dorsey, Biz Stone, and Evan Williams founded Twitter in 2006. Soon after, the group sought and received the organization's first round of venture capital (VC) funding. Although this amount has not been publicly disclosed, estimates have ranged from $1 million to $5 million.[8] Even at the high end of the range, this amount hardly is prodigious. Twitter management faced limited resources and, in all likelihood, an urgent need to show results. (Remember that 2007 was drastically different from the dot-com era.) Twitter no doubt followed one of two strategies:

1. Minimize its expenses and make its seed money last as long as possible.
2. Get as big as possible as fast as possible to raise more VC funding.

---

[8]See www.marketingvox.com/twitter-raises-over-35m-in-series-c-043192/.

In either case, Twitter had finite resources. It therefore chose to initially use the *free* open source application Ruby on Rails (RoR),[9] a Web-based development framework that may suffer from database scalability issues.[10]

Before continuing, a disclaimer is in order. Beyond its initial deployment of RoR, I do not know many specifics about Twitter's IT infrastructure (hardware, databases, and servers) now, nor did I back in April of 2009. As a privately held company, Twitter has no obligation to disclose its financials, much less these kinds of IT particulars.

In April 2009, Twitter began experiencing more than its fair share of growing pains. Many users experienced frequent errors accessing the site because the number of users had exponentially increased since the beginning of the year. These errors stemmed from "platform issues," as opposed to worms, Trojan houses, and denial of service (DOS) attacks. What's more, these issues occurred frequently enough that the site www.istwitterdown .com was created. In short, Twitter seemed to have outgrown the ability to support itself. The company was approaching a technological crossroads.

With that out of the way, let's turn to some specific questions examining Twitter's challenges.

WERE TWITTER'S FOUNDERS AND VCs SHORTSIGHTED IN NOT INVESTING IN A MORE ROBUST FRAMEWORK FROM THE START? No. For three reasons, neither Twitter management nor the VCs can be blamed for Twitter's infrastructure problems. First, hindsight is 20/20; it is very unlikely that either Dorsey or Twitter's investors could have predicted its sudden and meteoric growth. Who could have guessed that it would become one of the top 50 most visited sites on the Web?[11] Second, RoR had never been tested against such a large population. No one could have known that it would be unable to support so much traffic. Even ignoring the first two reasons, Twitter's initial VC funding was not large enough to allow Dorsey et al. to purchase and deploy a more powerful (read: more expensive) platform.

Let's assume for a moment that Twitter management had asked the VCs for more funds in round one specifically for this purpose. The VC firm would have been unlikely to provide these funds, because a more scalable and expensive framework would have been a pretty big and risky

---

[9]See www.forbes.com/forbes/2009/0622/software-internet-innovation-digital-tools .html.
[10]See www.techcrunch.com/2008/05/01/twitter-said-to-be-abandoning-ruby-on-rails.
[11]See www.alexa.com/siteinfo/twitter.com.

bet, especially since most start-ups fail. The VCs would have likely—and justifiably—viewed the costs of a premium platform as excessive.[12]

WHY COULDN'T TWITTER JUST SWITCH PLATFORMS?   Once it had become such a popular—if not profitable—site, Twitter could not just change platforms without missing a beat. Michael Arrington of TechCrunch wrote on May 1, 2009, that "switching off Rails may not solve all of Twitter's problems. They have nearly two years of infrastructure built up and would face many more growing pains if they switched frameworks or rolled their own."[13]

Arrington is right. To replace the RoR framework, Twitter would have had to invest considerable time and resources; you don't just replace IT infrastructure overnight. What's more, it's hard to imagine such a change without at least mild service disruptions at a time in which growth is essential.

WHAT'S TWITTER'S NEXT STEP   That depends on what Dorsey and the VCs want Twitter to be when it grows up. If they decide that Twitter would be best served as a stand-alone company, then they should probably bite the bullet—that is, buy sufficiently powerful hardware to support its viral growth. Note that Twitter has since received additional funding.[14]

If not, then they should look for an exit strategy soon. Too many system errors and "white screens of death" will only inhibit its growth and drive its users away or to comparable sites at a time when many question whether it can even become a viable business.

Enterprise 2.0 Lessons from Twitter

The Twitter example is an intriguing one. To be sure, most organizations have not faced—and probably will not face—the same technological dilemmas as Twitter. Most senior executives will *not* have to ask the question: "What to do now that we have outgrown our IT infrastructure during the past several months?"

At the same time, however, it would be foolish to dismiss potential lessons to be learned from Twitter for this very reason. The problems that Twitter faced surrounding its Enterprise 2.0 technologies are *not* entirely different from the prospective challenges that other organizations will face.

---

[12]Let me offer an analogy. Twitter would have been asking for high-end running shoes when it had not yet showed its backers that it could walk.

[13]See www.techcrunch.com/2008/05/01/twitter-said-to-be-abandoning-ruby-on-rails/.

[14]See www.marketingvox.com/twitter-raises-over-35m-in-series-c-043192/.

Going back a decade, eBay's remarkable growth taxed the capacity of its existing infrastructure during the late 1990s. At the time, the site experienced more than a few system outages and "white screens of death," resulting in angry and very vocal customers. For more information on eBay's early trials and tribulations, check out Adam Cohen's fascinating read, *The Perfect Store: Inside eBay*.

In fact, these challenges are arguably more similar than dissimilar; Twitter's issues were merely more acute and differ only in terms of degree. As a result, the company can provide four important lessons about Enterprise 2.0 projects.

THE LESS PREDICTABLE NATURE OF GROWTH Intelligent organizations have not historically purchased excessive technologies in terms of cost and functionality with zero intent of using them. (Whether these technologies were ultimately deployed is a separate matter.) For example, I have worked with many single-site hospitals as an independent consultant. Absent a merger or acquisition, each hospital would not have grown from 3,000 to 15,000 employees over the course of a few months (with corresponding increases in the number of transactions, system complexity, and support resources required). As such, management never found itself in a Twitter-like position of having to *unexpectedly* consider replacing suddenly insufficient IT infrastructure. On a broader level, many mature organizations implementing Enterprise 1.0 technologies knew years in advance that their legacy systems would eventually have to be replaced, even if many end users fought against the change tooth and nail.

In many places, this reality has changed. The Enterprise 2.0 world does *not* necessarily offer a clear and predictable technological environment in which even progressive management can foresee changes years in advance. (Of course, this depends on the type of application or technology, the industry, and a host of other factors.) I offer this disclaimer because different applications and technologies have different audiences. Returning to the example of a single-site hospital for a moment, an internal application rolled out to its employees by its very definition has a finite number of end users; the app is not available to the public at large. If the hospital had created a client-facing application, however, there is no practical limit on the number of end users who *might* utilize it. That very distinction should help the organization make an informed decision about the infrastructure required to support that application.

Sudden, unexpected growth may very well obviate the viability of a technology soon after an organization deploys it—or even before. In Enterprise 2.0, there is no long term anymore.

A POSSIBLE INABILITY TO IMMEDIATELY MEET BUSINESS NEEDS Many Enterprise 2.0 technologies offer organizations increased flexibility and scalability. SaaS, SOA, and agile development are just a few of the examples in this book. Despite this fact, however, organizations still might not be able to meet unexpected business requirements as quickly as required by stakeholders (senior managers, employees, suppliers, vendors, and customers). Perhaps this will be possible with Enterprise 3.0.

Such changes may include:

- Adding new functionality to support a proposed enhancement.
- Modifying applications to fix a previously undiscovered bug.
- Significantly increasing the existing bandwidth, scale, and capacity.

THE LIMITS OF "FREE" Despite the many virtues of open source software (OSS), the Twitter example proves that there are limits to free applications and frameworks. All else being equal, premium (i.e., nonfree) systems, platforms, hardware, and applications are more powerful and simply better at handling unexpected increased demands. Often they can just do more than many free OS equivalents. However, these premium technologies almost always cost more than their nonpremium brethren, sometimes by a considerable amount. Such costs may well be offset by their benefits. Chris Anderson makes this critical point in his book, *Free: The Future of a Radical Price*.

SYSTEM CHECKUPS Finally, organizations should *routinely* ask themselves if their existing frameworks can sustain both current and possibly unexpected usage levels. Performing system diagnostics, audits, tests, and evaluations should not be an annual or a biannual event. The last thing that an organization needs is an infrastructure- or technology-oriented bottleneck preventing it from reaching its full revenue and profit potentials. The technology sword cuts both ways. Exponential use of services and applications—and subsequent growth—is a net positive only for organizations with platforms capable of handling the extra burden. Those unable to handle this burden will yearn for simpler days.

Unstructured Development and Alternatives to the Waterfall

Enterprise 1.0 projects many times followed a linear trajectory consistent with the waterfall method of software development. In *The Software Developer's Guide*, Whil Hentzen writes that "structured development, or the waterfall method, gets its name from a visual interpretation of the process. A waterfall starts in one place, and then descends to a second level, and then a third, and then a fourth, but never goes back to a previous level. ... The waterfall method of software development starts out with an analysis of the problem, determining the requirements of the solution, and then moves on to a design of the solution, then the development (programming) of the design, then the testing, repair, and modification based on the testing, and, finally, the implementation."

As we will see in Chapter 14, the waterfall method of software development is no longer the only viable SD methodology. It may not even be the preferable method. With respect to SD, the relevant questions for Enterprise 2.0 projects become:

- Which method(s) will replace it?
- What skills do people need to work efficiently and effectively in these new models?

These questions cannot be viewed in isolation. If organizations expect to survive in an increasingly competitive world, they not only need a viable plan and the right technologies; they also need sufficiently skilled troops to implement those technologies.

Summary

Enterprise 2.0 projects differ from their predecessors in many fundamental ways. These differences mean that organizations need to adopt a more holistic perspective about technology. For example, using an Enterprise 2.0 technology to re-create a report because the "old system" had it entirely misses the point. A superior method involves asking if the previous report effectively conveyed the right contextual information and if that information was delivered effectively.

With the help of their partners, senior managers and end users need to make better decisions involving their organizations' goals and measures for success. Enterprise 2.0 technologies can help them do just that, but only if organizations embrace this new mind-set.

Next Steps

- Has your organization been relatively successful in implementing new technologies? Why or why not? What are the key areas that need to be improved?
- Are there parts of your organization's IT infrastructure that could not handle increased usage and transactions? What are they, and what could you use to replace them?

- If your organization's current technologies are inadequate, then are key players willing to embrace a different, more open mind-set? Can higher-level questions successfully replace hundreds or thousands of individual requirements?
- What's your organization's mind-set toward IT projects? Would a trial-and-error approach work, or do end users expect perfection upon rollout?
- While your organization may not resemble Twitter in any way, what can you learn from its example?

CHAPTER 3

The Role of IT in an Enterprise 2.0 World

Phil Simon

The best way to predict the future is to invent it.

—Alan Kay

Introduction

In the process of researching and writing this book, I have been simply amazed at how some organizations have deployed newer technologies. Beyond my own research, collaborating with so many accomplished and knowledgeable professionals has been very instructive. While these technologies are incredibly exciting, there is a limit to how much Kool-Aid I will drink. Much like their predecessors, Enterprise 2.0 technologies are not always successful, and they certainly are *not* elixirs for organizations on the ropes.

In May 2009, I read Jim Collins's latest book—*How the Mighty Fall: And Why Some Companies Never Give In*. I had read a review of it in *BusinessWeek* and was intrigued. The book had sparked great interest and debate. Collins and his team claimed to have uncovered the five stages of organizational decline. By understanding them, leaders could substantially reduce their chances of dying and becoming irrelevant.

Upon reading the book, I asked a friend of mine—an information technology (IT) director at a large retail organization—the following question: "What can IT can do to prevent an organization's demise?"

Pressed for time, he answered, "Stay out of the way." He then told me that he had to go to a meeting.

I wanted to say "That's it?" My brain started churning. Surely IT can do more than simply maintain basic applications, enforce security, manage upgrades of applications, and the like. However, IT's role has always been a complicated issue with many interwoven factors. Enterprise 2.0 does not change that; if anything, it makes the issue murkier.

Later that month, I started following a very heated discussion on the LinkedIn CIO Network group. A group member had posed the following question:

Were IT departments partially to blame for the financial crisis?

A maelstrom of replies followed, with answers across the board. Some said that IT could have—indeed, *should* have—been more proactive. For example, IT could have provided end users and senior management with business intelligence (BI) tools that, collectively, would have averted the economic calamity. What about simple audit reports that assessed transaction numbers and size? Some people honestly felt that IT could have stopped or at least could have mitigated the worst financial crisis since the Great Depression. (Note that IT here means departments and end users, not IT as a concept.)

On the other side of the aisle were those offended at the very notion that IT was in any way responsible so many firms' reckless lending practices. Since when did IT run the business? To those who insinuated that the IT systems were at fault, by the same rationale, do you blame the gun manufacturers for a senseless murder?

Somewhere in the middle were the moderates. While not burdening IT with much of the blame, perhaps IT could have at least asked some simple questions. To the extent that IT had access to this information, it was not unreasonable for IT to at least have broached a few concerns.

In the cases of Lehman Brothers and American International Group (AIG), audit reports were already in place, but this hardly meant that they were used, much less effectively. According to many accounts of these implosions, chief executive officers (CEOs) and their inner circles refused to listen when a few people asked questions. Lehman's Richard Fuld was so complicit in the meltdown that CNN actually named him one of the top biggest culprits of the collapse. Fuld completely cut off all communication with Lehman's senior-most risk officers. In other cases, the data coming out of these reports were only as good as the data put in, which typically incorporated economic assumptions that were way too optimistic and downright naive (e.g., home values will always increase). No rational, honest person can blame IT for that.

Collins's book and the LinkedIn debate made me think long and hard about the following question: What should be the role of IT in an Enterprise 2.0 world?

This is not a simple query—hence the need for an entire chapter about it. Depending on an organization's size, industry, financial resources, and myriad other factors, the role of IT may vary even among very similar organizations, much less vastly different ones. Nor is this question static. What technology cannot do today it may very well be able to do tomorrow. Twenty years ago, who among us could have conceived of constant updates via Twitter or being able to search billions of web pages in seconds via Google?

In order to properly answer this question, we first need to do three things:

1. Briefly describe Collins's model.
2. Put it into some type of context, since a model cannot exist in a vacuum.
3. Briefly describe IT's traditional charter.

Collins's Model

Collins's five stages are stated succinctly in the following paragraphs.

Stage 1: Hubris Born of Success

Organizations start out small, hungry, lean, and determined to succeed, but face long odds against success. Consider that most U.S.-based small businesses fail or close within a relatively short period of time. According to the U.S. Bureau of Labor Statistics:

- One-third of new firms fail or close within two years.
- Fully 56 percent fail within four years.
- Nearly 70 percent are gone within seven years.[1]

Now consider start-ups with plans to become the next Google or Amazon.com. While success rates vary by venture capital (VC) firm, a general rule of thumb is that VCs fund ten companies knowing that nine will fail. Despite those statistics, some startups actually do become successful. To be sure, the statistics vary a great deal by company size, region, industry, and time period. Think about how many dot-coms failed during the 1990s. The overall fact remains: It's not easy to build something from the ground up.

At the same time, however, Collins argues that this success causes the beginnings of a future cultural change to take root: A sense of entitlement to

---

[1] www.score.org/small_biz_stats.html.

future rewards replaces the ethos of hard work and intelligent management. Of course, management's tendency is to look internally, adopting a very healthy sense of self-worth and an inflated sense of confidence. Few people attribute this success to luck or good timing.

Stage 2: Undisciplined Pursuit of More

Buoyed by a smattering of early success, key players take the organization further astray. Rather than focusing on their core competencies or true strengths, organizations make questionable decisions justified by future growth or some other the grand strategy. Ideas such as getting big or pursuing quick gains supplant long-term, viable strategies.

Stage 3: Denial of Risk and Peril

As a result of the previous stage, organizations are now blind to the financial, organizational, or market-oriented problems facing them. At this point, management now looks externally, blaming the organization's deficiencies and struggles on bad luck, market conditions, or occasionally sloppy execution. Management often ignores or disputes data that show that the organization faces significant risk.

Stage 4: Grasping for Salvation

Facing challenges that can no longer be disputed, the organization often brings in a visionary leader with a new and game-saving strategy. Many believe that this new leader can return the organization to its prior prominence. Common tactics by this new leader include reorganizations, expansion into questionable markets or mergers and acquisition (M&A) activity.[2] Collins notes that it is difficult—but not impossible—for organizations to turn the corner. Pharmaceutical giant Merck & Company is one such example.

Stage 5: Capitulation to Irrelevance or Death

In the final stage, the organization realizes that the cause is lost and throws in the towel. Desperate measures have failed, the stock price has tumbled, and many employees have abandoned ship—or are looking to do so.

---

[2]For some of these desperation tactics and their ultimate outcomes, see the fascinating book *Billion-Dollar Lessons: What You Can Learn from the Most Inexcusable Business Failures of the Last 25 Years*, by Paul Carrol and Chunda Mui. I have never read a better account of absolutely horrible corporate decisions and their effects on employees, customers, and shareholders.

IT's Traditional Charter

Now that Collins's model has been explained, let's look at IT's traditional charter. Doing so will help us understand what IT can and cannot do, not to mention what it should and should not do. Historically, most IT departments have maintained responsibility for the following:

- Providing hardware
- Providing adequate security
- Providing information to lines of business (LOBs)
- Pioneering new technologies within the organization
- Providing audit capability
- Managing costs
- Challenging the business
- Managing risks

Providing Hardware

Information technology is still largely responsible for provisioning applications, personal computers (PCs), networks, and data. The designing, building, acquiring, and installing of applications, networks, and data are still largely IT's chief province. All IT departments are involved in implementing new systems, purchasing hardware, and so on.

Providing Adequate Security

Enterprise 2.0 has not absolved IT from its (arguably chief) role in providing a secure environment for an organization's customers and employees. IT still needs to ensure that information is secure. This has not changed. This prompts the question: With regard to security, what is different today and why?

In a fascinating white paper by the Jericho Forum entitled "Business Rationale for De-Perimeterisation," the authors argue that many organizations have insufficient security tools for the Enterprise 2.0 world.[3] The authors coin the term *de-perimeterisation* (*de-perimeterization* in the United States) to reflect the fact that technological advancements such as distributed computing, clouds, service-oriented architecture (SOA), and software as a service (SaaS) have caused a fundamental tension within many organizations, forcing them to reevaluate the need to keep all data local and

---

[3]www.opengroup.org/jericho/Business_Case_for_DP_v1.0.pdf.

theoretically safe. They go on to note:

> *Until recently most device and network security has been additive with, over time, a series of "sticking plaster" (Band-Aid) solutions being added. Interim solutions, such as VPN technology, are often applied everywhere as a "silver-bullet" with little regard for whether doing so is architecturally cost-effective; only with de-perimeterization are we able to realize an architectural mindset that will address these problems holistically.*

> *Most network based security controls and "solutions" such as Network Intrusion Detection Systems and Network Access Control are being added to shore up existing corporate networks in the misguided assumption that doing so provides "defense-in-depth" when an ever-increasing percentage of an organization's business is operating outside of the traditional perimeter.*

> *Many organizations have tried to segregate the corporate network into security zones, each behind its own firewall. While this can provide an interim step in an organization's transition to de-perimeterization (we use the terms shrinking the perimeter and micro-perimeterization), there is a worrying trend that some architects (and salespeople) regard this as synonymous with de-perimeterization. Widespread micro-perimeterization in fact adds network and management complexity, points of failure, and bottlenecks for network traffic, and is not viable in the long term.*

> *De-perimeterization requires security to be at the heart of the organization's distributed technology architecture, consistently implemented in end-user devices, application services, and surrounding the organization's critical information assets themselves—thus reinforcing what has been known for years but rarely implemented: that unless security is built in from the ground up, it will rarely be effective.*

Make no mistake. Security is still arguably one of IT's most critical functions. Securing applications, networks, and data is more important now than it was ten years ago. Of course, security should not be viewed in a vacuum. A secure system that does not help the business meet its goals is still of questionable value.

There are more dangerous and different types of threats and challenges facing IT departments. The architectural changes discussed in this book require IT departments to adopt a holistic approach to security. There are limits to what Band-Aids can do.

While security arguably remains the most critical piece of IT's charter, it is certainly not alone. The rest of this section details the other major responsibilities of IT.

Providing Information to Lines of Business (LOBs)

We are no longer in the 1980s. Access to information has been democratized in many workplaces. Many organizations have adopted reporting and BI tools that obviate the need for those same people to formally request reports from a central IT function. As a general rule, merely providing information to end users should no longer be part of IT's charter beyond establishing user accounts, enabling connectivity to databases, and dealing with connection issues.

Pioneering New Technologies within the Organization

End users may hear about the benefits of BI, SaaS, cloud computing, and the like. However, IT's security imperative means that those same people cannot download and install applications that affect the organization's data and, ultimately, survival. Firewalls and security policies still need to minimize external threats.

Enterprise 2.0 technologies offer more possibilities, benefits, and potential drawbacks than their predecessors. Unfortunately, due in large part to cutbacks necessitated by the recession, many IT departments now have fewer personnel to help the LOBs make sense of this dizzying array of choices.

The question becomes: Can LOBs pick up the slack and collaborate with IT to find the right technologies? The answer depends on two things. First, what is the relationship that the LOBs have historically had with IT? This is covered later in this chapter. Second, do the LOBs have sufficient technology skills and knowledge? This is covered in Chapter 19.

PARTNERSHIP WITH LOBs   In terms of its Enterprise 2.0 charter, in general IT should not dictate the organization's specific applications and use of *business-related* technology. That's not to say that chief information officers (CIOs) should be indifferent; it's the CIO's responsibility to ensure that technology costs such as hardware, software maintenance and licensing, and the like do not spiral out of control. It should work with LOBs to find technology able to meet business needs while not compromising the organization's security, data, system performance, and networks.

INNOVATION: THINKING LIKE GOOGLE   Perhaps the best example of the benefits of letting IT people play is Google. One of the most successful companies over the past ten years, the company has a highly publicized and successful policy of allowing "its engineers '20-percent time' so that they're free to work on what they're really passionate about. Google Suggest, AdSense for Content, and Orkut are among the many products of this policy."[4]

Of course, Google is unlike most organizations. Relatively few companies create technology products for the general public to use, employ the same technical caliber of staff, or have Google's deep pockets. However, there is no reason that IT personnel should not be allowed to noodle with different applications and see if end users would find them useful. In order for this to happen in any meaningful way, both the organization and IT management have to do the following:

- Embrace collaboration with LOBs.
- Staff the department with enough personnel to flush out new ideas.
- Do more than pay lip service to innovation.
- Retain so-called rock stars who develop useful applications and deploy technologies in innovative ways.
- Accept the fact that many ideas will not pan out and realize that this is not wasted time.
- Accept the fact that many technologies will become obsolete.

Providing Audit Capability

IT needs to ensure that end-user transactions are auditable. In many instances, IT has actually taken the lead in replacing legacy systems. Pre-Sarbanes-Oxley (SOX) systems in many cases did not allow for sufficient audit capability.

IT needs to look at existing systems and processes—in collaboration with the business—to make sure that the organization can do more than merely survive an audit. Rather, the organization should be able to provide auditors (be they the government or an individual firm) the information that they need as easily and quickly as possible, thus minimizing the overall impact (i.e., cost) of the audit on the organization.

If anything, audit capability has become more important since the passage of SOX.

Other Imperatives

For the sake of brevity, IT has traditionally done the following:

- *Managed IT costs.* For more on this, see Chapter 20, Sustainability and Green IT.

---

[4]www.google.com/support/jobs/bin/static.py?page=about.html&about=eng.

- *Challenged the business.* IT needs to ensure that technology supports the organization's overall strategy. (Of course, the organization may not know its own strategy, but let's assume for the moment that it does.) Redundant or overly customized systems that create administrative nightmares should not exist because end users fear slight changes to business processes. IT needs to keep informed of the latest developments in the marketplace to ensure that the LOBs have the right technology.
- *Managed risks.* For more on what constitutes acceptable risk for the enterprise, see Chapter 15, Enterprise Risk Management.

Depending on the stage in which the organization finds itself, IT departments will still need to perform these functions. Enterprise 2.0 does not change this.

Considerations

Having provided an understanding of both Collins's general framework and IT's traditional charter, it is now time to put them both into a business context. Before continuing, by no means does this book imply that *all* IT organizations and their IT departments are the same. Different organizations face different challenges at different times.

The following factors shed light on what IT can do, how much time it has to do it, and the constraints in which it has to operate:

- Stage
- Industry
- Other Considerations
- Regulatory environment
- Economic climate

Stage

Not all organizations will have similar definitions of acceptable risk, thresholds for pain, and obstacles preventing change. Consider the following three types of organizations:

- S1s and S2s are growing, confident, and vibrant organizations in stage one.
- S3s have stumbled quite a bit, finding themselves squarely in stage three.
- S4s are humbled organizations on the verge of plunging into extinction or irrelevance.

Note here that S5s are essentially beyond saving. No function, including IT, can resuscitate an organization in stage five, at least according to Collins.

S1s and S2s These organizations realize that they need to be relatively bold in order to succeed. Perhaps Google is the best example. While they were students at Stanford University, co-founders Larry Page and Sergey Brin did not merely want to create a marginally better search engine. Rather, their grand ambition was nothing less than organizing the world's information (along with not being evil). Early on, these organizations may not have much of an IT department or even a proper CIO. At these organizations, IT can theoretically make more of an impact because of the following:

- These organizations have less internal bureaucracy.
- Company owners typically consist of only the founder(s) and VC firms.
- As a result, these organizations can move relatively quickly in addressing problems.
- Their backers realize that they have to be bold to succeed.
- At least initially, any technology is added to a new or "greenfield" site—that is, one without existing technology infrastructure.

A small, privately held start-up cannot go to public markets to raise funds in the form of stock or bond offerings. It is beholden to its investors (typically VCs). While ostensibly limited in this regard, however, the same start-up need not face many regulatory obstacles, such as SOX.

Lest you think that IT is omnipotent at these organizations, remember that being small has its drawbacks. Specifically, IT may lack sufficient resources or IT infrastructure. The example of Twitter in Chapter 2 is a perfect case in point.

S3s S3s are arguably the most interesting types of organizations. In a way, they are the antitheses of S4s: While management at S4s may disagree about the problems or the solutions, S4s have fallen from grace (at least the key internal players know that much).

S3s are still in denial. They have had a certain level of success, but key players often do not see the writing on the wall. Some will argue that action is needed to return the organization to its prior prominence. Others will ignore the signs and the data, blaming external factors and openly questioning the need to divert from a strategy that got the company to this point.

S4s Relative to S1s, and S2s IT at S4s may not be able to make as much of an impact because of the following:

- S4s have a great deal more internal bureaucracy than S1s and S2s.
- S4s typically have more owners than most S1s and S2s. These typically include individual investors, banks, company officers, or even the

federal government via the U.S. government's Troubled Asset Relief Program (TARP), which purchased assets and equity from troubled financial organizations. What's more, these owners often have vastly different agendas and objectives.

- Not all owners will agree on the problem, much less on a recommended course of action.

At S4s, technology is added to a problematic site (brownfield) or "scorched earth" site (blackfield). If anything, S4s often have too much in the way of IT infrastructure and support—or at least not the right IT infrastructure and support.

Ironically, despite their vast differences, S1s, S2s, and S4s may view risk in a similar manner. Like S1s and S2s, S4s typically need to take drastic steps, although those steps will be very different. Typical mechanisms for S4s include slashing costs, M&A activity, or reorganizing the company. S4s really have nothing left to lose. Extinction or irrelevance (stage five) is essentially inevitable. Why not pull out all the stops?

The problem is that poorly conceived, last-ditch efforts rarely deliver their intended results. In *Billion-Dollar Lessons,* Carrol and Mui write about USAir's acquisitions of Pacific Southwest Airlines and Piedmont Airlines in 1987 and 1988, respectively. After the merger, "USAir's information systems couldn't handle the load. More than once, the computer systems broke down on payday, and armies of secretaries had to type paychecks manually. USAir's archaic scheduling system was also taxed to the limit."

Aside from bad marriages, even possibly beneficial partnerships or acquisitions may suffer from IT challenges, disparate cultures, misunderstood finances, and the like.

SUMMARY AND PARALLELS TO POLITICS   The early-twentieth-century French prime minister Georges Clemenceau once said, "Not to be a socialist at twenty is proof of want of heart; to be one at thirty is proof of want of head."[5] Translation: How you feel about wealth, taxes, and politics is typically a function of age. It's easier to say "Tax the rich" than to say "Tax me."

Along the same lines, stage matters a great deal for organizations. S1s are typically very different from S3s and S4s in terms of available resources, regulatory requirements, and financial means. It's a fallacy to assume that all organizations of all types have the same options at all points.

Regardless of stage, it is very difficult for IT to contribute in an optimal manner when the organization itself is failing. In fact, IT is arguably in a no-win situation in these cases. Fundamental questions about what the organization should do make it nearly impossible for IT to support any

---

[5]Note that a variation of this quote is typically misattributed to Winston Churchill.

coherent, overarching strategy. It is easy for management to complain that "IT isn't giving us what we need" when the organization doesn't *know* what it needs. IT cannot be expected to hit a moving target.

Industry

If we accept Collins's model as a whole, then we cannot view an organization's stage in a vacuum. Industry is another critical factor that drives the ability of IT to make an impact. Technology moves at a much different pace in the telecommunications and media worlds compared to more static industries such as agriculture and pharmaceuticals. Ask former Motorola execs about Iridium or Sony about digital music. Both companies lost hundreds of millions of dollars because they stubbornly resisted technological changes.

It is imperative for the tenor of IT organizations to reflect the industry in which the organization operates. Consider two examples. Imagine a strict, by-the-book IT department adhering to rigid rules at an Internet company. I can't imagine a better way to stifle innovation. Of course, this depends on the size and maturity of the company. For example, I would expect large, established Internet companies such as eBay and Amazon to employ proper change management procedures for one simple reason: the impact of a breach or process breakdown would be huge. What's more, often well codified business processes go hand-in-hand with intelligent IT management.

Other Considerations

Stage and industry are critical considerations in determining IT's role in a Enterprise 2.0 world, but they are not alone. Other factors that drive what IT should do and how it should do it include:

- *Competitive pressures.* Not all organizations face the same level of competition. It's hard to imagine an identical role for IT in retail and pharmaceutical organizations.
- *Regulatory environment.* IT does not operate in a vacuum any more than the organization that it supports does. Translation: Projects that IT might want to undertake need to be balanced against regulatory concerns. For example, projects without sufficient audit trails or transparency may increase enterprise risk, a topic that is covered in greater detail in Chapter 15.
- *Profit margins.* Companies such as Apple have been able to charge a premium for their products, largely because of the "wow" factor. Dell

Computer has historically competed on price, not features.[6] It's doubtful that Dell management allows its employees the same time to play as does Apple.

Three Viewpoints

Against the backdrop of Collins's model, IT's traditional charter, and real-world ramifications, now it's time to get philosophical and return to the chapter's core question: What should be the role of IT in an organization?

I will offer three different viewpoints on how many leaders have viewed the role of IT in an organization:

1. Hands on
2. Hands off
3. The enabler; the moderate view

Figure 3.1 depicts the continuum of thought with respect to IT's role in an organization.

Before continuing, a few disclaimers are in order. Regardless of your philosophical leanings about the normative role of IT, understand that no function in an organization can play Superman. IT is no exception. Consider the economic meltdown. Once the house of cards tumbled for many financial firms, IT had very few available levers to stop their organizations' collapses. Organizations that realized the extent of the danger had little choice but to go belly-up, seek a buyout, or go to Uncle Sam. Even those who may have traditionally spurned a more activist role for IT would have gladly let IT save the day, if only it could.

What's more, it's important to note that a CIO might need to adopt each of the following philosophies at different points. A CIO might normally opt for a hands-off approach but, during a crisis such as a security breach, rightfully believes that IT needs to temporarily adopt a more proactive role. For the sake of discussion, this chapter looks at IT's role under normal circumstances.

Finally, I don't expect all readers to agree with the content in this section, even those in the same organization.

Hands On	Moderate	Hands Off

FIGURE 3.1 IT Thought Continuum

---

[6]Note that this is changing, as Dell has recently rolled out "high end" laptops and desktops.

Hands On

There are two slightly different hands-on views, differing only in terms of the degree of trust between IT and the LOBs. The big-brother view can best be described as "IT knows best." The obstructionist view says that, if left to their own devices, LOBs will cause enormous problems not only for IT, but for the organization as a whole.

BIG BROTHER   Some believe that IT is omniscient and omnipotent. Under this viewpoint, business end users do not possess the skills or knowledge to constructively participate in the discussion about which technologies the organizations should adopt.

This viewpoint is the polar opposite of the hands-off impotent viewpoint. By understanding the tools and the organization's data, IT can go far beyond acting as a partner with each LOB. Here, IT can actually lead the business in new directions, primarily through the deployment of new technologies.

It's interesting to note that end users fearing a big brother as an IT department may also resist SaaS because they may not be able to access their data in the event that the SaaS provider experiences problems.

OBSTRUCTIONIST   The obstructionist view is closely related to the big-brother view of IT, with one notable exception: If left to their own devices, end users will cause the organization—and IT—quite a few headaches.

To be sure, I have seen some organizations adopt this approach, and it infuriates many end users. For example, I know of one IT department that has essentially handcuffed employees via onerous security and restrictions. These were so tight that employees could not perform their jobs and use technology effectively.[7] Excessive firewalls, passwords, time-outs, and policies meant that basic tasks would take five times as long as was necessary.

Proponents of hands-on approaches would argue that IT could have either prevented the organization's demise or at least minimized the bleeding. By asking questions about the prudence and actions of each LOB, IT would have slowed the tide.

Forcing businesses to make decisions based on intelligent data would have arguably given CEOs and presidents pause at a time when it was most needed. IT's involvement would have been here as good cop or legitimate business partner. Its detachment from the business would actually have been an asset, allowing for objective reflection on questionable business

---

[7]The head of IT actually told me that he wanted to prohibit people from using Microsoft Excel in the organization for audit purposes. You just can't make things like this up.

practices. By asking LOBs to explain their actions, IT would have forced the organization to take a much-needed step back.

The problem with both the of these hands-on views is that CIOs report to CEOs—and sometimes to the chief financial officer or chief operating officer. Absent some compelling reason, CIOs who prevent the business from doing their jobs are likely to find themselves looking for employment.

ENTERPRISE 2.0 AND STAFFING IMPLICATIONS Hands-on IT departments tend to have quite a few personnel working either with or against end users. As a result, more collaborative technologies such as SOA, open source software (OSS), and agile software development can be successful only if end users don't perceive IT as obstructionist.

Hands Off

There are two slightly different hands-off views, differing only in terms of intent: impotent and libertarian. The impotent view says that IT *cannot* do anything, while the libertarian view says that IT *should not* do anything.

IMPOTENT Under perhaps the most simplistic viewpoint, some have argued that IT cannot do anything to contribute to a business. In the case of the financial meltdown, IT could not have prevented it. Banks and mortgage brokers were determined and heavily incentivized to provide loans to those clearly unable to make the payments. Even if IT had provided safeguards in the form of audit reports or restricted system access, brokers would have gamed those systems to close questionable deals.

If bankers and mortgage brokers do not fully understand the risk created by collateralized debt obligations and other complicated financial instruments (or want to understand it), then how can IT possibly be expected to do the same? How can IT alert LOBs about questionable decisions when no one knows what's questionable?

In other words, IT *cannot* own the data and interpret it for each LOB, nor *can* it make beneficial recommendations on which applications end users need.

LIBERTARIAN This viewpoint is similar to the impotent one, but with one main difference: Libertarians feel that IT may be able to do some things beyond its traditional charter to prevent an organization's decline or demise. However, IT *should not* go down this road. Proponents of this view believe that IT will hurt more often than help the organization. Note that this view is very similar to that of the CATO Institute, a right-leaning think tank that believes that the federal government should only perform functions such as fighting fires, securing our nation's borders, and printing currency. The parallels for IT are providing end users with computers, relevant software, help desk support, access to information, network security, and system stability.

The libertarian IT perspective believes that IT can stifle an organization's innovation. IT is merely a servant to the business, proving support to each LOB as needed. As my friend at the beginning of the chapter mentioned, IT should "stay out of the way."

The hands-off camp would argue that no amount of hardware, software, or technology can possibly prevent an organization's demise. IT's involvement would have been ineffective at best and counterproductive at worst. Moreover, even if IT saves the day this time, it sets a dangerous precedent for end users that IT will always bail them out. Finally, from an audit perspective, IT's involvement increases organizational risk.

In sum, IT *should not* own the data and interpret it for each LOB, nor *should* it make recommendations on which applications employees need, even if it has the means in each case to do so.

ENTERPRISE 2.0 AND STAFFING IMPLICATIONS As expected, hands-off IT departments tend to have low levels of personnel, perhaps only help desk support and a few staff positions. Like hands-on departments, more collaborative technologies, such as SOA, OSS, and agile software development, also stand very little chance of being successful. However, this is for a much different reason: End users do not have the technical chops to undertake these endeavors independently, and IT does not offer sufficient support. Hands-off IT departments ideally should embrace SaaS and cloud computing more, but security concerns may make that impossible.

The Enabler: The Moderate View

Those who follow this view believe that IT is equal parts organizational problem solver, cop, and change agent. This is perhaps the most justifiable and most common view of IT's role.

Proponents of this view cite the need for IT involvement not IT obstructionism. IT should provide tools to help the LOBs identify risk. IT shares the blame with the rest of the organization. IT's role can and should be to intervene when the business makes questionable decisions.

Moderates would argue that when signs of impending financial doom began manifesting themselves in 2006, IT should have stepped up to the plate and asked if the LOBs needed better access to information or better information. As mentioned before, at many institutions, IT personnel had both access to this information and the business acumen to understand the problems. Those who spoke up had their concerns fall on deaf ears. Many CEOs refused to listen to IT folks telling them how to run the business.

ENTERPRISE 2.0 AND STAFFING IMPLICATIONS Expect to find more staff in moderate IT environments than in hands-off departments but fewer than in hands-on departments. In moderate IT departments, more collaborative technologies, such as SOA, OSS, and agile software development, stand a reasonable chance of being successful. End users do not butt heads with IT on a daily basis. The organization has determined that a particular project is important, necessitating IT's involvement. In this vein, IT can be seen as a truly strategic and valuable resource.

Under the moderate view, IT needs time to play with different technologies to see how it can help the LOBs. (See the example of Google and the "20-percent time" policy mentioned earlier in the chapter.)

The Changing Role of the CIO

The role of the CIO in an Enterprise 2.0 world is also changing on several levels. For example, the CIO is becoming more of a business partner and less the gatekeeper of all things technology. Depending on the type of IT department, many CIOs are now asking if current technologies are meeting the needs of the business.

This mind-set cascades down within IT departments as well. CIOs should be managing and coaching IT personnel to think of the business first, not technology. This may not be a new mind-set. Some have been making this argument for 15 years. However, it seems to be gaining more acceptance as technologies have become more user-friendly and many business end users now understand them better. In this sense, the CIO leads by example, ensuring that IT does not purchase and implement technologies in a vacuum. IT needs enough business savvy to question potentially dangerous decisions and requests from the LOBs.

In his book *Breakthrough IT: Supercharging Organizational Value through Technology,* Patrick Gray argues that the role of the CIO will change as IT becomes more of a commodity. As he explains in the following sidebar, many IT functions are moving beyond the traditional utility model of performing administrative tasks. Historically, these have included:

- Establishing network connectivity.
- Granting security.
- Creating email accounts.

These are no longer differentiators. Every IT department does this. Gray foresees a new role for IT.

Maximizing the Role of IT

For several decades, the role of organizational IT was a simple one: select, implement, and maintain technology assets and associated support functions. The CIO and most of IT management came from a technology or engineering background and were generally more comfortable in the icy confines of the server room than in the boardroom. As IT became more heavily embedded in the corporation, a funny thing started happening: Corporate technology worked so well that IT started being seen as a utility; you flicked the switch and anything from email to a cloud application would "just work." Like any other utility provider, no one wanted to hear from you until your costs grew too high, or the services stopped working. Corporate IT became the electric company.

Many IT organizations embraced the utility model, focusing on the nuts and bolts of IT and ignoring the business side of the equation. CFOs demanded ever-leaner cost structures, and CIOs diligently squeezed every penny out of their budgets. While cost cutting is certainly admirable, one can only cut so much. The continuing pressure to do more with less has many in IT feeling underappreciated and frustrated that their work is seen as a commodity.

CIOs have long lamented concepts like alignment between IT and the rest of the business. Many have felt unappreciated and undervalued by their C-suite peers. With an organization built around the utility model, it is easy to see why. Just as no CEO would invite the water company to a discussion of corporate strategy, a utility-based shop also finds itself left out of strategy and tactical discussions. Diligently tracking and reporting uptime and technology utilization is just about as appealing to CEOs as the phone company reporting the uptime of their lines and the performance of their network. Clearly the utility model of IT is unsustainable. This raises the question: What is the preferred role of IT?

Obviously, there will always be a utility element to IT. Any discussion about IT enabling business strategy or playing a more visible role within the corporation will fall on deaf ears if CEOs frequently cannot check their email. The trick is to acknowledge the utility aspects of IT and build them into a self-sufficient, low-cost organization within corporate IT, whether through outsourcing or insourcing these functions to an independent group with the autonomy to make decisions and manage its own budget. Far more important than minimizing the cost of these functions is minimizing the amount of time CIOs spend directly managing them.

With the utility aspects of IT consuming a lower amount of cash and, more important, requiring less management care and feeding, the CIO

(continued)

can start taking advantage of one of IT's biggest assets: its ubiquitous nature across the corporation. Few other business units have relationships and knowledge about every area of a business, including sales, marketing, operations, and finance. IT knows the systems and often has a strong grasp of the processes in each of these functions. Rather than merely waiting by the phone for the next request to build or modify a technical tool, IT can leverage this knowledge to suggest new ways in which business units can work together. IT goes from the handyman called for a specific job to the trusted adviser that provides tactical insight and helps plot a course for the future. The IT organizations that are successful at this transition often look and act like an internal consulting organization, more adept at talking about business process improvement and optimization than IT's usual technical domain.

As IT leverages its knowledge of the business, it should also apply more rigor and attention to its portfolio of projects. In any other business unit, it is the project-related work that becomes the focus and driver of the business unit's success. For sales, it might be a new tactic to push a particular product. For finance, it may be a new acquisition or spin-off. Most IT organizations are quite adept at managing projects. However, they often frame their projects as technical implementation efforts with milestones and the ultimate goal of the project revolving around the technology being implemented. Rather than focusing on the technology behind the project, IT should map the technology to business objectives. When business objectives are at the core of IT's project portfolio, each project can be analyzed in terms of risk, return horizon, and fit within the overall portfolio. IT's project work can now be viewed on equal footing with the efforts of any other business unit and its value clearly understood and quantifiable.

In an IT organization that has mastered the utility functions of IT, leveraged its unique knowledge of the entire business, and started managing its portfolio of projects as a group of investments in the company, discussions of alignment are no longer academic. IT is speaking the language of the rest of the organization. IT is delivering results that directly map to the organization's strategic and tactical goals. The technology is the grease that turns the wheels, rather than the sole focus of IT. When a complex new challenge surfaces, IT is then one of the first organizations brought to the table, rather than an afterthought grudgingly involved only when there is no other alternative.

Clearly, an IT organization acting in this capacity is not only more fulfilling for those who work inside it, but also is a source of competitive advantage to the organization that houses it. Many have lamented the relationship between IT and the rest of the business, yet this discussion

(continued)

(continued)

ultimately misses the point. IT is just as much a part of the business as accounting, finance, or sales. When acting in the role just described, IT will finally be regarded as such.

Patrick Gray is president of Prevoyance Group and author of *Breakthrough IT: Supercharging Organizational Value through Technology.*

Summary

One IT management philosophy is not inherently better than another. Different organizations in different phases of their life spans face different business and regulatory environments. As a result, they have different technological needs. Whether hands-on or hands-off or somewhere in between, all organizations must adopt Enterprise 2.0 technologies in a manner consistent with their individual philosophies. For example, expecting a traditionally hands-off IT department to effectively roll out a new collaboration tool with a disaffected and skeptical end-user base is the acme of foolishness. It's also unwise to expect a very hierarchical organization to embrace agile software development methods, such as those described in Chapter 14.

Next Steps

- Ensure that the business has realistic expectations for Enterprise 2.0 technologies from IT.
- If you accept Jim Collins's model, then which stage is your organization at?
- If the organization wants to open up and embrace collaborative technologies such as OSS, clouds, and SaaS, make sure that IT is on board. IT departments used to their traditional roles as guardians and gatekeepers will have to adjust to a new reality in which much lies beyond their control. Adjustments may have to take place by bringing in new CIOs or other personnel more open to embracing this new reality.
- De-perimeterization is huge. Take a cautious approach at first with regard to security.

PART II

Architecture, Software Development, and Frameworks

CHAPTER 4

Cloud Computing

Amy Wohl

For a successful technology, reality must take precedence over public relations, for Nature cannot be fooled.

—Richard P. Feynman

A Brief History of Cloud Computing

Originally, *cloud computing* was a vague term for a very vague and distant future in which computing would occur in a few remote locations without the need for very much human intervention. Infinite computing resources would be available for any need at costs approaching zero. Certainly, users would not need to know or care about how the computers, their software, or the network functioned.

In the real world, physical computing progressed differently. We cycled between periods when computing was more centralized (and seemed more remote and less accessible to users) and other periods when computing was right on user desktops. No one was ever satisfied.

Centralized computing failed to give users enough control and was too inflexible. Distributed computing made every user his or her own system administrator and was very inefficient.

In the past few years, as the cost of a unit of compute power[1] has continued to decrease—but the cost of humans with the skills to implement and manage computer systems has not—the vision of centralized computing has returned. It has taken several turns. Some computer scientists have suggested (and experimented with) a vast grid of computers, attached via the Internet, whose power can be combined for large-scale tasks when needed. In some cases, very large computing systems can be part of these grids

---

[1] Note that this is sometimes referred to as "computing power."

for specialized tasks. Others have suggested a computing utility that would provide just as much computing power as an organization needed, on an on-demand basis, much like electricity.

Eventually, as large Web users such as Google and Amazon built out enormous data centers for their own purposes, they realized that they could permit others to access these "clouds" of computing power at relatively attractive prices. The cloud computing era began.

Today, many companies are putting together very large data centers, sometimes as extensions of their own needs, sometimes just for customers to use. Originally the idea was that these clouds of computing would offer processing power and storage. Anything else would be added by the customer. As the idea of cloud computing became more popular, additional function has been added. Some clouds also offer systems management. Others are actually providing a set of applications as part of the cloud.

We could be grammarians and complain that applications are not supposed to be part of the cloud's vocabulary, but the market will sort this out. For now, most buyers think that cloud computing means computing resources on demand, perhaps including applications, delivered over the Internet.

Consumers and Small Office, Home Office (SOHO) versus the Enterprise

It is well to remember that every user, every application, and every cloud are not equal. For example, many of the early software as a service (SaaS) applications were designed for consumers, small businesses and home offices, and individual professionals. These applications (and the infrastructure behind them) are very different from what an enterprise (an organization with more than 1,000 employees) might need.

Individuals and small businesses are attracted by low cost, ease of use, and good-enough computing; that is, the application works well enough and is available most of the time.

Enterprises have high standards; essentially they want the power and control of their data center to be replicated in the cloud.

While we can satisfy the needs and demands of individuals and small businesses most of the time with most cloud infrastructures and SaaS applications, we are still working at meeting the higher demands of enterprises for quality of service, high levels of support, and very high availability, as well as security and data integrity. Enterprises also have to make their cloud computing investments compatible at some level with their ongoing usage of older (in some cases much older) applications.

A Cloud of One's Own

For most organizations, a decision on cloud computing will be a matter of choosing which cloud to use. (Many may use several, selecting different clouds for different purposes.) But for some large enterprises and government organizations, a cloud of their own may be an appropriate solution. IBM is already offering to build user-specific clouds, and several takers have appeared, including Wuxi City of China to support new entrepreneurs, the Vietnamese government institutions and universities to energize innovation in their country, and iTricity, a utility-based hosting service provider headquartered in the Netherlands. Sogeti, part of the global consulting firm Capgemini, has bought its own cloud to help it transform its company culture and move people into a Web 2.0 environment. Softex of Brazil will use its cloud to accelerate its software industry. This allows the organization to optimize the cloud for its own purposes and to make it available to its own constituency. In the near future, we would not be surprised to see some very large enterprises with clouds of their own (and some are in the works) and some systems integrators (SIs) who maintain clouds to service their customers' needs. Private clouds are somewhat controversial (i.e., some analysts claim a private cloud is not a cloud).

What Is a Cloud?

Interviewing customers and vendors makes it clear that the hype level is beyond amazing. I know that there is a point in any successful technology where it is used to label everything because it's so good at attracting positive attention, but I think we're close to reaching the saturation level here. I hope so. If everything is a cloud, then it gets very hard to see anything!

The confusion level is high. Everyone who is looking at clouds as a buyer, a seller, or a commentator (press, analyst, consultant—you name it) has their own definitions. I have a rule here. If you want to communicate with someone about clouds on a serious level, exchange definitions first. Otherwise, you may just be talking past each other.

In fact, a vendor executive I spoke to recently wanted to know if I thought cloud computing would enter the "trough of disillusionment" mid-2010. (This is a Gartner Research term for what happens to technologies as they go through their introduction to adoption cycles. Gartner says that after a Peak of Inflated Expectations comes a Trough of Disillusionment, followed by a Slope of Enlightenment and a Plateau of Productivity. I think there are so many rationales, pulling in so many directions, that it's hard to tell.)

Definitions of Cloud Computing

According to a National Institute of Standards and Technology (NIST) report,[2] cloud computing offers the prospect of dramatically increasing your computing power, being able to balance workloads with demand, and paying only for the services you use. Here is how NIST and a few of the leaders in the cloud computing marketplace define cloud computing.

NIST

A pay-per-use model for enabling convenient, on-demand network access to a shared pool of configurable and reliable computing resources (e.g., networks, servers, storage, applications, services) that can be rapidly provisioned and released with minimal consumer management effort or service provider interaction.

Gartner

A style of computing where massively scalable, IT-enabled capabilities are provided "as a service" across the Internet to multiple external customers.

International Data Corporation (IDC)

An emerging IT deployment, development, and delivery model enabling real time delivery of products, services, and solutions over the Internet.

University of California–Berkeley

Cloud Computing refers to both the applications delivered as services over the Internet and the hardware and systems software in the Data Centers that provide those services. The services themselves have long been referred to as Software as a Service (SaaS), so we use that term. The Data Center hardware and software is [sic] what we call a Cloud.

Cloud Manifesto

The key characteristics of the cloud are the ability to scale and provision computing power dynamically in a cost-efficient way and the ability of the consumer (end user, organization, or information technology [IT] staff) to make the most of that power without having to manage the underlying complexity of the technology. The cloud architecture itself can be private (hosted within an organization's firewall) or public (hosted on the Internet).

I believe the Berkeley definition and Cloud Manifesto definition come closest to the reality of what we are seeing in the marketplace.

---

[2]Jeff Erlichman, 1105 Government Information Group Custom Media, 2009.

Jeff Mell, author of the NIST report, believes that all clouds provide:

- On-demand self-service.
- Network access.
- Location-independent resource pooling.
- Rapid elasticity.
- Pay per use.
- (And perhaps) multitenancy.

Every pundit has some variation on that theme. I'd point out that many SaaS and PaaS (platform as a service, or computing infrastructure on demand) vendors, while providing the service on demand and permitting elasticity, sign contracts with users that presume some minimum level of service (and perhaps a maximum) with discounts for payments in advance or usage above a certain volume level. I think it's still cloud, it's just cloud trying to accommodate the cash flow needs of the service providers and the predictability needs of their IT buyers.

Today, cloud delivery models include:

- *Infrastructure as a service (IaaS)*. This is the Amazon and Rackspace model: computing power and storage delivered from the cloud. Users are responsible for the applications they run on top or the applications development and testing they engage in.
- *Software as a service (SAAS)*. The user sees this as on-demand software; the independent software provider (ISV) sees it as a distribution model for its software. More and more software in this model is designed specifically to exploit the Web; you should prefer it.
- *Platform as a service (PaaS)*. This deploys customer-created software for cloud delivery. Good examples are OpSource and Salesforce.com.

We're still not talking about private clouds; we'll get to them shortly, but for now think of them as clouds with limited access.

Cloud Architecture

I approached cloud architecture by thinking of it as a layer cake. Initially, it was a pretty simple one, including just some infrastructure and SaaS software, as shown in Figure 4.1.

But cloud architecture got complicated quickly, leading me to draw a cake with more layers, as shown in Figure 4.2. Initially, I thought of it just as a layer cake, adding management and (hopefully) applications integration. A user could now buy infrastructure from a platform vendor (Amazon,

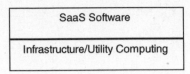

| SaaS Software |
| Infrastructure/Utility Computing |

FIGURE 4.1   Cloud Architecture 101

| Integration of Applications |
| SaaS Software |
| Management |
| Utility Computing (infrastructure) |

FIGURE 4.2   Cloud Architecture

Google, OpSource, IBM, etc.) with or without the management layer. Independent software vendors, or customers for that matter, could then add SaaS applications. Few have gotten to the top layer where they try to enhance the user experience by integrating the applications (which may be coming from multiple platforms and applications), offering them under a single sign-on and interface, and offering at least some data integration.

Michael Salsburg, an architect at Unisys, noted that he was thinking about a slightly different architecture. In his version (see Figure 4.3), management isn't a separate layer, but rather a layer that sits outside everything else and integrates and manages it.

I liked that a lot. In fact, I ended up altering my own chart as a result, as shown in Figure 4.4.

The layer cake has changed, with management moving out to the left, becoming a separate element that integrates all the other layers.

The cloud is in a constant state of flux. Improvements, both intellectual and physical, are welcome as we attempt to improve and better understand what clouds can do.

| Management | XaaS |
| | Utility Computing |

FIGURE 4.3   Managed Cloud Computing 1

Management	Integration of Applications
	SaaS Software
	Management
	Utility Computing (infrastructure)

FIGURE 4.4   Managed Cloud Computing 2

The Private Cloud: When Is a Cloud Not a Cloud?

To talk about cloud computing, it might help to first define it. The difficulty is there is a vivid debate occurring about just that subject.

The notion of a cloud (as a technical concept) first appeared in communications. Every diagram of networks, particularly multiple networks, was topped with a "cloud." The idea was that the cloud was beyond specific definition but that it included everything that the network might need and changed over time as technology and applications evolved.

It was natural for the biggest and most pervasive network, the Internet, to come to be thought of as a cloud.

Cloud computing takes the idea of processing at a distance (not a new idea at all) and translates it to the world of the Internet. Cloud computing has its precedents in time-shared computing, when in order to connect any remote user to the computing environment, expensive, secure physical connections had to be created. In the cloud computing round, we substitute the Internet (with or without secure connectivity) for those specific physical connections. This changes the equation enormously and makes access to the function of the cloud ubiquitous.

In the beginning it was easy. We had some clouds. They offered access to computing power and storage at a fee, usually per user per hour. All the clouds were public, in the sense that anyone with money (or, more realistically, a credit card) and an Internet connection could use cloud computing. But the term *cloud computing* quickly stretched to include not just the processing offering but other services as well as applications (previously referred to as SaaS) that the clouds enable.

But nothing appealing remains static and unchanged, and cloud computing quickly grew in multiple dimensions:

- Early cloud computing vendors like Amazon and Google added additional functions (often for additional fees), such as storage and development software.
- Additional vendors entered the marketplace, such as Rackspace and OpSource, each with its own focus based on its previous experiences, customer demand, and strengths.
- Large customers that were interested in the idea of cloud computing, but unwilling to place their information in a shared environment, wondered if private clouds were possible.

It is this interest in attracting enterprise business and providing additional security and privacy that has caused much of the controversy over the boundaries and definition of cloud computing.

Many cloud computing providers will now provide a private cloud for a customer, usually a large enterprise. Until recently, this meant building a new physical data center around a cloud architecture (virtualized servers, flexibility in scaling up and down, and the ability to support—and connect—users in many geographies). But it was entirely private and owned by the customer. Ownership, of course, is a flexible concept itself. IBM, for example, will build infrastructure, including private clouds, for customers and charge for them on a lease or lease-to-own basis as well as sell the new facility to the customer.

Although access to this private cloud would normally be via a virtual private network (VPN) over the Internet, the cloud was invisible and unavailable to anyone other than its owner and his or her invitees. Scalability was limited to the resources of the private cloud, and the customer was making a significant investment in capital infrastructure (or at least a commitment to it).

Recently, several vendors (Amazon and OpSource, e.g.,) have started offering "virtual private clouds" (or "private virtual clouds"). In this case, the customer contracts with its cloud vendor to create one or more private clouds within the vendor's larger public cloud. Subject to contract terms, the customer can choose to scale the private cloud up and down, enjoying the capital infrastructure investments and larger resources of the vendor, rather than being limited to the customer's individual organizational initiative. From within the public cloud that enables the private virtual cloud, the customer could choose to interoperate with other clouds (or other Web-based applications). Figure 4.5 shows public, private, and virtual private clouds.

And there's the controversy: Is a private cloud a cloud at all? Some claim that since a cloud, *by definition*, offers the ability to buy computing power (and other capabilities and services) on demand, without the need to buy the infrastructure, a private cloud is by definition not a cloud at all. These same debaters usually argue that a private virtual cloud *is* a cloud because it is simply a temporary (although temporary could be as long as the customer likes) piece of a public cloud, subject to scaling up and down, as any proper cloud computing offering is intended to do.

It's this kind of debate that convinces me that cloud computing is still pretty immature. Not that it doesn't work; it does. In fact, lots of customers are happily computing away in the cloud, for purposes as diverse as additional computing power; development and test environments of any required configuration; access to software more immediately and with fewer internal resource requirements than traditional, in-house implemented software; and the ability to create shared environments, outside the

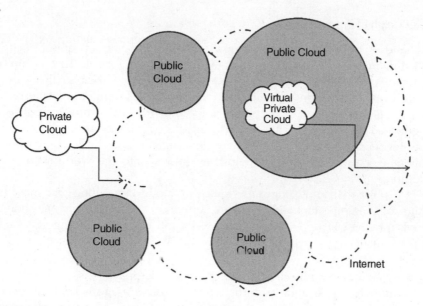

FIGURE 4.5 Public, Private, and Virtual Private Clouds

organizational firewall, where all kinds of workers (employees, contractors, suppliers, customers, and others) can collaborate.

Rather, we are all still testing the boundaries of exactly what we'd like cloud computing to be. Vendors want to take advantage of a hot new marketing term; customers bring their normal expectations to a new technology: They expect it to solve every problem. Cloud computing is no different than other technologies. It can offer extraordinary and growing capabilities that will make it attractive to most business customers for some things. But no technology will ever solve every problem, and it is when the users recognize the boundaries of a new technology and routinely use it for its strengths that a technology begins to mature and be genuinely useful.

Cloud Economics

Cloud economics has caused many ISVs, service providers, and customers to reconsider how they manage computing, especially large-scale computing for large enterprises. Hype abounds, from claiming that cloud computing can't be used by large enterprises to the noisy shout that cloud computing will kill IT.

The Death of Enterprise IT?

Whenever we get an important new technology, some are quick to rush to thinking it will replace everything that went before it. That is rarely if ever true. IBM is selling more mainframes today (albeit smaller ones) than ever. In addition to their traditional role as the engine of enterprise IT, mainframes are also becoming important for supporting specialized, dedicated applications. They are also increasingly important in the emerging economies, where developing government and business activities often look to mainframes to help them move onto the world stage and compete.

Against that knowledge, the idea that cloud computing will push IT into some unimportant and much smaller corner seems unlikely. We should look for smart IT departments using SaaS and cloud computing as a new option to:

- Support geographically dispersed users and applications.
- Allow for application patterns where baseline usage is low, but occasional usage is much higher, without the need to invest in capital structure and staff for peak periods.
- Try out new applications at lower risk.
- Move applications with little or no competitive advantage to a less expensive environment and use freed-up resources to better advantage.
- Consider the cloud architecture for the data center itself (private clouds) where the organization's need for data control or the support of existing proprietary applications makes that attractive.

Cloud computing won't be the whole thing and it won't put IT out of business. It will give IT new ways to choose how to best spend the organization's dollars, apportioning more to new development and less to managing the existing infrastructure.

A survey conducted by Applied Research West among 250 enterprise IT executives in June 2009 found that "widespread enterprise adoption of cloud computing is contingent upon solving access, security and performance concerns."

More than 80 percent of large enterprise IT managers are using or trying out cloud computing within their enterprises, and approximately 66 percent of respondents already have a dedicated budget for the cloud. Seventy-one percent expect their cloud computing budget to grow over the next couple of years.

More than 80 percent said they have some sort of private or public cloud computing solution in the works, at the very least at the trial stages. Half reported a full cloud deployment.

The biggest drivers for participating in public clouds were efficiency, reduction of capital costs, and amelioration of IT staffing issues. The key drivers behind adoption of private clouds were reduction of capital costs, agility, and staffing.

But the barriers to adoption show up, too. Approximately 90 percent of respondents said that access control is an important enabling technology in order to build cloud deployments; 89 percent said their organizations must have their network security ducks in a row in order to leverage the cloud; and 88 percent reported that server and storage virtualization were essential technologies in the cloud.

While the vast majority of organizations are deploying or considering cloud projects, respondents couldn't agree on what cloud computing is and is not. When offered five different definitions of cloud computing, survey participants could not concur on a single explanation as being "just right." (There's that definition problem again.) But participants in this survey did mainly agree that SaaS and cloud computing were different.

In an analysts' debate sponsored by BriefingsDirect (August 2009), there was a great deal of agreement that while a lot of enterprise IT budgets would go in the direction of the cloud, the cloud market was far too immature to support many enterprise IT requirements and concerns. Collaborative computing, for example, is moving into the cloud. Analysts also agreed that applications whose resource needs changed dramatically over time were good candidates for the cloud. Many also noted the potential cost-saving benefits of the cloud and felt that the day of the giant IT shop, where 80 percent of the staff is keeping the machines running, might be drawing to a close. However, they agreed that legacy applications are hard to move and enterprise IT will have to trust the cloud computing environment before it will choose to move many mission-critical applications to the cloud.

Cloud Computing *Is* for Enterprises

At the Uptime Institute's Symposium in April 2009, a conference where facilities management meets IT, I came face-to-face with a new McKinsey report on cloud computing that claimed that the economics made sense only for small and medium-sized companies, but not for enterprises with their own data centers. The analysis then compared the cost of using Amazon's service with the cost of a typical data center. McKinsey also assumed that the firm would move all of its computing to the cloud (we don't know of any organizations that plan to do that).

As you might guess, lots of conversation and controversy ensued.

Cloud computing may not be cheaper if all you are looking at is a comparison of hardware and an assumption of people costs. *The value of cloud computing lies elsewhere:*

- In the flexibility of being able to gain immediate access to additional computing (or to shrink your system when you don't need it).
- In the difference in time to market for new business opportunities.
- In the additional value (not included in the McKinsey study) provided in clouds that offer to manage the hardware (via systems software and other offerings) or to provide applications (SaaS). There is a brilliant explication of this by Balakrishna Narasimhan,[3] which I recommend.

Many large companies are already taking advantage of SaaS. Workday, Inc., for example, has clients for its human resources (HR) and financials with more than 20,000 employees.[4] Public clouds can be ideal places for large companies to use specific applications or obtain additional capacity. Private clouds (which may not be clouds at all, in the sense that the organization may own the hardware and software rather than temporarily rent its use) are intended primarily for large enterprises. I am certain that schemes that will make private clouds into capital-free propositions (if not available on a month-to-month basis) for any customer who needs one are already in or nearing the market. Much like rented or leased infrastructure today, you will be able to lease private clouds.

Vendor Strategies

There are many vendors that have chosen to enter the cloud business. In some cases, it was a natural adjunct of their own business. In other cases, they met a market demand and later realized that they could associate these efforts with an increasingly popular category.

Cloud vendors offer a variety of services, from computer power on demand and storage to developer tools, access to cloud-based applications, and private clouds.

There is no sound way of predicting which additional vendors will tie themselves to the cloud strategy. Of one thing I am certain: In so dynamic a market, we are sure to see at least one more company create itself from scratch and focus on cloud computing as its core business. That means not only are all the players not at the table yet, but some of them are not even in the room.

Some of the current players include Amazon, Google, IBM, Microsoft, OpSource, and Red Hat. Some of their offerings are summarized in Table 4.1, but note that while some offerings are well supported and relatively mature (if anything in the cloud market can be described as mature), others are in

---

[3]http://blog.appirio.com/2009/04/cloud-computing-savings-real-or.html.
[4]www.workday.com.

TABLE 4.1 Vendor Cloud Offerings

Cloud Vendor	Offering(s)	Target Market	Comments
Amazon	EC2, Amazon S3, Amazon SQS, Amazon SimpleDB, Virtual Private Cloud	Developers, ISVs, companies looking for additional capacity	Also partners with other players, such as IBM for development tools
Google	App Engine	Developers	Also offers a set of applications for individual users and small and medium-size businesses (SMBs)
IBM	Multiple offerings from development space on IBM clouds to private clouds; business analytics and large-scale financial analysis; Cloudburst	Large enterprises, ISVs	Cloudburst appliance creates a private cloud from enterprises' existing software
Microsoft	Azure (beta), Windows Live, Mesh	ISVs, developers, application consumers	Microsoft also offers applications from Exchange and Sharepoint to Office Web Apps
OpSource	Private Virtual Cloud	User organizations	Claims better security and performance
Red Hat	No clouds itself but Premier Cloud Provider Certification and Partner Program	Support for open source in the cloud	Partner: Amazon

various stages of experimentation and may be beta offerings. Also note that while some names appear similar, the services offered may differ. For example, the Amazon Virtual Private Cloud offering is rich but requires quite a bit of Web know-how to implement; the OpSource Private Virtual Cloud offering implements a cloud in a few minutes. Different private cloud offerings have different architectures; so far there is no agreement on exactly what a private cloud is or does.

Customer Strategies

Customers can have cloud strategies, too. If the customer is large, serving many constituencies, it can have a considerable effect in the cloud marketplace. Consider the following examples of the U.S. government and Wuxi.

U.S. Government

The U.S. government has moved into the cloud with its Apps.gov cloud, offering government-certified SaaS applications. The initial applications government agencies are offered include a collection of social applications, such as Twitter, Facebook, and YouTube. They can also try Salesforce.com and Google Docs. The government will be adding other SaaS offerings. The federal government is also considering using its own (private) clouds to support government agencies in the future, rather than building individual traditional data centers.

Wuxi

Wuxi is a medium-size city in China (population of 2 million) where IBM is building a private cloud, government-funded, for use by software businesses. The cloud will offer a place both to host the firm's IT centers as well as to host its software for access as SaaS applications. Twenty of the 2,000 software companies in Wuxi joined the cloud within weeks. The cloud will be funded by the local government, but expansion could be funded by the national Chinese stimulus package. IBM looks to a potential expansion to 100 Chinese cities and supporting 200,000 software companies in IBM-developed Chinese government clouds.

Standards and Interoperability

These two topics are together because they are so interdependent. It is standards, de facto or de jure,[5] that make interoperability possible, and it is the demand for interoperability that calls for standards.

But the timing of standards is a critical thing. Trying to create standards too early in a new market can have significant consequences:

---

[5]De facto standards are those that are based on a vendor's application programming interfaces and are created by the vendor's power in the marketplace. De jure standards are formal standards, agreed to by many vendors (and users) through a standards organization.

- Big players can force smaller players into using their specifications as de facto standards (think Windows), but that isn't necessarily good for users.
- On the Web, a very user-friendly and rich *user* interface could be more important than application programming interfaces (which users don't see or influence).
- In a survey, we asked users whether they would demand that clouds be interoperable. We think that it is unlikely that any one user or organization will be able to get all the services it wants from a single cloud. That cries out for being able to interconnect clouds easily and use services across clouds. Will we get that? Not easily, I think.

In the clouds, just what interoperability might be is going to vary from organization to organization. For a professional or small business, making it easy to sign on to multiple clouds and to move data from one environment to another may be enough.

In a large enterprise, much more interoperability will ultimately be required. This might range from:

- One public cloud to another.
- Between public and private (virtual or otherwise) clouds.
- Between public and/or private clouds and legacy data and applications (hosted internally).
- Between private clouds hosted in different environments.
- Between applications running on different types of clouds.

And at least a dozen other combinations we haven't thought of yet. We're going to need very good standards, widely implemented, for this to work. Otherwise, we are going to be back at selecting a single vendor and depending on that vendor to provide interoperability between its own cloud environments.

In discussing interoperability and standards, it's important to consider the role of open source. By adopting open source solutions, organizations move toward more interoperability. That argues for open source in the cloud, but, of course, even open source includes multiple (and not necessarily completely compatible) solutions to many problems. Open source can move cloud interoperability closer to its goals, but standards are still required.

Security

Some users (especially small ones in nonregulated industries) may be happy with consumer-level security—probably secure passwords. Keep in mind that consumers are doing banking, credit card shopping, and accessing health records—all applications that require a fair level of security—with relative satisfaction, if some nervousness.

But enterprises (even relatively smaller ones) will probably want more security. Just what they will want depends on their expectations. "As secure as my own data center" is a line we hear fairly often. In order to achieve suitable levels of security, we need not just the technology of security (which we understand pretty well), but also cross-platform governance, spanning security from the enterprise data center to all the clouds that enterprise employs. With both corporate governance and IT governance growing in importance and adoption, this is likely to be more broadly available, but early adopters will want to make certain that the clouds they choose offer the level of security and governance they require.

The Future of Clouds

This is an exciting time in the cloud computing market. It is a dynamic environment, with nearly every day bringing new revelations of cloud offerings, new partnerships, and new cloud users. Everyone wants to be part of the cloud as a platform provider or a cloud application or a user.

Do we know where this will end? We can probably project its reasonable ending. Too many vendors without the right experience or resources will enter the market and not all of them will succeed. Too many ISVs will try to field applications and only some of them will be real winners. And some customers will learn (once again) that nothing is the solution to everything. Of course, we don't know when this will happen or who the winners and losers will be. In the meantime it's going to be a lot of fun trying to sort it out.

Look for:

- Many vendors to announce SaaS and PaaS (platform as a service) offerings. Some user organizations will wait for their existing vendors to make announcements, because they enjoy their current relationships and feel this will offer better migration and interoperability for existing software. Other users will find what they are looking for in another vendor's offerings.
- Expectations to climb sky high as more vendors make many excited pronouncements about their cloud offerings; expect customers to be disappointed when they discover what they actually can do. This is a normal part of a new technology cycle.
- Cloud computing usage to expand quickly, especially in the individual user and small and medium-size business (SMB) sectors, where the

products will have to be very appealing and easy to implement and use to succeed.

- Every category of customer, including the largest enterprises, to use cloud computing for some things but almost no one (except some consumers and small businesses) to use it for everything.

In the meantime, enjoy the clouds—in this case they are not an omen of bad weather, but rather part of a sunny new computing future.

Summary

Cloud computing is still in its infancy, but it is already a very big baby. All of the large vendors have entered or plan to enter this market.

Clouds are being offered in many forms, from public clouds that anyone can use (but which may require technical know-how) to private clouds built for and owned by a single user. In between are private virtual clouds (public clouds that contain private clouds).

Cloud architecture will continue to evolve to permit additional layers of services to be offered. Cloud offerings will no doubt grow not just in number but also in variety.

It is unlikely that cloud computing will replace other on-premises modes, but it will likely grow to more than 30 percent of the market and conceivably even more. The trick for customers will be in deciding which applications to put in the cloud and which to keep closer to home.

Next Steps

- Identify new applications that could run in a public cloud.
- Identify existing applications that could run in a public cloud.
- Identify legacy applications that are likely to need to remain in your data center.
- Considering your organization's need for privacy or to support legacy applications, judge whether you are a candidate for a private cloud.
- Identify appropriate cloud vendors.

CHAPTER 5

Open Source: The War That Both Sides Won

Heather Meeker

First they ignore you, then they laugh at you, then they fight you, then you win.

—Mohandas Gandhi

Introduction

Most people know that the Cold War ended in 1991. In case you missed that, the capitalists won. Most people do not know, however, that around 2003 another cold war ended. This time, capitalists did not exactly win, but they did not exactly lose, either. This other cold war took place between two philosophies of software licensing: proprietary and free software. The free software movement is a technopolitical ideology that has been gaining ground since the early 1990s, based on the idea that software source code should be publicly available. Proprietary software is the kind we have all been familiar with since the 1980s—the kind with the click-to-accept end-user license agreements or big, expensive enterprise licensing contracts.

Microsoft's Bill Gates once famously called free software "communist."[1] Although that term was obviously intended to be an insult, in a way it was accurate as well. Academics who write about free software are fond of calling it a "gift economy"—which is a nice way of saying that some people will still do work in a system antithetical to private property rights. But in what might be one of the oddest developments of the business world, almost

---

[1]http://archives.cnn.com/2000/TECH/computing/02/11/free.software.idg/.

TABLE 5.1 Proprietary and Open Source Alternatives

Proprietary Product	Market Share	Open Source Alternative	Market Share
Microsoft IIS	30% (approx.)	Apache Web Server	50% (approx.)[a]
Internet Explorer	53%	Firefox	23%
Windows	86.56%	Linux	2.2%[b]

[a]Apache's share has fallen from over 70 percent, but appears to be in a plateau. http://ostatic.com/blog/apache-holds-steady-market-share-still-dominating-microsoft-iis.

[b]www.tgdaily.com/content/view/43824/140/. For more detailed information, see www.w3counter.com/globalstats.php. This percentage is much higher—about 23 percent—for server implementations than for desktop implementations.

every major technology company in existence today, including Microsoft, has embraced free software. That's right—they are all communists now. And their stockholders are not even upset about it.

This chapter seeks to explain how and why the strangest of bedfellows came to be so friendly, and what it might mean for the software industry.

A New Geography for Software

The growth of open source software over the past decade has been meteoric. In 1991, free software was a utopian dream of software hobbyists and *über*geeks. In 2009, it is considered an essential part of the knowledge tools of every businessperson, engineer, and attorney in the technology industry. In 2009, if you don't understand open source, you don't understand software. And in 2009, even your toaster has software in it. That means open source is central to every industry, not just what we normally think of as the technology sector.

Statistics are hard to come by the in open source world, because its essentially noncommercial nature means that statistics on open source usage are not within the grasp of any one source. Let's face it—writing was invented to calculate tax bills, and when a product is available for nothing, no one tends to keep track of its sales very well. But by conventional wisdom, the market looks like Table 5.1.

Open source is also notably countercyclical—but only in the sense that its use does not decline in times of economic stress. It is strong in good times as well. In a recent article, the *Economist* noted the growth, throughout the economic downturn, of organizations using or considering open source software—particularly in the United Kingdom, where adoption has lagged behind the United States and continental Europe.[2]

---

[2]"Born Free," *Economist*, May 28, 2009.

When UNIX Walked the Earth

Most people in the technology business have heard of open source, but many still do not quite know what it is. *Open source* is the term most commonly used to refer to free software. As in all ideological wars, the terminology one uses is fraught with peril. To understand it, we need to delve into some history and some technology.

The killer app of open source is the Linux operating system (OS). To understand why its development led to the open source movement, it is essential to know something about its progenitor, UNIX. UNIX was developed by AT&T Bell Laboratories in the 1970s and 1980s. Because AT&T had been in hot water with the U.S. Justice Department due to antitrust allegations, it was operating under a consent decree that required the company not to engage in commercial activities other than telephone service. AT&T responded to this by spinning off a research and development arm, AT&T Bell Laboratories, which was home to some of the brightest engineers of the time.

Two of these men were arguably the fathers of modern computing. Ken Thompson and Dennis Ritchie wrote an operating system called UNIX, but in order to write it, they had to invent a whole new computer programming language, which they called "C." UNIX was written to operate the computers of the day: minicomputers—a category that no longer truly exists today. A minicomputer was about the size of a refrigerator, cost about $100,000 in 1980 dollars, and did a fraction of what your cell phone can do today. C was a compiled language; in other words, the code written by the programmer had to be translated or compiled into a smaller, faster form to allow the computer to execute it. UNIX represented a revolution in computing, and suddenly became a very popular thing.

The consent decree restricted AT&T from licensing UNIX on commercial terms. So AT&T gave copies of UNIX to universities and others all over the world, on very permissive licensing terms and for practically nothing, and soon UNIX became the "commons" of computer research and development. Computer scientists began to share their improvements and innovations for UNIX. This was long before universities starting claiming the copyright in what professors wrote, and so there was nothing to stop them. When the consent decree was lifted, AT&T started a commercial licensing program for UNIX, under proprietary terms that did not allow the sharing of source code modifications. Each vendor developed its own flavor of UNIX, and from that day forward, UNIX forked into many incompatible versions.

The free software movement was started by some of the leading programmers of the UNIX era. They wanted to ensure that the privatization of an operating system that had benefited from community contributions would never happen again. So Richard Stallman, the visionary of free software, created a copyright license to set the rules for community contribution and sharing. That license was the GNU General Public License, commonly referred to as the GPL. This license required, as a condition of use of the software, that if you shared any copies of the software, even copies you had modified on your own, they must be shared under the terms of the GPL, which in turn passed along the right and obligation to share to all recipients. For this reason the GPL is sometimes called viral—its terms stick to the software forever. But the more politically correct, and legally accurate, way to characterize the GPL is similar to an easement or covenant in real estate title. The obligation to share the code runs with the title to the code, just as an easement or covenant might run with the land. It is a legal burden on the rights in the software that cannot be repudiated or avoided. Stallman called scheme of enforced sharing "copyleft."

By the mid-1990s, Microsoft had unequivocally won the computer platform wars. Apple, the only viable alternative, was waning as a computer company. That meant there was essentially one choice for a microcomputer operating system, and that was Microsoft Windows. Because of the economies of standardization, no private company was capable of competing with Microsoft in the operating system space. The reason Microsoft won those wars was that the older operating systems like UNIX did not run on the newer, cheaper, smaller Intel processors that were flooding the market and making computers truly accessible to the public. DOS and Windows did. But there were many die-hard UNIX users, particularly in academia and large organizations. After all, these programmers and system designers cut their teeth on UNIX in the consent decree era.

There were several attempts to write operating systems that would be useful alternatives to UNIX. In particular, many computer engineers wanted to be able to use a system that met all the specifications of UNIX and could interact with UNIX applications but that could not be privatized. The most successful attempt was Linux, which was written by Linus Torvalds, a young computer programmer in Helsinki. He wrote it as a school project. The first version of Linux was released in 1991.

Meanwhile, Richard Stallman had started the GNU Project, operated by the not-for-profit Free Software Foundation (FSF), whose goal was to write a free software operating system that was compatible with the specifications for UNIX. (GNU is a recursive acronym for "GNU's not UNIX.") Operating systems include many elements, only one of which is the so-called kernel that runs programs on your computer. A viable OS also requires development tools like compliers, debuggers, text editors, user interfaces, and administrative tools. The GNU Project before Linux was a car without an engine. It had not been able to develop a satisfactory kernel for its operating system. But it had the GPL, ready as a vehicle for licensing the entire

OS. When FSF and Torvalds got together, the GNU/Linux operating system was born. This is what most people call Linux today.

Up until the late 1990s, very few people paid attention to free software, Linux, and the GPL. Picture a small island nation where everyone is required to wear a special native tunic. That might be a human interest story for airline magazines or a subject for doctoral theses. But let one little oil well spring up, and all of a sudden everyone is getting measured for a native tunic. When Linux started rocketing to fame, the technology world at large started to pay attention to this new set of rules for software.

Linux emerged as a viable alternative to Windows in the corporate computing landscape. Once that idea caught on, free software was on fire. All it took to push Linux's popularity over the top was a couple of economic disasters—the dot-com bust and the terrorist attacks of September 11, 2001. The United States was in recession. Suddenly, big organizations were very, very interested in anything that could cut their costs. By 2003, Linux reportedly had a 23 percent share of the operating system market for enterprise servers, according to Interactive Data.[3] And as a corollary, free software was finally a software-licensing model no one could ignore.

Co-opted by the System

By 2003, a very strange phenomenon was at work. The only viable competitor for one of the most successful products in the world, Microsoft Windows OS, was a free good, the Linux OS. This competition intensified the ideological war between the free software advocates and the proprietary vendors.

First, there was the famous leaking of the 1998 Microsoft "Halloween Documents," internal Microsoft memos that acknowledged the competitive threat from Linux, particularly in the enterprise space.[4] Microsoft, usually through Steve Ballmer, took a publicly anti–free software view in the late 1990s and early 2000s. Almost without exception, the entire remainder of the technology industry took a neutral, wait-and-see approach. Many were skeptical about the risks of open source software, but at the same time they wanted to use the cheapest and best product, and they had no particular interest in a war of words.

---

[3]www.infoworld.com/t/platforms/microsoft-dominance-os-market-grows-idc-study-says-598.
[4]Microsoft later posted the documents here: http://web.archive.org/web/20010604100408/www.microsoft.com/ntserver/nts/news/mwarv/linuxresp.asp.

In the 1990s, some of the less vitriolic participants in the free software movement understood that antiproperty rhetoric does not go over very well in the United States, particularly among U.S. businesses. So they extended the olive branch and started the Open Source Initiative, which took a more inclusive approach, building bridges between free software and industry. This organization, started in 1998 by Eric Raymond and Bruce Perens, two luminaries of the software world, used "open source" to describe a variety of licenses, not all of which had the copyleft features of the GPL, but all of which allowed sharing of source code modifications.

In retrospect, this building of bridges was inevitable. The fact is that, even in 2009, Linux is mostly of interest to corporate users. The average consumer still does not use a Linux personal computer—though Linux cell phones, digital video recorders (DVRs), and other small gizmos are widespread. Linux remains a product that has a do-it-yourself aspect to it, and most individual consumers don't like that—and don't care a whit about access to source code. In fact, they would probably pay money not to see it. A large company that needs to run big servers may be able to run them more cheaply and effectively using Linux than proprietary alternatives. But that requires employing technical personnel, at least some of which is a sunk cost for an enterprise regardless of which kind of software it uses. Individuals neither have nor want technical support staff. So, for open source to survive, there had to be cooperation that cut through the rhetoric. Free software and business needed each other.

In 2009, the transformation is complete. Informal figures suggest that about 80 percent of open source development is now performed by corporations and 20 percent by individual hobbyists, whereas the figures 10 to 15 years ago were probably exactly the opposite. IBM has become famous for its support of Linux. Google has spearheaded the Open Handset Alliance platform for mobile, and the Symbian platform has also become an open source cooperative effort. Intel, IBM, Hewlett-Packard, Cisco Systems, and even Microsoft all sponsor open source initiatives. Almost every major technology company allows its engineers to perform open source development as part of their work or contribute to open source on their own time.

What Is Open Source?

If you are a programmer or already understand why access to source code is important, then you can probably skip this section.

Open source is the term almost universally used to refer to free software, by all but the most vehement free software advocates. The quintessential element of free and open source software (sometimes called OSS or FOSS) is availability of source code and the freedom to change and redistribute it.

"Free" is used in the sense of *libre* rather than *gratis*, and refers to access, not price. As the Free Software Foundation pithily says, "Think free speech, not free beer."

It's not possible to understand open source without understanding what source code is. Most computer users understandably do not understand source code, because it is transparent to them. Modern computer languages, like C, C++, or Java, are compiled languages. This means that the program file that runs on your computer is not the same file the programmer wrote.

A computer program is nothing more than series of instructions. For instance, I have a program for getting to work in the morning. It is:

- Wake up.
- Shower.
- Get dressed.
- Make coffee.
- Answer hysterical emails from clients in Europe.
- Read open source news.
- Eat breakfast.
- Go to work.

Obviously, each of these steps consists of many tasks. Computer programs are also a list of tasks, but they are more formalized and detailed. You could easily write a program to find news stories about open source. It might say:

- Open Firefox browser.
- Go to search page.
- Type in "open source."
- Click on Search button.
- Display results.

In turn, one of these steps (Type in "open source") can be further broken down:

- Display the blinking caret in the search box.
- Get a keystroke.
- Display the keystroke in the search box.
- Store the keystroke in a buffer.
- When the keystroke is "enter," stop getting keystrokes.
- Send the text in the buffer to the server as a search query.

Even these steps represent many actions or calculations by the computer. When we break them down to their very smallest components, they are the addition or subtraction of binary numbers that take place in the computer's processor. But obviously, no programmer wants to spend all day writing ones and zeros. That is why programming languages exist. Each line of code written by a programmer represents many substeps, and the programmer does not have to reinvent the wheel to write a simple instruction.

The instructions written by the programmer are called source code. The computer cannot process source code. So there are interpretation programs known as compilers that translate the high-level instructions into the ones and zeros the computer can understand. This translation is called binary or object code, and once produced based on the source code, it is saved in a file in that form. (On a Windows system, these files have the extension ".exe" for an executable file.) Binary code is usually smaller in size than source code and cannot be changed by a user. If you wish to change software, you need to change the source code, then regenerate the binary code. The custom and practice of distributing programs in binary code instead of source code developed in the 1980s when computers were becoming standardized. Today, most commercial programs are not available in source code form. This is a business decision that is made by software vendors to maximize the efficiency of distribution and the ease of support, but it is also a way to force the user to depend on the vendor for bug fixes and changes. For obvious reasons, many vendors are reluctant to relinquish this control and, ultimately, revenue.

Open source, therefore, is important because it liberates users to make their own changes, provide their own support, or hire anyone who is sufficiently skilled—and not necessarily the original vendor—to do those things. OSS enables competition, in a way: disrupting the monopoly on support and maintenance that vendors enjoy by virtue of binary distribution and the intellectual property rights they use to enforce that model.

The Costs of Free Software

We all know that freedom is not free. Any technical manager also understands that free software is not free. Information technology (IT) managers assess OSS against proprietary software by measuring total cost of ownership (TCO). This includes not only license fees (in the case of proprietary software) but the following:

- Maintenance costs.
- Support costs.
- Security costs associated with necessary hardware investments.

Open source and proprietary vendors alike claim that their model produces the lowest total cost of ownership.

In fact, the jury is still out on which side is right, and realistically there is no one right answer. Some open source projects benefit hugely from the community development and maintenance model, and thus truly spread out the costs of support and maintenance. Some open source projects do not enjoy a robust user or developer community, and using them simply becomes an in-house maintenance cost that may be difficult to outsource because there is no one vendor to commit to it. Most licensees are agnostic about the software they choose. It can be open source or it can be proprietary, but it must be cheaper, faster, and better.

The kind of software that lends itself best to open source is standardized software. It is no accident that the so-called LAMP stack (Linux, Apache, MySQL, and PHP/PERL/PYTHON) is the core of the open source world. These projects are an operating system, Web server, database, and scripting languages. Add to that Java (recently made open source) and the Firefox browser, and you can do about 90 percent of the computing you need to do, particularly for Web-based systems, using ubiquitous, free-of-charge software with a huge potential pool of developers and maintainers to serve you. Proprietary software seems to work better for high-level and specialized applications. In an economic sense, this is rational. No one wants to pay to reinvent the wheel. They want to put their money into developing the latest and greatest—the electronic stability control system. The basics work better as a common good, freeing up the technology sector to work on improvements.

But there are other costs to free software as well. First among these are the costs of tracking and managing OSS within an organization. The problem with open source, from a business management perspective, is that it flies under the business process radar. Proprietary software costs money, and because it does, businesses know how to track it. A commercial license requires a check, which requires a purchase order, which requires the signature of a purchasing manager, which requires legal review. But open source, for the most part, is free of charge and can be downloaded by anyone from the Internet. Corporate firewalls may restrict access to it, but don't underestimate the ingenuity of your engineers to circumvent any restrictions you implement. Software engineers are notorious for grabbing what they need off the Web in the wee hours of the morning to hit their release deadlines. In the corporate world, if a tree falls in the forest and no one has to pay for it, it doesn't make a sound. Open source eludes all the business controls that exist for proprietary software.

At the same time, OSS is in ubiquitous use in the corporate world. When you add that to the difficulty in tracking it, you have a huge informational problem. While there are organizations that make tools to help track open source, and some of the conventional development tools—like a concurrent versioning system (CVS) or bug tracker—can also help do so, most organizations quite simply do not know what open source they are using. Add this to the fact that organizations now regularly outsource software development to other organizations or to divisions in far-flung countries, and you have an information and communication problem that has just begun to be addressed, and will only get more unmanageable over time.

Although the phenomenon is not quite as common as it once was, corporations tend to wake up one day and realize they have open source problems. In the worst case, this comes in the form of a lawsuit. But usually this realization comes from the board level, or from a general counsel who has come across an article about the legal risks of open source. When that happens, there is a mad scramble to find out: What are we using? Are we using it correctly? Is our proprietary software at risk? Do we need a written policy for open source use? And so forth.

Having gone through the process many times, I can say from personal experience that formulating and implementing an open source management policy at any company larger than a raw start-up is a 6- to 18-month process. It can be disruptive and expensive, and requires management-level decisions that divert focus from day-to-day operations, expensive legal advice, analysis of automation tools, and in-house education. This, too, is one of the hidden costs of open source. But the good news is that once an open source program is in place, it is cheaper to maintain than to start, and developing and implementing a good open source policy improves in-house technology; improves relations among engineering, legal, and management; and actually can help attract better engineers to the company—not to mention paving the way for taking advantage of the business benefits of open source.

Is It a Virus? Legal Risks to Using Open Source

Businesspeople and lawyers worry a lot about the legal risks of using open source. As is usually the case with anxiety, it is at once too much and not enough. This section outlines the legal risks to using open source. There are two major risk areas: infringement risk and compliance risk.[5]

A dozen years ago, when I first became interested in open source, the main area of risk people worried about was infringement. To understand the difference between infringement and compliance risk, one needs to

---

[5]Most free software advocates would cite patent risk separately in this list. For a discussion of patent infringement and why I do not consider it uniquely risky for open source, see www.philsimonsystems.com/nwot_extras.html.

understand dual nature of open source. Open source is both a development model and a licensing model; these models sometimes overlap and sometimes do not.

In the development model, many users or developers contribute changes and improvements to the software in a community code base. The code base has a gatekeeper—usually called a committer—but that person's decisions about what to include or not include in the code base are supposed to be driven by the consensus of the community. This is different from the proprietary development model, where the entire software project is developed by one company, its consultants, and its employees, and the direction of product growth is a matter of corporate preference. The difference between these two models was famously described by Eric Raymond in his seminar article "The Cathedral and the Bazaar."[6] The cathedral is the work of one man's vision—a Brunelleschi or a Sir John Soane—who is funded by a patron. That is proprietary software development. The bazaar is a marketplace of ideas, codified into software code, where the direction of development is driven by what features are most demanded by the community, anyone is free to "fork the code"[7] base to make his own version, and the development is funded by the sweat equity of many individual authors.

The difference between the cathedral and the bazaar is the reason that infringement risk was the initial concern of most lawyers. In the mid-1990s, most intellectual property (IP) lawyers believed open source to be categorically too risky to use. This was because they felt the contributions of many authors could not be properly tracked to ensure that the intellectual property rights to the contributions actually belonged to those authors. This was not by any means an unfounded concern. The people most likely to know how to make contributions to software projects are—you guessed it—professional computer programmers. Those programmers are employed by organizations that own, more or less, all the intellectual property in the software they produce. If they contribute to an open source project, it is likely that the IP rights in what they contribute are owned by the company they work for. What's more, it is also likely that they lack the corporate authority to license that intellectual property to the project.

Intellectual property attorneys in the 1990s, therefore, assumed that open source would be impossible to clear from an intellectual property perspective. They were not wrong in theory, but time proved the infringement risk to be negligible. In fact, open source may be riddled with small elements that are, technically, infringing. But apparently no one cares enough to do

---

[6]Raymond's article is available online at http://catb.org/~esr/writings/cathedral-bazaar/.

[7]"To fork the code" is developer slang for taking the code of an application, modifying it, and creating a separate and distinct version of that application.

anything about it. As of today, there have been no lawsuits over copyright or trade secret infringement by open source projects, notwithstanding nearly 15 years of robust open source development.[8]

What has turned out to be a significant risk, however, is compliance. This risk stems from the open source licensing model, not the development model. Software can be developed by a community or not, but if it is proffered under an open source license, it is OSS. Anyone using OSS is bound by the terms of the license that applies to it. But, it turns out, these licenses can be very difficult to interpret and difficult to comply with.

This is where the notions of "viral" and "nonviral" open source come in. These are the terms used by lawyers, but they are more than politically incorrect; they are misleading as well. It's more useful to think of them as copyleft (or free software) and permissive. Permissive licenses are easy to understand. They say, in essence, anyone can use my code, and don't come crying to me if something goes wrong. The compliance requirements for permissive licenses are minimal—only extending to placing correct notices on products that contain the OSS. Not that this cannot be a challenge; some permissive licenses have poorly drafted notice requirements that can be nonsensical, like requirements to put notices in a "user manual" for software used in an embedded system.

But some open source licenses leave lawyers and laypeople alike in a quandary. As much as people complain about lawyers and legalese, there is some method to their madness. Licenses written by nonlawyers tend to be imprecise, idiosyncratic, and confusing. Consider the following "beer-ware license":

"THE BEER-WARE LICENSE" (Revision 42):
<phk@FreeBSD.ORG>wrote this file. As long as you retain this notice
    you
can do whatever you want with this stuff. If we meet some day, and
    you think
this stuff is worth it, you can buy me a beer in return Poul-Henning
    Kamp

---

[8]The *SCO v. IBM* case was the closest thing, but was not actually a copyright infringement case, except in later pleadings. For details, see my article "SCOing, SCOing, Gone" in *Linux Insider*, March 23, 2005. The facts of the *SCO* case are presented in great detail on www.groklaw.com. The suit was also unmeritorious, and if anything it underscored the difficulty of making infringement claims based on widely used software. Copyright claims in the software area are notoriously fact-dependent, and much of copyright law—the doctrines of merger and *scenes à faire*—works against copyright claims. See http://people.freebsd.org/~phk/.

Admittedly, being called upon to interpret such a document is one of the more interesting tasks that a lawyer may be asked to do. But clients, above all, want certainty in their legal positions, and "beer-ware" is anything but certain. Is the author serious? Is an ale sufficient? What about a light beer? Any chips with that?

Most open source licenses are more serious, but some are notoriously difficult to understand. The GPL reads more like a polemic than a legal document, and while it purports to be written in plain English and layman's terms, most people find it anything but plain. Lawyers find it crazy-making. One of the most difficult questions is its scope. The Free Software Foundation takes a nearly unqualified position that all software linked to GPL software[9] must be covered by GPL as well. This is why the term *viral* is employed—the GPL tries to reach entirely new software that interacts with GPL software, even though the overlap may be the minimum necessary for the code to interact. Thus, it "infects" code that lies adjacent to it.

But this kind of terminology is one of the reasons that businesspeople worry too much about open source. In truth, GPL does not "infect" new code in the sense that it would cause proprietary code to somehow be automatically licensed under GPL. If you try to put GPL and proprietary code together in the same program, the GPL terminates, and you no longer have the right to distribute the GPL code. Therefore, a noncompliant program is simply infringing, and cannot lawfully be distributed. That is a bad-enough situation—potentially requiring product recalls or reengineering—but it does not grant free licenses to an organization's proprietary software. A better analogy than a virus is two cogs with teeth that don't match. GPL and proprietary software just don't fit together. If you have two cogs with different teeth and you try to make them mesh, one doesn't just magically change the others so they work together; they just break.

The New Green

Back in the 1980s, when I was a computer programmer, we were not politicized. We ate junk food and watched *Star Trek* and wrote code. But today, software engineers are just as doctrinaire as everyone else, but instead of pontificating about carbon footprints, they crusade about open source.

In 2009, software engineers coming to the workforce from college or graduate programs are open source junkies. They are completely steeped

---

[9]Linking is the process of combining routines in a modular fashion into one program. For details, see Chapter 12 of Heather Meeker, *The Open Source Alternative: Understanding Risks and Leveraging Opportunities* (Hoboken, NJ: John Wiley & Sons, 2008), on technical concepts relating to open source.

in the open source ideology; hiring them and giving them a paycheck does not change that in the least. They are like law school graduates whose first interview question is about your law firm's pro bono program. To attract engineers to your company, you are going to have to explain how you contribute to open source. In this sense, open source is the new green—it is the feel-good medicine of the programmer world. Even if your company does not want to approve use of open source from a business or legal perspective, your engineers will push you to not only use it but contribute to it as well.

Open source is the new green in another way, too. The technology sector has slowly come to the understanding that organizations using open source can make money. As one venture capitalist explained it to me, he wants his dollars to be used where they make the most difference, so he prefers to invest in organizations that build on top of open source platforms. As to whether pure open source companies—those with open source products—can make money, the answer is yes and no. They can make money, but not from licensing OSS.

There are two ways they go about it. One is the age-old razor blades model—offering an open source product as a teaser to sell something else: hardware, services, other software, or software with additional bells and whistles. Thus you have the business models of Tivo (hardware), Google (online services), Red Hat (services), and Oracle (additional software). These are all viable businesses that have leveraged open source to their advantage in a strategic way.

There is also the dual licensing model pioneered by MySQL. In this model, the company offers the software under a copyleft license (usually GPL) or a commercial original equipment manufacturer (OEM) license. Those who do not want to abide by GPL, or who want professional support and warranties, choose the commercial license. It is the same software in either case. This was like the time I got a new roof for my house. The roofer asked, "Do you want the roof with the 10-year guarantee or the roof with the 20-year guarantee?" I asked, "Is it a different kind of roof?" He said, "No, it's just a different guarantee."

For many years, people have asked me, usually with incredulity: "How can you make money with open source?" Having been a lawyer in Silicon Valley for 15 years, I usually reply that none of my clients actually makes money, according to generally accepted accounting principles (GAAP). But as anyone in the Valley knows, making money is often not a question of the income statement but of the mergers and acquisitions (M&A) exit. Organizations like Oracle buy up open source organizations at a rapid clip. That may be because they are trying to avoid the competition that those organizations represent, or it may not, but it means a payday for the target and its investors. So the answer is: You can make money with open source one way or another. You just need to understand the open source model and how it works in business.

The Future of Open Source

We have learned over the past 15 years that the war of words was a draw. Neither open source nor proprietary software will ever kill the other—at least not anytime soon. It is clear that today all technology users and developers are operating in a mixed environment. It is clear that today, to understand technology or technology licensing, you need to understand open source.

The most credible threat to open source may come from within. Some glimmers of this were clear in the GPL version 3 discussions of 2007 and 2008. The Free Software Foundation wanted to tighten the conditions for use of free software, most notably to require those who made the software available over a network—as in an application service provider (ASP), software as a service (SaaS), or cloud computing environment—to share their modifications under the copyleft model. (Currently under GPL these activities do not constitute distribution, and thus do not invoke the copyleft requirements to share source code.) This illustrated two potential chinks in the open source model. First, there were a few catfights between the FSF and its constituencies as the rules were rewritten. Some corporate commentators opposed the FSF's ideas and engaged in a behind-the-scenes campaign to temper the requirements of GPL version 3. The Linux kernel maintainers, including Linus Torvalds, engaged in a public spat with the FSF, publishing an open letter criticizing some of the proposed requirements of GPL version 3. It was clear at that point that the free software zealots were risking taking positions that made themselves irrelevant—opposing software patents, digital rights management (DRM), and other elements that they felt threatened the free software model. Businesses sent the clear message that although they had reluctantly accepted the free software rules represented by GPL over the years, they were not willing to cede to the free software movement the authority to change those rules.

Second, cloud computing is truly a fly in the free software ointment. As the world moves to smaller devices, more connectivity, and thin client applications, the copyleft obligations of GPL may become less relevant, because they will more rarely be triggered. Software developers will not be required to share their source code, and there will be less appreciable difference between copyleft and permissive licenses.

Similarly, the enforcement of licenses like GPL depends entirely on copyright law. That works well in places like the United States and Germany, where cases have been filed and settled, and there is a keen interest in open source compliance. But countries with spotty records of copyright enforcement happen to be the very places that outsourced software development is most popular. The more emphasis there is on a truly worldwide software industry, the more free software developers will have to rely on moral suasion rather than a legal stick. Of course, for software developed and licensed under permissive licenses (like the Apache project), these risks are irrelevant. Those licenses do not require significant IP enforcement and do not have copyleft requirements whose trigger mechanisms must be strategized.

In other words, open source will survive if it is the true communist ideal, rather than a flawed reality that requires a despotic state to impose it. Marx believed that the fetters of government would someday melt away before the irresistible force of humanity, leaving in its place a workers' paradise that did not require the Berlin Wall to prop it up. The future of open source therefore remains to be seen. It may tell us as much about the nature of people as it does about software—that is, how much they will cooperate without being forced to do so.

Summary

Open source has come a long way from its roots. It has evolved from an esoteric technology used by geeks to running some of the largest applications of major corporations around the globe. Foolish is the organization that universally dismisses the benefits of OSS. A balanced perspective on OSS is required, however. Understanding the legal risks and operational challenges of OSS is essential if organizations expect to see a bang for their buck.

Next Steps

- *Get the facts.* If you think your company is not using open source, think again. The first step to recovery is admitting you have a problem. Talk to your engineers. Ask them what open source they use and like. Don't be surprised if they understand open source licensing better than your lawyers do.
- *Be the peacemaker.* Anyone in your organization who is either evangelical or vitriolic about open source probably is not seeing the whole picture. Most private organizations use open source but don't build their businesses around it. However, it's important to listen to your colleagues' concerns and address them head-on. If management, legal, and engineering don't see eye to eye, you will never be able to develop an open source policy that will actually be followed. Having no open source policy is not good, but having one that everyone ignores is worse.

- *Take a trip to the candy store.* If you don't know about the LAMP stack and other popular open source software, do some digging. Go to www.sourceforge.com and see what's there. The amount and quality of it may surprise you.
- *Keep your eyes on the prize.* Don't get sidetracked by rhetoric. Open source software is a business tool. Use it when it works, and don't use it when it doesn't. The rest is just for amusement value.
- *Catch up on your reading.* If you want a deeper dive into the details of open source licensing in business, take a look at my book *The Open Source Alternative: Understanding Risks and Leveraging Opportunities*.

CHAPTER 6

Software as a Service (SaaS)

Amy Wohl

The future has already arrived. It's just not evenly distributed yet.
—William Gibson

Introduction

Software as a service (SaaS) is not a new idea but rather a new name for a concept that crops up at intervals, each time strengthened by technology that is better suited to provide its features, technologists who have a better understanding of what customers require and what the market will require for financial success, and customers who are better educated as to what the concept can offer them. It is a method of providing and distributing the functionality of software that permits an individual or an organization to benefit from its use without taking on its implementation or ongoing management. This means it can often be used more quickly, at less expense, and by individuals and organizations without the internal resources to implement and support complex, modern software and systems.

SaaS is offered by a dazzling array of potential players. They include traditional independent software vendors (ISVs) moving to the Web, new net-native software vendors building their business on the SaaS models, and a variety of platform players who offer an infrastructure on which ISVs can host and market their software. Some platform players are interested in creating an ecosystem around applications or infrastructure tools of their own; others are interested in providing aggregation and marketing as a service. From the end user's point of view, SaaS may also be offered by resellers, offering ISVs or platform players branded solutions (with or without their own solutions and services added into the value proposition) and by huge hosting organizations with vast customer bases of their own, such as Internet service providers (ISPs) (Web hosters) and telcos (telephone companies). In the future, SaaS may also be offered as part of services such as banking, financial services (investments, retirement planning, etc.), health care, or e-commerce, vanishing entirely into the service and not recognized as software at all.

Today, perhaps half of business organizations are using at least one SaaS application, and more than half of nonusers are considering SaaS. Many research firms believe that by 2010 through 2012, about 25 to 30 percent of all new software will be delivered on SaaS platforms. That means a substantial amount of software will move to this new technology and a substantial number of buyers will buy some (but probably not all) of their software using SaaS. Keep in mind that some software will be deemed too valuable or too risky (in need of high levels of security) to go outside of company control; other software will simply not be possible or economically justifiable to rewrite to the new platform.

For small, new firms and individual consumers, SaaS may represent a more compelling solution, and much higher percentages of usage may be found in these markets. The SaaS market started out as a complement to the traditional software market. Many vendors thought of it as a way to sell a tweaked version of their existing software to smaller firms it had previously been too expensive to market to or support. Software start-up firms entering the SaaS market, of course, built software optimized for delivery on the SaaS platform. Some initially also targeted the small and medium-size business (SMB) market, but others focused on the enterprise market from the start. In any case, large enterprises (those with more than a few thousand employees) have looked at SaaS for at least some applications from the start. Financial services, professional services, and retail firms have been particularly aggressive in adopting the SaaS model. We are still at the beginning of the SaaS market. The larger players (Microsoft, IBM, Oracle, and Adobe) are now entering into the market, as well as telcos and ISPs of every size all over the world. New forms of SaaS vendors (platform providers, aggregators, integrators) are coming into the mainstream. New applications of every kind are coming on line. And large enterprises have the choice of building their own SaaS architecture internally to take advantage of the efficiency, speed, and flexibility of SaaS, while maintaining the control and security they may require. This now may take the form of private clouds. For more on this, see Chapter 4 on cloud computing.

Steve Mills, executive vice president in charge of IBM's $20 billion software business, believes that SaaS is really a service business and that there are a lot of services already being delivered that we are not yet counting, such as Automatic Data Processing (ADP) and other payroll services, as well as airline and entertainment ticketing services—a huge market. We'd agree, noting that it is this market where the software disappears inside the service it provides. That will be the big business opportunity in the future.

The game has only just begun. According to a study by Rackspace, a hosting company, performed in March 2007:

- Fifty-one percent of respondents already use an SaaS application and 72 percent of those SaaS users are considering additional SaaS applications.
- Sixty-nine percent of respondents see SaaS as the preferred software delivery method of the future.
- Thirty-four percent of respondents that are not currently using an SaaS application are considering it.
- The 420 participants (of 2,788 queried) in the survey were Rackspace customers and varied in size from firms with annual revenue of $1 million to those with $1 billion in revenue.

What Is Software as a Service?

SaaS is simply software that is delivered from a server in a remote location to your desktop, and is used online. Typically, it is used via a browser interface, although some SaaS software uses its own interface, designed to provide special characteristics for its application or its users. Initially, SaaS software existed only in real time, within an online connection; when the connection was interrupted, the user had no data and no application. As SaaS evolved, the online-only model remains as the predominant model, but it has been joined by SaaS applications that live on an appliance (a server managed by the SaaS vendor) on the user organization's premises, as well as by other SaaS applications that place interfaces, applications, and data on users' desktops and mobile devices (laptops, smartphones), synchronizing them to the online versions to keep everything up-to-date. This allows users to work without interruption, whether they have an Internet connection available or not, and to handle airplane rides, black holes in the network, and network failures (mine are mainly due to my ISP, but some users find theirs are mainly due to their SaaS provider's software).

Some do not take to the notion of parking their data or applications on a server they do not control and cannot physically touch or see lightly. Some IT professionals believe SaaS is not mature enough for any but the most casual usage, often citing variable and unreliable performance and the possibility of lost or corrupted data. We'd note that the best SaaS providers (and why would you use anyone else?) use professional data centers, provisioned and staffed beyond the resources of all but the largest enterprises. Data that is too valuable to risk either should not be exposed to Web-based storage or should be backed up on your own premises as well as on the Web. Good practices don't change because a new method of software distribution becomes available.

SaaS is a fundamental change in the software market and a strong disruptive force:

- It empowers users to select software and implement it without having to wait for information technology (IT) to find the time and resources to provision them. It offers a new concept of *time to value* that can be compelling for marketing departments, product developers, and others in a rush to get something begun.
- It permits small companies, with little or no internal IT, to have access to the same applications that were previously available to only the largest enterprises. Just as the spreadsheet made data and the ability to manipulate it available to any company, SaaS makes sophisticated data analysis and management tools available to companies of any size.
- It offers an opportunity for a new generation of software companies, exploiting the Internet as their platform, to challenge the current incumbents, who must decide whether to defend their turf or divide their resources between supporting and marketing existing applications on traditional platforms and trying to build and market SaaS applications that have a different design philosophy and may require different marketing plans.

Nothing's New: SaaS's Historical Precedents

While the term *SaaS* is relatively recent, its concept is not. Much like many of the technologies discussed in this book, SaaS is more of an evolution than a revolution.

Ancient History: Time-Shared Computing

Nothing is new—and neither is the idea of using software from a remote, managed location. In the 1970s, this was called time-shared computing. It was expensive and not very flexible, because in the pre-Internet era, accessing a remote server meant implementing a private data network. This was a decision not taken lightly and a game mainly for large companies trying to offer their locations access to the same software or to collect data (such as daily sales) promptly. Adding a piece of hardware or a new application to the environment was difficult, time-consuming, and expensive. These networks often used whatever they had for long periods of time because the change process was so daunting. Integration across applications from multiple software vendors was a task for highly skilled (and very expensive) systems integrators (SIs), typically adding to their specific knowledge on the customer's dime. Custom code could be unpredictable.

TABLE 6.1 Breakdown of ASP Models

ASP Type	Service	Customer
ASP software aggregator	Provides Internet access to (popular) software	Individuals, professionals; SMBs
Traditional ISV	Adapts its own software to Internet with minor changes; provides hosting	SMBs
Net-native ISV	Writes new software for the Internet	Consumers to midmarket enterprises

The ASP Market, the Dot-Com Bubble, and Why It Didn't Work

The Internet changed all that. Suddenly, there was a ubiquitous, standard interconnection mechanism. Anyone anywhere could be connected or disconnected easily. With a little work, we could make them secure. Quickly, developers realized there was an opportunity to offer access to software applications over the Internet. The application service provider (ASP) round was on. Table 6.1 presents a breakdown of the three major ASP models.

By 1998, hundreds of companies had decided that they could acquire licenses to existing software, host it for access via the Internet, and be ASPs. A much smaller number set out to build software that would take advantage of being Net native—built to run across the Internet and exploit it. But the ASP round didn't last. Most of the early ASPs were unsuccessful. Some ended up as part of a few larger firms. Many simply disappeared. The players, however, noted what hadn't worked and continued, many turning up in other start-ups or joining firms that survived the Internet bubble.

The mistakes in the late 1990s and at the turn of the twenty-first century were readily identifiable in retrospect.

Products Based on Technology Bets, Not User Needs

Early ASPs were either existing ISVs or new start-ups. Most of them entered the online market because they believed they had a good application, not based on interaction with users (via focus groups, user observation in usability labs, or trial usage) to assure that the software they were building was something users actually wanted and needed, offered in a form users could readily consume. They took the view that if they built good technology it would attract customers. This supply-side view of the demand for technology rarely works today (although we still see developers offering products based on this model).

Few Business Models

Most ASPs had no business models. They priced to the market, frequently not charging enough to cover their costs, or pricing valuable services well below what customers might be willing to pay for unique or convenient services. Many had no idea how they would actually make money—they just assumed they would.

A New Distribution Channel via the Internet

Many of the original ASPs were ISVs looking for a new way to get their software to market. Typically they were technologically astute but knew little about marketing. Everyone thought that simply making applications available on the magical Internet would be enough; users would find them through word of mouth—viral marketing. These ISVs rarely built marketing plans into their business models, nor did they allocate marketing budgets. Unfortunately, while online software has many benefits, customers must still be sold, and marketing to create product awareness and brand recognition is vital.

Data Center Distractions

In the beginning, almost every ISV thought it was important to build and control his own data center. This meant significant capital investments and large budgets for technical staff. Also, the ISV either had to start with a very small data center (a server in the back room wasn't unusual), hoping to add to it as customers arrived, or had to bet on the future with a very large data center, requiring a major financial investment. In the first case, the ISV and its customers were vulnerable to unacceptable performance during peak periods and downtime caused by unscheduled failures; in the second case, the ISV (and its investors) had to bear the high cost of a large data center that was rarely used to its capacity.

Educating a New Market

The market was completely uneducated as to the value of online application software and its infrastructure. It would take several years of education, examples, and success to educate the market. In 1999, my company performed a primary market research study on the ASP market, interviewing 100 ASP vendors (mainly ISVs) and 100 potential customers (half large enterprises, half smaller ones). Only a small percentage of the large enterprises knew much about the ASP model; almost none of the smaller ones did.

What's Different This Time?

All of these mistakes have been corrected in the SaaS round.

Market Requirements

Most SaaS vendors have gotten much better at listening to potential buyers. Applications are written with user requirements in mind. New SaaS applications attempt to match what the best application in their category offers and then go on to provide more—a better interface, better integration with other applications, more features (especially Web features).

Stronger Business Models

While there is still a lot of room for improvement in SaaS vendors' business models, they've come a long way from the ASPs of the late 1990s, when there might be no real business model at all. Today, most SaaS vendors plan to monetize their software (or the third-party software they license for distribution) by either making a charge for each user or each transaction (rarer) or by using an advertising model where the user is exposed to presumably relevant ads in exchange for access to the software. Sometimes the two techniques are combined: Ads are used to support a trial usage period, and then the user is invited to switch to a premium service (no ads), with better support, more features, and a subscription fee. For business applications and larger customers in the midmarket and the enterprise market—as opposed to the consumer and small office, home office (SOHO) market—SaaS vendors go straight to a subscription basis, often with a multiyear commitment.

Better Financing

SaaS is now a respectable business that has an excellent chance of generating positive cash flows and profits. In some cases, it has also permitted successful initial public offerings (IPOs) and mergers and acquisitions (M&As), all providing profitable exit strategies for investors. With the popularity of SaaS, venture capitalists have swarmed into this market, investing in company after company, often on terms that would have seemed lavish a few years ago. Not only do investors bring money for additional development and more substantial marketing investments, but they also bring their networks of contacts, offering new arrays and access to both partners and customers. They also bring more seasoned management skills, so they can mentor SaaS start-ups or nudge them into hiring more appropriate management as their companies grow in size and sophistication.

Market Focus

Almost all the original ASP vendors thought they were in the SMB business. Some of them still are, selling largely to companies with 5 to 200 users and 20 to 500 employees. Others are selling all over the demographic game, from very small businesses with fewer than five employees to large enterprises with thousands. A few packages are useful to everyone, regardless of size; most are not. In fact, most SaaS vendors attempt to focus on a particular part of the marketplace, generally based on the skill sets of their existing staff. They may choose a company size to focus on, or they may prefer to specialize in one or more vertical markets such as insurance, health care, or local government. Often they pick both. Companies outside their selected demographic may find them and choose to become customers, but they are usually not actively marketing to multiple demographics unless they have multiple product and marketing strategies (like Salesforce.com and Intacct).

Outsourcing for Outsourcers

Between the ASP round and the SaaS round, most of the ISVs discovered that it was better to partner for infrastructure than to invest in and run it themselves. This decision was assisted by the rise of a new layer of players who were interested in providing infrastructure (computing power, storage, systems management, perhaps billing) for SaaS, but not SaaS applications and generally not marketing. These new SaaS data center providers are not all alike. For example, platform as a service (PaaS) providers like OpSource provide hosting, billing, and some marketing and support. Salesforce.com is both a successful SaaS ISV and a PaaS provider that has built an ecosystem of partners that write not just on their platforms but on top of their applications as well. JamCracker is both a PaaS provider and an aggregator that sells selected ISVs' applications, providing cross-application integration, support, and marketing.

A Better-Educated Market

While the ISVs were moving toward Net-native applications and the market was moving toward a partnership approach with ISVs partnered with PaaS providers, the users were experimenting with SaaS. They found that it could offer them access to applications much more speedily than the traditional decision-and-implementation process could. Decisions could be made quickly because there were few up-front fees to pay and SaaS was treated as an expense rather than a capital expenditure. Many applications could be accessed within hours or days, rather than the months it could take to prepare a traditional software application. Often, although ISVs expected their

SaaS applications to be used mainly by SMBs, they found that individuals and departments in enterprises were users, too, attracted by the easy access and ease of use. Both word of mouth and better use of formal marketing spread the word, leading to significant success for some vendors. Several vendors have more than one million users, and Salesforce had more than $1 billion in revenue in 2008. Success, of course, leads to more interest, attracting additional users to the market. According to Interactive Data, it is estimated that about 70 percent of companies will use SaaS within the next few years and more than 25 percent of new software will be delivered via SaaS.

Customer Expectations

This section discusses SaaS from the customer perspective, addressing questions such as:

- Who uses SaaS?
- What do customers want?
- What are the challenges and choices?

Who Uses SaaS?

It is a computing industry myth that SaaS is appealing only or mainly to consumers and the SMB market. The myth's origins are easy to trace. In the early days of the ASP market, traditional software vendors wanted to downplay the importance of online software. They either ignored it entirely or considered it a possible complement to their existing business, a way to sell to the SMB market without disturbing their current and lucrative enterprise and midmarket customers. In fact, from the very start, online software has appealed to customers in companies of every size. It is particularly appealing to users who cannot get that kind of functionality quickly and easily—if at all—either because they do not have the resources of an IT department or because their IT department cannot give their needs an appropriate priority.

Table 6.2 sums up the issues. In large enterprises, SaaS will not be used (at least not yet) for mission-critical applications. But it will be used to support remote locations and users, infrequently used and specialty applications, and applications that are shared with outsiders—contractors, consultants, suppliers, customers—whom IT prefers not to permit inside the firewall. SaaS will often be challenged as unable to provide a suitable level of service, or to support integration with internal applications or the level of customization large enterprises prefer. All of these challenges can be met, but perhaps not at a level that a large enterprise would find satisfactory.

TABLE 6.2 Who Will Use SaaS?

Organization/User	Type of Use	Challenges
Large enterprises	Non–mission-critical applications	Level of service
	Remote locations and users	Application
	Infrequently used applications	Integration
	Applications shared with nonemployees	Customization
SMBs	Large-scale applications	Vendor selections
		Application
	Support of remote locations and users	Integration
	Applications shared with nonemployees	Complex, unpredictable bills
Individual professional workers	Multilocation work	Identifying reliable vendor
	Shared applications	Application integration

In the SMB market, SaaS provides a way for organizations to have access to applications that they would otherwise not be able to implement and support, because SaaS provides not just software but implemented software, managed and supported. It allows the SMB to compete more equally in the marketplace with larger firms. And, of course, it offers the smaller organization the same advantages for remote and external users that it offers larger firms. For SMBs, the challenges are in selecting vendors, since they will often need to do this with less formal assistance than customers in large enterprises who can use their IT departments as advisers. They will also have to deal with integrating multiple SaaS applications and with the problem of predicting costs in an environment where one is billed on a usage basis. Individual users often are very loyal SaaS users, especially since many SaaS products are free or very inexpensive in their individual versions. SaaS vendors often hope to use these individual professional users as advocates, helping to sell larger installations of their products over time. They will, of course, not get much support, since individual SaaS software is often offered with minimal support, so caution should be taken in selecting a reliable vendor and in using it for serious business work. A user might, for example, want to keep off-line copies of his or her files.

What Do Customers Want?

Customers are drawn to SaaS for a number of reasons, of which cost savings is often mentioned, but rarely first. What customers are looking for is easy access to function, and access as quickly as possible. SaaS is particularly appealing when compared to conventional software with its long decision process, followed by a lengthy design and implementation process. Many SaaS products that can be accessed immediately (within an hour) would take weeks or more to set up as an internal application. More complex applications that would take a few weeks or a month to implement in an SaaS environment (mainly for formatting and connecting data) might take months to a year or more in a traditional software environment. The issues most often mentioned for considering SaaS include:

- Cost savings.
- Faster time to value.
- Skill savings.
- Support for remote workers.
- Support for non–mission-critical tasks

COST SAVINGS This is a tricky issue. Customers often try to compare the subscription fees from an SaaS vendor to the cost of a software package, forgetting that a software package requires hardware, perhaps additional complementary software, and IT resources to implement, manage, and support it. All those are included in the SaaS offering, so the prospective buyer must calculate those costs, too, to get an accurate comparison. Remember, too, that customers need SaaS vendors to make an appropriate profit to continue to invest in their service and have an incentive to stay in business; otherwise, customers will be in for an unpleasant surprise!

FASTER TIME TO VALUE This is perhaps the best incentive for using SaaS. It's already there, waiting for the customer to use it now. Implementation time is minimal, ranging from minutes to weeks, allowing customers to get on with their projects and reap the benefits of collaboration, project management, sales campaigns, or whatever the SaaS software provides without weeks or months of waiting, to say nothing of the uncertainty of whether the implemented application will actually match customer expectations. In SaaS it should be right there for the customer to see and try; it works or it doesn't work. Of course, modifications are sometimes possible (see the subsection on customization), but what the software does and whether it matches the customer's needs should be quickly apparent.

SKILL SAVINGS When customers buy an application from an SaaS source rather than via the traditional software route, the skill to implement, manage, and support the software is supplied by the SaaS vendor. This allows customers with small or no IT departments to more readily use complex, sophisticated applications, perhaps with some fee-for-services help from either the ISV or a third party. Larger customers can conserve their IT resources for mission-critical applications by judiciously employing some SaaS applications in their IT mix. This is particularly important when a technology or philosophy change is sweeping through the IT industry, since trained and experienced staff in the new skill sets will be very scarce until the new techniques have had a chance to settle in.

SUPPORT FOR REMOTE WORKERS   Many companies use SaaS entirely to be able to support an increasingly geographically distributed workforce. This can be as simple as more employees working from home or as complex as workers spread out across the globe. For many companies, projects are not completed just by employees but rather by teams that might include employees, suppliers, customers, and consultants, working across various locations and time zones. A shared space, with shared supporting applications, becomes a critical part of getting work successfully completed. That is one reason why so much SaaS software, regardless of which vertical industry it is directed toward, is likely to include collaborative elements.

SUPPORT FOR NON–MISSION-CRITICAL TASKS   Many enterprise chief information officers (CIOs) tell me that they are not ready to place their mission-critical tasks or data on SaaS infrastructures; they are concerned about issues like security and data integrity. In fact, a well-run SaaS vendor with an impeccably run professional data center partner behind it might well offer more security and data integrity than all but the best-run IT shops, but we will save that argument for another day, because the CIOs are ready, it's clear, to move some of their non–mission-critical tasks to SaaS. Which tasks vary from company to company, but frequently named applications include human resources (HR), electronic mail, and collaboration, as well as specialized applications that are used only by small groups of users.

Case Study: Southern Oak Insurance Company

A case in point is Southern Oak Insurance Company, a residential property insurance company located in Florida, started in 2004. It was looking for systems to handle processing for its agents and its claims. It looked at Better Insurance Processing Technology (BIPT)'s TiVA system because it is used by other insurers in its market and its agents were already familiar with it. The system allows 24/7 access anywhere in the world and allows Southern Oaks to give its business partners immediate

(continued)

access to the systems with appropriate authority levels. Southern Oaks started using the BIPT system in early 2005 with 1,000 to 1,500 independent agents and 40 internal users; today there are about 4,500 users. Originally, BIPT offered Southern Oaks a three-year agreement with a one-time license fee plus a storage fee based on the premium dollars and a volume discount. BIPT is also charging a setup fee and an annual maintenance fee. Custom programming is charged separately and performed by BIPT; Southern Oaks has done quite a bit of that to meet government regulations. Now it renews the contract on a year-to-year basis. The BIPT software is integrated with Southern Oaks' claims system for data exchange and the accounting software. BIPT has done a good job, in Southern Oaks' estimation. The system has had almost no downtime and has done a good job at rating properly. Of course, there are always things that could be prettier, such as when the underwriter is looking at risk, there could be an easier way to see claims without exiting the current position (via a better interface and higher level of integration). One of the issues is that BIPT has multiple customers and everyone wants something slightly different, so there are some compromises. Southern Oaks uses other SaaS products, which made it more willing to try the BIPT product; its staff had also had some experience with BIPT's previous in-house software in other organizations. Southern Oaks did look at some competitive products that it thought might be more flexible, but it was concerned about the stability of the rating engine. BIPT was selected as the most stable environment.

Challenges and Choices

Organizations face several SaaS-related challenges and choices with respect to the following:

- Integration.
- Customization.
- Vendor selection.
- Standards.

INTEGRATION Nearly every company, regardless of size, has existing applications. That means SaaS applications may have to connect to some of these applications to optimize the flow of information and work. Many SaaS applications are now capable of connecting to legacy (existing) applications through the SaaS application programming interfaces (APIs) or through connectors written for specific applications (this works best if you have a mainstream application with few customizations). Of course, the more integration a firm needs between SaaS applications or between SaaS applications and legacy applications, the more time it will take to get everything just right and the more skilled labor will be required to connect everything together. It is worth noting that service-oriented architecture (SOA) is often helpful here, on multiple dimensions. First, wrapping legacy applications in SOA may make it easier to connect them to SaaS applications. Second, if you are in the process of considering moving to SOA architectures for some of your more important existing applications, you can consider how to use SOA to connect them to the SaaS applications you are planning to use. Third, many SaaS applications use SOA methodologies that you may be able to tap into in implementing your integration strategy.

Case Study: Webalo

Webalo is an eight-year-old firm that helps companies take their information and make it available on mobile devices so that mobile executives can quickly make business decisions. It is particularly interesting because it is using SOA to deliver an SaaS solution. Webalo is not an application, but rather a platform that sits between users and their devices and the applications and data they need to access.

At a 300-store retail jewelry chain, the executives get information on inventory, sales, and other necessary data on their mobile devices, provided as a service by Webalo. The service is all about simplicity. It can be offered hosted or it can be provided on the customer's site on a Webalo appliance, in which case it will still be a supported service, pushing or pulling updates (as desired) to the user devices. The service supports a range of tools for administration plus a client piece that supports devices for off-line function, including a generated interface for the device. Wizards help the administrators get the applications and data connected to the user devices. An early version of the application is in full production; a second version will become available shortly. At first, Webalo only supported business intelligence (BI) data; now it is opening up to more data sources, such as web sites, web services, and other databases. Webalo can federate data across a number of resources. About 30 customers are live on this early version of the service, mainly midsize companies, especially in the retail and financial services sectors. Webalo expects that the service will be popular in its appliance form with larger firms, such as larger banks and Fortune 500 companies.

(continued)

Many large firms want to innovate new uses of tech knowledge on a limited basis in tough economic times and then come out quickly as the economy improves, in a very competitive position. The product is priced in a traditional subscription model, starting at $25 per user per month, discounted when users get to an annual fee at volume. Most organizations start with a pilot for a few users on a monthly basis and then move on to 100 or more users on an annual contract. Although Webalo can sell directly, it expects that it will make many of its sales through partners in the telco industry and other partners. Webalo's big advantage is simplicity; it can move access to the mobile devices without the need for programming.

CUSTOMIZATION   Customization is an issue of where you are willing to compromise. Some organizations have committed to trying to run off-the-shelf software with no customizations beyond menu-based configuration choices. They will save a lot of money and time but give up some choice. Other organizations will feel it is worth the price in dollars and time to have an application look and behave exactly the way they want it to; they should keep in mind these are not only up-front costs, but also substantial ongoing costs that must be paid every time the ISV updates the software and customizations must be redone to accept the update. Some SaaS ISVs try to offer a best-of-both-worlds approach, offering customization both to their partners and to internal IT via APIs and tools. These customizations will ride on top of future upgrades without the need to be rewritten, but they are, of course, limited by the rules of the API environment.

VENDOR SELECTION   Vendor selection might be the single most important task for a customer deciding to use an SaaS application. Customers should look for not only a vendor that has a compelling application with the right functions, but also a vendor with an excellent reputation for service and support. This includes knowing something about the extent and robustness of vendor infrastructure (it is best that there be at least two locations, with your data and applications backed up so that an outage on one is invisible to users), and whether the vendor owns it or uses well-respected third-party infrastructure players (better). Customers above the individual user level should also seek a service-level agreement (SLA), where the SaaS vendor sets out what penalties will be available to the customers should agreed-upon service levels (performance, uptime) not be met. Any serious forays into SaaS demand that customers require references from existing customers, preferably customers of a similar size using similar services. Check them out. It's also wise to do a little Web searching to see if the vendor's reputation seems to survive the forums and communities boards where disgruntled customers air their gripes. A bit of this can be overlooked, but a tsunami should require an adequate explanation.

STANDARDS Some SaaS vendors are as proprietary as any traditional software vendor. Others are devoted to industry standards. Until we have strong standards for data and applications in the SaaS space that make it easy to move from one vendor to another, taking your data with you, it's wise to be aware of exactly what you're getting into. If you are putting a large enterprise's email system into a proprietary setup, you should make sure that it is widely available elsewhere or that the code can be escrowed on your behalf and updated on a regular basis to protect your interests. You should also see how you are going to update your data (outside the SaaS vendor's system) on a regular basis. SaaS does not change the rules of wise IT management; it just changes where computing is done. Don't pick an SaaS vendor on price alone. If your SaaS vendor isn't making a profit, it will not be able to provide good support or to improve the software (if it is its own). A good vendor is one that will endure, and to endure it must make a reasonable profit. Keep that in the selection equation.

Summary

With reasonable care, a company of any size can use SaaS for many applications, saving time and money and being well satisfied with the results. This is a young industry with new vendors and new events occurring all the time. Part of using SaaS is keeping an eye out for changes that you can exploit—and emerging issues you may need to address.

Next Steps

To see if SaaS makes sense for your organization and in what form(s), do the following:

- Survey your staff to see which individual and departmental SaaS applications are already in use. You may want to use them as building blocks.
- Consider current departmental requests for new applications to see which could be well satisfied with SaaS solutions.
- Ask colleagues in your industry if they are using or planning to use SaaS solutions. Ask which ones and why.

- Use IT as an adviser on whether particular applications can be run in the SaaS environment and how to meet the organizational guidelines for security and data integrity.
- Put together a filter to qualify SaaS vendors for ad hoc, departmental, and organizational applications. Include not just the features of the SaaS solution, but the service reputations and service offerings of the vendors.

CHAPTER 7

Service-Oriented Architecture

Tushar K. Hazra

The greatest challenge to any thinker is stating the problem in a way that will allow a solution.

— Bertrand Russell

Introduction

In today's turbulent economy, many organizations have decided to modernize and rationalize existing business functions and processes. To find the panacea for cost reduction, organizations have charged business and information technology (IT) managers, executives, and visionaries to pursue and lead the initiatives that can influence organizations' top lines and bottom lines. You plan to align your business and IT strategies in such a way that your business organizations feel empowered and engaged from the beginning of your IT initiatives, and both business and IT can collaborate throughout the life cycle of such initiatives.

In this day and age, foolish is the organization that fails to consider the use of service-oriented architecture (SOA). No doubt many practitioners are using this notion today. SOA is one of the latest and most widespread emerging concepts in the industry—and you very likely receive a myriad of reading material on SOA in daily emails or trade journals. However, as you get started, some questions may arise:

- Are you ready to chart the course for your initiatives?
- Can you leverage the power of SOA to reduce the cost of delivering services to your customers and subsequently increase your revenues?
- Can you truly empower your business? And how can you deliver the business value of SOA for your enterprise?

The answers to these and other associated questions rely primarily on recognizing the essence of a service, establishing the principles of SOA, and building the foundation for an SOA-driven enterprise.

This chapter offers a synopsis of SOA from the perspective of a service: covering the primary benefits that can be achieved and realizing the challenges that must be resolved. It also presents an overview of a road map that emphasizes the SOA essentials relevant to delivering business services to customers. Further, we outline an adoption strategy that can help you leverage SOA—listing steps that can impact your ability to increase revenues using SOA. Finally, we review several real-world lessons learned along with a set of best practices that seem most effective and have been cultivated by many practitioners in the field.

What Is Service-Oriented Architecture?

Although the concepts of SOA and services have been around for a while, there's still not much of a consensus on defining SOA. So let's begin with a basic description of SOA.

A *service* is a logical representation of a repeatable business activity, function, or process step that is exposed for access and has a specified outcome. It is a black box to the service consumer, in that it is expressed in a manner that is independent of how it is implemented. As shown in Figure 7.1, for an account holder, a service is to obtain his or her account information irrespective of how the bank provides the information.

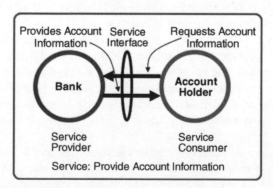

FIGURE 7.1 A Simple Example of Service
© EpitomiOne, 2009.

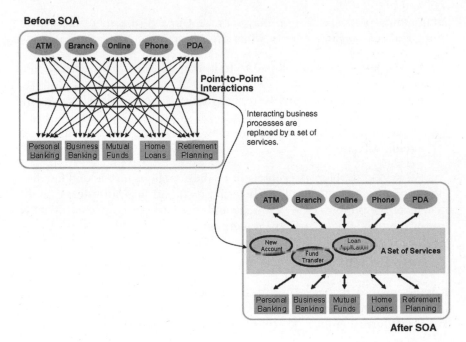

FIGURE 7.2 Benefits of Service Orientation
© EpitomiOne, 2009.

Service orientation is the approach of representing and integrating the functions of a business in terms of a set of accessible services and the outcomes that they produce. As shown in Figure 7.2, service orientation represents how interacting business processes between the bank and the account holder (via his or her access media) are replaced by a set of services.

Service-oriented architecture is an architectural style for creating enterprise business architecture and associated IT infrastructure that exploits the principles of service orientation at both the business and the IT level. As shown in Figure 7.2, bank business systems or applications utilize the identified services to deliver specific business values to account holders.

Most dictionaries define *architecture* as the overall design or structure of a computer system unifying both hardware and software components. So SOA can be appropriately described as an approach that encapsulates various business functionalities and capabilities as components of the architecture, with "service" as the unit of such components. At a minimum, a particular service may represent one of the specific business functionalities—regardless of whether this service is:

- Newly designed or developed to transition an existing functionality in-house.
- Bought from a third party to replace the existing functionality or component.
- Created by wrapping or transforming an existing functionality as an interim solution.

For system developers or integrators, these options may sound familiar. However, for chief information officers (CIOs) and line-of-business (LOB) managers, the promise of SOA is huge and real—and can prove to be of the essence in building collaborative enterprise.

Business Benefits of SOA

It is essential to recognize the business benefits of SOA to achieve early buy-ins and adequate collaborations from the business sponsors and the associated teams. From a business perspective, these major benefits are:

- *Improved performance and efficiency (aka better productivity).* This relates to rationalizing existing business applications, consolidating redundant systems, and modernizing legacy applications. This benefit works both ways—isolating a legacy application as a so-called black box behind the wrapper, and connecting two or more silo and disparate applications.
- *Increased business value delivery via responsiveness and reaching out to critical business functions.* This addresses the ability to serve multiple business needs and also interoperability to connect and work with multiple services. This benefit adds to the agility of an enterprise with flexible service-level agreements (SLAs) or contracts.
- *Higher availability and business continuity with procedural and regulatory compliance.* This refers to making effective use of pay-per-use concepts of a service and reducing the complexities from the interdependencies of existing applications. This benefit leverages the modular and plug-and-play nature of a service in providing continuous availability and built-in redundancy for continuity of operations.
- *Adapting to new and changing business needs via reuse of services.* This reflects the granularity and modularity of the services. This benefit offers the extensibility of services to effectively deploy or roll out replicable solutions across the enterprise. It makes change management a less daunting task than traditional systems integration.

Technical Benefits of SOA

Once the business benefits are recognized, then the focus of SOA should turn toward the technology imperatives. Primarily these imperatives relate to readying the organizations involved or the entire enterprise. From a technical perspective, primary benefits of SOA are:

- *Ease of transition and transformation in modernizing legacy or existing applications.* This refers to developing black-box services by using wrappers for legacy applications and advanced technologies such as enterprise service bus (ESB) or XML-based technologies to create a layer of separation for evolving services in existing systems. This benefit focuses on refreshing the technology iteratively and incrementally.
- *Use of open standards instead of proprietary solutions.* This refers to the portability of services from one platform, language of implementation, or environment to another without affecting the external interface or function of the services in use. This approach can help you create new services that can truly focus on delivering your organizational business functionalities.
- *Achieve improved return on investment (ROI) and total cost of ownership (TCO).* This relates to using the investments in technology, tools, and human resources (HR). The financial component of the investments is amortized over time and is recognized for budgetary considerations. This facilitates creating a transition path for transforming existing business functionalities to newly developed or acquired services.
- *Detangling the complicated, coupled, or interdependent applications.* This presents the potential of reusing services and the ability to abstract and separate services from one another. This benefit creates opportunities to replace services with equal or better capabilities.

While most of these benefits yield significant bottom-line benefits for a business organization or the entire enterprise, the objectives that get the most attention—and are sometimes the most elusive—are improving business efficiency and optimizing business value delivery via service reuse. In practice, effective delivery of tangible business value consistently can accentuate the top line of the company or agency.

Essentials of SOA

SOA essentials for LOB managers and executives begin with a set of services founded on business processes. Obviously, an existing or new IT infrastructure must support the services, tools, technology, frameworks,

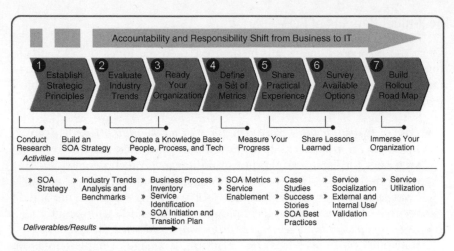

FIGURE 7.3 Major Activities in SOA Delivery Approach
© EpitomiOne, 2009.

and reference models. Building a successful SOA-based enterprise also requires effective use of industry standards, best practices, and regulatory compliance.

For LOB managers as well as business and IT executives, the most critical component of leveraging SOA essentials is collaboration between the business and IT. Figure 7.3 provides a high-level overview of the SOA delivery approach to demonstrate the importance of business-IT collaboration. Business organizations play a significant role in executing the overall road map for rolling out SOA across the enterprise. Strategic business-IT collaborative activities such as those suggested in Figure 7.3 offer a cursory view of the level of involvement that LOB managers can anticipate while working with their IT counterparts on SOA initiatives. Many companies and agencies consider a service design capability that incorporates basic visual modeling standards, frameworks, and reference models across the enterprise.

Before proceeding with an enterprise-level SOA initiative, most IT organizations promote support for an enterprise-level architecture capability and maturity model to formalize a foundation of the existing architecture. To support incremental maturity, the delivery approach presented here is based on the concepts of model-driven architecture (MDA), created by the Object Management Group (OMG). The MDA approach helps practitioners to abstract and to visualize business requirements in the form of platform– and implementation technology–independent models. This approach consists of three major phases:

1. Business modeling
2. Transformation
3. Deployment

During business modeling, business users own and participate in identifying the business requirements and helping IT teams visualize the business models. During transformation, the IT teams take charge of transferring business requirements into technical specifications, and they solicit the participation of users in critical decision-making processes. Finally, in the deployment phase, users and IT teams coordinate integration of the SOA-driven enterprise. Business teams then take over the final delivery while IT offers ongoing support. Therefore, during these phases, LOB managers can witness a swap between the business and IT teams in their responsibilities and accountabilities.

The list of deliverables for each phase can be categorized under several models:

- *Business modeling—platform-independent service model.* A set of conceptual and logical diagrams that includes the business service model and the business service interaction model.
- *Transformation—platform-specific service model.* A set of physical, implementation, and deployment diagrams that comprises the interface interaction model and the interface realization model.
- *Deployment—deployment model.* A set of deployable and tested services that consists of service interfaces and test services that can be integrated with existing applications or systems.

The LOB managers use these models to measure the level of progress made by the IT teams at any time. LOB managers periodically review these models with IT teams to change the direction of an initiative, to mitigate risks, or to enforce corrective measures. The deliverables and milestones, substantiated with business/IT collaboration at a project level, promote joint education and awareness programs.

During business modeling, LOB managers focus on these aspects of the services:

- *Identity and granularity.* This aspect includes what a particular service is, which business functionality it encapsulates, how it may have been created (for existing services), and how it can be used to build another service.
- *Coupling and interdependencies.* This aspect entails how existing or packaged (including wrapped legacy applications) services integrate with others and the dependencies they may have.

- *Interactions between identified services*. This relates to the exchange and sharing of information between two or more services.

Key service-related concepts that emerge during the transformation include:

- *Contractual agreements*. SLAs identify requirements and contracts needed with service providers.
- *Compliance*. Interfaces and interactions between service providers and consumers via broker or enterprise service bus (ESB), including how they will be developed and supported using existing or new technology, tools, patterns, frameworks, best practices, and industry standards.
- *Financial obligations*. Cost and operational support benefits that can be leveraged from the development or acquisition of a service to its maintenance or maturity.

Finally, during deployment, LOB managers focus on these additional elements of SOA:

- *Usability*. The proof of a concept or prototype of service interfaces, including the prospects for reuse.
- *Impact analysis*. The impact of testing and integration of services to the business model of the organization or the entire company, including regulatory considerations.

LOB managers consider the cost, ease of integration, and reusability benefits for each of these areas while evaluating how they can impact the bottom line. The next section addresses several steps LOB managers can take to achieve their revenue goals while adopting SOA.

SOA in Practice

Figure 7.4 presents a comprehensive set of steps for adopting SOA. All seven stages of the SOA adoption call for alignment between LOB managers and their IT counterparts.

The adoption life cycle is preceded by a preadoption stage during which the business teams (under the supervision of LOB managers) must identify and review their existing business functionalities and investigate how the associated business processes can be improved using SOA. This exercise is often referred to as making the business case for service orientation.

During the stage of establishing strategic principles, most LOB managers build an SOA adoption strategy based on their enterprise needs, including revenue goals, customer satisfaction objectives, and the reuse plans for

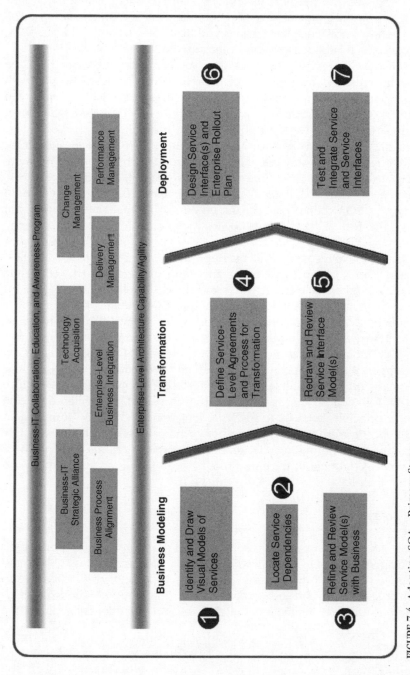

FIGURE 7.4 Adopting SOA—Primary Steps
© EpitomiOne, 2009.

123

desired services. In the next two stages, while evaluating industry trends and readying their organizations (or the enterprise), LOB managers focus on creating a knowledge base that can address the challenges, issues, risks, and concerns related to delivering anticipated revenues.

The next stage involves defining a set of metrics that can help the managers measure the progress of their initiatives and link results with the performance metrics used in negotiating SLAs or service contracts with providers. This is the stage in which initial services are designed, developed, and deployed for the respective business organizations.

In the following two stages, LOB managers can leverage and create concrete examples of services and share lessons learned from deployment of services with other practitioners. These two stages let managers review the revenues generated by the SOA-based services. The final stage is about building an SOA rollout plan for the enterprise. Here, LOB managers can engage the rest of their enterprise and achieve enterprise-wide revenue goals.

In addition to recognizing all the steps just mentioned, practitioners must consider a mechanism (e.g., governance and management) to efficiently orchestrate and execute the activities and deliver results listed in Figure 7.4 while managing, monitoring, and maintaining SOA initiatives.

SOA governance can and must coexist with corporate, IT, and enterprise architecture governance bodies prevalent in many organizations. Fundamentally, it is "more than just providing governance for SOA efforts—it is how IT governance should operate within an enterprise that has adopted SOA as its primary approach to enterprise architecture."[1] Hence, SOA governance must be founded on the existing governance principles, while embracing the new principles relevant to service orientation.[2] In practice, it must help practitioners govern the interactions between business and IT teams as they embark upon incorporating relevant policies, procedures, and best practices into services throughout the enterprise.

Lessons Learned

Most practitioners consider "lessons learned" sessions to emphasize their due diligence for SOA initiatives. They often start as business-driven and executive-sponsored investigative initiatives. In general, it is advisable to conduct lessons learned sessions even before jumping onto the SOA bandwagon. These sessions most definitely can help practitioners evaluate the

---

[1] www.ibm.com/developerworks/webservices/library/ws-soa-govern/.
[2] T. K. Hazra, "SOA Governance: Building on the Old, Embracing the New," *Cutter IT Journal* 20, no. 6, June 2007.

current state of their organizations and assess the effective best practices embraced by other practitioners in the industry. Let's consider the experiences of two companies in which LOB managers employed SOA in achieving their target revenues.

A U.S. Insurance Company

The first case is that of a U.S. insurance company with four lines of business (LOBs). The senior executive in charge of an individual LOB took a proactive role in introducing service orientation to the company. A limited amount of information was available on the industry trends and on relevant benchmarks for employing SOA in the insurance industry. As a result, the manager opted for an iterative, incremental approach in deploying SOA. Early introduction of lessons learned sessions jump-started the process of readying the key resources of the company. (In a way, this resembled the agile software development approach discussed in Chapter 14.)

The manager identified five major business functionalities, as these components were directly connected to the revenue goals of the LOB. Major difficulties experienced in this case stemmed from defining the dependencies of the services and removing their coupling with other applications and services. Several business applications were identified as redundant and retired over a period of six months. Several SOA development initiatives also were outsourced, and that caused major complications for the initiative teams in identifying the service interfaces and dependencies. The manager promoted use of the delivery approach described in Figure 7.1, and the first set of services was deployed over a period of nine months. The LOB is currently working on deploying six other major services and has already increased revenue by 11 percent.

Health Care Company

The second case study involves a health care company with two major LOBs: personal and commercial. The senior leadership decided to promote the use of SOA in its national benefit administration and claim processing system for the commercial line of business. The CIO offered his help to the line of business with a set of awareness programs educating LOB resources.

The business and IT teams had prior collaboration experience. Major difficulties encountered were identifying the services to be enabled and defining the interfaces between the services and existing applications. During business modeling, several redundant business functionalities were identified, and the business teams involved also worked to eliminate different silos. Several risks were identified and mitigated early in the SOA delivery process; this made a significant difference in the bottom lines of the LOB. The commercial line of business has four major services deployed using SOA, and the personal line of business is now leveraging the commercial LOB's core competencies.

Best Practices

It is important to emphasize different prerequisites to do SOA right. In the current economic climate, it is absolutely essential to pursue two major efforts:

1. Assess your situation while considering your options for transition to the SOA-driven enterprise.
2. Resolve most of the initiative planning challenges in the early stages.

Most practitioners cultivate a set of best practices to manage the SOA initiatives effectively. From my experience, I have collected seven such best practices so far. Even though these best practices may not be equally important to each one of us or for every project, they tend to promote successful SOA deployments for a variety of organizations.

- *Practice 1: Start with a focus on business and keep it that way.* SOA is a business-driven initiative. It starts with understanding the business requirements and continues beyond delivering business functions as services. Once a service is deployed, it is essential to devise a plan to maintain, manage, and monitor the health of a service and how it works. It is essential to keep known stakeholder business units involved in each and every step of an SOA initiative—and throughout the life cycle of a service.
- *Practice 2: Identify (and prioritize, when necessary) each service and validate the strategic goals behind it.* Once again, each service supports one or more business functions and ultimately connects to a strategic goal of the organization. It is essential to validate that each service has a purpose to exist. Once a business case is made to have multiple services, it may be necessary to consider prioritizing the deployment of services based on their impacts to the company business goals—or the criticalities in achieving the goals.
- *Practice 3: Leverage existing business architecture, supporting infrastructure, and technology investments.* In deploying or moving to an SOA, it is imperative to assess the current state of the organization. Utilize the existing knowledge, expertise, and resources, as well as current investments in technology, tools, or infrastructure. Leveraging business

architecture and its model(s) allows practitioners to focus on the business requirements first before delving into the technology utilization challenges. Business processes play a significant role in defining the scope of an SOA initiative.

- *Practice 4: Ready an enterprise with a comprehensive awareness program that includes both LOBs and IT.* Most practitioners today are familiar with the concepts of SOA. For many businesses, the concepts of service and pay per use are nothing new. However, it is necessary to allocate substantial time for the practitioners to become aware of the scope and limitations of SOA. What's more, they need to understand how services:
  - Can be integrated with the architecture of an enterprise.
  - Can be supported by the existing infrastructure to begin with.

  Both business and IT practitioners must align their goals and objectives behind embarking upon SOA initiatives. This will ensure that risks, challenges, and issues can be resolved effectively.

- *Practice 5: Think of the big picture and yet build small.* Reuse of a service cannot be retrofitted. Reuse is not a derivative of an SOA initiative. Rather, practitioners must build for reuse with a big-picture blueprint that presents a detailed road map for the enterprise in deploying SOA. However, services must be deployed iteratively and incrementally over a period of time. This will allow the rollout process to utilize the lessons learned from the previous iterations. It also allows help practitioners to revisit Practices 2 and 3 and take advantage of the activities performed there.

- *Practice 6: Plan for the governance of each and every service.* It is essential to make each service comply with government mandates, industry regulations, and organizational policies. A service in and of itself has no value until it complies with a set of established principles:
  - Government mandates or regulations
  - Organizational policies and procedures
  - Industry standards
  - Accepted best practices across the organization

  Governance cannot be retrofitted, either. This practice can provide a consistent approach to using services effectively—and will help practitioners to maintain the maturity of SOA initiatives.

- *Practice 7: Measure, monitor, and manage the progress of SOA initiatives all the way—each step at a time.* To paraphrase W. Edwards Deming, no progress can be managed unless it is measured. An SOA initiative is no exception. For many practitioners, measuring and monitoring SOA initiatives adds a new dimension to their attempt to improve the overall performance of the enterprise. This leads to a successful deployment of SOA in supporting the business operations.

Over the past ten years, I have revisited and refined these best practices many times while working with other practitioners. These best practices have come to help me in providing consulting services for review, evaluation, and maturity assessment of SOA initiatives to many organizations.

Summary

The concepts of SOA, a model-driven delivery approach, and suggested steps to adoption described in this chapter are based on my experience from the trenches. All the steps and the approaches presented here may not be equally applicable for all organizations to initiate their SOA efforts. However, the binding principles will accelerate the formation of collaborative enterprise.

For many LOB managers, revenue goals consist of multiple financial factors, parameters, and constraints. Most LOB managers use a set of best practices available to them from their IT counterparts or from research analysts. A plethora of information is also published in trade magazines and on the Internet today that describes the key difficulties in reaping the revenue-related benefits of SOA. An essential step for success is for managers to identify and prioritize their prospective business service candidates first in a visual model. Managers must instill a business-first approach in their teams. These services can then be transformed using a set of SOA technology, standards, and best practices. This step can influence business and IT collaboration—the critical component of service orientation. To make a significant impact on revenue goals, LOB managers usually focus on the following characteristics of their business-driven services:

- *Service granularity and its ability to form other services.* This is to abstract a service so it can deliver specific business functionality and be easily managed. The granularity of a service promotes composing other services.
- *Service coupling and its interoperability with other services.* This characteristic helps in detaching a service from another. Many companies are using an ESB to enhance interoperability of loosely coupled services.
- *Service reusability and its portability to multiple environments.* This is perhaps the most important feature in making a direct impact to the bottom line. To support users effectively, focus on the quality of service interfaces.

Currently, the standards, frameworks, and reference models supporting SOA initiatives are improving and SOA governance processes are still maturing. As a result, LOB managers can use various tools that can help them assess the health of their SOA initiatives and achieve their desired objectives.

Next Steps

The future of SOA is bright, prosperous, and vibrant. Many organizations in the United States and elsewhere are already making efforts to successfully build service-oriented enterprises (SOEs) today. The core business value of employing SOA today is in delivering to the enterprise agility, improved performance, and enhanced productivity. It is imperative when organizations try to change that they feel the crunch to survive as well as to excel. For some organizations, the benefit of SOA may be in service reconfiguration flexibility (as the business transforms). For example, consider the changes necessary to drive ease of information access in days by businesspeople and not in weeks by technical specialists. Critics suggest SOA is not here to stay forever. (What technology is?)

With that in mind, what really is the future of SOA? Where are we heading?

- SOA is a mainstream approach today. It has been turning into the fabric of each and every complex enterprise (i.e., a company or an agency). The practicality of service enablement has become the key delivery point of SOA. As a result, the promise of SOA is still very much alive.
- The next-generation SOA embraces Web 2.0 technology evolution. As Web 2.0 technology emerges rapidly, so does the feasibility of SOA leveraging the practical benefits of Web 2.0. Consider the combination of SOA and portals, and we will quickly recognize that Web 2.0 can help companies and agencies to leapfrog into a community of service users.
- The ultimate push of SOA and transformational Web 2.0 is the collaborative enterprise. As the technology evolves, standards mature, and established architectural frameworks gain popularity and momentum in use, SOA will lead the businesses to achieve consensus-driven, collaborative, and customer-oriented business goals effectively.

CHAPTER 8

Managing Mobile Business

Bhuvan Unhelkar

We will communicate with each other without the use of technological devices, but through our mind.

—Edgar Cayce (*On the Millennium*)

Introduction

Mobile technologies have revolutionized the way in which many organizations operate. Mobility provides two crucial advantages to organizations: *location independence* and *personalization*. The past decade has seen the rapid development of the Internet, the advent of cloud computing, and the lowering of costs of both mobile hardware and services. As a result, mobile technology has become a viable—and some would say essential—way of conducting business. Hugely successful organizations such as Apple Computer have been able to fundamentally alter the user experience, forcing other organizations to change the way they conduct business, interact with key constituents, and collaborate with one other.

As a result, organizations should not view mobile technologies through a limited lens (e.g., mainly as support mechanisms for existing processes). Rather, mobility can drive innovation and can make current business processes more flexible, dynamic, and efficient. Indeed, mobility can introduce new business processes altogether and obviate the need for antiquated ones. Through mobility, organizations can instantaneously customize (read: personalize) specific services used by customers, vendors, and employees, now capable of being individually identified and located through their mobile devices. Organizations can customize services to meet the different needs of different end users at different times.

This chapter introduces mobile technologies in a business context. This is followed by description of a mobile enterprise transition and management

(METM) framework. This transition framework is based on people, processes, and technologies involved in moving to a mobile business. Finally, the chapter discusses the advantages and risks associated with mobile technology adoption, with an eye on how organizations can mitigate these risks.

An Introduction to Mobility

Figure 8.1 depicts this nature of mobility and how it extends the land-based connectivity. The inner squares in this figure indicate land-based connectivity between enterprises, functional units, and other fixed devices. This connectivity evolved from the initial centralized connectivity of the mainframe, followed by the client-server connectivity, and finally resulting in the Internet connectivity (business to business [B2B] and business to customer [B2C]). The Internet-based connectivity continues to further evolve through eXtensible Markup Language (XML), service-oriented architecture (SOA), and the evolving Web 2.0 and beyond. However, as depicted by the outer squares in Figure 8.1, the external wireless connectivity, by its very nature, is between an individual and the business or between two individuals. A mobile device is a far more personal device than a desktop personal computer (PC), for example; an individual can carry a phone around and is not chained to a desk or a PC.

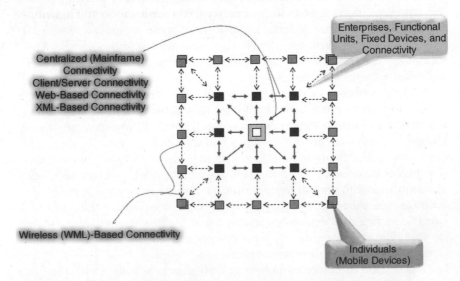

FIGURE 8.1 The Unique Nature of Mobile Connectivity in a Business Context

Organizations need to embrace the personalized nature of wireless connectivity, as shown in the external squares in Figure 8.1. The individuality of mobile gadgets and their ability to be location-aware is a crucial consideration of mobile business. What's more, the cost of these individual mobile devices, their networks, and their operating expenses are also a part of these considerations. So, also, are the process aspects of the business that need to make good use of the handheld gadgets.

Mobile technologies are affecting the cultural and social fabrics of many societies. They are changing value systems, like work ethics and social protocols. As a result, organizations "going mobile" need to consider the following:

- How to mobilize their existing land-based connectivity paradigms.
- How to incorporate wireless connectivity in a new paradigm that enables creation of previously unknown and far-reaching businesses.

The Mobile Enterprise

At a high level, mobile business can be defined as evolution of both internal and external business practices through the adoption of suitable mobile technologies and processes resulting in a mobile enterprise. M-businesses primarily want to engage with customers and business partners in *location-independent* and *time-independent* manners. This allows them to provide customers with new and valuable services and products.

Moreover, m-businesses also want to exploit the location and time independence of mobility to improve internal business processes. Because of the dynamic and instantaneous nature of mobile technologies, m-businesses can be in close and even constant contact with customers, partners, other external partners, and internal stakeholders.

Mobile strategic partnerships form a significant part of a successful mobile enterprise transition. Setting up and conducting mobile business requires a substantial interaction between the business and the following groups:

- Its mobile users.
- Mobile content and application service providers.
- Legal and regulatory agencies dealing with mobile compliance.
- The mobile network operators.

Mobile businesses create and provide contents and services for the customers, and the mobile network operators enable transmission of those contents over their networks. An organization's mobile suppliers and clients, through their mobile supply chain management (SCM) and mobile customer relationship management (CRM) systems, exercise considerable influence over the mobile business. Network operators are in an excellent position to leverage the following:

- Location data generated in their networks.
- The business's authentication information, user preferences.
- The billing relationship with their customers.

The area of strategic consideration for "going mobile" includes a part of the business of its suppliers and clients due to their significant interdependence on each other due to mobility. An understanding of these mobile relationships ensures that the partners are adequately prepared to collaborate with each other, on both technical and social levels.

Strategic mobile business is a complicated beast because it necessitates an understanding of each of the following:

- Application of mobility to external and internal business processes.
- Intelligent use of mobile devices.
- The study and understanding of the changes to organizational structures.
- Changes to operational arrangements.
- New and improved customer relationships.
- The social and cultural effects of mobility.
- The effects of mobile business on the physical environment and ecosystem.

As the preceding list indicates, mobility is an involved concept that goes beyond mere use of mobile gadgets for automation.

Strategic use of mobility is holistic in nature. It needs to consider both the internal and the external factors influencing the business. Benefits of mobility may not be immediately apparent, as they may be cloaked in environmental factors currently not visible or obvious to organizations still finding their way.

More than anything, mobility is a technology about different groups of people. Customers' and employees' views on ease of use and privacy are paramount to the success of mobile business. A mobile enterprise also needs to understand the potential benefits offered by mobility in globalization of business. Wireless networks, satellite communications, and the associated gadgets and processes of mobility can do tremendous things, but only if they are properly understood in different countries and cultures.

Mobile customers and employees are able to roam freely around the world with their mobile gadgets without losing connectivity to the business. Mobility is global and local at the same time.

Risks and Considerations

Businesses moving to mobile platforms need to consider each of the following factors:

- Different approaches to the content carrier versus the business partner that is going to provide the contents and services.
- Pricing model for the relationship with the carrier and the partner.
- Ownership, privacy, and security issues in terms of mobile contents.
- Licensing to ascertain and use location information on customers in order to promote business.
- Quality of service (QoS) based on mobile network technologies and their coverage.
- Collaborations and service-level agreements (SLAs) with location-based service providers
- Strategies for the development and management of contents for mobile services.
- Managing the changes to the business model and organizational structure resulting from mobile technology adoption.
- Managing the changes to the relationships with clients and suppliers resulting from mobile technology adoption.
- Development of mobile applications that will create value for customers.
- Integrating online and off-line contents and services in order to provide a unified view to users.
- Using extranets and intranets to enable clients and partners in the dynamic decision-making process required in mobile business.
- Handling quality and testing issues related to dynamically changing business processes.
- Providing for regulatory compliance by business, especially in a global mobile context.

Business Expectations from Mobile Technologies

Organizations are not alone in being able to realize major benefits from mobile technologies. Customers, employees, and business partners of any one organization can expect to see improvements on a number of levels.

Improved Business Processes

Mobility allows organizations to reengineer fundamental business processes. The new and reengineered processes utilize mobility's location and time independence. Business process modeling notations (BPMNs) and unified modeling languages (UMLs) activity diagrams are of great value in assisting organizations to optimize processes.

Dynamic Customization of Products and Services

Mobile technologies equip organizations to dynamically modify and update their offerings—and offer new products altogether. In other words, customers need not sit at desktops to download updates or patches. Of course, the types of updates required will hinge on many factors, including specific products, location, urgency, and the like.

Accessibility and Communication

Mobile technologies can improve accessibility and communication on many levels for many types of end users. Customers and employees can access information in different ways and different information altogether. Mobility means that employees, customers, and businesses are much more available to one another if they choose to be. For example, an airline passenger can access flight times while being driven to the airport in a taxi without actually calling the airline. The passenger can obtain this relevant information through a text on her mobile device. Similarly, accessibility to sports scores, medical information, and other types of information is increasing every day. Rapid growth and availability of hot spots is enabling connectivity around airports, hotels, restaurants, schools, and universities.

Cost Reduction

Mobile technologies enable organizations to reduce operational, marketing, services, and support costs. The return on investment (ROI) of mobile technologies in business is a crucial factor considered by the decision makers in formally using them.

Personalization of Products

Customers are increasingly demanding services tailored to their individual needs, as books such as Chris Anderson's *The Long Tail* illustrate. Anderson writes that "there's still demand for big cultural buckets, but they're no longer the only market. The hits now compete with an infinite number of niche markets, of any size. And customers are increasingly favoring the one with the most choice. The era of one-size-fits-all is ending, and in its place is something new, a market of multitudes."

It is hard to think of a technology more suited to meeting customers' increasingly diverse needs than mobile technology. Customers' needs are highly personalized—not only for a customer but also in the *context* in which the customer is looking for that service. Mobile technologies provide an opportunity for business to *tailor* its offerings that are specific to a particular customer at a particular location. Furthermore, such personalization significantly improves the overall experience the customer has with the business.

Adding Value to Customer Service

Through mobile technologies, employees can spend more—and more efficient—time with customers. Employees can use mobile devices connected to their organizations' enterprise servers to access mobile enterprise applications, such as CRM. Employees can garner a better understanding of their internal inventories and respond immediately to the changing customer demands.

Organizational Structure

Mobile technologies allow for greater collaboration. Organizational and team structures can concurrently be leaner, more responsive, and ultimately more effective. Flexibility in team structures is positively enhanced by mobile usage.

Ability to Reach a Wider and More Dispersed Audience

This goal is significant in mobile technologies, as it enables the organization to tap into audiences (and potential customers) that it would not have otherwise had access to. Furthermore, this extension through mobility is at a global level, because through the roaming features of the modern-day mobile gadgets and networks a customer need not be in the vicinity of the business in order to transact with the business. City, country, or region does not matter, especially when the business wants to access and provide services to the registered customer.

Environment and Sustainability

This goal of mobile technologies enables an organization to launch green initiatives through use of mobility. Mobility has the opportunity to provide environmentally responsible business strategies. For more on green information technology (IT), see Chapter 20.

Ability to Capture Data at the Source

With mobility, there is considerable reduction in duplication and errors in sourcing of data for the organizational systems. Portable mobile and wireless devices enable critical data to be captured at the time and place of its creation, which, in turn, helps reduce mistakes in capturing data and improves data information quality. For example, a radio frequency identification (RFID)–enabled inventory management system will directly provide stock levels to the system and will not have any translation.

Improved Management Understanding and Control

Mobile technologies enable management at all levels of the business to be involved in the decision-making process. Therefore, there is high potential for integrated decision making by the various stakeholders in the business, leading to much improved management understanding, structure, operation, and control of business than before mobile technologies.

Generating Content for Services

Mobile technologies allow organizations to generate timely and relevant content by facilitating user input in the content-generating process. Mobile technologies ensure sourcing of content, a major activity for mobile business. Transitioning of business is able to generate content through various sources, including user input, regular Web services–based updates, subscriptions from other service providers, and so on.

Workplace Flexibility

Mobility provides great opportunities for teleworking. Work need not be limited by office space and office hours in the mobile age, and therefore the concept of work itself is evolving with mobility. Mobile technologies enable people with families to balance their work and personal lives, as well as people who are physically challenged due to sickness or past injuries to find a new avenue of offering their skills and services in the workforce. However, great care needs to be taken to ensure the privacy of mobile employees. Personal quality of life of workers should not suffer due to mobile intrusion. A carefully implemented "working away from workspace" plan can help alleviate the challenge of loss of privacy in the workplace, improve employee morale, and also potentially reduce staff turnover.

Virtual Team Formation

Mobility opens up enormous opportunities on many levels, not the least of which is the creation of virtual teams. The niche skills of employees, consultants, and managers are no longer limited by physical location; these people can easily get together to serve the needs of a particular customer. Furthermore, such virtual teams can also lead to a reduction in staff numbers, as they enable the business to tap into the skills of consulting professionals outside the business for shorter and specific durations. The purpose of such reengineering of processes is *not* focused on staff reduction; however, it does lead to a much leaner team structure.[1]

Improved Disaster Recovery

The ability of the business to resume its operations as quickly and efficiently as possible after a disaster is enhanced by mobile technologies—mainly due to the lack of dependence on a single location in terms of carrying out operations.

The Mobile Enterprise Transition Framework

The framework for mobile enterprise transition (MET) provides a path for organizations to realize maximum value from the use of mobile technologies. This framework enables the business to balance its risks in adopting mobile technologies. For example, adopting mobile technology quickly is risky in that it may not be fully matured and may have numerous unresolved issues. Another factor to consider at early-stage entry by a business is the high cost involved in all introductory levels of mobile technologies. However, if a business is late in adopting mobility during a specific period of time and the competitors do so, then there is a great chance that the business will be left behind in terms of technology adoption and it may not be able to catch up with its competitors. These are some issues that the management is facing today.

When an organization decides to incorporate mobility into its business, it is a strategic decision that can be implemented using the MET process framework. This transition framework is made up of four major dimensions: the economic, technical, process, and social dimensions, which deal, respectively, with the why, what, how, and who. Practical experience in dealing with MET issues suggests that MET encompasses, in addition to mobile processes, technical issues as well as the sociological impact

---

[1]www.theleanway.com/.

of mobile transformations. Furthermore, mentioned in the goals of MET, and also based on practical experience in dealing with MET, a business hardly ever embarks on this transition unless there are sufficiently justified business reasons to do so.

Economic Dimension (Why)

The business drivers for incorporation of mobility in business are a strategic decision that is based on the primary question of why to mobilize. This strategic decision leads to instantiation of an MET process framework that can take the business to a global mobile playing field. This decision by the organization to adopt mobility is a part of the business dimension of the MET. The business/economic dimension of the MET framework is primarily concerned with the costs, competition, customers, employees, convenience, and usage of mobility.

Technical Dimension (What)

The technical dimension focuses on the technologies that underpin the MET as well as the framework's deliverables. Issues discussed in this dimension include devices/gadgets, programming, databases, networking, security, and architecture of mobile technologies participating in the MET. The technical dimension includes the understanding and the application of the following:

- The different mobile hardware devices and gadgets.
- The different issues of Global Positioning System (GPS)–enabled gadgets (3G).
- Wireless networking and security.

Organizations must prioritize these technical drivers in terms of their relative importance for the organization as it undertakes a mobile transition.

Process Dimension (How)

This process dimension of the MET methodological framework deals primarily with the following questions:

- How to model and conduct business transactions.
- How to ensure quality.
- How to manage the changing relationships of the business with its customers and employees.

This process dimension is concerned with the business processes, their modeling and engineering, and how adoption of mobility by the business affects its customers.

Social Dimension (Who)

The social dimension of the transformation process focuses on who the players in the MET are and how they influence, and are influenced by, the MET process. Typically these are the clients, employees, and other users of the business. The issues that face these users when they interface with a mobile business include usability and privacy, and the way their relationships change with the organization. The changes to work formats, including telecommuting and changing organizational and social structures, are all part of this social dimension of the MET.

Figure 8.2 shows the four mobile dimensions. This figure also shows the four evolutionary and revolutionary tiers of mobile business transitions: m-informative, m-transaction, m-operative, and m-collaborative. As the organization evolves from one usage to another, it also maps with the four dimensions of the MET.

Phases of Mobile Enterprise Transition

There are five major phases of MET:

1. Discovery
2. Innovation
3. Integration
4. Adapting
5. Review

An organization moving to a mobile business would progress through the following phases to bring about a change in its operations, organization, and processes.

Discovery

Discovery is the first phase of transformation that is actually a diagnostic activity in order to ascertain the current state of the organization with respect to its mobile maturity. The discovery of the state of the organization is based on the demographics of the organization, together with the existing mobile maturity of the organization. The details of the demographics of a transitioning organization are discussed in greater detail in the later in this

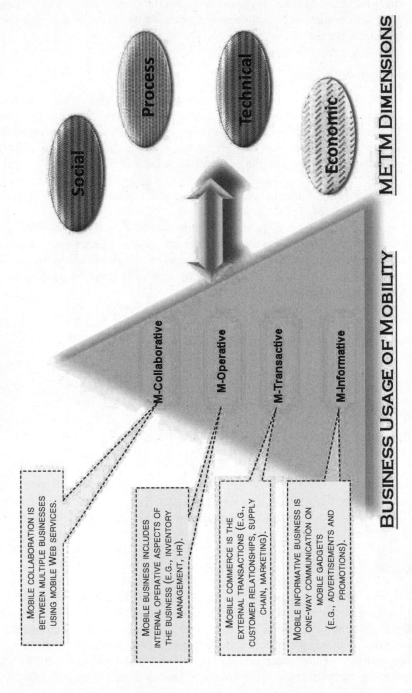

FIGURE 8.2 Mapping Business Usage of Mobility with MET Dimensions

chapter. This important diagnostic activity can help an organization under-stand the amount of effort required and the possible time line for such an effort when it undertakes MET. The four different mobile maturity levels are the preliminary, ad hoc, advanced, and managed states. An organization that merely provides mobile gadgets to its employees and also aims to deal with its clients with very basic processes can be considered only at a pre-liminary level of mobile maturity. The next stage is ad hoc use across the organization, followed by advanced use in all processes and organizational structures. Finally, there is the most mature state, in which the organization is mobile managed.

Innovation

The innovative activity of the organization undergoing MET is focused on the strategic thinking and strategy formation aspect of the plan for the transitioning business. Innovation deals with the new and creative ways of using mobility in all aspects of business. Therefore, innovation considers both internal and external process requirements, studies the external environment in which the business exists, and also deals with the departments and similar organizational units in terms of prioritizing the effects of changes on these units.

Integration

The integration activity of the MET brings together the internal as well as external business processes that would result in a unified view of the busi-ness to its users. The business processes and supporting systems in the current state of the organization are studied carefully in order to effectuate the necessary changes in those processes and systems due to mobility, as required by stakeholders and as demanded by the industry. While exist-ing processes can be merged together with the help of mobility, there are also completely new processes that need to be engineered with the use of mobility. To be successful, organizations must internally and externally inte-grate processes and systems. Process modeling tools and techniques can be very helpful in this regard. They can also allow organizations to anticipate changes to the existing processes brought about by mobility.

The integration of mobile devices and business processes is crucial for MET to be successful. Changes to the business processes are more robust and lasting when organizations adopt a holistic view of mobility. Agreements with service providers and technology partners, enablers, and network oper-ators need to be finalized during integration. Finally, the contents and corresponding content management systems (CMSs) also need to be inte-grated with the processes. The CMS database is also integrated with the existing technologies in the organization, such as the existing software systems and applications, existing databases, and existing security mechanisms during integration.

Adapting

The adaptation of the organization to the new technology, mobile in this case, permeates all aspects of the organization. This includes its organizational structure, its software systems, and its people. Therefore, adaptation also includes training activities.

The employees are trained during this activity on the new and reengineered mobile business processes. At the same time, some existing old processes may still be required by the business due to operational reasons, and they can be part of the transition considerations. Therefore, depending on the complexity of the business processes, there can be a parallel execution of the old processes as well as the new processes. The adaptation of the technology and the training of the employees need to be complemented by potential training for business partners and even for customers that are dealing with large and complex transactions with the business. The training provided to employees during the MET helps them with their customer service and support responsibilities using mobile devices. Employees are trained to provide responses to customer calls for support, and that response is provided with a high level of personalization. The transitioning organization, with its adaptation and training, creates a high level of service standards, delivery periods, response times, and customer orientation, leading to a new customer-oriented business culture. Creation of this customer-centric unified business view is one of the significant goals of a mobile business.

Review

After the adaptation, the organization evaluates the outcomes of its attempts to incorporate mobile technologies. The implemented software, system solution, and changes to organizational structures are evaluated and the effectiveness of the transition is measured. This measure is reported as a review and feedback to those responsible for the transition and also to the business stakeholders. As a result of the review, further enhancements are possible. Hence the review process should make provisions for these enhancements in all dimensions of the business. Organizations should incorporate into the MET framework both the experience gained from the transition as well as the issues discovered.

Business Value of Mobile Technologies

A strategic framework for adoption of mobility by an enterprise leads the organization on its path to achieving its stated goals. These enterprise goals are based on a number of factors, including the demographics of the enterprise (i.e., its size, location, and the type of business). The goals of the enterprise transition must ensure that it aligns the mobile enterprise with its mission and values. MET aims at generating good value for its stakeholders. Strategic considerations in mobile business start with an assessment of the current status of the enterprise in terms of its current mobile usage and maturity. This assessment leads to the identification and investigation of the various business processes in the organization and also an analysis of how the MET can be applied to them. These business processes support the overall goal of the enterprise.

Metrics

The MET should also propose a mechanism (metric) to identify and measure the criteria for optimization and improvement. Changes to business processes due to mobile technologies must be measured before and after the changes.

Many organizations use the following as mobile process metrics:

- The speed of response.
- Its relevance to the situation and location.
- The calculations of dynamicity of mobile groups.
- Quality of service (QoS).

These metrics provide a set of measurable criteria rather than an ad hoc understanding of improvement resulting from the MET. The MET should ensure involvement from the stakeholders so as to understand their perceptions of the goals in relation to mobile enterprises, and mobile strategic considerations include a systems approach to the transition. Furthermore, the organizational structures and behaviors need to be understood in order to strategically apply mobility to them. Enterprises may be abstracted in terms of their structures (what they consist of); their processes and functions (what they do, how they change, and how they bring about change); and the technologies they use. Mobile strategies study the organizational structures; model the processes; and implement and measure the networks, databases, and devices. The understanding and measurement of these various organizational factors provides a good grasp of how mobility can help improve the performance of such an enterprise. Socially, however, advertisement and customer solicitation need to be carefully and sensitively considered. The offerings of the enterprise in terms of products, services, quality, as well as sustainability are studied within the context of the MET framework.

Mobile Organizational Structures

Mobility is forcing organizations to adopt a different perspective: Customer-centric views are replacing department-centric views. Organizational and team structures are affected by the way mobility changes management of human resources as well as the social and cultural issues in managing the transition to a mobile enterprise.

Consider the traditional need for a hierarchical organization structure. Customer requests need to pass through a number of different departmental circles in order to reach the right person. This is abating, as customers now often have direct access managers and employees responsible for providing the service.

Mobility changes the way in which organizations structure themselves, their employees, their roles, their responsibilities, and their reporting hierarchies. Mobility is causing organizations to flatten and loosen their structures; the hierarchical and rigid organizational structures of the premobile era are dwindling. Mobility is causing communication channels to overlap and intersect in many unforeseen ways.

Mobile Content and Services

Mobile content and services have enabled many organizations to form strategic alliances. Perhaps the best example of this is Apple's partnerships with different application developers for its iPhone.[2] Many software organizations develop cool bells and whistles, sharing revenue with Apple. To be sure, these partnerships have been extremely profitable for all concerned and are serving as a model for other mobile organizations. BlackBerry maker Research in Motion is one of many companies developing its own version of Apple's app store in response to the immensely popular iPhone.

While mobile operators (MOs) are able to capture location data, that data is incomplete. In order to be able to tailor their services to individual customers, MOs need to combine it with data available from content providers. This combination of location-specific services and mobile contents provides excellent opportunities for businesses to create market differentiation. Content providers have an incentive to work with network

---

[2]http://online.wsj.com/article/SB121789232442511743.html?mod=googlenews_wsj.

operators; only together can they brand the service offered by the network operators. During the early stages of an MET, organizations must formulate their strategies in terms of how they combine the offerings of the operators and the corresponding content providers. Alternatively, the organization itself might need to provide the content. In such cases, the content provider must develop a mutually beneficial strategy with the network operator as it undertakes MET.

Consider the following scenario. A network operator and a content provider offer services such as sports scores or a traffic update. At times, the operators have a high degree of control over the distribution of mobile content. This control over the mobile network allows their operators to create greater profit margins for themselves. In so doing, they can brand or co-brand the service depending on the brand image of the service provider. In the sports score example, a network operator can provide the sports score as its own, or if the service provider is a well-known sports association, then the operator can co-brand the score with the sports association. Privacy and security concerns of customers need to be considered in the branding of the services during an MET, as it requires sharing of location and related context information by network operators with trusted partners. The network operators are usually keen not to reduce their role to mere providers of the infrastructure for the content sought by the customers and users of services. As a result, they are typically reluctant to participate in a business model wherein the content developers have direct access to the location- and context-specific data that allows them to deal directly with the consumers. The network operators can participate in a shared revenue model with their partners wherein they retain the right to bill the customer and, thereby, maintain some sort of ownership of the customer for the entire package of service being offered to the customer. While the content developers are free to set prices for their services and attract customers, they end up with a slice of the overall revenue obtained from the customer in this shared business model.

Service providers need to make an appropriate choice from a range of mobile technologies that are available to them in order to provide their services. For example, the selection of a mobile technology in order to ascertain the location and context of the customer can provide great opportunities for the service providers to customize their services. This is also the difference between a successful mobile content and service provider organization as against the one that is merely partnering with a network operator. Location- and context-specific data can be obtained from GPSs, Bluetooth, RFID, and even local area networks (LANs). When a service provider accesses, stores, analyzes, and uses such location- and context-based information of existing and potential customers, it also has the opportunity to bypass the need to partner with a mobile network operator. However, at the same time, such service provider business may then also be limited to the specific locations where there is an opportunity for interfacing with willing customers through LANs or Bluetooth technologies. The advantage of going alone and not partnering with a network operator to provide the service also needs to be balanced with the possible time lag before the customer base for the service provider is large enough for the business to be effective. Therefore, in terms of strategic decision making during the early stages of MET, it is vital that the business undergoing MET gives due credence to the network operators, the content, and the service providers.

Mobile Business Application Considerations

The transitioning mobile business has to consider various business applications and the changes to these applications and packages resulting from mobile technology adoptions.

Customer Relationship Management

Mobile customer relationship management (M-CRM) must create close relationships with customers by providing value. Customers want reliable and fast service, and CRM provides those services to enable the business to gain more customers. The CRM is crucial in a mobile business as it is the system that provides the business with the ability to directly contact the customers and users. Furthermore, personalization of the customer's interaction is extremely valuable in M-CRM. An example includes automated voice interaction that takes into account the ethnic diversity and vocabulary. Customers are not interested in the internal functioning of an organization. The combination of technology, software, people, and reengineered business processes converges to provide value through CRMs.

Supply Change Management

Supply chain management (SCM) is perhaps one of the best uses of mobile technologies. Enterprise Resource Planning (ERP) vendors such as Oracle offer mobile SCM applications that "enable users to perform many common warehouse and shop floor transactions through hand-held radio frequency devices, personal digital assistants and truck-mounted radio frequency scanners. Transactions can be carried out on these wireless devices at the point of use, offering real time transaction processing, improved data accuracy and increased mobility and convenience."[3] What's more, mobile SCM gives

---

[3] www.oracle.com/applications/order_mgmt/MSCA.html.

organizations much greater flexibility in monitoring and controlling many documents and their delivery statuses, such as order status.

Procurement Systems

Procurement has a broader meaning and includes purchasing, transportation, warehousing, and inbound receiving of goods ordered. Mobile procurement systems provide more updated and relevant information on internal movement on goods. This results in improved inventory control and more efficient purchasing processes.

Human Resource and Payroll Systems

The human resources (HR) systems in mobile business provide opportunities for improved internal HR management due to personalization of time sheets and payrolls. Enterprise bargaining, subsequent agreements, and other responsibilities of HR are also modified due to the use of mobility. Further changes in HR systems due to mobility include changes to job roles and definitions, shift management, security of goods and premises, and delivery of services. Similarly, mobile technologies are also used creatively in payroll applications to save time and enhance value to employees. While the HR systems change and manage rosters, their rosters are linked to the payroll to automatically generate a pay list based on the automated roster instead of using a human supervisor.

System Integration

Mobile business applications need to integrate the disparate systems running in organizations. Here, system integration is more than the mere provision of interfaces (typically XML-based or Wireless Markup Language [WML] interfaces) for each system. Rather, the complete system brings together contents, applications, security, and transmission networks.

Knowledge Management

Mobility can enhance knowledge management (KM) within an organization by making it more robust, accurate, reliable, and accessible. End users can update key documents—or add new ones—anywhere and at any time. To get to this point, organizations must utilize search capabilities that rely on mobile inputs. (For more on knowledge management, see Chapter 10, Enterprise Search and Retrieval.)

Specifically, mobility facilitates this linking and correlations between silos of information in a dynamic manner, as the access to the information silos is no longer restricted to a physical location. Mobility also provides an excellent opportunity for organizations to improve their environmental responsibilities by recycling products and streamlining goods movements. So-called environmentally intelligent systems have an opportunity to incorporate mobility in them that will help the organizations using such systems to improve their environment-related performance, such as carbon emissions (discussed in Chapter 20).

Balancing Personal Services with Privacy

If businesses have learned anything from e-commerce, it is that customers are willing to provide personal information in exchange for personalized services. Perhaps mobile customers are more concerned about usefulness and degree of personalization of service than privacy threats. However, the potential for misuse of personal information is real and raises several questions, such as:

- Who would have access to the location information?
- Can users not have their locations tracked?
- How secure is the information?

Mobile organizations must follow solid business practices regarding the management and use of location data. Building trust with customers is certainly a good business practice. What's more, it will also avoid a more restrictive regulatory climate if self-regulation ultimately does not work.

Most customers look at a mobile business as more than a business that is merely converting its existing services to mobile services. A customer wants the business to provide new and unique services that will make formal use of the location and time independence provided by mobility.

Many mobile customers want highly personalized services provided to them. When these services are delivered via mobile gadgets, organizations have an enormous opportunity targeting specific individuals.

Personalization is one of the unique advantages of mobile technologies for customers. The personalized nature of mobility means that organizations need to consider mobility separately at the individual, organizational, and collaborative levels.

Summary

This chapter has approached mobile technologies as a means of creating and improving mobile business. Mobile technologies are unique as they provide location independence, personalization, and time independence. The four-dimensional framework for mobile enterprise transition and management (METM) is made up of economy, technology, process, and society. While the advantages of mobility can be significant, so are its challenges and risks. The mobile technology layers, their strategic impact on businesses, and the balancing of various drivers, such as costs, functionality, and privacy, were discussed. However, the technology discussions only underpinned the process for mobile enterprise transition (MET). A business decision maker needs to follow the five phases of MET outlined in this chapter. Each industry and organization within the industry has its own nuances that need to be catered to in adapting mobile technologies. For example, organizations developing and selling products need to consider the product life cycle management with the help of mobility, whereas organizations providing services need to enhance their business processes and their contents in order to provide value to their customers. The rapidly advancing wireless Internet resulting in numerous wireless broadband services has a major impact on mobile businesses. The impact of social networking and social engineering resulting from mobile technologies is just as great. These technologies are literally changing the landscape of our social fabric. Organizations need to continuously dip into research, case studies, and advisories to remain on top of the mobile game. Things are moving very fast.[4]

Next Steps

- Investigate the current state of your organization. Where is it in terms of its mobile maturity?
- Create a mobile enterprise transition project that will deal with business transformation for a mobile business.
- Identify the areas in the business that will benefit from the mobile technology features of location independence, personalization, and time independence.
- Discuss each of the four dimensions of mobile enterprise transition with corresponding stakeholders—the economic dimension being the responsibility of senior management/decision makers, the technology dimension residing with the IT director/chief architect, the process dimension with the business/departmental management, and the social dimension with the marketing/HR people.
- Create a mobile enterprise architecture (MEA) that is specific to your organization.
- Update the project plan for mobile enterprise transition with the five phases: discover, innovate, integrate, adapt, and review.
- Implement the mobile enterprise transition project.

---

[4]For additional information on this topic, please see http://philsimonsystems.com/nwot_extras.html.

CHAPTER 9

Social Networking

Jay Miletsky

What we have to learn to do, we learn by doing.

—Aristotle

Introduction

For anybody who never got to enjoy life among the popular crowd, there's a golden opportunity waiting for you—a virtual (pun intended) gold mine of friends and followers anxious to make you feel more wanted. It's a place where people you don't even know will happily peruse your summer vacation photos and comment on how great your new hairstyle looks, and people you'd be too shy to approach in real life will actively post quiz results to your wall so you'll have firsthand knowledge of what they consider to be the five greatest Molly Ringwald movies of all time. It's an environment in which generations can close the gaps, as people who once held authoritative positions, such as parents and bosses, can now share the same "friend" classification as fraternity brothers and one-night stands. It's a magical place where we can all have a louder voice, even if nobody ever actually hears us speak.

Welcome to the world of social networking, brought to you by Facebook, Twitter, LinkedIn, and any one of the hundreds of other relevant sites where people meet and greet and congregate and share. According to a July 2009 report by Forrester Research, nearly 33 percent of U.S. adults (55.6 million) visit a social network at least once each month—nearly doubling the number of users from just one year earlier. And where people go, so go the businesses, as the Association of National Advertisers reports that in 2009, over two-thirds of all organizations have explored ways of using various social media, including social networks, as a vital means of reaching their audiences.

Note that, for the purposes of this chapter, it's important to distinguish between *social media* and *social networks*. Although the two terms are often (and incorrectly) used interchangeably, *social media* is the umbrella term for the wide variety of tools and applications that give the Web its social capabilities—capabilities that allow a community to come together, communicate, and build upon one another's opinions and ideas. These tools include email, instant messaging, blogs, and others. A social network, in contrast, is a site that uses one or more of these social media tools for the primary purpose of promoting connectivity and interaction—to facilitate people communicating with other people. While many of the rules I discuss through the remainder of this chapter apply to social media in general, the focus of this conversation will center on social networking.

But while agencies everywhere are rushing to create Facebook fan pages and Twitter strategies for their clients, many organizations are taking matters into their own hands, owning their social networks through enterprise solutions that bring the conversation to their home turf. Engagement here isn't limited to interaction with consumers, but rather it extends to vendors, suppliers, and perhaps most important, employees.

Why Social Networking? Why Not Just Use the Public Forums?

Everything has its purpose and reasons for existing. Chicken noodle soup is a wonderful meal when you're sick, while split pea might be better to order in a restaurant. The existence of one doesn't necessarily negate the need for the other. Social networking is no different, which is why so many networks exist and people continue to flock to them. Similarly, the existence (and popularity) of public forums does not negate the need, impact, or usefulness of the enterprise solutions for networking.

There's no question that organizations can and do benefit from implementing Facebook and Twitter strategies (as well as more niche networks that make sense for a given industry). But these have their limitations, and many larger organizations have discovered the benefits of maintaining their own enterprise systems that simply cannot be achieved (at least not as easily or as effectively) with more public networks.

Benefits of Social Networking

Because of their flexibility, enterprises can utilize social networking tools in myriad different ways and realize a number of different benefits. They include:

- Greater access to different audiences
- Improved branding opportunities
- Increased control over the conversation
- Greater access to user information
- Real-time market research
- Improved customer service

This is by no means a definitive list. Like many of the other Enterprise 2.0 technologies discussed in this book, social networking tools are evolving as we speak. An organization is doubtless introducing a new social networking application right now that will result in unexpected benefits (and perhaps a few unanticipated problems). The following subsections discuss some of the most common benefits that organizations adopting social networking tools can expect to realize.

Greater Access to Different Audiences

With over 250 million people on Facebook alone (as of the time of this writing), it's not surprising that for most organizations, the focus on social networking has been on engaging consumers as a supplement to or replacement of their traditional marketing efforts. But consumers represent only one audience that organizations can tap into. Vendor and supplier relations can be vastly improved through communication on enterprise networks, with conversations ranging from delivery issues to invoicing, contracts, partnerships, and supply chain improvements.

Perhaps even more important are the benefits derived from increased and improved interaction among employees. The contributions this population can provide to their company cannot be stated strongly enough. Social networking helps engage employees for purposes of living the brand through multiple touch points, improving morale and increasing productivity.

Social networking on the enterprise level helps improve employee relations by giving each member of the workforce a platform to have his or her voice heard—an empowering forum that brings employees out of their cubicles and gives them direct access to human resources (HR), key executives, and each other, no matter how far apart they are spread. Like a virtual suggestion box or brainstorming session, employees can use internal social networks to collaborate on a variety of topics and play a more important role in corporate development—all while key executives can harvest previously inaccessible ideas that could ultimately help improve the brand, the product, service mix, and the corporate environment altogether.

Improved Branding Opportunities

Without getting too detailed about the methods and importance of brand building (especially in a digital age), consistency in look, feel, voice, and action plays an important role in maintaining the integrity of the brand.

Enterprise solutions (depending on the technology being used) give organizations control over the look and feel of their social networks. Social networks owned and operated by the enterprise can develop a look and feel that works seamlessly with the standard corporate site, while ensuring that content is completely its own (no ads by Google or other unwanted information), presented in a way that makes the most sense for the brand and the visitor.

But branding is about more than a look and feel. Building a brand is about building trust. Through their social networks, organizations have the opportunity to relate and respond to their audiences in ways that traditional marketing simply cannot provide. It affords them the opportunity to present a more human side to the organization, putting a voice to the people behind the brand with more transparency—in stark contrast to the complete absence of human personality from standard mass media advertising. The more human the voice comes across through social network engagement, the more human and relatable the company becomes, ultimately increasing trust in the brand.

Increased Control over the Conversation

Although most public networks will allow the owner to control the conversation, enterprise solutions provide increased ownership over all content, controlling and steering the conversation in ways that reflect what is important to both the brand and the audience. Organizations can instigate conversations, curtail other ones, alert their audience to updates, and provide instant online solutions to issues that they detect within any given discussion. It is a fully controlled environment in which connections are made on very specific topics with less of a chance for conversations to dissolve into a disorganized mess. For example, a recent scan of Sun Microsystem's fan page on Facebook has one user leaving a Wall post about the "fake" Apollo moon landing, while another compares a cloud security webinar to a wedding party. A quick look at their consumer-facing enterprise forums resulted in far more serious-minded posts around more specific topics, adding real value to both the company and the visiting audience. Sun developers and enthusiasts, faced with a decision between the Facebook fan page or Sun's own social network for a place to engage in real conversation with their peers and with the brand, well . . . is there really any debate?

Greater Access to User Information

Plain and simple, enterprise solutions allow organizations to collect as much user data as they would like (and their audience is willing to give), before granting them access to the network, including any contact information needed to run direct marketing campaigns in the future. Moreover, enterprise networks allow organizations greater details and insight into audience movements to better plan calendars of content to which individuals will respond.

Real-Time Market Research

While they still provide valuable insights, focus groups cannot reach the same audience as social networks. Engaged users can be tapped directly (asked a question online or presented with a specific conversation topic) or observed indirectly (having their online conversations viewed without encroachment). Given the chance to speak their minds, individuals are not shy about leaving their opinions and taking an active role in the brands they or their employers use. To be sure, enterprise solutions provide the fodder and platform for these very telling conversations to take place. What's more, detailed analytic studies can give brands invaluable insight into the types of people who are more actively engaged, their sentiment toward the brand, and their passion for it. Aggregated, this information can create a solid base for making future decisions regarding the marketing and development of products and services.

Improved Customer Service

As much as consumers love the endless maze of menu options they get faced with each time they call customer service, and as much as people relish discussing their issues with overseas representatives whose thick accents can turn a simple question into a hour-long ordeal, social networking has become a resource for individuals to gain direct access to companies when problems arise.

On a broader scale, companies have taken advantage of enterprise solutions to provide media-rich resource centers, including how-to videos, downloads, question-and-answer boards, and more. Live chat sessions allow consumers to speak with support professionals without any language barriers and engage in conversations that can include helpful links and reduce corporate expenditures (employees handling support can often oversee multiple online chats as opposed to one phone call during each session).

Social networking allows companies to monitor online conversations to gauge any growing discontent among its market and solve issues before they become too pervasive. Further, consumers that discuss their issues openly not only give other consumers the opportunity to solve their problems (saving the company time and effort), but give companies the benefit of providing a public response, further building brand trust and potentially solving problems for others before they happen.

Impediments, Solutions, and Resolutions to Progress

As often proves to be the case when it comes to emerging media, organizations are so quick to jump on the bandwagon that they fail to take the necessary time to fully understand its subtleties. (Ironically, many of the same organizations have been slow in adopting some of the exciting new technologies discussed in this book.) Regardless of the technology employed, the social network itself is simply a tool—the platform that is used to facilitate interactions. But tools alone don't do the job—the world's fastest car won't win a race if nobody knows how to drive it. Social networks can be launched, but that's only one part of a far larger effort that requires specific work and understanding.

Social Networking Requires a Different Approach

From a marketing standpoint (both internally and externally), brands typically measure effectiveness based on impressions. Print, TV, radio, roadside billboard, pay-per-click advertising, and other such methods are worked into strategies based on the media planners' expectation of total possible impressions. Similarly, traditional public relations (PR) tactics also gauge effectiveness by total impressions through media placements and editorial coverage. Because campaigns typically run for a finite period of time and then go dark when return starts to fall off, impression-based marketing forms a wave pattern, as shown in Figure 9.1.

Whereas traditional marketing is often measured by overall impressions during times when campaigns are running (resulting in a wave pattern), social networking is measured in engagement, which grows with each new communication and plateaus in between, resulting in a stepped pattern.

By contrast, success in social networking is measured in engagement rather than impressions, as consumers are spoken *with* rather than spoken *to*, and more intimate connections are made. When done correctly, engagement will grow with each new communication and plateau in between, in effect replacing the traditional waves with a less volatile stepped pattern, also shown in Figure 9.1.

The significance of this difference goes far beyond measurements of reach and success; it speaks to the ways in which brands communicate

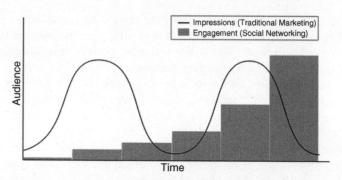

FIGURE 9.1 Impact of Traditional Marketing versus Social Media

with their markets through social networking—a style whose nuances are often misunderstood by brands that rush into social networking but maintain their traditional marketing mind-sets. Traditional advertising sends a one-way communication: *Here's who we are, here's what we sell, and here's why you should do what we want you to do*. Markets don't have a voice or any real options other than to either listen to ignore each message. Traditional marketing is meant, by design, to be one-sided—it speaks to the masses and provides limited, if any, capabilities for market retort or opinion.

True market engagement, however, occurs only when the audience has a voice and the ability to directly respond to all communication efforts. In this sense, marketing becomes a conversation—in a public forum—in which individuals have direct access to the brands they buy, sell to, and work for. *Individuals* is the key word in that last sentence. To take full advantage of the power of social networking, folks in the corner office need to start relating to their market on an individual level, rather than grouped together as broad-based demographic profiles. Communication needs to be more personal and less promotional, more transparent, timely, consistent, and valuable. It needs to reflect brand without the marketing jargon that is more reflective of traditional marketing methods.

Engaging with audiences requires a conversationalist mentality, breaking down the walls that keep outsiders at arm's length.

Meaningful Content Is Required

People love to punish their future selves. We do it all the time. *"Sure, lunch next Tuesday sounds great—see you then!"* is all well and good until about 11:00 a.m. next Tuesday morning when we start wondering why we agreed to lunch in the first place and frantically jog our imaginations for believable reasons to cancel.

Many a future self has been punished thanks to social networking. At the outset, executives agree to stay on a steady schedule, imagining that a blog post here and there won't take too much effort. It usually isn't until after the network is up and running that they realize...

It *is* an effort. Content development can be a rigorous process that is time-consuming and difficult to do well. Properly developing effective content for a social network requires adherence to specific points:

- *Update content regularly.* Maintaining a successful social network requires making a commitment to keep it updated with new content on a regular basis. Much like developing a media plan with advertising scheduled months in advance, content needs to be planned out ahead of time, keeping to a firm yet flexible schedule. Posting entries on a seemingly random basis or missing scheduled updates is a sure way to lose core visitors who can easily become confused or indifferent, taking their social networking elsewhere.
- *Maintain a friendly but brand-oriented voice.* Social networks offer organizations the opportunity to communicate in a friendlier, more conversational tone—but care needs to be taken to avoid letting this more casual style dilute the image and lifestyle that the brand represents.
- *Keep content relevant.* For the most part, social networks on the enterprise level are based on a central theme, even when multiple subconversations are taking place at once. Developers need to ensure that new content remains in line with what the audience wants to talk about and what the brand wants them to discuss.
- *Remain transparent.* Because social networking is a conversation, users want to know who they are talking to and where communication is coming from. Unlike the canned quotes in traditional press releases attributed to executives but written by publicists, people who engage in social networking expect the real deal. If a blog on a social network claims to be from the CEO, then it really does need to come from the CEO.
- *Don't sell.* With social networking, brands are sold based on the individuals who represent them. Thought leadership through the provision of useful content and the development of active online communities becomes a far better seller than direct marketing pitches.

Management Needs to Stand Behind Its Network

They put the money out to build an enterprise-based social platform, so it stands to reason that upper management stands behind it and encourages its use internally, right? Not necessarily. All too often, upper management takes the approach that money and technology are all the network needs. But there is another asset required that is easily overlooked because it is intangible: firm support from upper management for the active use of enterprise social networking, especially among the employee population.

This can be prove to be a sticky wicket, however, as management could be seen as speaking out of both sides of their mouths, and employees may not be sure of which side to listen to. On one hand, managers want employees to take advantage of social networking functionality within the enterprise—respond to blogs, add to the corporate wiki, and so on. On the other hand, many organizations continue to block their workforce from using public networks like Facebook or Twitter, or even accessing YouTube or instant messaging while at work. Collectively, these actions convey the message that social networking isn't regarded as a valuable employee function, and that even internal network collaboration could be a trap. Employees are well aware that unlike the public networks, where it is easy to maintain one's anonymity, the enterprise network offers no safe havens—IT can easily track down which employee said what, when, and how long they spent saying it. Even worse, many employees of larger organizations work in cubicles where all of their computing is visible to passersby: *Sure, upper management says "Go, go, go," but my immediate boss glares at me every time he sees me on the corporate blog and reminds me that we have a deadline to meet.*

This creates a quandary, and it's one that only upper management can solve through the following:

- *Guidelines.* Employee handbooks and corporate guidelines can no longer exist without consideration of social media applications, tools, and how employees are expected to use them. This is especially true of employees' use of social networks outside the enterprise and in the public domain, as their association with the company can mean that all of their online behavior is ultimately a reflection (positive or negative) of the brand. New guidelines will provide employees a much-needed map as to what is and what is not considered acceptable use of online engagement.
- *Training.* Midlevel managers can't be left in the dark. They need to know that upper management is onboard and behind the enterprise system, encourages its use among lower-level employees, and sees it as a boon to the company rather than a drain on resources. More important, this training needs to teach midlevel managers *why* social networking is important and how the company plans to benefit from its use among employee, consumer, and other populations.

Itchy Trigger Fingers

Nobody likes to be criticized, and corporations are no better at accepting criticism than individuals are (in fact, they're often worse!). Social networking tools are forums for ideas and opinions, and centers where individuals can have a voice. Because of this, they set an ideal stage for the following:

- Disgruntled consumers to express negative opinions about their experience with a brand.
- Disgruntled employees to vent their frustration at other employees and management.
- Other forms of communication not anticipated or desired by senior management.

These negative comments, of course, are visible and available for anybody on the network to see—not exactly the kind of notoriety that most organizations want to be made public.

This is where the disparity between information technology (IT) and PR becomes very visible. The traditional IT response is to immediately delete any negative commentary. The PR response usually involves turning a negative into a positive, responding openly to any negative comments, and showing its audiences that the organization is listening to them. This builds trust. Social networking is perhaps at its absolute finest when consumers and employees are not the only ones with a voice. Organizations also benefit from the ability to speak out and present themselves as the good guys: *We're listening, and we want to make your life better.* In terms of branding, it's perhaps the most effective sales pitch possible.

That is not to say that all comments, no matter how scandalous, should be left on open forums. There is a fine line between a comment that is mere slander with no critical value ("This brand is terrible—I hate it") and genuine disappointment ("I tried this brand and was unhappy because of . . ."). The same applies to constructive criticism. While the following quote may be negative, it can help the organization improve the customer experience: "One of the areas I think your brand could improve is . . . ." Management needs to determine where this line needs to be drawn, but not be too scared by negative reactions, ratings, or reviews. If handled properly, they can reflect positively on the brand.

Does Return on Investment (ROI) Exist in the Social World?

It's one of the more frustrating and confounding debates among social media marketers: *Does engagement through social networking provide any solid financial return?* It's a great question and one that unfortunately doesn't have a solid answer yet—at least not one that has swayed the majorities in one direction or the other. Enterprise social networks can face particular difficulty in terms of measuring returns. In part, this stems from the fact that the expense is greater than simply maintaining a presence on a public forum, but also because the audiences can be so diverse. It's one thing to build a calculation model for social networking efforts that are aimed at engaging consumers—even a fairly rudimentary comparison of gross sales to social networking activity over a period of time would give some indication of actual benefit. But calculating ROI becomes significantly harder when we turn the enterprise network's focus on employees.

Because many employees don't generate direct revenue, it's harder for IT managers, HR directors, and chief technology officers (CTOs) to make the case for social networking within the enterprise as a benefit whose expense is warranted. More often, the better measure is not in revenue generation but in cost savings.

Social networking offers additional benefits to organizations willing to embrace them, including:

- *More efficient communication across large geographies.* Enterprise social networking collects information that was once shared only in conference rooms and hallways, and later through emails. All of this content is collected in a centralized system of blogs, wikis, and other tools, as well as central repositories for files and other larger, digital content. Access to this information isn't regulated to where in the world (or even where in a single building) an employee is located, cutting down costs on all communication vehicles from overnight shipping to travel and hotel expenses and more. (See Chapter 17 for information about the benefits of wikis and other collaborative tools.)
- *Getting it right the first time.* Not only can tools be shared across the enterprise, but so can success stories, research, instructions, and motivation. Why should one employee in Hackensack, New Jersey, begin the expensive process of starting something new from scratch (potentially even more expensive if it's done incorrectly), when a coworker in San Francisco, California, has recently gone through a similar process and chronicled her success on the enterprise network?
- *Fewer outside consultants need to be paid if employees can collaborate more effectively.* A company's greatest resource is its own employees. While they may be concentrating on their specific job functions, these are the people who know the organization and the brand best. They have the most to gain from seeing the company they work for grow. The thoughts and ideas they can bring to the table cannot be underestimated. Enterprise-based collaboration on specific topics may result in free (and profitable) solutions that may otherwise have cost a considerable amount for an outside consultant to develop.

Examples of Social Networking Tools

While independent software vendors (ISVs) can build just about any application, existing social networking applications already enable many of the benefits discussed in this chapter. In particular, Yammer's flagship product and Vialect's Noodle application are just two of the innovative social networking tools on the market. Each is modular, meaning that organizations can enable piecemeal functionality. For example, organizations that merely want employees to share information and collaborate better can start there. Months later, however, buoyed by the early success of the tool, those same organizations might want to introduce communication tools. In other words, social networking tools are identical to other Enterprise 2.0 technologies in the sense that features can be "plugged and played" as circumstances warrant.

Best Practices of Social Networking

Social networking as used within organizations is often referred to Enterprise 2.0. The term incorporates a range of social networking and collaborative tools that have evolved into business use from the consumer space. A good number of the tools considered here have entered under the radar. These tools and technologies provide a number of advantages to the enterprise, including:

- Access to talented new employees who expect availability of these types of applications on the job.
- Improvements in collaboration, yielding benefits in innovation and ability to adapt.
- Enhancement of communications and improved decision making based on wider input.
- Improvements in collaboration, yielding benefits across a wide range of areas, including capability of different departments to work closely together, closer integration with elements of the supply chain, and ability to better work with individuals located outside of the firm.
- Improved productivity and efficiency due to a new capacity to immediately add new data or mashup applications to quickly assemble online application components.

Social networking concepts and tools have evolved considerably in the past five years. In reality, their origin goes to a much earlier time.

(continued)

Social networking is really the current state of evolution of Web-based interaction and communications, which have evolved from diverse components, including email, instant messaging, development of bulletin boards and other earlier group communications methods, and development of the Internet itself. Collaborative tools have been developing both online and off-line, and in the past have included such things as virtual meeting rooms, videoconferencing, and the like. All communications and collaborative tools and methodologies have now moved to the Web. So, videoconferencing can be done using the Internet rather than dedicated networks; voice communications and voice mail can be handled through the Web using voice over Internet Protocol (VoIP); and email and messaging moved over to the Web very early. All of these technologies have been combined and recombined to create new offerings that have become easier to use, accessible to all, and increasingly integrated. The integration of these communications technologies has yielded what we call social networking. It is a continuing evolution.

During the past five years, social networking sites have moved into specialty areas, with one of the important ones being LinkedIn, a social networking site designed for business. General sites such as Facebook and MySpace have continued to evolve toward greater levels of customization and personalization, permitting users to develop new experiences and share them online. Social networking has also become increasingly accepted, and the issues that it raises in terms of security and exposure have also come more to public attention.

It is difficult to determine which industries are ahead in adoption of Enterprise 2.0. Usage is promoted by two things principally: the need for collaboration and the entry of new technically savvy employees from the schools. Because of this, as one might expect, probably the strongest initial adoption of social networking tools is within education, where various learning management systems have evolved that provide social networking tools such as bulletin boards, instant messaging, wikis, conferencing, and so forth. These systems include both proprietary solutions, such as Blackboard and SumTotal, and also a number of open source products, such as Moodle.

Another area in which social networking is important is in software development. In software development and within IT, familiarity with social networking tools is likely to be universal. In fact, one strong area of use will be found within the open source community and with organizations and individuals who participate in open source projects. These projects require collaboration across long distances and involve

(continued)

(*continued*)

technically savvy individuals who are willing to work with the available social networking tools to collaboratively solve common problems. Social networking is also becoming extremely important in the recruiting and human resources sector, which stretches across all firms. In specific industries, technology organizations tend by far to be in front.

The risks posed by social networking and Enterprise 2.0 applications can be significant and need to be monitored. Because these communications tools easily creep into an organization, they frequently enter below the radar and may avoid the usual organizational controls on incorporation of new technologies. There are risks arising from communications, such as potential release of sensitive information and dilution of intellectual property rights. There are risks at the application level of creating unknown weak points in corporate data security, particularly where mashups are used to draw information from diverse sources using embedded security clearances. There are risks of abuse, such as employees spending too much time using applications like Facebook, or inappropriate communications that may involve the corporation in litigation. There are also issues of intellectual property rights regarding information that is posted to social networking sites.

While these risks are significant, it is also important to provide the widest possible latitude in use of these new technologies so that the organization is able to keep up with the technology and obtain the substantial benefits that it promises. Corporate governance needs to embrace social networking, understand its functions and technologies, and fit it into a universal security scheme. This includes creating frameworks for use of social networking sites, training, and advising of employees regarding appropriate usage.

Quantification of returns for social networking tools is extremely difficult and fraught with problems. As with any attempt to determine a return on investment, many of the benefits are intangibles. This means that a positive contribution may be known and the technology may be seen as valuable, but placing any form of exact monetary figure on the result is next to impossible. There have been some studies on costs, but nothing that could be considered absolute.

Another issue is that social networking is really an evolution of the current state of digital communications and Web-enabled collaboration, so it is hard to determine whether benefits come from keeping up with the technology or come specifically from the use of social networking. It should also be noted that social networking is part of a much larger trend within the firm toward modularization, workgroup organization,

(*continued*)

and decentralization. Many organizations are outsourcing large portions of their processes and retaining in-house only those things they consider core processes. Collaborative tools, social networking, increasing standardization, and requirements for virtual teamwork all combine in creating a new vision of the enterprise from which components cannot be individually isolated and evaluated.

Brian J. Dooley is an author, analyst, and journalist with more than 20 years' experience in analyzing and writing about trends in telecommunications and IT. He has written six books, numerous user manuals, hundreds of reports, and more than 1,000 magazine features. Projects include user manuals, market research, technology research, magazine features, case histories, white papers, online documents, Web pages, and multimedia.

Summary

Social networking has taken the Web and turned it into a global conversation. Organizations, well aware of its popularity, are increasingly eager to explore ways of leveraging its reach and power. Bringing the solutions in-house through enterprise social networking solutions can provide a number of benefits, including cost savings, increased collaboration, and improved research and service. However, they also may present specific impediments to progress. Organizations need to understand and face these impediments, learn how to shift from a traditional style of communication, and stand firmly behind social networking to truly reap the rewards.

Next Steps

The following are some steps for getting started with social networking:

- *Step 1: Set goals*. Determine why you want to begin a social networking program; what you plan to get out of it; and how it will benefit the company, brand, and market in general. If possible, establish these goals numerically, with benchmarks outlining user and engagement levels that need to be reached within certain time frames. Goals should be set for each audience that will be reached—consumers, employees, vendors, suppliers, and partners.
- *Step 2: Organize and plan*. Teams need to be assembled and team members need to be clearly aware of their roles. Long-term social

networking success largely comes down to organization, and the sooner this gets established the better.

- *Step 3: Build versus buy*. Decide if your organization wants to build or buy. There are some good free platforms available; however, it does take time and resources to deploy them. Buying a platform may not get 100 percent of the functions that you require, but it may cost you less. There are pros and cons for each path. Organizations should consider each option and choose what is best for them.

- *Step 4: Determine and schedule content*. Although social networking is current, with conversations occurring in real time, topics should be scheduled in advance and a calendar of content maintained at least two months ahead of time. While it will be important to remain flexible and alter topics on the fly when necessary, content calendars should take into consideration information that various parts of the companies want to communicate, such as marketing, PR, business development, HR, customer support, and possibly even investor relations.

- *Step 5: Establish a voice*. Communication via social networking should take a less marketing, more conversational tone, while still maintaining the brand's integrity. Establish a voice that will represent the company on the network.

- *Step 6: Drive traffic*. I really don't want to be one more author to write that "if you build it, they will come" doesn't actually work on the Web, but unfortunately it is true. Marketing strategies need to be put in place to alert users that the network exists, indicate how they'll benefit, explain why they should come, and encourage existing users to come back more often and invite other users to join.

PART III

Data, Information, and Knowledge

CHAPTER 10

Enterprise Search and Retrieval
Damien Santer

*Well, allow me to introduce myself to you as an advocate of Orna-
mental Knowledge. You like the mind to be a neat machine, equipped
to work efficiently, if narrowly, and with no extra bits or useless parts.
I like the mind to be a dustbin of scraps of brilliant fabric, odd gems,
worthless but fascinating curiosities, tinsel, quaint bits of carving,
and a reasonable amount of healthy dirt. Shake the machine and it
goes out of order; shake the dustbin and it adjusts itself beautifully
to its new position.*

—Robertson Davies (1913–1995)

Introduction

Mankind has been managing information since time immemorial, from
"Where is the nearest waterhole?" carved on the wall of a cave to a massive
World Wide Web of unstructured data that research scientists and eight-year-
old children alike can contribute to and consume equally. Admittedly, there
were a few iterations between these two examples. However, the challenge
of finding information in an efficient and practical matter applies equally to
all of these.

Web search first came to light in the early 1990s as the explosion of
content on the Internet transpired. New challenges appeared on a daily
basis, not the least of which was finding efficient ways to leverage this
amazing mass of content. Unlike traditional information systems, the Web
was completely unstructured and suffered from the following limitations:

- The layout of a Web page lacked standards.
- Web sites and content had no clearly defined relationships between
  them.
- There were no hard-and-fast rules of taxonomy and structure.

As a result, from an information management standpoint, the Web soon became quite unseemly. Web search did more than create a need for the ability to retrieve information from structured sources based on business rules and database queries. It manifested the need for search and retrieval tools to possess an ability to understand (in a nonsentient sense of the word) content and provide a facility to search based on relevance to keywords and topics without the assistance of a taxonomy or ontology.

Information systems have been used in corporate and government organizations for many decades, and the challenge of finding information within enterprise systems significantly predates Web search. The challenges of enterprise search and retrieval (ESR)—albeit through a smaller repository than the World Wide Web—are still quite significant.

The initial challenge of Web search is that of the apparent ability to understand the meaning of content. Once this is solved, Web search scales without too much further thought. Conversely, the myriad of technical challenges to be met by ESR includes:

- Organization or industry-specific idiom.
- Ensuring that content is served in compliance with internal security policies and access control mechanisms—often on a per-repository basis.
- Extending reach into legacy applications that are not browser based and predate service-oriented architecture (SOA) and web site application programming interface (WSAPI) initiatives.
- Merging of results from structured and unstructured data sources in a meaningful way.
- Determining the relevance of the results and ranking them in a way that is efficient for the user.

Technical challenges aside, the commercial challenges of ESR are no sneezing matter. With license fees often running into the millions of dollars, realizing a return on the investment of ESR is not always a given, particularly for large multinational corporations to which outsourcing and offshoring process-driven functions are viable options.

It is often said that organizations' most valuable assets are their employees. In fact, an organization's true asset is the experience, expertise, and knowledge held by individuals within the organization. The value of this is often underestimated and difficult to quantify.[1] As such, over the past 20-something years, organizations have devoted innumerable hours to the creation and management of information and organizational knowledge

---

[1]Although, to be sure, people like University of Southern California professor John Boudreau have done a great deal of work around human resource metrics.

through varying fields of applied enterprise content management (ECM). However, it is only in the past few years that any significant effort has been expended in the development of technology to allow us to further leverage that investment.

The first wave of such investment was seen in the enterprise portal movement of the late 1990s. The thought leaders of the day were advocating investment in the provision of a single front end to information residing in multiple disparate repositories—effectively desiloing[2] the information. Such initiatives were met with significant concern by the individual repository managers, as questions such as how to securely control access to information through the portal were raised.

Subsequently, it has been realized that bringing the information to users in a manner prescribed by the organization is simply not enough. Empowering the users to not only locate but also access and work with information on their own terms is paramount.

What Is ESR?

Historically ESR has been quite an esoteric field, with most organizations taking a pragmatic, repository-specific approach to search. The major information systems vendors have generally provided their own search tools specific to the needs of the individual repository. As a rule, they do not stop to think about the overarching need for a ubiquitous solution that extends beyond the perimeter of any specific application, nor about the magnitude of the challenge of providing extensibility into unknown and undefined data sources while maintaining data security and integrity.

The ability for users to search a specific repository does not truly constitute enterprise search. While useful, search within a specific repository of content relies on users knowing in which repository the information they seek resides. There are two extremely common challenges faced by users of information that this approach does not resolve: first, the collation of information on a specific topic from multiple (sometimes unknown) sources, and second, the identification of material relevant to a subject without prior knowledge of what will be found and from where. In order to resolve these issues, ESR must reach horizontally across the enterprise.

---

[2]While desiloing is, strictly speaking, not a word, it has become commonly accepted to represent the paradigm of the ubiquitous access to information horizontally across the organization.

Content Acquisition

Content acquisition in the Web search arena is quite a simple matter, as even though the World Wide Web is a massive, unstructured, geographically disparate entity, all of the content on the Web follows a few key rules:

- All content on the Internet is published in HTML.
- All content on the Internet can be retrieved with the HTTP protocol, which is well documented and defined.
- There are defined standards for the inclusion of meta information.
- All information that needs to be indexed is publicly viewable.

Conversely, the acquisition of content can be considerably trickier, even if that content stems from structured, centralized systems in the same data center, managed by the same team. ESR generally uses three mechanisms for content acquisition:

1. *Crawling*. This can be very similar to the methods used by Web search engines. Crawling is most commonly employed for intranets, web sites, file systems, and sometimes databases.
2. *Real-time query*. Content would be stale if not indexed. Real-time query is most commonly employed to facilitate the retrieval of the most meaningful results.
3. *Feed*. This is programmatically inserting content or meta into an index.

By way of example of a real-time query, surf to Google and try the search "convert 100 USD to AUD." You will immediately notice that the search results do not simply consist of traditional links, but the answer to the question itself is displayed in line with the other results. Consider that this in the realm of ESR. Exchange rates, stock levels, prices, and service-level agreement (SLA) statistics are but a few examples of information within the enterprise that may be searched for, and would be stale if held in an index for even seconds—let alone minutes or hours, which may be the case depending on the acquisition cycle of the ESR solution.

Content Relevance

Relevance is paramount to ESR. One of the most common pain points of existing ESR solutions is that users do not manage to find the content they are looking for in a timely fashion—in extreme cases it may be quicker for them to log into a repository and find the information they seek manually.

The acquisition and indexing of content is but a small part of ESR; once acquired, a means to ascertain the relevance of the content to any given search query is required. Search queries may be long-winded natural language questions, short lists of keywords, or complex Boolean queries—each of which must be interpreted by the search engine and parsed before processing can begin. Search engines use relevance algorithms comprised of complex mathematical processes, including document vectors, latent semantic analysis, and statistical analysis alongside methods such as heuristics to determine relevance.

Relevance algorithms vary from simple implementations of term count model (TCM) or term frequency–inverse document frequency (TF-IDF) to complex multidimensional algorithms such as Google Page Rank, which among other things leverages an in-linking algorithm. TF-IDF and other such algorithms are centered on the prevalence of the query term within a document, adding weight for rare terms.

The issue with this approach is that the number of instances of a given phrase within a document does not necessarily indicate relevance. For example, I may be searching for "decongestant" and "heavy machinery" to ensure I can safely operate my forklift while medicated. The PDF document may state 30 times, "Do not operate heavy machinery while using this decongestant," which obviously does not help, but would be matched by a TF-IDF algorithm.

Other factors considered by complex search algorithms include:

- *Text match.* Either partial match, phrase match, or exact match.
- *Concept search.* For example, a search for the term *iron* may return results for raw materials or for electronic household goods.
- *Spell-checker and thesaurus.* Looking at common misspellings of words, as well as organizational- or industry-specific idioms and acronyms.
- *Query expansion.* Including lemmatization and stemming for morphological analysis and use of synonyms.
- *In-linking.* Additional relevance based on quality and quantity of inbound links.
- *Source biasing.* Certain repositories may hold content considered authoritative; that is, the intranet hosting HR policies would be more relevant than an employee blog to a query for the leave application process.
- *Date biasing.* Content of a specific age may be more relevant if it was authored recently, or alternatively closer to a specific date or event.
- *Mandated results.* Organizations may wish to mandate that a specific piece of content be returned for certain queries regardless of relevance.

Systems based on in-linking place additional value on a piece of content that has multiple links to it from other pages that are authoritative in their own subject matter. Relevance in the context of ESR is not just a popularity contest. Oftentimes the most valuable content in the enterprise will not be linked from intranets or other Web-based systems, but rather be stored in customer relationship management (CRM), ECM, Enterprise Resource Planning (ERP), or other proprietary business systems.

Heuristics are a set of logic rules to be applied to the ranking process. An example of relevance heuristics may be to add weight for documents that match the entire search term as a phrase above those matching individual terms, or to increase weight for documents that have elements of the search query within the document title.

When determining relevance within the enterprise, the application of algorithms and heuristics is not always adequate. Industry- and organization-specific idioms, policy documents, and taxonomical structures must be taken into account.

Taxonomies organize and classify information. The term *taxonomy* originated in the scientific field in which scientists struggled to classify and categorize the world and all of the creatures in it. Taxonomy derives from the Greek terms *taxis*, arrangement, and *nomos*, method, manage, or law. Taxonomy is a controlled method of organizing content into a logical and unambiguous structure to provide a foundation by which users store, search for, and retrieve information. Taxonomy provides conceptual structure and enhances clean navigation design. The value of an ESR increases dramatically with the introduction of a content taxonomy.

The taxonomy defines the domains of the content's metadata and the valid combination of all metadata dimensions (what some might call facets). Industry, for instance, is a common taxonomy dimension. By defining a set of industry codes, you define the range that the industry identifier of your content assets can take.

For example, the Acme, Inc. part number B213457-235 is unlikely to be found as a string in a manner not relevant to a search for the same. However, in the context of ESR, returning a list of documents containing that part number is not sufficient. An ESR solution that can leverage the organization's taxonomy is infinitely more valuable.

Let's look at an example of ESR within Acme, Inc., a fictional organization using ESR (universal search) across the enterprise. Consider specifically an account manager receiving an inquiry from one of Acme's customers for a new part number the account manager has previously come across. Traditional ESR when searching for the part number B213457-235 will return a text-based list of links to documents referencing this part number, without understanding the context or relevance of the reference. While this provides users with access to the information that they need to research in order to respond to the client request, it does not provide any hard-and-fast answers.

ESR, when integrated with the organization's taxonomy and key content repositories for real-time query, can return valuable results to the users—showing that B213457-235 is actually an oversized rubber band that is manufactured by Acme, Inc., is stocked in three of Acme's U.S. warehouses, wholesales for $9, retails for $24, has four optional accessories, and is out of stock in Los Angeles and New York but there are 3,500 units in Cincinnati—in much the same way that Google can convert 100 USD to AUD.

Query Processing

At query time, the ESR solution will analyze the query string, applying the methods just described herein to the query before executing the internal query against the index.

Some search engines use Boolean operators[3] within query strings. In this case, the Boolean operators are parsed and the appropriate logic is applied to the results set.

A list of results will then be returned. These results will then be ranked for relevance to the initial query term. The ESR solution should then verify that the user has access to the content returned. In the case of late binding security, this query is executed against the source repository's authorization system. In the case of early binding security, this is against an internal database.

Results Serving

Once the ESR solution has identified which results from the index (or configured external sources) are relevant and that the user has access to view the results, the results will be returned to the user as HTML or to the requesting system, usually in XML in the case of search as a service.

Many ESR solutions use a text-based results list that is quite similar to that of Google, displaying a title, snippet, link, and buttons for collaborative and other functionality.

Several attempts to update the presentation of search results from text-based to graphical visualizations have been made over the past few years. However, the simplicity and cleanliness of the previously mentioned format are hard to surpass for efficiency.

The two visualizations that have been gaining popularity in recent years are mashups and a resource description framework (RDF).[4]

---

[3]Boolean operators include terms like *and*, *or*, and *not*. For example, if trying to avoid results pertaining to large cats when searching for the term *jaguar*, one may use the query *jaguar and vehicle* or *jaguar not feline*.
[4]www.w3.org/TR/PR-rdf-syntax/.

MASHUPS   Prolific information technology (IT) author, analyst, and journalist Brian J. Dooley defines mashups as:

> *lightweight integrations of one or more Web applications used to create a synergistic result, with the outcome often delivered through the Web. Although use of data from Web sources has been going on for some time, mashups represent a new level of functionality characterized by ease of use, programmatic access to data (e.g., through APIs [application programming interfaces]), combination of data from multiple sources, and sharing of results. Many of the earliest mashups involved charting data—including apartment advertisements, real estate, and even Flickr photos—to Google Maps. Since about the year 2000, the possibilities have been growing steadily, in presentation-oriented and data aggregation applications, as well as in more sophisticated process-oriented applications. The use of mashups has since grown quickly within the consumer sector, and it is now heading into the enterprise space.[5]*

ESR mashups do things such as displaying all search results from a CRM database in their geospatial context on a map.

RESOURCE DESCRIPTION FRAMEWORK   Resource description framework is a foundation for processing metadata; it provides interoperability between applications that exchange machine-understandable information on the Web. RDF emphasizes facilities to enable automated processing of Web resources.[6]

Security

When implementing any new information system (IS), organizations go to great lengths to ensure that the information within the new system is adequately secured and accessible only by its intended audience. ESR represents a unique security challenge, as rather than having its own content to secure, ESR is intended to give users access to all of the content across the enterprise from a single interface—that is, all of the content they legitimately have authority to view. A modern organization may rely on in excess of a dozen different information systems. Let's look at a scenario—Acme, Inc., a fictional global conglomerate (see Table 10.1).

Supposing for a moment that Acme, Inc. is pre–single sign-on (SSO), a user would have different credentials for 10 of the 13 systems and may only have access to certain applications that are required for the performance of

---

[5]www.cutter.com/content/architecture/fulltext/updates/2009/eau0914.html.
[6]www.w3.org/TR/PR-rdf-syntax/.

TABLE 10.1 Information Systems Used by Acme, Inc.

System	Purpose	Authentication and Authorization
Microsoft Exchange	Email and calendaring	Active Directory
Exchange Public Folders	Email collaboration	Active Directory
Microsoft SharePoint	Corporate intranet	Active Directory
Microsoft Windows File Server	File sharing	Active Directory
Lotus Domino Team Rooms	Project and product team sites	Notes .ID files
Interwoven TeamSite	Corporate extranet	System Internal
EMC Documentum	Document management system	System Internal
IBM Filenet	Electronic records management system	System Internal
AS400	Inventory and manufacturing management	System Internal
SAP	Enterprise Resource Planning	System Internal
Salesforce.com	Customer relationship management	System Internal
Oracle	Custom business apps	System Internal
Microsoft SQL	Custom business apps	AzMan and Active Directory

his or her job. When implementing ESR, it is imperative to ensure that none of the work done by the security or applications teams to ensure the integrity of the organization's data is undone. For obvious reasons, the office junior has a very different level of access within any given application compared to the chief financial officer.

ESR can be described as consisting of two sides, the first being content acquisition and relevance and the second being query processing and result serving. For similar reasons to the aforementioned desire not to index certain types of real-time information for fear it will grow stale, in most cases it is necessary to enforce security in real time.

Early binding security entails access control being processed and stored at the time a document is being indexed. The obvious flaw with this approach is that should an employee be terminated or have his or her access privileges changed, the changes will not be reflected in the ESR solution until that content is next indexed—which may be anywhere from minutes to weeks, depending on the nature of the content itself. This can lead to scenarios whereby users have access to information through search that they are not otherwise permitted to access, or conversely are not able to find information through search that they have been granted access to.

Conversely, late binding security checks for access to information at serve time rather than at the point of index. This approach removes the aforementioned risk; however, it has a trade-off in performance, with each result being validated postquery.

Search and Information Architecture

Information architecture (IA) has become increasingly important in recent times. Information systems continually increase in complexity, and the requirement for seamless integration between systems is becoming more and more prevalent. While often confused with usability, information architecture is a discrete field focused on providing a common structure and method of organizing and describing an organization's information. Similar to usability, information architects strive to maintain focus on the fact that at the end of the day, it is a human being who will interact with information systems, not a computer, and for that reason systems should be intuitive and a pleasure to use.

Information architecture is most commonly applied in areas such as library systems, content management (both ECM and Web content management [WCM]), Web and portal development, database development, technical writing, enterprise architecture, and software architecture.

Organizations considering ESR can be faced with a chicken-and-egg scenario:

- *Option A*. Devote time and resources to improving the information architecture and state of content management within the organization.
- *Option B*. Devote time and resources to deploying ESR within the organization.

ESR is by no means a silver bullet capable of doing away with the requirement for a well-constructed and well-defined IA. However, upon analysis of the motivation for either Option A or Option B, it becomes apparent they are not mutually exclusive. Such initiatives tend to be focused on increasing organizational efficiency and empowering users with access to timely, relevant information. Oftentimes a combined approach returns the best result. Harvesting the low-hanging fruit provided by ESR can bring immediate returns to the organization while longer-term strategies are implemented.

The Business Case for ESR

As the volume of data and information produced by enterprises continues to grow, the strategies needed to manage the information increase in
complexity, also increasing the budget required.

Much of the information produced remains locked in proprietary
applications—data silos if you will. Users must login to the specific repository in order to access and work with the information.

It is estimated that up to 80 percent of content in the average enterprise
remains unstructured, stored in word processing formats, in spreadsheets,
and on intranets, and that content volumes are exploding at a rate close to
200 percent per annum.

With the explosion of content, many organizations' file servers have
more than one commonality with Father's toolshed—full of bits and pieces
that may be needed some day, without really knowing what exists, where
it is stored, what condition it is in, and if it will ever be used again.

The cost of this storage is not the only consideration in this case. Having
large numbers of your employees lost in a virtually endless sea of unwashed
information can be devastating to productivity.

Knowledge workers can spend nearly ten hours per week simply searching for information and in excess of eight hours researching and gathering
information—not to mention the countless hours wasted re-creating content
that already exists but could not be found at short notice.

The potential savings from implementing ESR can be enormous, as
employees are able to find key information faster, allowing them to make
better decisions. Enterprise 2.0 is all about doing more with information.
Nothing embodies this concept more than ESR.

Total Cost of Ownership

ESR tools come in all shapes and sizes, with vendors choosing different
metrics by which to charge. The two primary shapes of ESR offerings are
software and *appliance*.

ESR software requires a server upon which to run as well as an operating
system, each of which must be purchased and maintained individually. In
contrast, the purchase price of ESR appliances includes hardware and a
preinstalled operating system that is often transparent to administrators and
is configured through a Web-based console.

Some of the metrics by which vendors charge include the number
of users, the number of processors, the number of servers, or the number of documents in the index, each of which will present a different

value proposition depending on the use case and the organization. Likewise, the appliance and software models also represent different value propositions.

Consider the following factors when evaluating the TCO of an ESR solution:

- Infrastructure (hardware and operating systems)
- Database engine
- License fees
- Connector/adapter fees
- Consulting and integration fees

An exhaustive examination of the risks and considerations for each of these factors is beyond the scope of this chapter and would require quite a bit of site-specific knowledge to be of any significant value.

Forms of ESR Deployment

Enterprise search has been a service in one form or another on most corporate intranets for more than a decade. There are three typical forms of ESR deployment:

1. Repository search
2. Universal search
3. Search as a service

Repository Search

The most prevalent form of ESR found in the enterprise is a repository-specific search solution, or search across a small group of selected repositories such as file shares and intranets. Repository search may use the *baked-in* search functionality of one of the primary repositories in use or may use a separate *pure-play* solution, such as the Google Search Appliance, Autonomy, or Endecca.

The advantage of repository search is that it is quick and simple to implement with complexity and cost kept low by the careful selection of the repositories being indexed. Security requirements can often be quite straightforward—particularly for deployments involving a suite of products from the same vendor, such as Windows Server, SharePoint, and Exchange.

The low-hanging fruit with repository search is generally horizontal information intended for use by the majority of the members of the organization, such as policies and procedures, staff manuals, product and marketing information, as well other team sites and intranets or, alternately, an implementation specific to a contact center, help desk, or other knowledge group.

Universal Search

Universal search is the holy grail of ESR—complete and seamless integration of all of the organization's content to a single, universal search experience. Universal search nearly always uses a pure-play ESR tool.

Universal search provides better return on investment than repository search, but that return does come at a price. Universal search generally involves a seeming plethora of repositories, and unless the organization has SSO, each often requires its own authentication and authorization scheme.

The end game of universal search is to provide ubiquitous access to all of the organization's content from a single interface that may be attached to the intranet or be a system in its own right.

Search as a Service

ESR can be implemented as a utility, providing wholesale services to other applications within the enterprise. Search as a service places ESR firmly into the organization's IA, often as an SOA component. This means that the ESR team is responsible for the acquisition of data into the index and maintenance of the solution, but rather than only providing search through the ESR user interface, the search results can be syndicated to other applications programmatically via APIs.

ESR in Action

Let's go back and have another look at Acme, Inc. Acme is a fictitious global conglomerate operating across the Americas, the Asia-Pacific region, Europe, the Middle East, and Africa. Acme manufactures a wide variety of products ranging from wrought-iron anvils to backpack rockets designed to aid in the capture of a roadrunner. Acme employ 3,000 staff worldwide, 1,800 of whom sit between sales, marketing, product management, finance, operations, service, and support, and 1,200 of whom work in manufacturing and logistics.

Acme has identified that its employees—specifically the 1,800 knowledge workers—spend up to eight hours per week searching for information and an average of a further four hours re-creating content that already exists in the organization that they were unable to find.

TABLE 10.2 Project Team for Fictitious ESR Implementation

Role	Responsibilities
Program manager	Overall responsibility for the outcome of the program
	Control of the strategy and vision of the project
	Relationship management to the business
Business representatives	Provide business requirements and direction to project team
	Participate in user acceptance testing
Project manager	Successful management of project delivery
	Operational management of the project team
Enterprise architect	Work with the business and project team to ensure ESR is delivered in a way that reflects the business objectives
Information architect	Ensure adequate taxonomy and other corporate IA available to the project team
	Deliver search as a service
ESR architect	Design overall ESR solution
ESR engineer	Work with repository specialists to implement ESR solution as designed by ESR architect
Business analyst	Work with users to gather and analyze requirements
Repository specialists	Work with ESR engineer to prepare repositories and integrate ESR solution with repositories

Project Team

Acme has created a strategic program team to address ESR. This project team will be responsible for the architecture, planning, deployment, and ongoing management of the ESR solution as well as liaison with the business, as shown in Table 10.2.

Implementation Plan

Let's look at a typical ESR project implementation plan. This plan is intended to be quite high level, and assumes knowledge of and integration with traditional project management rigmarole.

TASK 1: TALK TO THE BUSINESS   It may sound obvious, but it does get forgotten, especially when providing technologies to the business that are seen as "utility" by IT. Identify your key stakeholders and work with them, as they will know the processes followed by the teams they manage and have ideas as to where timely access to relevant information will create efficiency for the organization.

TASK 2: IDENTIFY AND PRIORITIZE CONTENT Before embarking on an ESR project, identification of key content across the enterprise that should be in the index and of security policies and corporate procedures that affect the use of the information are important.

Organizations with massive amounts of content often don't know where to begin with ESR. There are two fatal mistakes.

Because of the complexity of cross-repository security and integration with many disparate systems, striking the balance between achievable and insignificant is often difficult. Organizations that try to do it all at once often come unstuck, with individual department managers, repository managers, or security architects objecting purely to try to avoid what they foresee to be an insurmountable challenge when, in all reality, some careful planning and the right approach can all but guarantee the success of the project.

Some ESR vendors will convince you that your requirements are so simple they can be achieved out of the box and that an out-of-the-box implementation will take three to five days. Unless we are talking about repository search, this is usually (and I do say "usually," as there are exceptions) not quite accurate. Your requirements may well be met by the feature set of the solution and an out-of-the-box implementation of the solution will take three to five days. This much is true. Configuration, customization, implementation, training, and the implementation of the requisite cultural change to embrace and adopt ESR will, once again—generally speaking—take longer.

Other ESR vendors will tell you that the barrier to entry for real ESR is significant and that you can look forward to the happy company of a team of their consultants occupying one of your meeting rooms for six months. Once again, the reality of the matter is that, as usual, when deciphering sales-speak, the reality of the situation is somewhere in the middle of what the vendors are telling you.

> *ESR Vendor 1.* ESR is set-and-forget. Sign on the dotted line and away you go—no more to pay, until next time.
> *ESR Vendor 2.* ESR is a complex solution that requires constant maintenance, tuning, and management. You really need a dedicated team of subject matter experts for this who understand the algorithms and underlying technologies.

The implementation of ESR does not necessarily require your own army of PhDs. Each of the tier 1 pure-play ESR solutions has its own distinct advantages. Some solutions require more maintenance and tuning than others in order to provide relevant results. Those that do often have superior feature sets to allow for the customization of the core engine, modification of the heuristics to cater to specify business rules, and tight-knit integration with taxonomy or ontology in the assessment of relevance. As with most things in life, there are horses for courses; however, the comparison and benefits of individual ESR solutions are unfortunately outside the scope of this chapter.

TASK 3: DEFINE THE OVERALL ESR ARCHITECTURE   Refer back to three earlier sections in this chapter: "Search and Information Architecture," "The Business Case for ESR," and "Forms of ESR Deployment." The rewards are real and significant.

Review the organization's content priorities and be realistic. If you are the chief information officer (CIO) of a dot-com portal employing 35 people, 25 of whom are engineers, then repository search for your portal is most likely what you seek.

If however, you are the CIO or IS manager of Acme, Inc., with 1,800 knowledge workers relying on the tools you provide, then universal search or search as a service is most likely the right fit. Oftentimes search projects stall when vendors start presenting licensing quotes to cover the 40 terabytes, 35 million documents, and 200 million database rows you wish to search against.

TASK 4: PLAN CONTENT ACQUISITION STRATEGY   Refer to Table 10.1 for a list of repositories in use at Acme, Inc.

Before you even begin to determine which of these should be crawled, which we should have a connector for, and which we should be querying in real time, let's examine which you actually want to index.

Rather than go through the repositories one by one, for the sake of brevity I'm just going to pick on those that generally give people pause.

TASK 5: PLAN CONTENT SECURITY STRATEGY   The complexities of a security strategy for ESR provide material for a book in its own right, so please do not take the brevity of this section as an indication of complexity or the lack thereof. Take care formulating your security strategy for ESR. Take time to ponder the age-old question of early binding security or late binding security—perhaps rivaled only by the other age-old question of transubstantiation versus consubstantiation.

Implementing ESR can also expose previously unknown security issues in the content repositories themselves. On more than one occasion—particularly when indexing Windows File Shares—a client has come running up to our consultant visibly disturbed, chanting, "Turn it off, turn it off—they can see everything," or words to that effect.

Correctly implemented ESR adheres to the security policy of the source repository. If there are file structures or applications that either do not enforce security correctly or do not have adequate security applied, users of the ESR solution may well be given access to material they were not intended to see.

TASK 6: DEPLOY ESR As mentioned above, this is not intended as an exhaustive implementation guide for ESR, but rather a high-level guide to some of the nuances of ESR and a proverbial heads-up to some of the traps for young players.

Best Practices

With ESR, start small but plan big. The rewards are there for the reaping. As a result, it will pay to make your architecture extensible and scalable. Choose an ESR solution that provides flexibility and doesn't require massive reengineering in the event that you find you need to add another repository halfway through the project.

ESR should be an integral part of your information architecture and also your enterprise architecture. Work with the repository owners and the business to ensure that you have identified the key information required to be indexed and that you are leveraging all of the available meta and taxonomies. Further, work with your enterprise architects and the business to ensure that processes are updated, appropriate cultural changes transpire, and proper training is received in how to best leverage ESR.

ESR is a specialized field; ensure that your project team is well versed in the technologies as well as the strategic goals for the ESR solution.

Start with more than just a file server or the intranet. After talking to the business, decide where you can return real value quickly with minimal risk and effort. Plan a staged rollout, working with individual departments or repositories as appropriate to your business over a reasonable period of time. Rome wasn't built in a day, after all.

In order to get the most from your ESR, you need to maintain it. It requires ongoing effort and investment. The good news is that the return on investment is also recurrent. The reality is as repository vendors release new versions of their software and as the business evolves, there will be further effort required to continue to enjoy the efficiencies created by ESR.

Summary

ESR is a technology for the future and will be a mainstream channel for content delivery to users in the enterprise. There are three common forms of ESR deployment: repository search, universal search, and search as a service. ESR solutions are available as software only or as an appliance. ESR can be a user-facing technology or an SOA component to be used by other software. A well-planned ESR program can be self-supporting through return on investment (ROI) based on increased productivity and efficiency of knowledge workers.

Next Steps

- With your newly acquired knowledge of ESR, take another look at the information systems used by your organization and talk to some of the business unit managers about how their staff members work with the data, information, and knowledge.
- Google the following and try some of these queries:
  - Convert 100 USD to AUD
  - QF31
  - Convert 143 pounds to kg
- Now think about what queries against your CRM, ERP, and other structured systems could provide value to your users in line with search results.
- Log on to each of the main content repositories within your organization and have a play with the baked-in search functions. Consider what life would be like if you had the ability to interpose results from all of these systems in a single interface, in order of relevance to your query term.
- Run some scenarios through the ROI formula. A conservative efficiency increase may be 5 percent, and an aggressive efficiency increase may be 25 percent.
- Get some information on some of the ESR solutions available and consider a pilot for your organization.[7]

---

[7]For more information on sources of ESR information, please see www. philsimonsystems.com/nwot_extras.html.

CHAPTER 11

Enterprise 2.0 Business Intelligence

Brian P. Morgan

In God we trust, all others bring data.

—W. Edwards Deming

What Is Business Intelligence, and Why Do We Need It?

At its core, business intelligence (BI) aims to get superior information into the hands of decision makers. This information will allow for better decisions—that is, those based on hard facts rather than warrantless assumptions. The often-recited mantra for BI has typically been the turning of "data into information." To begin a discussion on BI, this is as good a place to start as any.

At the risk of stating the obvious, without BI in the equation, you're stuck with just data. To be sure, many organizations already have plenty of systems in place generating larger and larger volumes of data. These systems in turn typically do a good job of churning out reports that have been defined for the given system. However, reports alone are very limited to what they can present on the screen or printed out at a given time. For example, looking at one summary report leads to the question, "Why is this number like that?" To answer that question, you need another report. The second report will surely beget further questions. This is where BI *starts* coming into play.

Information technology (IT) research and advisory firm Gartner Research stresses the importance of BI, defining it as:

> the top technology priority in Gartner's 2008 CIO survey[; it] can have a direct positive impact on a company's business performance, dramatically improving its ability to accomplish its mission by making smarter decisions at every level of the business from corporate strategy to operational processes. BI is particularly strategic because it is directed

toward business managers and knowledge workers who make up the pool of thinkers and decision makers that are tasked with running, growing and transforming the business. Tools that let these users make faster, better and more-informed decisions are particularly valuable in a difficult business environment.[1]

Business intelligence is an umbrella term encompassing a number of technologies, such as key performance indicators (KPIs) and data mining. BI is oftentimes synonymous with online analytical processing (OLAP). OLAP is the wonderful technology that brings you such buzzwords as "drill down" and "slice and dice." At the risk of propagating more business jargon, it is valuable to know what these terms mean. To better explain OLAP, let's continue the example of the summary report.

Before continuing, a disclaimer is in order. Many readers may in fact already be using BI in their organizations.[2] To be sure, BI is certainly not a new technology. In fact, the very term *BI* has been part of the corporate parlance since the mid-1990s. However, many organizations that have implemented BI tools have not exactly set the world on fire. In fact, statistics on successful BI deployments are arguably more discouraging that those of IT projects in general. By some estimates, more than seven in eight BI projects fail.[3]

BI 2.0

Basic BI can easily provide more information to end users who previously had to go to different sources or different parts of the organization. Equipped with better information, they can now make better business decisions. Note that "can" and "will" are two entirely different things. Better access to information does not mean better decisions. BI doesn't prevent people from making mistakes or errors in judgment. This is really just scratching the surface of what BI can do.

In their book *Database Management Systems*, Patricia Ward and George Dafoulas write that "a trigger defines an action the database should take when some database-related event occurs. They are associated with a single table within the database and are specific to an Update, Insert, or Delete operation or a combination of these against rows in the table. ... They are

---

[1]Press release (Orlando), "Gartner Identifies the Top 10 Strategic Technologies for 2009," October 12–16, 2008, www.gartner.com/it/page.jsp?id=777212.

[2]For a very brief history of BI, go to www.philsimonsystems/nwot_extras.html.

[3]www.ncc.co.uk/aboutncc/press_rel/Business_Intelligence_Implementations_fail_to_meet_objectives.cfm.

TABLE 11.1 KPI View

	Indicator Name	Amount	Target	Variance
↑	Total units sold	78	45	32
↓	Remaining inventory	15	25	10
—	Profit margin	24.5%	25%	0.5%
↑	Solar panel growth	50%	20%	30%

automatically executed whenever a specified event occurs and a condition is satisfied."

BI indicators can work in conjunction with these triggers. When an organization meets a target value, the trigger automatically sends an email to affected parties. For example, if the number of sales of solar panels exceeds 35, then the BI tool sends an email to the manager of the warehouse. Also, while BI tools certainly allow for one-offs and ad hoc querying, commonly used indicators can easily be reused and shared to key personnel.

Organizations can also set up several of these indicators (KPIs) that can easily indicate where attention should be paid, as shown in Table 11.1.

With these metrics available, plain data can be transformed into knowledge. End users can take operational actions and make managerial decisions without the need for significant digging or hypothesizing.

Measuring BI Maturity

A good way of looking at how BI can improve your business is by measuring your organization's IT maturity. Consider the following three broad groups:

1. *Reactionary*. Putting out fires as they occur. The organization has no time for a vision because all available time is spent resolving issues.
2. *Steady*. On top of the business. Management is able to spot trends as they occur and can react *before* any significant impacts arise.
3. *Strategic*. Anticipating issues before they arise and predicting industry trends. The organization has models in place and has strategists who can put their fingers on the pulse of the company and its health.

It should be evident to the reader now how BI can actually make organizations more mature. For example, reactionary organizations can graduate to steady. Having provided a taste of the flexibility of the basics of OLAP and BI, the chapter now focuses on what organizations need to do to successfully effect the adoption of BI.

BI Challenges

Like each of the other technologies in this book, there is opportunity in chaos. With regard to BI, its benefits can be enormous. However, there is no shortage of obstacles to successfully implementing a BI project. Some of the main roadblocks that consistently doom BI projects are discussed next.

Lack of Strong Project Sponsorship

While there are projects of all different shapes and sizes, a successful BI solution requires strong executive sponsorship and buy-in from the different parts of the organization. Further, an organization's BI strategy must align with its overall business strategy. Organizations accustomed to formalized decision-making methods and rigid processes may struggle using tools that provide immediate, actionable feedback.

Without executive and senior sponsorship, too often you will be fighting for resources to continue improving the BI content. Small implementations of BI work fine, but if you ever want to permeate the technology throughout the organization, you cannot count on everyone agreeing that BI is the required killer app. Due to busy schedules and comfort with antiquated processes, the adoption of BI is often not as easy or as contagious as one might expect. Strong sponsorship is the best way to ensure that the work done on any BI project will be leveraged by those who get what BI offers as well as those who are slower to adopt the technology.

Dirty or Nonconformed Data

Data quality concerns can turn a project of several weeks into one of several years. Taking a small subset of clean data to complete a proof of concept (POC) is typically a necessary starting point. Often it ensures readiness on both IT *creation* and the business *consumption* sides. However, one little victory does not win the war. There is a significant difference in realizing success with a small set of data for a POC and taking enormous volumes of varied data into a production-ready system that will be the basis of many critical business decisions.

While data quality is one of the most significant challenges in setting up BI, there is good news: The process of setting up BI is a fantastic way of understanding and detecting the cleanliness of data. This process is also known as data profiling. By the nature of what they deliver, BI tools very quickly expose areas where data is bad. Continuing with our example, imagine that on August 6 a new office is added in Toronto with two new salespeople. Due to an error by a new employee in human resources (HR), the dimensional (also known as referential) data that the cube uses has

TABLE 11.2 Month-to-Date (MTD) Sales by Region with Errors

	8/1	8/2	8/3	8/4	8/5	8/6
East	23	20	15	30	28	25
Central	5	3	7	2	10	8
West	15	55	22	10	19	18
Mike Portnoy						2
John Petrucci						3
All locations	43	78	44	42	57	56

not been updated properly. You would now see your three summary-level regions alongside the two new Toronto salespeople—not exactly what you would want your firm's decision makers seeing (see Table 11.2).

While these are two of the biggest challenges facing BI projects, in her article "The Seven Pillars of BI Success," Cindi Howson lists important considerations for organizations about to embark on BI journeys:

- Measure success.
- Develop a data strategy.
- Manage the program well.
- Ensure executive support.
- Choose appropriate tools.
- Standardize on a platform.
- Align BI strategy with business.

The Data Warehouse

Consider the following. All BI efforts are based on data. Organizations will eventually, if not immediately, need data from disparate sources. (For more on this, see Chapter 12.) As such, organizations need to establish a way to pull this data together. Once pulled together, the data needs to be in a format conducive to reporting. This is where a discussion on data marts and data warehouses comes into play.

Data warehouses and data marts are related but separate things. The former tend to be massive firmwide reporting stores. Data marts tend to be much smaller, focused on a specific part of the organization. At this point, it is worth pointing out that there are two generally accepted key founders of data warehousing: Bill Inmon and Ralph Kimball. Each has a different methodology for implementing the data warehouse:

- *Top-down*. Tackle the larger data warehouse as one big firmwide initiative (Inmon).

- *Bottom-up*. Build several data marts and stack them together to represent one cohesive warehouse (Kimball).[4]

Regardless of the approach taken, organizations should ensure that their different data sets are aligned. In the previous example, imagine what would happen if HR data had a different set of employee IDs than the sales tracking system. This is where Ralph Kimball's insights on conforming dimensions using a BI bus matrix are instrumental.

A BI bus matrix visualizes relationships among data. These relationships are powerful and important, regardless of the specific approach to data warehousing and BI desired by the organization. The BI bus matrix is an invaluable tool for assisting organizations in understanding and aligning their data.

Kimball's book, *The Data Warehouse Toolkit*, provides everything that one needs to know on building successful data warehouses. Not surprisingly, the book follows his bottom-up approach.

Having attended several of his classes, I clearly have a bias toward Kimball's approach. The lower risk of building smaller data marts that will be pieced together into a larger data warehouse with a quicker return on investment outweighs the risks of doing the big-bang approach. Given the age of shrinking IT budgets, organizations are pressured to deliver projects and prove their worth as quickly as possible. Doing so will increase the chances of securing more funding for future expansion.

Make no mistake: Data warehouses and marts are costly. Outside of the obvious technology costs in disk space and processing time, organizations have to consider the following:

- Requirement and vendor analysis.
- Data cleansing.
- Development and production support of a large IT project.

This raises the question: What are the alternatives? Most of the large BI vendors allow you to connect to various sources directly, and the BI metadata (data about data) will act as a logical data warehouse. Additionally, tools like Composite exist that can create a virtual data warehouse (among other things).

While these virtual data warehouses may seem like the best approach, there are many downsides, such as slower report performance (your BI process has to do extra data retrieval or at least wait for it), multiple points

---

[4]For more details on how the methodologies differ, you can see the ITNirvanas article *Kimball vs. Inmon*, www.itnirvanas.com/2009/02/kimball-vs-inmon.html.

TABLE 11.3 Virtual versus Physical Data Warehouse

	Virtual Data Warehouse	Physical Data Warehouse
Price	Pro	Con
Flexibility	Pro	Con
Time to market	Pro	Con
Reliability	Con	Pro
Performance	Con	Pro
Enterprise-worthy	Con	Pro

of failure, and so on. Bill Inmon has taken a clear stance against the virtual data warehouse.[5]

In most cases, Inmon is spot-on. However, certain situations call for the flexibility of a more nimble approach like the virtual data warehouse. Regardless, organizations should be aware of both approaches (see Table 11.3).

Let's be clear: Data is a commodity in and of itself. Not surprisingly, many firms base their entire business models around collecting and providing data to firms for BI as a product. What's more, these firms are in turn banding together to provide even more complete sets of data for customers to leverage—that is, data with more dimensions and measures. In 2008, the NPD Group, GfK Chart-Track Limited, and Enterbrain, Inc. collectively created a global view of video game sales previously simply not possible (see Table 11.4).[6]

TABLE 11.4 Year-to-Date Top Video Game Sales Ranked by Units as of July 2008

Rank	Title	Total	U.S.	UK	Japan
1	Grand Theft Auto IV	6,293,000	4,711,000	1,582,000	—
2	Super Smash Bros: Brawl	5,433,000	3,539,000	213,000	1,681,000
3	Mario Kart Wii	4,697,000	2,409,000	687,000	1,601,000
4	Wii Fit	3,604,000	1,433,000	624,000	1,547,000
5	Guitar Hero III: Legends of Rock	3,475,000	3,037,000	412,000	26,000

---

[5]"The Virtual Data Warehouse—Transparent and Superficial," *Information Management*, March 2004, www.information-management.com/issues/20040301/8205-1.html.

[6]Press release, February 2, 2009, www.npd.com/press/releases/press_090202.html.

While seemingly inconsequential at a top level, this data can be aligned with internal sales data to find trends and patterns using internal BI tools. The results can be huge. If company ABC can access to this information while XYZ cannot, then XYZ is at a disadvantage. In either case, the companies make marketing, research and development (R&D), and sales decisions based on information. The difference here is that ABC is making these decisions with superior access to facts and trends relative to XYZ.

Key Factors

Consider the following when attempting to understand the objectives of a BI project.

Defining Success

BI is not a secret sauce. If an organization does not know how to define key requirements, then BI will not magically show it the way. Remember that the success of BI within an organization is a function of the end users who consume the new information.

In his article "Sales Success: Measure Results but Manage Activities," Dr. Rick Johnson indicates that the clear measurement of results is a necessary—but not sufficient—condition for the successful management of sales. Only with clear measurement can organizations appropriately manage sales activities.[7] Having the right data available at the right time is critical in sales management or, for that matter, any role.

One of the cardinal mistakes of many BI projects is that decision makers lack a fundamental understanding of what they are trying to measure. To paraphrase W. Edwards Deming, we cannot manage what we do not measure. In other words, organizations should not expect BI—or master data management (MDM) for that matter—to perform miracles. By itself, no BI tool will:

- Magically cleanse data.
- Automatically consolidate duplicate records.
- Define key dimensions or measures by themselves.

At the same time, however, effectively used BI tools will absolutely shed light on previously hidden issues and trends. In turn, this will likely prompt more questions critical to a firm's success.

---

[7]Dr. Rick Johnson, "Sales Success: Measure Results but Manage Activities," December 23, 2008, www.4hoteliers.com/4hots_fshw.php?mwi=3619.

Need for Information

The introduction of BI tools often causes a bit of disruption in many organizations. End users are often faced with fundamental questions about how they do their jobs. Specific queries include:

- How is the data ultimately consumed?
- What do you do with this information?
- Why do you need this report?

BI is hardly unique in that end users frequently cite existing reports as requirements for new ones. This rarely makes any sense, because BI is about so much more than just reports. Creating an OLAP cube to essentially mimic a dated, minimally useful report is more than a waste of time; it completely misses the point.

When defining BI requirements, intelligent practitioners take any given report and constantly ask, ". . . and then what is done with it?" This traces the report to its ultimate purpose. To be sure, some reports will be specifically formatted. Examples include those for public reporting and those that meet regulatory requirements. However, often business users are too comfortable with their current business processes. As a result, they ask for the same report and fail to realize the significant areas for improvement.

Consider a temporary protected status (TPS) report that requires five manual changes. The end user then passes it to someone else who makes five more changes. The second recipient ultimately publishes a set of analytical reports to senior management. Through the very process of gathering requirements necessary to implement BI tools, these assumptions can be challenged. End users can now understand these manual changes and determine if BI can eliminate each of these manual steps automatically. (Short answer: BI can probably do this and a great deal more.)

Also be mindful of the dangers of excessive requirements gathering. To be sure, technical business users need to know the specific data that functional folks need to be stored. A specific need should be driving requirements, not a gut feeling. In other words, the eventual output is paramount to the steps required to get there.

Scope

Like most technology projects, scope creep is a very serious threat on BI endeavors. On one hand, the project sponsor wants the project to meet the objectives originally requested at or under cost, deadline, and so on. As the project evolves, however, either the sponsor or the other key small and medium-size businesses (SMEs) are bound to request more capabilities.

This is especially true on agile projects in which end users see results very quickly. On waterfall projects, no one may know what's coming until the very end of the project. Managing that expectation—communicating the cost of any changes to the original plan—is critical to a successful project. The difficulty here versus regular IT projects is that many see BI as the new toy that gives them all the data they've ever wanted. While this is somewhat true, projects and sponsors are not compelled to cram everything into a Phase I.

In Phase II, the BI tool can be expanded to deliver additional functionality once the organization is live and initial milestones have been achieved. In this sense BI is identical to other technologies. Like a kid in a candy store, senior managers must enforce restraint. Once the sugar high of adding all these new features finally hits home, the bellyache of missing your project deadlines will become very apparent.

The Best BI for the Audience

All forms of BI are not for everyone. For instance, an organization should not expect its senior executives to use interactive OLAP. It's unlikely that they will have the time to slice and dice data, unearthing valuable trends. This is an example of a potential misuse of BI. Understanding the audience and how the information will be consumed is crucial to a successful BI deployment. Senior executives likely have planners doing sophisticated data analysis for them. As such, they could benefit from KPIs or a dashboard of custom metrics.

For others, be aware that not everyone will adopt the most robust technology available to them. Similar to all IT projects, organizations need to understand the composition of their audiences:

- Power analytical users
- Nontechnical users
- Those who fall in between

Understanding this breakdown of your audience will allow the organization to customize its BI solutions so that each recipient receives maximum benefit from the underlying information presented.

At all costs, organizations need to minimize the chance for improper use of a BI tool. For example, consider a nontechnical user who incorrectly manipulates an OLAP cube, causing others to potentially make decisions based on the wrong number.

Recent BI Trends

This chapter has provided a background in the basics of BI and how to effectively implement a solution. The chapter concludes with a discussion of the latest BI trends. Each reader must decide the following:

- Which parts of BI are important to the organization
- The vendor(s) with which to work
- Upcoming trends to ensure that no BI solution is obsolete before activated

BI has come a long way since its inception. Like the other technologies discussed in this book, BI continues to evolve. The evolution and maturity of BI only increases an organization's opportunity to make it more pervasive and more useful.

The following technologies and upcoming trends are expanding the importance of—and potential uses for—BI:

- In-memory OLAP
- Data mining (DM)
- Unstructured data/BI search
- Mobile BI
- BI competency centers (BICCs)

In-Memory OLAP

Before detailing the benefits of in-memory OLAP, consider the limitations of traditional OLAP. If not properly modeled, the OLAP cube can have significant performance issues of the inherent nature of the tool. For example, traditional OLAP cannot easily analyze 10,000 employees without groupings. In these cases, an OLAP cube, which should be built for *analysis*, is forced to become an ad hoc reporting tool. Worse, sometimes that very cube is used as a professional report creator.[8]

Collectively, these limitations are largely responsible for the unjustifiably negative perception of OLAP in certain circles. Again, these are all instances of the tool not being used appropriately. Additionally, performance to create cubes sometimes takes days if not optimized efficiently. Ultimately, large cubes can easily exceed several gigabytes in size when stored as a discrete file.

The natural evolution of the computer server industry over the past 20 years has been nothing less than staggering. With regard to OLAP, the change to 64-bit architecture and availability of cheaper RAM now makes it possible to run these OLAP cubes directly in memory. To be sure, in-memory OLAP is no silver bullet for improving the issues with OLAP discussed earlier. Still, tools that leverage in-memory OLAP can significantly improve cube

---

[8]In golfing terms, this is analogous to not being able to putt with your driver. The tool just wasn't meant for its ultimate use.

performance. Since it is already loaded into memory on the server and not physically on a disk, the system has no need to go to disk or network for retrieving the response to a request. Again, since there is a cap on the size of your memory, there are bound to be limitations to the size of the cubes you can create, but this segment of BI is certainly one that seems likely to continue to grow as server capacities continue to grow.

Data Mining

More and more organizations are using BI for data mining (DM) in interesting ways. First, DM has shown an amazing ability to find previously undetected trends. The example in Chapter 1 of Wal-Mart discovering that customers buy beer and strawberry Pop-Tarts during hurricanes is one of the most publicized examples of data mining. Data volumes are larger than ever and will only continue to grow. Consider the Internet, now essential for just about every business. These days, many organizations are tracking many metrics, such as:

- Visits to their web sites.
- Links clicked on the web site.
- In some cases, *user-viewed* material (for tracking views of advertising banners).

To store this surfeit of data, organizations require significantly larger data warehouses, measured not only in terabytes but in petabytes (1 petabyte = 1,000 terabytes). Extracting value out of this enormous data requires tools equipped for heavy lifting. One cannot realistically expect stalwarts such as Microsoft Excel and Access to find value in a sea of data in any reasonable period of time.

In his article "IBM SNAzzy Knows Your Circle of Friends Better Than You Do" (SNAzzy stands for Social Network Analysis for Telecom Business Intelligence), Jack Loftus describes a case in which DM creates information in an unlikely way. "The purpose of this snazzy snooping, as explained by Big Blue researchers, is to spot 'churners' on a cell network who might influence their circle of friends with 'profit-threatening behavior.'" According to this reasoning, when one person ditches a cell network for greener pastures, she can inspire her friends to do the same. IBM claims that SNAzzy can do the following:

- Recognize this behavior.
- Alert the carrier.
- Allow it to swoop in with retention materials.
- Possibly keep its remaining customers happy.

Loftus goes on to write that "it does this by mapping out call behavior, time, and a bunch of other heavy metrics that seem to be copy/pasted right out of the NSA."[9]

Privacy concerns aside, one cannot overstate the importance of proactively spotting trends and making better, more informed business responses. DM is clearly a game changer for any organization looking to stay ahead of its competition. In this example, being able to predict which customers may leave provides organizations with incredible insight and related opportunities. Put simply, this knowledge is simply not available without BI.

Data mining is continuing to open doors never imagined before through exciting new technologies and concepts. One burgeoning trend is sentiment analysis. In his *New York Times* article "Mining the Web for Feelings, Not Facts,"[10] Alex Wright sheds light on a simply amazing use of technology. Through mining Web content such as blogs and online reviews, some firms are "translating the vagaries of human emotion into hard data." As opinions are formed online and positive or negative sentiment grows, organizations can react quickly to information that simply is not available without BI. Wright writes that "in early May, the ticket marketplace StubHub used Scout Labs' monitoring tool to identify a sudden surge of negative blog sentiment after rain delayed a Yankees–Red Sox game. Stadium officials mistakenly told hundreds of fans that the game had been canceled, and StubHub denied fans' requests for refunds on the grounds that the game had actually been played. But after spotting trouble brewing online, the company offered discounts and credits to the affected fans. It is now re-evaluating its bad weather policy."

Technological predecessors to BI allowed organizations, to a limited degree, to react to issues *after* they have occurred. Enterprise 2.0 tools such as BI have allowed organizations to become more mature, more strategic, and more proactive. Rather than just triaging situations with damage control, they can proactively spot trends and sentiment. The implications for business are huge.

Unstructured Data and BI Search

With an estimated 80 percent of all business data being unstructured, organizations can use BI to leverage otherwise unusable data. For the most part, if volume doesn't make it impossible, organizations should manually add structure to this data by tagging it. If not, they have options through BI.

---

[9]Jack Loftus, "IBM SNAzzy Knows Your Circle of Friends Better Than You Do," August 2, 2009, http://gizmodo.com/5328265/ibm-snazzy-knows-your-circle-of-friends-better-than-you-do.
[10]See www.nytimes.com/2009/08/24/technology/internet/24emotion.html

One such option is data mining. Trying to find patterns across seemingly random data sets can uncover useful patterns. However, expect to find many useless patterns. Set your expectations appropriately.

BI search is a tool that offers amazing promise. Organizations can use BI search to extract value from largely unstructured data. By definition, BI search is simply searching among transactional or unstructured data. However, most organizations using BI eventually use the following:

- Many OLAP report views.
- Non-OLAP reports.
- Volumes of content within each of them.

Through BI search, end users can enter a keyword that returns related reports and content. In this manner, BI search is very similar to enterprise search and retrieval (ESR), a topic discussed at length in Chapter 10. Moreover, the ability to search unstructured data (otherwise unusable in some cases) provides a valuable tool capable of extracting additional value out of a sea of data.

Note that there is hope for unstructured data. Tools such as Google Squared can convert unstructured data into structured data. While this site may have limited viability in the consumer world, there is a great deal of potential in the business world for this capability.

Mobile BI

While the notion of mobile BI may seem facile, effectively using it isn't as simple as it sounds. A small mobile screen may well not be the best mechanism to deliver a BI tool. Let's start by pointing out the clear strengths of mobile devices like the BlackBerry as demonstrated in Table 11.5.

TABLE 11.5 Pros and Cons of Mobile BI

Pros	Cons
Mobility	Small screen
Supply ample information through killer apps such as email and calendar	Limited application functionality
Instant messaging	Limited disk space/processing power
Phone	Slow bandwidth (although this is clearly improving)
GPS	

Targeting company executives' mobile devices to contain the critical metrics to keep their fingers on the pulse of the company is typically where these initiatives start. No other single business user's time is as valuable as that of the top brass, and ensuring that the content they need is available when they need it is increasingly becoming a standard practice.

Until the limitations of business mobile BI change, OLAP in its true form is unlikely to be a good remote solution because it requires heavy interaction, a lot of bandwidth, and processing power. That said, the iPhone, with its larger screen and greatly improved interface, is quickly becoming a target of BI. QlikView has already released an interactive BI application specific for the iPhone.[11]

BI Competency Centers

Many organizations have established BI competency centers (BICCs) that essentially serve as governance committees. BICCs are comprised of senior technical and business personnel and focus on the following areas of a BI:

- *Behavior/culture.* Training and internal promotion of BI.
- *Infrastructure.* Central infrastructure, license management, and data governance.
- *Process improvement.* Providing central consulting services and a best practices repository.

In a nutshell, BICCs provide best practices and serve as a center of excellence (CoE). BICCs attempt to maximize the benefits received from BI across an organization. BICCs provide a kind of steering committee for everything related to BI and facilitate the following:

- Faster and more cost-effective time to market of solutions.
- Constant improvement of solutions through central governance.
- Standardization across all implementations.
- Co-ownership of BI between the lines of business (LOBs) and IT.

A specific goal of a BICC might be to routinely survey all license holders of the firm with the intent of understanding their usage and satisfaction with the organization's current BI offerings. BICCs can produce invaluable insight into improving processes within different parts of an organization.

---

[11]Neil Florio, "Delivering on the Promise of Mobile BI," www.qliktech.com, www.dashboardinsight.com/dashboards/screenshots/delivering-on-the-promise-mobile-bi.aspx.

Do different pockets of the organization have similar processes but use different metrics or BI tools? BICCs can identify areas for consolidation and improvement. Finally, BICCs can reduce costs by cutting the licenses of nonusers, supported by audit logs.

For more information, see Aiman Zeid's article, "Your BI Competency Center: A Blueprint for Successful Deployment." It contains more detail about starting a BICC.

Open Source BI

Like any IT project, deciding on a vendor is a complex process for any organization. Fortunately, because BI is a fairly mature technology, organizations have many options. Popular and mature technologies result in open source variations, as discussed in Chapters 5 and 16. While still young, vendors such as Pentaho and JasperSoft have compelling stories to tell. This is especially true in light of the uncertainty brought about by the recent merger and acquisition (M&A) activity. Open source BI (like any open source software) means that organizations no longer have to deal with vendor end-user license agreements (EULAs) and forced upgrades.

Too Much BI?

Some organizations simply have too much technology. A Forrester Research survey states that "just under half of companies polled said they use between three and five BI products throughout the enterprise. Another 10% reported deploying between six and nine BI products, and around 15% said they use an astounding 10 or more BI tools enterprise-wide. Just over 20% boasted using just one or two BI products."[12]

Excessive BI can result from the following:

- Lack of enterprise coordination—departmental silos (working in isolation from others).
- Haste to jump on the latest trend.
- Immature vendors that could satisfy only some of a client's requirements.

With BI firms maturing, many organizations will need to consolidate their BI tools. Doing so will not only allow them to leverage their best practices and infrastructure, but also allow significant cost savings from software

---

[12]SearchDataManagement.com editorial team, "Key Considerations for Business Intelligence Platform Consolidation," SearchDataManagement.com, http://search-datamanagement.techtarget.com/news/article/0,289142,sid91_gci1348011,00.html.

purchases and maintenance. Before consolidating, however, organizations should conduct true vendor and requirements analyses.

Summary

As organizations make more decisions based on hard facts, the proliferation and evolution of BI tools will no doubt continue. The future of BI is very exciting; its value is only growing. More and more organizations are realizing BI is a requirement, lest they fall behind their competition and lose money. The next years should be even more exciting. The federal government is using BI to track funds spent by organizations receiving financial assistance via the American Recovery and Reinvestment Act (ARRA) of 2009. BI will continue to be at the forefront of technology, as more examples of its creative uses come to light.[13]

Without BI, end users search for data and the meaning behind it, but never really get what they want. They only get enough to meet their needs, and sometimes not even enough. The question for organizations of all sizes will change from *whether* BI should be used to *how* it should be used.

Next Steps

- Having a vision of BI in your organization and successfully implementing that vision are two very different things. Be aware of the gap between theory and practice.
- BI requires data, and data is best consumed for reporting when it is loaded into a data warehouse.
- Is BI top-down or bottom-up?
- What type of information is best suited for mobile BI at your organization?
- Is your data clean enough for BI?
- What, if any, are the key metrics that BI might help your organization answer?
- Are the end users at your organization ready for BI? Do key end users make decisions from the gut more often than based on hard data?

---

[13]Dr. Ramon Barquin, "ARRA Will Be a Boon for Business Intelligence," June 16, 2009, www.b-eye-network.com/view/10641.

CHAPTER 12

Master Data Management

Dalton Cervo

Insanity: Doing the same thing over and over again and expecting different results.

—Albert Einstein

Introduction

Today's business environment requires organizations to find a way to differentiate themselves from their competition and thrive amid increased pressure to succeed. To be sure, traditional routes, such as looking at an acquisition or attempting to develop a new product, are viable and often necessary options. Often overlooked, however, is a typically underutilized resource: the organization's own data. To gain and sustain a competitive advantage, an organization should start by understanding and leveraging its data.

While data in general is extremely important to an organization's success, master data bridges intelligence by the way in which it interacts with other data. Master data is the centerpiece supporting and connecting transactional data from multiple business areas, such as sales, service, order management, purchasing, manufacturing, billing, accounts receivable, and accounts payable (AP).

Master data consists of information critical to operations and business intelligence (BI) about the following entities: customers, products, suppliers, partners, employees, materials, and so on. While often nontransactional in nature, master data supports transactional processes and operations, as well as BI via analytics and reporting. Master data is normally used by multiple functional groups and stored in disparate systems across the organization. Since it is commonly stored in isolated systems, the possibility for inaccurate and/or duplicate master data exists.

In summary, master data is persistent, nontransactional data defining a business entity for which there should be one consistent and understood view across the organization.

Master data management (MDM) has arisen mostly to solve the need to achieve a single view of master data across the enterprise. Historically, there has been a huge proliferation of data due to cheap storage and increased digitization. Furthermore, compartmentalized solutions have added to the fragmentation of information considerably, magnifying data duplication and lack of a common entity identification.

Organizations came to the realization that the most effective way to address this growing problem is by having a single source of master data with high standards of quality and governance serving the entire business.

The State of the Union

Imagine a company with perfect systems, data, and processes. Let's call this Utopia, Inc. Utopia never has any issues resolving discrepancies among systems, because all enterprise information exists in one place with one set of consistently applied business rules. End users perfectly understand how to create, edit, store, and retrieve data. Reports give each level of management the information that they require, allowing them to make optimal decisions without Band-Aids.

Now let's return to reality. This utopian entity does not exist. Most organizations suffer from an inconsistent and fragmented set of master data spread out across multiple disparate systems throughout the enterprise. For example, different customer relationship management (CRM) systems might contain multiple instances of a customer record with different details and transactions linked to it. While not an exhaustive list, these redundancies often stem from the following:

- Mergers and acquisitions (M&A).
- Years of multiple distributed software and business applications.
- Inconsistent business rules among different applications.
- Multiple database technologies and application architectures combined with previously immature integration solutions.
- Proliferation of data warehouses.
- Lack of audits.

Because of these reasons, most organizations suffer from fragmented and inconsistent data. The net effect is that organizations face unnecessary and increased operational inefficiencies, inconsistent or inaccurate reporting, and ultimately incorrect business decisions. If utilized properly throughout an organization, MDM can address those problems, help organizations to operate more effectively, and understand their own data to achieve strategic objectives.

In a report entitled "MDM's Monumental Momentum," Andrew White of the Gartner Group writes, "The prime reason for MDM's emerging popularity, and the principal failure of data quality strategies and solutions to date, has been the development and deployment of enterprise applications that have remained isolated. Enterprise applications—whether it's ERP, CRM, or SCM—they've all become silos of information within the enterprise. As a result, the data has been duplicated over and over again."

The Business Case for Master Data Management

But why is MDM important? Quite simply, MDM gives organizations the opportunity to improve both their data and their internal processes. Organizations that ignore these issues exacerbate the following:

- Increased costs stemming from superfluous operational overhead.
- Higher risk of audits and regulatory violations.
- Poorer BI and analytics, adding to customer frustration and missed opportunities.
- Customer/partner/vendor/employee dissatisfaction and consequently unrealized revenues.
- Possibility of duplicate vendor and customer records, increasing the risk of possible overpayment.

MDM does much more than just bring data together. It involves an entire set of processes, services, and policies that go along with it. The three main reasons most often used to justify MDM are cost reduction, risk management, and revenue growth, as shown in Figure 12.1.

Cost Reduction

Potential areas for cost reduction include:

- Operating costs due to inefficient business processes, needed workarounds, and redundant tasks.
- Inventory management, delivery errors, shipping fines, product returns, and wasted direct marketing due to inaccurate data.
- Information technology (IT) costs, including consulting and software maintenance fees, plus necessary tools and resources required to maintain and reconcile redundant systems.

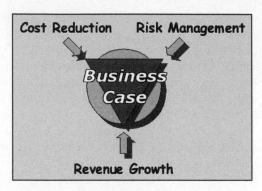

FIGURE 12.1 The Business Case for MDM

Risk Management

Potential areas for risk management include:

- Legal compliance, such as compensation, privacy, pricing, and contracts.
- Regulatory compliance, such as financial reporting, Sarbanes-Oxley Act (SOX), U.S. Patriot Act, and Basel II.
- Mitigation of frauds, lawsuits, audit findings, loss of certifications, fines, and penalties.

Revenue Growth

Potential areas for revenue growth include:

- Enhanced customer satisfaction due to better understanding of customer needs.
- Better marketing programs and channel management.
- Strategic mergers and acquisitions.

MDM offers a collection of processes, policies, services, and technologies that create and maintain consistent and accurate lists of master data. MDM is not merely a fix to system, data, and integration problems; it equally addresses *business* problems. As such, to be successful, an MDM must represent a joint and coordinated effort between IT and different lines of business (LOBs).

There is no one recipe for making the case for MDM. Organization A might suffer from such poor data quality that it can barely function. Organization B may face severe and strict government oversight.

In any event, organizations first need to recognize the strongest probable benefits of an MDM initiative and build the business case around them. Next, they should estimate how much they are losing by *not* realizing all the benefits of having a timely, accurate, and consistent set of data delivered to the organization. This is sometimes referred to as alternative-based costing (ABC).

Often, the best way to measure the potential benefit of MDM involves determining the amount of money that an organization spends with reactive activities in place to compensate for a suboptimal set of processes and tools.

MDM Approaches and Architectures

Information architects and managers sometimes say that a true MDM solution should address two fundamental business areas: operational and BI. However, it is often not possible—or even advisable—for an MDM initiative to address both of them. This section outlines the three major types of different MDM initiatives:

1. *Analytical MDM.* Addresses BI.
2. *Operational MDM.* Addresses business operations.
3. *Enterprise MDM.* Addresses *both* BI and operations.

Each has a somewhat different objective and carries distinct levels of complexity, risk, and impact. Organizations should perform detailed analyses to decide which approach is required. At a minimum, an MDM project must take into consideration business and IT requirements, time frame, resource availability, priority, and the size of the problem to be addressed.

Figure 12.2 depicts the level of intrusiveness of each MDM approach.

Naturally, more intrusive MDM projects involve both higher risks and higher likelihoods of disrupting organizations' daily operations. It is

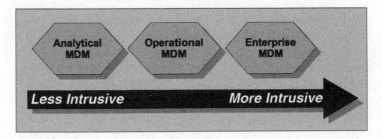

FIGURE 12.2 MDM Approaches

important to notice that the figure does *not* suggest a sequence or phases to be adopted when implementing an MDM solution.

Later in the chapter, potential architectures are described to allow organizations to facilitate a phased deployment. Approaches and architectures *cannot* be considered independent of each other. This chapter evaluates both at the same time.

Analytical MDM

Historically, analytical MDM has been the most commonly adopted MDM approach. This stems mostly from the relative simplicity of leveraging data warehouse projects. Figure 12.3 depicts a common architecture adopted by organizations implementing an analytical MDM approach.

Figure 12.3 Quadrant 1 shows that an extract, transform, load (ETL) process gathers data from disparate operational systems. Ultimately, the data is stored on an enterprise data warehouse (EDW). EDW and associated data marts become the source of master data for BI and analytics. Since EDW is now a single source from an analytical perspective, it is also the centerpiece for what can be called MDM services.

Analytical MDM is the quick-hit approach. While organizations can quickly make a tremendous impact with respect to reporting and BI, with the analytical MDM approach, relatively minimal inputs yield corresponding outputs. Specifically, organizations fail to harvest the benefits of the MDM services back to their operational data. What's more, by relying on a data warehouse, the analytical MDM approach does not enforce any regulatory or audit requirements.

In this architecture, a physical copy of the multiple data systems across the organization is performed. It requires the provisioning and maintenance of another system to host this information. It also creates the possibility of another fragmented and incomplete data system to exist.

Operational MDM

Once implemented, organizations can easily leverage operational MDM in the analytical world. For this reason, many organizations commonly use operational MDM as a first step to achieving enterprise MDM. Operational MDM can be accomplished via three different architectures:

1. Single central repository architecture
2. Central hub-and-spoke architecture
3. Virtual integration or data federation

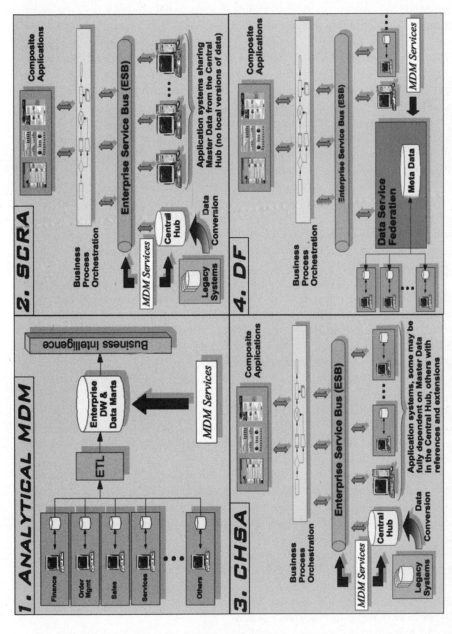

FIGURE 12.3 Comparison of MDM Architectures—Quadrant I-Analytical MDM, Quadrant II-SCRA, Quadrant III-CHSA, Quadrant IV-DF

213

Note that a service-oriented architecture (SOA) with an enterprise service bus (ESB) and business process orchestration is not required to make the MDM repository or the federation system available, but it is the most common and effective architecture.

SINGLE CENTRAL REPOSITORY ARCHITECTURE (SCRA)   In this architecture, a single central repository within the operational environment serves as the source of data to an integrated suite of applications and processes. Only one physical copy of master data exists.

It is important to emphasize that this approach may obviate the need for certain applications. In other words, after the consolidation of data, an organization may not need all of its previous applications. Required applications dependent on that data might need to be rewritten.

SCRA guarantees consistency of master data. However, it can be very expensive—if not impossible—to implement due to potentially inflexible off-the-shelf applications in use (although SCRA could actually be the easiest and cheapest to maintain). SCRA could potentially require a massive data conversion effort, depending on the size of the organization and the number of disparate systems.

In Figure 12.3 Quadrant 2, multiple legacy systems go through a data conversion step to bring data into a central hub. This conversion normally takes place in phases to minimize impact and lower risk of concurrently converting multiple legacy systems. When the central hub is operational, it is then used by application systems that would either replace legacy systems or add new functionality to the organization. In this particular case, new application systems do *not* have their own versions of master data.

CENTRAL HUB AND SPOKE ARCHITECTURE (CHSA)   This is a more common variation of SCRA. Like SCRA, CHSA has an independently deployed common repository. However, CHSA does not require that all applications and processes are fully coupled to the hub.

The major advantage of this architecture is the efficiency of a central hub hosting the master data, combined with the flexibility to support spoke systems operating relatively decoupled. This flexibility is important when integrating commercial, off-the-shelf (COTS) applications with your MDM solution.

Some of the applications can act as spoke systems with independent data models, but cross-referenced and synchronized to the central data. To be sure, CHSA alleviates some of the problems presented by SCRA, but CHSA can still require a massive data conversion effort and interface new layers between the hub and its spokes.

In Figure 12.3 Quadrant 3, multiple legacy systems go through a data conversion step to bring data into a central hub. Again, this conversion normally takes place in phases to minimize impact and lower risk of concurrently converting multiple legacy systems. When the central hub is operational, application systems then access it to either replace legacy systems or add new functionality to the organization. Spoke systems are synchronized and integrated with the central hub.

DATA FEDERATION (DF) Under data federation, also known as virtual integration (VI), the data is *not* copied into an independent repository. This is a fundamental difference compared to the previous two methods. A DF system virtually aggregates data from multiple sources into a single view by maintaining a metadata definition of all sources. Data across multiple sources is collected in real time, and services provided can be reused by many process applications.

In Figure 12.3 Quadrant 4, a data service federation (DSF) system collects real-time data from multiple existing sources. The data is *not* physically copied into the federated system. Information about the data in each source is stored on a metadata repository. It is further used to determine which system and data element to access based on requests performed to the DSF.

Enterprise MDM

Enterprise MDM is a combination of both operational and analytical MDMs. As such, it can be implemented by combining the architectures previously discussed.

A data warehouse solution could be added to any of the three operational MDM architectures. As an added bonus, most of the MDM services that would be needed in the warehouse are already functional in the operational system, making the maintenance of your data warehouse much easier.

What's more, the ETL function of the analytical MDM should be much simpler since organizations now maintain fewer systems from which to extract data. The data should also be cleaner, standardized, and already consolidated.

Data federation offers another potential solution. DF could be expanded to provide a view into multiple departmental data warehouses in addition to operational systems. Through this method, DF becomes the single point to resolve complex BI queries. This solution reduces both organizations' costs and complexity by lowering the need for an extra and expensive database server. However, there's no free lunch here.

DF technology takes a toll on performance of the operational and transactional data sources that it queries. It requires that transactional data sources are always on. This is in stark contrast to batch load data at preset and convenient times as normally done by data warehouse implementations—for example, at 4 A.M. while few users are accessing the system. BI queries can be quite complex and aggregate a multitude of data. Data warehouses are normally optimized to support those queries, making a DF implementation for this purpose potentially enviable. If organizations go this route, then they should proceed with caution and with extensive load testing to confirm viability.

Selecting the Right MDM Approach

As discussed previously, organizations typically use three main reasons to justify an MDM implementation: cost reduction, risk management, and revenue growth.

But once an organization selects its main area of focus for its business case, how does it decide which MDM approach to implement?

Enterprise MDM represents a combination of analytical and operational MDMs. To be sure, organizations can use enterprise MDM to solve virtually any data and integration problem. For some issues, however, enterprise MDM is simply overkill. This section aims to recommend the right solution to each problem, ensuring that organizations do not attempt to kill an ant with a machine gun.

Note that Table 12.1 should be used only as a general guideline. Further, each of the three business cases overlaps the others to an extent; one does not start where the other ends. One could correctly argue that by mitigating certain risks, organizations lower the costs of doing business. This, in turn, raises questions of whether this should be in the cost reduction category instead. Also, better data could reduce costs and improve marketing, and consequently grow revenue.

MDM Services and Components

Again, MDM entails much more than bringing master data together: It is a collection of processes, policies, services, and technologies required to create and maintain consistent and accurate lists of master data.

Integrating master data in a single source facilitates the employment of services and components needed to create and maintain a set of consistent and accurate information. The combination of integrated data with proper services and components makes an MDM program successful. On one hand, migrating multiple systems into a single source alone will *not* do the job. This may well result in the typical "garbage in, garbage out" (GIGO) outcome. On the other hand, it is practically impossible to apply MDM services and components when data is fragmented across the organization. Integrated

TABLE 12.1 Business Rationale for Different MDM Approaches

Business Case	Recommended MDM Approach	Rationale
Risk mitigation	Operational MDM	The biggest concern is control. Implementing MDM on a data warehouse (analytical MDM) will not help, because operational data must be regulated to minimize risk and increase compliance.
Cost reduction	Operational MDM (maybe enterprise MDM)	Most likely, the majority of costs are related to operations (see the section on the business case for MDM). This means that an operational MDM is sufficient. However, inconsistent and incorrect data may also have a huge cost impact on wasted marketing campaigns. As a result, enterprise MDM may be required, depending on the situation.
Revenue growth	Analytical MDM	Revenue growth is mostly related to better strategic decisions. Analytical MDM only should suffice in most cases.

data is a necessary but not sufficient cause of a successful MDM endeavor. A complete solution requires proper *services* as well.

Data Quality

Data quality is likely the single most important reason that organizations tackle MDM. Trusted data delivered in a timely manner is any organization's ultimate objective.

DATA PROFILING Data profiling involves understanding organization data and is the first step to correcting or converting it. Many organizations underestimate or even ignore this requirement, ultimately wasting a great deal of money solving the wrong problem. Data profiling or discovery should be the initial step when starting a data cleansing project. Organizations often overlook the need to profile their data before migrating it into a master data repository. Many organizations go to data conversion projects without understanding the specific data being converted, only to be surprised midway through the MDM project.

DATA VALIDATION, CLEANSING, STANDARDIZATION, ENRICHMENT, AND CONSOLIDA-TION Data validation involves improving the quality of enterprise data. The ultimate aim of data validation is to prevent previously bad data from entering the new system (e.g., accepting only "M" and "F" values for gender on an employee).

Data cleansing or scrubbing involves correcting corrupt, invalid, or inaccurate records. For example, an organization eliminates invalid characters or extra spaces from a set of data records.

Data standardization is about conforming your data to a list of established rules and standards (e.g., replacing all variations of Incorporated—Incorporated, Inc, Incorp, etc.—with Inc.).

Data enrichment involves augmenting data (e.g., add +4 to U.S. zip codes).

Data consolidation is about eliminating duplicates. Data cleansing, standardization, and enrichment are means for increasing the ability to identify and consequently eliminate duplicates and improve consolidation.

DATA QUALITY METRICS (DQMs) Data quality metrics (DQMs) measure the quality of data so proper actions can be taken to prevent a recurrence of previous issues and a deterioration of data quality. Quoting Lord Kelvin, "If you cannot measure it, you cannot improve it." DQMs can be separated into two categories: monitors and scorecards. Monitors are used to detect violations that usually require immediate corrective actions. Scorecards allow for a number to be associated with the quality of your data.

To increase overall data quality, organizations should do the following:

- Establish a baseline or score of the current state of data quality.
- Determine improvement targets tied to business objectives.
- Use the ongoing scorecards to gauge results.

Both monitors and scorecards should be qualified according to one of the data quality dimensions:

- *Completeness*. Level of data missing or unusable.
- *Conformity*. Degree of data stored in a nonstandard format.
- *Consistency*. Level of conflicting information.
- *Accuracy*. Degree of agreement with an identified source of correct information.
- *Uniqueness*. Level of nonduplicates.
- *Integrity*. Degree of referenced data.

With regard to each of these data quality dimensions, there are a multitude of details and nuances outside of the scope for this chapter. For now, suffice it to say that it is important to understand that data quality is a very complex, time-consuming, and ongoing process that should not be overlooked.

Data Governance and Stewardship

Most organizations have multiple groups sharing the same set of data, resulting in the obvious question, "Who owns the data?" To properly answer this question, organizations must establish roles of data governance and data stewardship. Moreover, they need cross-functional teams to enact standards, policies, and procedures. Only then can organizations maintain the integrity of the data established by the MDM project.

Remember that before beginning an MDM initiative, organizations maintain multiple isolated systems serving the needs of different factions—some better than others. In most corporate environments, each faction is responsible for its own data. A change of mind-set is in order. After the MDM project, no longer will each have full control over its data. Since the data will now exist in a centralized hub, end users may lack their previous flexibility.

Once data is shared by multiple LOBs, any changes to the centralized information can have huge implications. For this reason, it is essential for organizations to enforce data governance and stewardship. Doing so will more effectively represent those multiple LOBs and ultimately maintain the common data in a far superior fashion.

By forming teams specialized in a particular master data entity, organizations can effectively act as stewards of their data. Individual teams may focus on customers, products, suppliers, partners, employees, or materials. These teams need to work with multiple LOBs to ensure that the best interests of those groups are reflected in the data.

The data stewards can either be from the same department or be a combination of individuals in assorted areas. It is imperative that all LOBs are represented, *either* directly or indirectly.

Data governance is part of data stewardship. It is the vehicle by which organizations establish, monitor, and enforce standards, policies, and procedures. Data governance has the authority over the management of data assets and performance of data functions.

An operational or enterprise MDM project without data governance and stewardship is bound to fail. Moreover, these two functions should be established as early as possible. For each, scope, roles, and responsibilities should be clearly defined and communicated to all affected groups. Confirming understanding and getting acceptance are essential for organizations to avoid internecine conflicts in the future.

Analytical MDM does *not* involve operational data. For that reason, data governance and stewardship are less important—in fact, possibly even most likely unnecessary. As described previously, analytical MDM is normally implemented as a data warehouse project to support business intelligence reporting. Normally, there is a single team responsible for performing that function for one or more of the data entities, making the issue of control a moot point.

As a rule of thumb, if you have multiple lines of business competing for the maintenance of the same set of data, you need a governing body to oversee the activity and look for the best interests of the entire organization.

Metadata Management

Metadata is defined as data about other data. While ostensibly simple, there is quite a bit behind that simplistic definition. Before we get into a wider description of metadata and its management, let's discuss why it is needed.

It is quite amazing to find out how different LOBs have different—and sometimes conflicting—definitions of an apparently simple data element. LOBs, operating in silos, sometimes disagree over definitions, but ultimately a common understanding normally prevails. However, as organizations combine data elements into a shared MDM repository, the need for clear and firm definitions becomes patently obvious.

Metadata management enhances understanding of data elements across the organization. It provides the proper description of and business rules associated with each data element in an MDM repository. In the case of a data migration effort, metadata should describe each of the following:

- The source of the data's value.
- The transformations performed.
- The business rules applied to it.

Metadata must accurately describe the master data and the specific applications that depend on it.

Organizations typically manage their metadata via a repository. A metadata repository is not necessarily an application accompanying an MDM solution. Organizations can implement their own metadata repository using a normal set of database tables if they don't have the budget.

Similar to data governance and stewardship, metadata management is less critical when implementing an analytical MDM. But don't be deceived. There are certain aspects of metadata management that should not be overlooked even with an analytical MDM. For example, the ETL functions of an analytical MDM are much better managed and documented with a metadata repository.

Metadata management is extremely important. To that end, organizations need to conduct detailed analysis of their particular MDM implementations to identify to what extent they employ such management.

Hierarchy Management

Hierarchy management entails managing data relationships. As such, it could also be referred as relationship management or categorization. In essence, it is a type of grouping.

This type of MDM service is closely related to the particular master data entity implemented. For instance, if the entity is customer, then hierarchies can be used to represent company organizational structures. If the entity is product, then it can be used to represent product lines or taxonomies.

From a BI perspective, hierarchical organization of data is essential. It allows for a vastly superior understanding of market and industry segmentation. The volume of master data can be quite overwhelming. Classifying this data hierarchically is a critical first step to make the most sense of the information. The results can be applied to market campaigns, cross-sells, and up-sells.

From an operational perspective, hierarchy management is also critical in improving efforts to maintain master data. Some LOBs such as sales may have a vested interest in hierarchical organization for means of territory segmentation and sales commissions.

It is doubtful that single hierarchical representation for each data entity will meet the needs of all LOBs within any large organization. Multiple representations are not uncommon but add to the project's cost. Maintaining a single hierarchy per data entity can be very challenging already. As the different perspectives grow, organizations risk compromising the main reason that they engaged in an MDM project in the first place: an agreed-upon view of master data across the entire organization. Finding the right balance is key.

Most likely, the MDM repository will have relational relationships (e.g., a customer has multiple addresses or accounts). These types of relationships are inherent to the structure of the repository and are conceptually different from hierarchy management. What's more, hierarchy management may *not* be supported by your MDM repository.

Master Data Life Cycle Management

This category encompasses the diverse activities related to the actual structure, design, load, creation, modification, retirement, distribution, synchronization, and access of master data.

The amount of effort required for most of these activities depends on the decision either to buy a COTS MDM solution or to build one internally. Existing MDM solutions provide the infrastructure to manage most of these activities. However, customizations are not uncommon, depending on an organization's particular situation. Obviously, organizations that decide to build their own MDM repositories face much more time, effort, and expense than those that opt for COTS solutions. However, organizations with unique requirements may have no choice. A cost-benefit analysis is typically appropriate, with the help of an experienced consultant.

Summary

Foolish is the person who believes that MDM is exclusively a technology issue. It's as much—if not more—of a business capability issue. MDM initiatives can be successful only by combining people, processes, and technologies. Further, MDM projects must be coordinated efforts between business and IT.

MDM requires bringing many disparate data elements, systems, and processes into a common framework. It also requires aligning multiple business units into an integrated set of data, processes, rules, standards, policies, and procedures.

Getting executive buy-in and full sponsorship throughout the entire MDM project is of utmost importance. A strong change management process, with extra focus on communication and training, should be put in place to guide the organization in this endeavor.

Organizations do not need to consolidate all data entities in a single project or phase. A staggered approach often makes the most sense. An organization may start with a customer-based MDM project and then move to products, vendors, and others.

The ultimate goal is to have a single version of the truth, completely understood by all LOBs. It is a long and tenuous road but very worthwhile in the long run. If done right, the outputs more than justify the inputs.

Next Steps

Questions

- What data entity or entities will I start with in my MDM project?
- What am I going to focus on for my business case: cost reduction, risk management, or revenue growth?
- What MDM approach is the right fit for my business case?

- What MDM architecture is most appropriate for my organization?
- Buy or build? If buying, what vendor or vendors should I select?

Checklist

- Executive buy-in.
- Change management process (readiness assessment; sponsorship; communication; education and training; coaching; measurement systems, rewards, and reinforcement).
- Data governance and stewardship: early and ongoing.
- Data quality management: early and ongoing.
- Other MDM services: metadata, hierarchy, and master data life-cycle management.

CHAPTER 13

Procurement in Chaos

Brian G. Rosenberg

If opportunity doesn't knock, build a door.

—Milton Berle

Introduction

There has been an increased focus on the procure-to-pay (P2P) process over the past several years. This has resulted in a growth in conferences focused on P2P, consulting organizations specializing in P2P improvement, and solution providers all offering the silver bullet that will solve all your procurement problems.

The sudden interest in P2P should not be surprising, but it should be surprising that it has taken so long for the spotlight to be put on a part of the business that is so vital to the profitability of so many organizations. *Procure-to-pay* refers to the entire process by which organizations buy and pay for goods and services, from the request for the product from the operations staff to the issuance of the purchase order, receipt of the goods, and finally payment of the invoice. What could be more important than how your company spends its money?

Yet understanding and controlling the procurement process has not been a priority in most organizations. When it comes to automation, the focus has been on the front-end, customer-facing process (such as point of sale for retail organizations or patient tracking for health care), or the back-end human resources and financial processes through an Enterprise Resource Planning (ERP) solution. P2P has simply not been given the attention that it needs. The result is a chaotic purchasing environment.

Is your purchasing in chaos? The following are typical characteristics of purchasing in chaos:

- *Manual processes.* In a 2008 survey by International Accounts Payable Professionals (IAPP), two-thirds of respondents stated that an overreliance on manual and paper-based processes was the biggest challenge that faced their financial operations. Paper-based processes lead to lost and buried paperwork and long delays in obtaining approval, which in turn leads to staff finding work-arounds or ignoring the process altogether.
- *Weak controls.* Approval processes do not occur, or occur after the fact and are therefore a rubber stamp rather than a true approval.
- *Rogue buying.* Negotiated contracts and/or best pricing are ignored in favor of personal relationships or conveniences to the requestor rather than ensuring that the best price is obtained.
- *No three-way match.* Payments are issued without assurances that the product or service in question has been received and without the ability to match the price against an established contract.
- *Limited information.* Purchasing leadership does not have access to actionable information as to what is being purchased. Vendor contracts are negotiated without the benefit of historical purchasing information, and contract compliance is challenging to monitor.
- *No visibility to commitments.* As purchase orders are not always created and invoices are sent directly to operational staff rather than accounts payable (AP), there is a significant delay in recording of expenses, and the company is not able to determine the true value of its commitments at any time.

Does Procure-to-Pay Matter?

Regardless of their role, every executive should have an interest in procure-to-pay automation, as it can have a significant impact on the bottom line. As a finance leader, addressing P2P will ensure more accurate financial statements, increased profitability, and better controls. As an information technology leader, it is important to be aware of the different available technologies to ensure that the best technologies are selected and that they will work well together. As an operations leader, changes in the P2P process will significantly change the way that operations staff members interact with vendors and with corporate staff. P2P process improvement is coming as organizations realize the benefits, and will have an impact across the enterprise.

Even large, well-funded public organizations do not have the technology in place to be able to understand and control their procurement process. The technology used to create and issue purchase orders often varies from one location to the next, with some using the company ERP software, issuing purchase orders manually or using another system, or others not issuing purchase orders at all, but rather just calling in their orders to the vendor. Without this technology, establishing controls over these processes and cashing in on this opportunity is almost impossible.

Yet within chaos lies opportunity. A savvy executive can identify significant improvements through standardization and automation of the procurement process. The results can be better financial controls, lower costs of products, reduced overhead, and better relationships with operations staff and vendors.

What Is Procure-to-Pay Automation?

One of the challenges in understanding procure-to-pay automation is that the term is used inconsistently. Many products and services marketed as a P2P solution in fact address only one small part of the procurement process. It is common for these solutions to have overlapping functionality. The reality is that for most organizations, multiple solutions may be necessary to solve their procurement needs. Selecting the best technologies that will work well together and create consistency in the process is a key challenge that must be overcome.

Generally, *P2P automation* refers to using technology to streamline part or all of the procurement process. The common components of the procurement process that are automated are discussed next.

Requisitioning

Requisitions are generated by operation staff that wish to purchase goods or services. In manual environments, requisitions are often completed on paper, or requisitions are not created at all as orders are typically called in to the vendor directly. The objective of automation of the requisition function is to provide a method for the operations staff to complete the requisitions electronically, often selecting items from a limited catalog or template of items that they are permitted to order.

Approval of Requisitions

Most organizations require approval prior to a purchase being made. In a manual environment, this requires completing a form to request goods and forwarding that form to the approvers. This often leads to delayed and lost paperwork. Manual approval processes have long proven to be ineffective, as approvals are often not obtained or obtained after the fact due to the time required to obtain them. Workflow automation solutions allow for these invoices to be routed electronically, reducing approval time.

Issuance of Purchase Orders

Once a requisition is approved, a purchase order is issued to a vendor. Without automation, purchase orders are called in to vendors or faxed. In a highly automated organization, purchase orders are sent electronically with acknowledgments being returned electronically from the vendor.

Receiving Invoices

The most common way for invoices to be submitted from vendors is by mail. Upon receipt, invoices are manually entered. In automated AP departments, invoices can be received electronically using a method such as electronic data interchange (EDI) or e-payables. Invoices that are received manually can still be scanned and have information extracted using advanced data capture, creating a fully electronic environment.

Issuing Payments

The end of the era of the paper check has long been predicted. In the consumer world, it has essentially become a reality, replaced by credit and debit cards, as well as online banking services. In the world of business-to-business commerce, it has taken a much longer time for adoption to occur. However, a combination of Automated Clearing House (ACH) and procurement cards is quickly increasing the volume of payments processed electronically, steadily reducing the number of checks issued by many organizations. See Figure 13.1 for an overview of the procure-to-pay process.

Technology and process solutions designed to automate procure-to-pay come in a variety of forms, but most subscribe to the same basic tenets and incorporate some pieces of these functions:

FIGURE 13.1 Procure-to-Pay Process Overview

- Creating paperless procurement environments.
- Reducing time required for each step of the procurement cycle.
- Increasing the number of transactions received or sent electronically.
- Increasing visibility of information, including company spend.
- Eliminating manual processes.

Certain forms of P2P automation are rapidly approaching maturity, such as document imaging. Others are experiencing much slower adoption rates, as they are not being prioritized within their organizations. The Paystream Advisors Financial Automation study in 2007 found that 47 percent of the surveyed respondents used imaging and document management, with another 9 percent of respondents in the deployment stage. However, when asked the same question about approval workflow, only 27 percent were using this technology and only another 4 percent were in the planning stage.

In this chapter, we explore different technologies available to organizations that would like to take advantage of this opportunity and gain control over how their organization spends its money. We will discuss the benefits to automating your procurement operation, as well as the challenges that will need to be faced. The number and variety of these technologies is significant, as the market has responded to this need in many different ways, and new options are being added to the marketplace every day. Our focus will be on understanding some of the most common categories of products available and how each might impact your business operation.

Benefiting from P2P Automation

In any information technology project, the case for change must be made, and that business case will focus on why change is necessary. When it comes to procure-to-pay, the benefits should prove to be overwhelming, and the case for change will focus on the "what" to do rather than the "why."

The number-one benefit from procure-to-pay automation is simple: It will save money. Automation will allow your organization to better understand how it spends its money and act upon that information to increase compliance to contracts, negotiate better pricing, rein in maverick buying, negotiate and take more discounts, and prevent vendors from overcharging. Elimination of manual processes will speed up the procurement process, eliminating costly manual steps and ensuring that work is not duplicated. Procure-to-pay is the process of how your company spends its money—and automation of procure-to-pay is designed to help you reduce the amount of money that you spend.

There are many aspects to the benefits of automation of P2P. There are financial, technical, audit, operational, and logistical considerations and benefits. When evaluating the reasons to automate procure-to-pay, it is easiest to summarize them into the categories discussed next.

Visibility

Visibility (and accuracy) of information should be one of the key objectives of procurement automation. A well-run company is one in which there is visibility of all financial activity. When reviewing the data in financial systems, an auditor should be asking not only what is in the system, but what is *not* in the system. To ensure accurate financial statements and compliance to audit requirements such as Sarbanes-Oxley, effort must be taken to ensure that all transactions are properly reported.

In a chaotic purchasing environment, many hidden transactions may exist. For example, if purchase orders are issued manually, there is no visibility to commitments that have been made. If there is no three-way matching, such as purchase order (PO) to receiving to invoice, there is no visibility to ensure that the goods have been properly received prior to issuing payment. If invoices are received directly by operations staff and sent for approval before being recorded in the financial software, these likely valid liabilities are not reflected and cash flow decisions are being made based on incomplete data.

Prior to automation, most organizations followed this antiquated and manual practice for paying invoices:

- AP would send vendor invoices directly to the department managers who ordered the products.
- Department managers would then sign invoices.
- Department managers would then send the invoices to AP for payment processing, but not immediately.

The last two steps in the process were typically the biggest bottlenecks. Department managers often held on to invoices—not exactly their highest priority. Aside from forgetfulness, sometimes they purposely delayed signing invoices because they would put them over budget. Many managers submitted them in the next month when their budget numbers had improved.

What was the result of this antiquated process? For the accounting department, financial statements were simply inaccurate, with liabilities understated and a large cash-flow impact coming later. For the AP department, calls would be received from vendors asking for payment for invoices that they did not have, and operational decisions were being made based on incomplete information. Eventually, the invoices would be submitted, negatively impacting profit and cash flow for a future period and creating a backlog in AP. Through automation (document imaging and workflow), organizations are able to eliminate this practice and create visibility to the invoices from the initial point of receipt.

Understanding and Controlling Spend

It's become a cliché to say that "information is power." Yet with information we can better understand our operations and how we spend our money, and then make informed decisions about how to make it better. Without automation, spend information is compiled across multiple systems, obtaining information directly from vendors, and assembled based on general ledger (GL) coding or in many cases just educated guesses. The first step to reducing your costs is to understand what you are buying and what you are paying for it.

When reviewing our own personal finances and determining how to lower our bills, we demand to know the details. It isn't enough to know that we spent $500 this month on utilities; this doesn't tell us what to do to lower those costs next month. We want to know how much we spent on phone, on cable, and on electricity. On a personal level, when reviewing our cable bills, we may want to know what we are paying for extra movie channels. A procurement executive should be able to expect the same level of detail to be available. The devil (and the opportunity) is always in the details.

Using the visibility of information obtained through P2P automation, a procurement leader is able to evaluate vendor and employee compliance to contracts and agreements, and adjust behavior to increase that compliance. Are vendors charging the agreed-upon prices? Are operations personnel buying from vendors for the best price? These questions are vital to understanding where the opportunity is to reduce costs.

Once we know how much we spend on products and how we purchase them today, we can identify where better pricing can be negotiated. We can then take that information to vendors to attempt to negotiate better pricing. When you know what you buy, how much you buy, and what you pay for it today, you are in a much stronger negotiating position.

Audit Controls

Chaotic purchasing environments create significant risk for fraud, which could include vendor fraud or employee fraud. If purchasing is not controlled based on established contracts and pricing, there is opportunity for vendors to influence staff who make purchasing decisions so that their decisions are not necessarily in the best interest of the company. Or worse, an employee could be bribed to accept invoices for higher dollar amounts or for services that were not performed. Procurement fraud almost always involves some type of collusion between an employee and a vendor.

In addition to fraud, incorrect payments can take place due to processor errors or simply not catching vendor errors. Without a process of validating receipts such as three-way matching, a vendor could short-ship a product. Often, vendors duplicate-ship products. As a result, both packages are accepted and paid for, increasing the amount of money spent and the inventory on hand. The three-way matching process is critical to ensure that payments are issued only for goods received, and issued only one time.

Reduce Processing Costs

There have been many studies done of the cost to issue a purchase order. Some of these incorporate the entire requisition-to-check process while others focus on a specific portion of it. Estimates range from $25 to $95, but the actual numbers can be significantly different from one organization to the next. However, all of these studies agree that there is a cost, and that the cost contributes to making the case for procurement automation.

Why is this process so expensive? In a manual environment, a single purchase requires a large number of manual steps involving many different people within the organization. Forms must be filled out, approvals must be obtained, purchase orders must be issued, and receipts must be entered. The invoice must be entered, matched, and a check produced. Each of these steps consumes time—and as each step is automated, costs are reduced.

Reduced processing costs are one of the key drivers of change in procure-to-pay. As organizations grow, they consider alternatives to hiring additional staff in purchasing and AP functions. Centralization of these functions is considered, which can produce even more savings opportunities through efficiencies in volume. Reduction of staff is a tangible form of return on investment (ROI), which can help to get a P2P automation project prioritized.

Procure-to-Pay Leadership

Who is the leader of procure-to-pay within your organization? It is not uncommon for there to be no clear answer. Often payment is considered a financial responsibility, with procurement often decentralized and with purchasing activity occurring at many levels of the organization.

This separation of responsibilities has produced many inconsistencies in the procure-to-pay process and has been a challenge to procure-to-pay automation. Purchasing, operations, and AP departments often have conflicting goals and limited or contentious relationships. The operations department's primary objective is to get the products they want quickly, with minimal paperwork and without concern to cost. The goals of purchasing are to get the product at the lowest price possible. AP's goal is to pay the invoice quickly, avoiding phone calls from the vendors.

When negotiating contracts, purchasing often is going for best price regardless of terms, which may result in negotiating discounts that are hard for AP to achieve or negotiating payment terms incompatible with company cash flow objectives. In decentralized purchasing environments, it is not uncommon for organizations to have multiple contracts with the same vendor, often with different terms and different pricing. With centralized organization and leadership, there may be no awareness of these differences.

As organizations realize the opportunity to improve the procure to-pay process, they increasingly have reassessed the way that the procurement is organized. Establishment of a single corporate procure-to-pay leader or executive has become increasingly common to create and implement a single procurement vision. This is usually done at the beginning of a transition to centralization of procurement and/or AP functions.

However, these new procurement leaders face significant challenges in both understanding the current state and implementing their vision.

Automation Risks and Challenges

Recently, the newly appointed procurement leader of a Fortune 1000 retail company shared his vision of the future state of his procurement organization and discussed the challenges of getting there. Although the retail merchandise spend was being tracked through a merchandising system, the nonmerchandise spend, which represented hundreds of millions of dollars, was not visible. The procurement leader understood the need to gain control over this spend, but the number-one challenge was clear. In an environment where most purchases were completed manually, he simply had no information to be able to truly understand the current environment. In addition, without the data necessary to evaluate the opportunity, it would be complicated to prioritize the project with his executive leadership.

This is unfortunately not an unusual situation. Many P2P leaders struggle with obtaining the budget necessary to automate. In decentralized environments, there is not enough information to truly understand the extent of the problem and use that information to build the case for change.

The following are the most common challenges for organizations that have recognized the need for change in their procurement processes.

Prioritization

When it comes to information technology (IT) projects, budget and time usually are given to the projects that are customer-facing, such as point of sale for retail organizations or patient tracking for health care providers. It is very challenging for back-office functions to gain the attention of leadership for procurement automation. The case must be made for change.

Differing Technologies

Technology is often a significant barrier to automation of procurement functions. In most cases, it is simply the lack of proper technology. Even at organizations with the latest technologies in other areas of their operation, they are still issuing purchase orders manually, or their purchasing is completed on a variety of different systems, often due to legacy software that has remained after a merger or acquisition. While there may be desire to and interest in implementing advanced features such as workflow and EDI, there may still be significant work to be done just to get the enterprise to the same place in use of basic technology for issuing and receiving purchase orders.

Inconsistent Processes

Partially as a result of the differing technologies that may be in use today, often there is wide variation in procurement processes from one facility to the next, creating a significant barrier to procurement automation. If each facility has differing approval limits, or has no approval limits at all, deploying workflow for requisition approval may require that each facility's approval limits be set up and maintained separately, or may require a significant effort to define and deploy systemwide standards. Large organizations often have a shocking variety of practices when it comes to processes such as when a purchase order is required, how to address returns to vendors, from whom products should be purchased, and payment terms on invoices. Deployment of technology is a great opportunity to force standardization of processes, but making those changes with the operations staff can be a barrier to rapid and successful deployment.

Cultural Change

Environments where there are limited controls leave authority to local staff that may have become used to making their own purchasing decisions. Automating and standardizing approval and purchasing processes may restrict the vendors they can buy from and the items purchased, limit their authority, or force them to obtain approvals that they were not obtaining before. In some cases these changes will be welcomed, but in other cases there will be resistance.

Even in highly automated organizations, the system can be bypassed. One of the most common causes of rogue buying (buying outside of established contracts and processes) is the need to procure something quickly—the pressure to buy something fast to meet the needs of a customer or of the internal staff, such as a physician who desires a specific implant from a specific vendor for a surgery.

Decision Paralysis

Another significant challenge is when organizations are unaware of the procure-to-pay automation options available to them. Others are simply overwhelmed by the large number of options that they may consider, many of which have conflicting or overlapping capabilities. This often leads to decision paralysis, with the project being shelved as no clear decision can be made. In most cases, it is better to put in place basic forms of automation than to do nothing at all.

Procurement leaders are challenged to cut through the noise and get their most important question answered: Which of these technologies will help me to run my business better?

Leveraging Your ERP

In many cases, we find that leadership believes that they have automated the procure-to-pay process as part of the implementation of an enterprise system, such as an Enterprise Resource Planning (ERP) software package. These large, complex software packages are designed to address all back-end functions from accounting to human resources to procurement. Executive leadership is aware of a large investment in these packages and considers the work in this area to be done. They may not be aware that the software functionality was not fully implemented, that their ERP may lack certain automation functionality, or that they did not purchase this functionality when it was available. Often we find that procurement automation is not a priority in the ERP implementation, with focus being given to replacing existing functionality rather than implementing new functionality.

The first step to automating procure-to-pay is to ensure that you are using the basic functionality commonly available in an ERP system, such as maintaining an item file, inventory control, issuing purchase orders electronically, receiving, and matching purchase orders to invoices. These functions are a standard part of most ERP systems, yet it is constantly a surprise how many organizations have not implemented these functions, even when they already own the software to do so.

As we explore procure-to-pay automation solutions, it is important to understand the relationship between procure-to-pay automation and ERP software. Many procurement solutions are positioning themselves as an alternative to using ERP for the basic functions related to purchasing and AP. However, an ERP system is the foundation for an organization's back-end data, and there is value in doing as much as possible within the ERP product. Having all the data in one system ensures the ability to view data from one module to the next, tracking every aspect of a transaction from requisition to procurement to payment to general ledger posting, and adding in associated transactions such as returns and reclassifications. When basic procurement functions are performed outside the ERP, often these connections are lost and research becomes more time-consuming.

Why do some organizations ignore the capabilities within their ERP? In many cases, the ERP software is originally purchased because of the bells and whistles, but these functions never get implemented. Due to the large cost and complexity of an ERP implementation (much of which is due to the cultural and process change that often goes with it), the focus on these new functions is lost along the way and the money is spent essentially to replace the functionality that existed before. The fancy new features get forgotten, the new controls are not put in place, and the reporting to take advantage of all the data being collected is never designed.

An executive for a major ERP vendor (the vendor wanted to remain anonymous) recently expressed that "only 30 percent of our customers are leveraging the full procurement capabilities of our software. Many of our customers are not even aware of the extent of features that exist to automate procurement using products they already have or could add onto their system at a minimal cost."

Once we expand beyond the basic procurement functions described and begin to discuss advanced forms of P2P automation, we often move beyond the capabilities provided by the applications of ERP software vendors. While ERP providers offer functions such as workflow, critical functionality such as imaging, data capture, and others discussed in this chapter are often provided through third-party applications.

Generally, organizations should complete their base procurement functions within their financial system of record. What's more, they should put that money and effort budgeted for other software to use on advanced automation technologies.

Technology Overview

Leveraging your ERP system is just the first step of P2P automation. Many other powerful technologies exist that can significantly improve your procurement processes.

There are many technology options, and we do not have the opportunity in this chapter to explore them all in depth. The next section discusses vendor portals, a rapidly developing technology that will be a key part of P2P automation in the coming years.

Other technologies that are commonly used for procurement automation include purchasing cards, advanced data capture, approval workflow, and electronic invoicing. More information about each of these technologies can be found in the supplemental materials on the RPI Consultants web site at www.rpic.com.

Vendor Portals

Another rapidly growing form of procure-to-pay automation has come in the form of vendor portals, web sites that allow a vendor to interact with the purchasing and/or AP department electronically. While still in the early stages, vendor portals are showing significant promise in streamlining communications and improving relationships between organizations and their suppliers.

The term *vendor portal* is used rather broadly and can encompass one or all of the following functions:

- Sourcing
- Vendor information management
- AP self-service
- Purchase order flipping

Sourcing

Sourcing represents one of the most common uses of vendor portals today, though use is primarily within the public sector. Vendors are encouraged to create a log into the portal and indicate the type of products or services they are able to provide. When the company has a need for that product or service, it posts a request for proposal (RFP), which is received by all vendors in that category, and they have the opportunity to respond to the RFP from within the vendor portal.

Portals can create significant flexibility in how RFPs are presented to the vendors and how responses are received. Vendors can be asked to fill out qualifying questions, submit backup documentation electronically, and perhaps upload a spreadsheet of prices that can be easily compared to those offered by other vendors. Reporting can provide comparisons of responses and help with selecting the winner. Using sourcing functionality, procurement departments can identify direct savings opportunities and reduce the labor associated with reviewing RFP responses and ensuring that all registered vendors get an equal opportunity to respond.

Vendor Information Management

Allowing vendors to manage their contact and remittance information represents perhaps the simplest form of a vendor portal, but through its simplicity has proven to be a very effective and easy-to-implement tool. Vendors are able to log into the vendor master file and change their information, such as their address and contact name. Usually the change then needs to be approved by the person responsible for maintaining the vendor master file. This can be an effective way to reduce checks returned because they went to old addresses, as well as reduce labor required to maintain the vendor file.

AP Self-Service

AP self-service refers to allowing a vendor to view information about its invoice status online. In a manual environment, the accounts receivable staff from the vendor has to call the AP department for payment information. This requires time on their part to make the calls and time for the AP customer service staff member to research and resolve the issue. Using a vendor portal, the vendor can view the information on its own, looking up its invoices to see if payment has been issued, and if not, when payment will be issued.

Self-service can significantly reduce the number of phone calls to the AP department, but it is unrealistic to expect it to eliminate them. If a vendor is not able to find information about a particular invoice, perhaps because it has not yet been received in AP, then it will need to call to get information. If an invoice is not paid, the vendor portal must be able to display sufficient information to allow the vendor to resolve the issue; otherwise it will just lead to a phone call or email. Self-service can be particularly troublesome in a cash-poor organization. You can't tell vendors that "the check is in the mail" because if they have self-service, they can see the truth.

Purchase Order Flipping

Purchase order flipping is a growing solution to addressing the high level of invoice-matching discrepancies common in many organizations. The vendor logs into its vendor portal, pulls up an approved purchase order, and flips it, creating an invoice that perfectly matches the items and prices on the purchase order. AP will then review the invoice (likely electronically). The invoice should match without incident, as it is exactly the same as the purchase order that generated it.

Purchase order flipping is still a relatively new use of vendor portals and has proven effective where low levels of discrepancies already exist. Certain industries, such as health care, experience very high rates of invoice matching discrepancies due to discrepancies in contract pricing. In theory the vendor should be billing only in the amount of the purchase order, as that is the legal document requesting the item, and by shipping the item the vendor is effectively accepting that price. In some industries, this purity of a purchase order is ignored. Time will tell if these industries force their vendors to change their practices to get to the point where flipping is the natural course of creating invoices.

Dynamic Discounting

Perhaps the use of vendor portals with the most potential to produce savings is dynamic discounting, though that potential has yet to be proven. It is a common practice for organizations to negotiate prompt payment discounts with their vendors, such as a 2 percent discount if an invoice is paid within 10 days of the invoice issuance. With dynamic discounting, the discount negotiation is made with the vendor on an invoice-by-invoice basis if desired.

Discounts can be negotiated in advance, with sliding discounts based on the specific number of days. Perhaps the 2 percent net 10 discount becomes 2.1 percent if paid in 9, but 1.9 percent if paid in 11 days. Alternatively, the discounts can be fully dynamic, with the vendor having the option to log into their portal, view an invoice waiting for its due date, and offer the carrot of a discount to get that money paid faster than the contracted due date. Therefore a company with a working capital shortage can attempt to quickly cash in its receivables.

Dynamic discounting is still in its infancy, though many P2P professionals anticipate that it will grow rapidly in the next five years. Applicability to your organization may be heavily based on your cash flow being able to support paying vendors faster when discounts are offered, as well as the interest of your vendors in offering the discount in exchange for faster payment.

The basic premise of the vendor portal is simple: to get the vendors to do the work for you. Rather than calling the AP department, vendors can look up the status of invoices themselves. Vendors are able to manage their own addresses and other remittance information, cutting down the time required for AP staff to do this work manually. Reduced work for the AP staff can lead to direct savings. For the MGM Mirage in Las Vegas, implementation of a vendor portal resulted in a reduction of six positions in the AP shared service department.

Vendor portals are still a very new technology. In the IAPP 2008 Membership Benchmarking Survey, only 8 percent of respondents indicated that they are using a form of vendor portal today. Adoption appears to be most common in the public sector, where sourcing functionality is of particular importance. However, this is expected to rapidly change and is a technology that should be considered and tracked closely over the next few years. Solutions are currently offered by a variety of different software providers, and recently several of the ERP vendors have begun to provide vendor portal software as an option.

Summary: Rethinking Procurement

P2P automation can allow your organization to reconsider all aspects of how these functions are completed and how they are staffed. Rather than simply layering technology on top of your current processes, this is an opportunity to start from scratch and design a procurement operation for the future.

In a highly automated procurement environment, all aspects of the operation are paperless. Requisitions are completed online and submitted for approval electronically. Purchase orders are sent electronically to vendors. Invoices are received electronically, or scanned and run through data capture, converting the invoice to electronic data to be loaded into the payables system. Invoices are paid automatically based on established terms or early in order to obtain prompt-payment discounts.

The staff required to maintain the P2P operation will change. Rather than the focus being on entering data off paper to create purchase orders or invoices, staff will analyze information to determine opportunities to negotiate better prices, increase contract compliance, identify bottlenecks in the procurement process, and reduce invoice matching error rates. This new P2P operation may require a different skill set than the one in place today, with a focus on analytical and problem-solving skills over fast typing. However, it will be a staff focused on identifying opportunities to save time and money.

The procurement operation of the future is the procurement department of today for many progressive organizations. The future can be here today for your organization as well.

When considering procurement automation, it is not possible to ignore the compelling value of centralization of procurement and AP functions. A recent study by the Hackett Group found that there has been a 50 percent increase in the use of shared service centers over the past three years. Those that have shared services have been expanding their use, with 82 percent of respondents indicating that they are increasing the number and types of transactions completed from their service centers.

Centralization of procurement and payment functions can be a significant cultural change, but can also be the most rapid way to adopt new automation technologies and obtain the benefits from those technologies.

Shared service centers create true consistency in processes and reduce the risk of staff falling back on the old ways.

There is significant opportunity for procurement leaders prepared to embrace change and new technologies.[1]

Next Steps

The procurement automation solution categories outlined are by no means meant to be a complete list of all of the options that are available. To do so would require a complete book of its own, if not several books, and the options are growing every day.

Regardless of which path is taken to P2P automation, it is important that every company step back and evaluate its current procurement process to determine where improvements can be made, through technology, standardization, or process change. Here are a few suggested steps to begin that process:

- *Create a P2P vision.* It is always a mistake to let the technology dictate the vision. The first step in an automation project should be to determine your vision of the future of P2P at your company. Determine how each function will be performed, if centralization will be a part of the change, and what benefits will be achieved. This P2P vision will be the blueprint for all future automation projects, leading toward the goal of your new P2P operation.
- *Understand your current capabilities and limitations.* Before looking at other technologies, take the time to understand what is available within your organization now. Understand the capabilities of these technologies, but also the limitations. If multiple software providers are in use for the same function, compare the difference and understand the pros and cons of each option. Even if you will likely replace the software, understanding what works and does not work about your current software is the next step to understanding what you need.
- *Determine priorities.* Obtaining the budget to implement your entire vision at once may not be achievable. Determine priorities based on need and the time line to get to your future estate. Perhaps implementing purchasing cards is a higher priority as it has no cost, or perhaps advanced data capture is a priority because your AP department is

---

[1]For additional information on electronic invoicing, advanced data capture, approval workflow, and purchasing cards, please see http://philsimonsystems.com/nwot_extras.html.

short-staffed and you can avoid replacing those positions. Each business is unique, and the priorities will vary.

- *Design and sell the future state.* Once you have selected the areas to focus on, design the future-state processes based on how you want them to perform. Get internal buy-in to the future-state to ensure you have full support. Provide this information to the software vendors, and ask them to demonstrate their software based on your process design.

- *Narrow down technology options.* The technologies related to procure-to-pay automation are varied and are changing all the time. Narrow your choice down to a few options that meet your needs. Many of the software providers are developing new features and functions that may or may not come to fruition, but focus on what they offer today. Look for strong, stable organizations with a proven track record.

PART IV

Management and Deployment

CHAPTER 14

Agile Software Development
Roland Cuellar

It is not the strongest of the species that survive, nor the most intelligent, but the one most responsive to change.

—Charles Darwin

Introduction

Traditional software, using what we commonly refer to as "waterfall" methods, is predicated on stable requirements and clear expectations. With stable requirements that are fully elaborated in some detail and clear expectations of exactly what the system should accomplish, information technology (IT) teams can develop detailed work breakdown structures, estimates, schedules, and work plans. In most cases, with this level of stability, IT teams can get within an acceptable variance of the estimates. In a nutshell, traditional waterfall processes are designed to hit fixed targets. We can put in change control boards and we can try to lock down the requirements in some attempt to keep the target from moving, but the unfortunate reality of modern enterprise systems is that the requirements are not fixed at all.

As technology, regulations, and business environments all change, it is very likely that there will be significant goal and requirements changes over the development time frame. This represents a serious challenge to the ways that most organizations develop software. How do we reconcile the need to accept and even embrace change when the processes that we have put in place are designed around the idea of requirements stability?

Limitations of the Waterfall Method of Software Development

The traditional waterfall cycle of software development (SD) tends to follow this familiar arc:

- Gathering and analysis of requirements (two months)
- System design (two months)
- Software development (four months)
- Testing (two months)

This entire process can take close to a year of substantial effort and spending before organizations realize any business value. In addition, it is highly likely that over this time frame, the business requirements will change. The business should be responding, in real time, to the changing landscape; but most of our SD processes are not designed to deal with that change.

Late changes to requirements—or new ones altogether—typically result in substantial impact to a project. Often, developers must return to the design phase (square one). The challenge for IT is how to meet changing needs and still be fast, precise, and nimble. In other words, IT needs to be agile.

Perhaps the chief limitation of the waterfall method is that it cannot adapt quickly enough to the realities presented by our current economic and regulatory environments. Moreover, it does not foster the kind of team-work, communication, and collaboration that organizations need in order to succeed. Consider the following three groups involved in most SD projects:

1. Business analysts (BAs)
2. Designers and software developers
3. Software testers

Each group has its own line of reporting on the organizational chart. What's more, each throws huge documents and other deliverables over the wall to the other side in arm's-length transactions.

To boot, there is usually no love lost between them. Developers become frustrated when requirements are late, unclear, incomplete, or even wrong. The testers are frustrated because the software is late and full of bugs. For their part, management and the business analysts are frustrated because they continue to pour money into the effort with no incremental payback nor any certainty that the system will even work until it is well into the testing phase, which is a very late time to discover that an application is insufficient. Each side blames the other, and the resulting animosity, schedule slips, and unmet expectations result in yet more governance and controls being put into place. This in turn frustrates everyone even more.

Some have asked if there's a better way to develop software. Fortunately, there is: agile.

Benefits of Agile Methods

Measuring SD effectiveness and efficiency is enormously difficult. Each organization, project, and team is different, so making comparisons is difficult at best. However, patterns are emerging that lead us to believe that agile SD has strong economic and cultural benefits to the organizations that successfully adopt it. Most organizations adopting agile methods have reported software time to market and/or productivity gains of 30 to 40 percent, along with increases in business partner satisfaction and IT employee satisfaction. For example, CapitalOne Financial Corporation reported a 30 to 40 percent hike in productivity in its IT development efforts in a recent *InfoWeek* article.

In *The Business Value of Agile Software Methods*, Dr. David Rico and his co-authors detail the economics of different SD models. They report the following based not only on their study of many organizations, but also on the results of other surveys performed by organizations such as IBM:

> *We found 79 studies with quantitative data on the benefits of Agile methods. They cited an average of 26% improvements in cost, 71% improvements in schedule, and 122% improvements in productivity performance. Quality improvements averaged 75% and customer satisfaction improvements averaged 70%. Over 29 of these studies had the data necessary to estimate an average return on investment of 2,633%.*
>
> *At least 26 of these studies involving over 726 programmers yielded an average productivity of over 21 lines of code per hour. This is roughly 10 to 20 times the productivity rate associated with traditional methods. At least 21 of these studies involving over 323 programmers yielded an average defect density of about 2 defects per thousand lines of code.*
>
> *All of these factors combine to make Agile methods more productive to use than traditional methods. Agile methods result in lower maintenance and total life cycle costs due to greater productivity and efficient defect removal. On average, Agile methods are about 25 times more efficient than traditional methods.*

Any organization can probably take its existing processes and tweak them around the edges and get a 3 to 6 percent improvement. But getting improvements of this magnitude is altogether different and will typically require a fundamentally different process model. For clues as to how and why these improvements are achieved using agile methods, let's explore some other engineering disciplines for alternative ideas on how to attack the problem of SD.

Alternative Engineering Models

Let's discuss several alternative engineering models that illustrate the different problems of SD in new ways. These models suggest alternative process solutions as well:

- Just-in-time (JIT) inventory management
- Cellular manufacturing
- Closed-loop control systems

Consider for a moment these three other engineering disciplines and their successful models. Think about how we might apply this thinking to problems related to SD. These three models provide important clues about how to design a better software engineering model.

This section shows how agile SD methods borrow from process control, work-cell thinking, and lean, pull-based inventory management systems. In the end, agile methods produce a deceptively simple but highly effective SD process.

Just in Time: Borrowing from the Toyota Playbook

Imagine that there were no networks or shared disk storage. This is a world of only individual, unconnected workstations and printers. Requirements would have to be printed out in full by the analysts and walked over to the designers. The designers in turn would create their blueprints, printing out everything to give to the developers. The developers would need a full copy of the requirements on paper along with the blueprints. The developers would write code, printing it out as well. They would then deliver the code to the testers, and so forth down the line.

If this were how we really had to work, then organizations would be drowning in paper or inventory, since everything would have to be moved around so many functional silos. Make no mistake here: SD has inventory and lots of it. This is interesting, because this inventory is electronic and it moves around on our networks—we don't see it. Rest assured, however, it is there, it is huge, and it requires a great deal of financial and physical resources to hold and manage.

Other disciplines such as logistics and manufacturing have very successfully dealt with the problem of inventory management. To that end, the agile community has borrowed very successfully from the Toyota playbook to address issues of intermediate inventory and work in progress as well as their impacts upon cycle time, cost, and quality.

LITTLE'S LAW Many manufacturing firms utilize pull systems and just-in-time methods to reduce inventory and accelerate delivery. A mathematical model called Little's Law is widely understood in inventory management circles. It basically states that the more work in progress that you have going on at any one moment, the longer it will take to deliver a completed product.

This law makes intuitive sense. If I am simultaneously building 100 birdhouses in parallel and it takes me one hour to build each one, then it will take me 100 hours before I produce any completed birdhouses. However, if I build them one at a time, then I can deliver the first birdhouse in one hour. The last birdhouse still doesn't come out until the 100th hour, but delivery of the first birdhouse is greatly accelerated. By reducing my work in progress from 100 birdhouses at a time down to just 1 at a time, I can reduce my delivery time hugely for many of the birdhouses.

PARALLELS TO TRADITIONAL SD So, what does Little's Law have to do with traditional SD? Quite a bit, actually. For example, most SD also takes place in huge parallel batches. The process of gathering and analyzing hundreds of requirements often takes months. After that time, those requirements are turned into design documents. After that point, the coding of the requirements begins. In this large batch model, it often takes anywhere from nine months to a year before anyone sees anything of value. In fact, most of the value is saved for the very end of the development process. Ouch.

Consider the SD equivalent of the manufacturing JIT/pull method. It would entail the following with just one requirement:

- Analyze it.
- Design it.
- Code it.
- Test it.

The entire process might take only one or two weeks if I were working on only one requirement at a time. By reducing the work in progress from all the requirements down to just one or two at a time, the delivery time for those few requirements can be greatly accelerated. Working in this fashion allows for a continuous flow of working software, delivering a few more working requirements every few weeks. As a result, software testing can begin sooner, as can any necessary modifications. What's more, by building the first birdhouse completely before starting the next, developers can learn how to do things better so that the quality of the birdhouses continues to improve.

For now, let's think of it this way: The more requirements we try to do at once, the more slowly the work flows. To get speed, we need to greatly reduce the number of critical requirements addressed concurrently. Just like cars on the highway, the more we have at once, the slower they go. Remove most of the cars from the highway and the remaining ones can fly.

Cellular Manufacturing

Now let's look at the cellular manufacturing model. In a typical mass-production line, each process step is scaled and locally optimized to work on very large batches. A machine might stamp out thousands of parts a day. These parts are then placed on pallets, ready for the next step in the process. This is often locally efficient but globally inefficient. Consider the delivery time problem discussed in the previous section. The intermediate work products flow very slowly from one machine to the next. Finally, the finished product comes out at the end.

To be sure, SD is very different from manufacturing on a number of levels. However, it is absurd that most organizations use SD processes rooted in this mass-production model. Consider the following:

- A requirements machine spits out tons of requirements.
- The requirements are then put on the forklift and taken over to the design machine.
- The design machine spits out huge designs.
- The designs are delivered in bulk to the SD machine.
- The development machine spits out mountains of code.
- The code is forklifted over to testing.

There are three major flaws with this model:

1. Large-batch thinking dominates this way of working, ultimately delaying delivery.
2. Hidden defects and other quality issues typically go undetected until the testing phase.
3. This model tends to create animosity between the different functional silos.

Consider the work-cell model in a manufacturing context. In a work cell, each necessary function is pulled together to create the whole product. Work takes place in small batches. In a manufacturing environment, this might mean putting all sorts of tools around each other so a single part can be completed very quickly by a very small, coordinated team. By bringing the tools together in close proximity, and working in smaller batches, an entire product can be built rather quickly.

Now consider the work-cell model in an SD context. A business analyst, a lead designer, three software developers, and two testers all work very closely together. The analyst elaborates just a few requirements at a time, often with the help of the designer, developers, and testers. The designers, developers, and testers all work together on understanding the one or two requirements at a time. They also agree on how the testing will be done and collaborate on the design. The individuals bring their own special skills to the team, but they all work together to jointly produce a working requirement. In a very short time, the completed requirement is delivered with the benefit of having had input and support from everyone: the business analyst, designer, developer, and tester (see Figure 14.1).

Better communication and the obliteration of the traditional "us versus them" mentality yields enormous benefits, including decreased development time and fewer bugs. Cross-functional teams emerge, each of which is capable of completing specific functionality from beginning to end. In other words, the process creates semiautonomous units able to minimize the number of handoffs required across organizational boundaries.

Thanks to their greater communication and collaboration skills, work-cell teams can move much faster and produce higher-quality products.

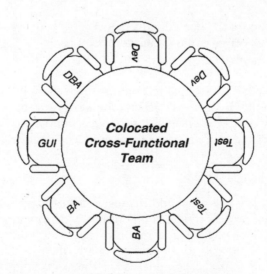

FIGURE 14.1 Cross-Functional and Colocated Development Team

What's more, they can break down organizational silos and begin to actually work together.

Closed-Loop Control Systems

The third model is closed-loop process control. Thermostats, refineries, cruise-control mechanisms, heat-seeking missiles, and lots of other sophisticated devices in our world use this model. By way of background, there are two basic kinds of process control mechanisms: open-loop and closed-loop.

In open-loop control systems, the output signal has no effect on the controlled variable. For example, the operation of a washing machine has the duration of washing and rinsing set in advance. In this case, the control is executed on a purely time-related basis: soak for five minutes, wash for ten minutes, and rinse for five minutes. Note that the actual cleanliness of the clothes is never measured and has no impact on the wash cycles.

Compare this process to that of a thermostat. The temperature is measured and compared against the desired state on a frequent basis. This allows the thermostat to adjust to changing conditions such as warmer and cooler parts of the day. Obviously, feedback loops are essential in closed-loop controllers. A detector measures the output signal of the controlled process, and the difference between the actual measurement and the desired outcome becomes an input back into the process.

Open-loop systems such as the washing machine are relatively simple if the following are known in advance:

- Characteristics of the operating elements.
- Relationships between the inputs and outputs.
- Expected disturbances.

This knowledge is essential to establish both the rules and the schedule that govern the process. As a result, open-loop systems *cannot* tolerate changes, disturbances, or errors. Closed-loop controls are capable of correcting for process disturbance and compensating for errors in the model.

Parallels to Traditional SD

Software development is first and foremost a *process*. The traditional waterfall development process model is unfortunately an open-loop, single-pass process with little or no feedback. In this model, after finishing the requirements phase we proceed to the design phase, then to the development phase, and finally to the testing phase. Each phase is time-controlled for a period of three months, for example. This is kind of like saying that the rinse cycle will go for three minutes. At the end of this single pass, out comes the software. This is the first and pretty much only opportunity to see if it works (e.g., whether it still meets our needs).

Think of the limitations of this model. By this time, team members have spent thousands of hours on these projects. The needs may have changed, even if everyone did what they were supposed to do. (This is hardly a safe assumption.)

Open-loop processes do not present much—if any—opportunity for early feedback, much less correction. To be sure, intermediate documents such as requirements documents or design specs offer at least a foundation on which to build applications. However, those documents cannot possibly determine whether the ultimate product will work or meet the business's needs. Add to this that the product will be actually delivered at some point in the future and that business needs are moving targets. No business sponsor can look at design documents and tell whether the software will function according to plan, be delivered on time, or meet its objectives.

Agile processes, in contrast, are closed-loop systems. They use high degrees of iteration and feedback to converge on the solution. By using the small-batch thinking mentioned earlier, agile processes take only a few requirements at a time and can deliver several working requirements every few weeks. This allows for the building, testing, demonstrating, and integrating of the software to start early and often.

Agile processes provide an enormous amount of feedback-based data that can be used in two important ways. First, feedback can help modify the product and make changes as necessary to requirements. Second, feedback can continuously monitor and correct processes, teamwork, and communications. As a result, agile teams have many opportunities to improve both the product and the process; the basis for these improvements is *not* intermediate documents but actual running code.

Summary of Engineering Models

Agile encompasses the best of all three engineering models. It can use JIT inventory management to expedite the delivery of critical requirements. Agile can utilize the work-cell concept to bring the resources closer together. Finally, it can utilize closed-loop process design to give us feedback early and often.

Agile Process in a Nutshell

So what is this process that utilizes Toyota thinking and closed-loop process control to achieve such remarkable improvements for SD projects? Like all feedback systems, it is deceptively simple looking but very powerful, and it looks like Figure 14.2.

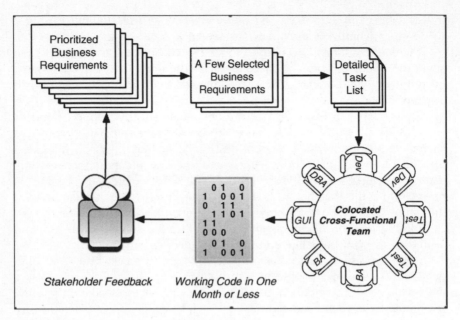

FIGURE 14.2 High-Level Agile Development Process

Consider the following steps before beginning an IT project using agile methods:

- Get a list of high-level business and technical requirements together but do not elaborate them in great detail just yet.
- Prioritize those requirements by business value, risk, or some combination thereof.
- Assemble a cross-functional team including both business and technology, and move them within close proximity to one another (work-cell model).
- Pick a few requirements as a starting point. For those requirements and those only, go to the next level of detail on requirements specification and begin development and testing with a goal of completing them within a month. That's right: The goal is to have working, tested software for these requirements within one month. Remember, the more requirements you start on at once, the slower you will go (small-batch, JIT thinking).
- Break those few business requirements down into all of the detailed tasks needed to complete the functionality, including design tasks, development tasks, testing tasks, documentation tasks, and so on.

- Develop working code for just these few requirements quickly.
- Demonstrate the working software to stakeholders and get feedback in the form of defects and change requests (feedback control).
- Perform a lessons learned exercise with the team to see how process improvements can be made in the next iteration (feedback control).
- Repeat with the next small set of requirements and a slightly improved process.

Within a few months:

- You will have a fair bit of actual working software that has already been developed, tested, and seen by stakeholders.
- You will have a continuous feedback loop working that will allow you to much more accurately measure both progress and correctness.
- You will have a constantly improving process.
- You will have an option for early deployment if there is business value in what has already been created.
- You will have many opportunities to make revisions in the face of changing business needs.
- There will be no surprises at the end since everyone has had many opportunities to see and review the software.
- The highest-priority requirements will be working early.
- You will be agile.

If only it were that easy. Like most organizational process changes, making this work at an enterprise level may be very difficult, depending on the organization's culture, processes, and employees.

The Agile Landscape

There are many agile processes out there, all of which embody these same process design standards: small batches, fast iterations, feedback early and often, continuous process improvement, and integrated teams.

Scrum is probably the most widely used agile method today, although many organizations use extreme programming, feature-driven development, and others. Scrum has reigned supreme perhaps because it can be effective from small five-person projects up to projects involving hundreds of staff on large enterprise programs.

The origins of scrum go back to a 1984 paper in the *Harvard Business Review* titled "The New New Product Development Game" by Hirotaka Takeuchi and Ikujiro Nonaka. The authors surveyed several Japanese product-development firms, such as Canon, Honda, and NEC Corporation, to see how these firms have been so successful in global consumer product development. These firms quickly converged on engineering solutions by utilizing highly nonlinear approaches with cross-functional teams. They also used shorter, more frequent iterations to achieve such amazing results. Many U.S. organizations used very linear, phased approaches. Several notable SD leaders, including Ken Schwaber, Jeff Sutherland, and others, latched onto these ideas, utilizing them very successfully on SD projects. Together, they devised the agile SD process that we now call scrum.

The Benefits of Simplicity

The agile methodology depicted in Figure 14.2 appears simple, almost *too* simple. Remember that for the past two decades most organizations have been following extremely structured SD processes. Highly iterative processes such as agile SD fly in the face of their structured counterparts.

Note that the agile method lacks the traditional phases, phase-gate sign-offs on requirements, and development cutoffs. Agile teams still produce designs and documentation, and they still test. They just do all of those things in a short amount of time for each requirement. Perhaps agile SD's single greatest strength is its development of truly cross-functional teams that collaborate for an extended period of time. Of course, the agile methodology increases the importance of organizations retaining key employees, a topic addressed in Chapter 19.

The Manager's Perspective

Managers are typically charged with producing financially meaningful results and providing transparency, metrics, intermediate work products, and other leading indicators of financial success while simultaneously meeting controls. In many ways, the agile process increases management's ability to achieve its goals.

Deliver Value Early and Often

One of the problems with traditional SD has been the lack of options for early delivery. Projects are either on time (rarely) or late but never early. All of the cost is front-loaded and all of the value is back-loaded. This makes the economics of many IT projects challenging, to say the least. Traditional methods resulted in a very long spending phase with no opportunity for early payback. Agile projects often have the ability to deliver value earlier to the organization.

For example, on some agile projects not fully completed, teams have built enough working software after a few early iterations that there was real business value in what had been accomplished so far. The business and IT were able to deliver some early functionality into production that automated a business process or made some previously unavailable data accessible. By releasing this value early, organizations can reduce time and costs or satisfy customers sooner than with traditional SD.

The implications for IT projects are huge. Agile projects can fund themselves sooner because they generate savings, revenue, or benefits back sooner. This in turn increases stakeholder satisfaction sooner. Follow-on iterations can build out more of the system until such time that it is fully functional. These options for early delivery can yield enormous benefits on project economics such as net present value (NPV), payback period, and so on. Think of agile iterations as financial options that can be exercised via early deployment when conditions warrant.

Visibility and Transparency

Many times, organizations are nearly finished with the requirements phase or the design phase and are theoretically on track. The truth is that, in a single-pass system, it is very difficult to know if the project's schedule is going to hold. To be sure, system design on schedule is unequivocally a good thing. However, that alone does not tell organizations the following:

- Will the code be on schedule?
- Will testing be on schedule?
- Will the product work during integration testing?
- Will the resulting product actually meet the customers' needs?

Few people in the organization can read a complicated IT design document and tell if the resulting system is going to work; surely the business end user is not one of them. This raises the question: How are they supposed to get any meaningful input into whether the system will work and be on time?

Agile solves this problem. By producing actual working software every few weeks and demonstrating that software to stakeholders, managers see a much more accurate view of many things. These include:

- Progress (percent of functionality completed).
- Whether the product will meet expectations.
- Quality.

IT and the business sponsor begin to develop a mutual sense of trust. The business now sees actual working features as the measure of progress. This provides the organization with a much more meaningful measure of the team's progress and risk. Agile SD allows business sponsors to accurately see things before the product's final launch.

Appropriate Controls

The agile process can be a defined, repeatable, auditable process. Many Fortune 500 firms have adopted the agile methodology on a large scale. While different from traditional SD, agile SD is certainly not immune to issues related to Sarbanes-Oxley and internal audit. Most of the common IT governance frameworks do *not* dictate how to achieve control, traceability, and risk mitigation. They typically ask that firms develop processes and controls that will meet the different types of risk. For more on enterprise risk management, see Chapter 15.

Through the controlled usage of agile methods, many organizations have been able to achieve significant benefits and have done so while still passing an audit. To achieve this, organizations need to do the following:

- Design and document a standard internal interpretation of the agile process.
- Clearly define the appropriate deliverables and process artifacts.
- Develop internal audit points for evaluating agile process compliance.

It is important to note that the appropriate deliverables and artifacts necessary to reduce project risk might be very different for an agile process than for a traditional waterfall SD process. These very different processes have different process risks that may need to be mitigated through different controls.

Most organizations using agile SD on a large scale actually maintain two development processes. They have the traditional process with traditional controls used on traditional projects. They maintain a separate agile process with its controls for projects where time to market, close collaboration, and the need for frequent review and feedback can be used advantageously.

Limitations of Agile

Like each of the technologies discussed in this book, agile SD is no silver bullet. What's more, its methods can be used inappropriately, yielding suboptimal results. This next section discusses some of the agile method's limitations.

The Soft Stuff Is the Hard Stuff

Ultimately, delivering new products to market ahead of the competition will not be achieved by processes, tools, or architectures. It will be achieved by people who can tolerate bureaucratic processes, political infighting, and inefficient methods. The vast majority of developers would love to perform at their highest level, if only they could.

Addressing the People Side

Cross-functional and colocated teams do not need many formal processes or much management muscle to get things done. (For more on the challenges of projects spanning different time zones and cultures, see Chapter 17.) Agile means that business and technology constituents improve their intergroup and intragroup communication. In other words, there is no need to go up the ladder, across the org chart, and back down again in order to make something happen. When organized appropriately, the teams are able to truly become self-organizing and empowered teams. (These are buzzwords, but to see it actually work in the way that it was meant is inspiring and liberating.) Animosity across department boundaries drops, and true collaboration rises. Agile team members have described feeling that they are almost like a small, entrepreneurial company in which everybody works together toward short deadlines and does whatever is necessary to deliver the product.

In organizations that have embraced the agile method, IT staff satisfaction and morale have dramatically improved as measured by staff surveys. In addition, business partner satisfaction has also increased significantly, stemming from the following:

- Shorter delivery cycles
- Demonstration of working code (no surprises at the end)
- Much more meaningful communication
- Teams' ability to respond to change

When organizations measure team and business partner satisfaction before and after agile implementations, they often see benefits such as those depicted in Figure 14.3.

Figure 14.3 displays internal team survey results showing substantial increases along a number of parameters, such as communication, teamwork, team empowerment, team performance, planning, quality, and so on, after agile adoption (solid line) compared to before (dashed line).

While this way of working will not suit everyone, most team members respond very positively to working in this manner. One of the key roles of management is to create an environment where people are motivated and

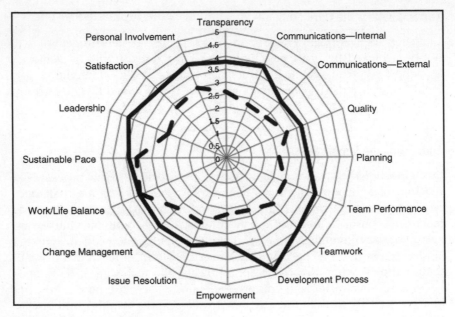

FIGURE 14.3 Actual Team Survey Map

able to perform at the highest levels. This means creating the appropriate team structures, communication mechanisms, interaction models, and measurements. This soft side of management is often the hardest problem to solve.

Agile's emphasis on the team structure and communications—along with its emphasis on actual delivery—resonates with a large percentage of the staff. Energized and motivated people can do almost anything.

Achieving Enterprise Agility

Having seen many successful corporate agile adoptions, and a few failed ones, certain patterns have appeared that give guidance on how to design a successful program.

It's Not a Technology Thing

Too many people in IT management see changes of this nature as "technology things." They start to look at tools, architecture, process maps, and artifacts way too early. In other words, they miss the critical ingredient in managing a successful migration to agile methods: organizational change management. If there is a single predictor of agile process transition success, it is the management team's ability to lead organizational change.

Moving to agile methods requires many people to change how they do their jobs, including developers, testers, architects, product owners, business analysts, and managers. People do not change easily, and getting large groups of people to change is notoriously difficult. Leading the change will require strong people skills surrounding communications, leadership, and motivation.

However, so-called soft skills are necessary but not sufficient conditions for the successful adoption of agile methods. Supporting changes in metrics and expectations are also necessary; only they can drive the changes in appropriate organizational behavior. The biggest challenges in large-scale process change will not come from technology, tools, or architecture. They will come from people.

Transition Road Map

It always concerns me when I talk to a manager who says, "We tried agile and it didn't work. We sent everyone to training and then started them up on a project and it was a failure." This is hardly the way to lead change. Without question, there are several viable ways to lead a successful organizational change to agile methods. Consider the following high-level plan that has worked well in several large firms. The idea is to actually use agile thinking to manage the migration to agile. Organizations should follow these steps:

- Start with a few small pilot projects and provide them with substantial support, including training and mentoring.
- Try to get some early wins and solve some early challenges.
- Gather feedback and make corrective adjustments in the next wave of projects.
- Formalize the process, artifacts, audit points, and training plan.
- Begin the scaling process.

By taking on successively larger and more complex projects, organizations will quickly develop advanced capabilities built on earlier successes and learning. Again, the agile methodology has shown demonstrable results (e.g., double-digit improvements in time to market, quality, and team satisfaction). However, realizing these improvements will not happen overnight. In most large organizations, this transition has taken well over a year and has required significant time and budgetary support from the senior leadership team.

Additional Challenges of Agile

Pure agile methodology emphasizes fungibility of resources, summarized in the mentality that "just about anyone of the team can do just about anything that needs to get done." In the real world, this often is not attainable in a practical sense. Development projects often require specialized work that needs specialized skills, such as database tuning, setting up new network segments, and coding new Web services. These cannot be picked up quickly. What's more, they often require specific system access for production rollout, bug fixes, or database changes that the information security department will not give out indiscriminately, often due to regulatory, compliance, and business continuity reasons.

Senior managers need to decide on budgets for the fiscal year in advance. This means that project scope at a high level must be determined up front. This requires architectural decisions and some high-level design and analysis. Similarly, interdependencies between systems force architects and IT managers to know requirements and system impacts up front and coordinate all of these projects closely, requiring some level of prescriptive project planning (i.e., waterfall).

Agile works best when all of the members of the performing team can work together in the same location. This can conflict with today's more flexible work arrangements and sourcing strategies, such as a mobile workforce, work-from-home arrangements, and a geographically dispersed (i.e., global) workforce. Note that colocation and globalization can peacefully coexist when most of the team is at one particular off-site location.

Having an empowered performing team is a key tenet of any agile methodology. Agile requires individual members to communicate very openly in a group setting and to feel empowered to act proactively and take charge whenever necessary. Some people may find this difficult due to their personalities or backgrounds. Management has to be open to staff taking some risks, learning from mistakes, and adapting. This may not work as well at a company where the company culture is highly risk-averse or heavily top-down in its decision-making process.

There is the temptation to neglect system documentation, making it difficult for team members to review and know about each other's work at a detailed level and for new team members to get up to speed. Then again, this can happen regardless of the methodology if the team is under immense time pressure or the individuals simply lack the discipline or motivation to create/maintain the appropriate documentation.

(*continued*)

Agile teams will often need to interact with waterfall teams, creating interesting project management challenges. For example, when the waterfall team requires a fixed scope to be delivered by the agile team, performers on the agile team must plan proactively and sufficiently in advance to meet the dependency. In another case, the agile team may not have all the information or resources needed to react quickly to a new scope item if the key resource or decision maker has not yet been engaged according to the waterfall project's more prescriptive resourcing plan or if scope/requirements have been locked down within the waterfall project.

Agile methodology tends to work best on small enhancement streams for established systems or where scope can be unitized in small chunks and the business can be flexible about when to expect a given chunk. A classic example is building a web site for marketing and selling products and services. Agile can also be a good fit when the business prefers to see its requirements reflected in a live system ("make it blue—no, red") before making them final. Agile might not be as efficient as traditional project methodologies on large projects in which the scope is well understood and fixed, such as converting a large legacy system to a new (but not bleeding-edge) technology platform (e.g., COBOL to Java) with minimal change to its business functionality.

Ben Lewis is currently an IT compliance manager at a Fortune 500 company in the financial services industry. He has spent nearly five years on agile software development teams in various roles: developer, tech lead, project manager, and agile scrum coach.

Summary

Agile software development is often a misunderstood process. Many feel that it is a lightweight process that is suitable only for non–mission-critical programs. This thinking is simply erroneous. Agile is founded on tried-and-true science and engineering principles, including just-in-time inventory management, closed-loop feedback systems, engineering work cells, queuing theory, and the Toyota Production System. In fact, agile SD has a stronger engineering foundation than traditional methods of SD.

While the process is deceptively simple, the transition to agile methods at the enterprise scale can be difficult for organizations mired in antiquated development methods. The adoption of agile SD will impact many other internal processes, standards, audits, and practices. Finally, let's not forget the people issue, for it is the most difficult change of all.

However, despite the pains of change, organizations that embrace agile SD should see significant benefits.

Next Steps

- Execute several smaller pilot projects that are very well supported by training and have team members who have successfully worked on agile teams in the past. If you do not have any such people in your organization, then get outside help.
- Monitor the teams closely and help to clear the organizational blockages that will almost surely keep them from delivering as fast as they could.
- Learn from these teams. Capture best practices and lessons learned and leverage them on the next round of projects.
- Begin an additional wave of projects with teams that are seeded from the initial teams so that each new team has at least one member who has successfully delivered on one of the previous projects.
- If you are a publicly traded firm, begin to develop the formal agile process complete with process checkpoints, artifacts, expected deliverables, audit points, and so on. Also plan to brief internal and external audit on your new process and its control points.
- Develop broad organizational communications related to the agile program. Address why you are making the change, the benefits to the organization, the challenges, the plan, and so on. Plan on repeating this broad communication at least quarterly in order to keep focus on the goal.
- Develop role-based training programs that include formal instructor-led training, online training, informal brown-bag sessions, and so on so that there will be a variety of channels by which staff can begin learning.
- Develop a cross-functional management team composed of managers from application development, architecture, production operations, business, quality assurance, and so on. This cross-functional management team will be responsible for both clearing the blockages to agile adoption and championing the agile process within the functional area(s).
- Continue to slowly scale out with more projects while always being protective during the early phases of the program. Avoid any spectacular, large-scale, high-cost project failures caused by a lack of oversight, training, or experience. Early failures will give the process a bad name and may cause you to abandon the plan before it really has a chance to succeed, thereby destroying one of the best opportunities currently available for dramatically improving IT performance.

CHAPTER 15

Enterprise Risk Management
Robert N. Charette

Risk is like fire: If controlled it will help you; if uncontrolled it will rise up and destroy you.

—Theodore Roosevelt

The High-Risk Society

British Prime Minister Harold Macmillan was once asked by a reporter what would influence his government's decisions the most.

"Events, dear boy, events," was his answer.

Enterprise managers today no doubt can empathize with Macmillan's answer. What manager today—business or government—doesn't feel that his or her decisions are not being increasingly shaped by events and forces that seem more numerous, more consequential, and more unpredictable in nature than a decade ago? What manager is not being asked to do more with less and in less time? What manager today believes that his or her decisions don't entail more risk today than ten years ago as a result?

In a 2008 IBM study performed before the recent financial troubles really took hold, nearly two-thirds (62 percent) of corporations with revenues over $5 billon reported they had experienced at least one material event in the past three years, and almost half (42 percent) of these same corporations admitted that they were not well prepared for it.[1] Smaller corporations were barely better: Some 46 percent of enterprises with revenues experienced a material event, and 42 percent of those acknowledged that they, too, were not well prepared for it.

---

[1] IBM, "Balancing Risk and Performance with an Integrated Finance Organization," IBM Global CFO Study 2008.

In fact, if we turn the clock back to 1996 when economic conditions were good, Michael Mandel, the economics editor for *BusinessWeek*, was asserting *then* that we were living in what he called the *high-risk society*.[2] To survive, let alone thrive, in such an environment, Mandel claimed that everyone—individuals, organizations, and governments alike—urgently needed to develop a keen ability to manage the risks associated with the rewards created.

If we fast-forward from 1996 to today, what are some of the events we have experienced? In no particular order, we have seen:

- The explosion of the Internet.
- A dot-com boom and bust.
- Major corporate accounting scandals such as Enron and Tyco.
- The institutionalism of terrorism.
- Major wars in Iraq and Afghanistan.
- Natural disasters such as Hurricane Katrina and a killer tsunami in the Indian Ocean.
- A global financial meltdown.
- A global flu pandemic.

Against this backdrop, the globalization of competition, government deregulation of industries, the streamlining of business processes, and improvements in technology to which Mandel referred have intensified the development of the high-risk society.

Management professor Gary Hamel (with Liisa Valikangas) wrote a few years ago in a *Harvard Business Review* paper, "The Quest for Resilience," that the world is becoming more chaotic than the majority of organizations have the ability to adapt.[3] Evidence of Hamel's observation of increasing chaos is abundant. For instance, consider 11 great organizations—ones that by their discipline were able to sustain improved performance—that best-selling author Jim Collins listed in his 2001 book *Good to Great*.[4] In less than eight years:

- One has gone bankrupt (Circuit City).
- Another (Fannie Mae) has been taken over by the government.
- A third (Wells Fargo) received a $25 billion financial bailout from the government.

---

[2]Michael Mandel, *The High-Risk Society* (New York: Random House, 1996).
[3]Gary Hamel and Liisa Valikangas, "The Quest for Resilience," *Harvard Business Review*, September 2003, 52–63.
[4]Jim Collins, *Good to Great: Why Some Companies Make the Leap ... and Others Don't* (New York: HarperBusiness, 2001).

Collins has even had to write a new book, *How the Mighty Fall*, to try to explain why; in part he blames organizational "denial of risk and peril."[5] (Note that Chapter 3 explains organization and information technology [IT] departments within the context of Collins's model.)

An Ernst & Young report called "Board Members on Risk," conducted during the economic boom time of 2006 found that some 72 percent of company board members said risk had increased from the previous two years, with 41 percent saying it had increased significantly.[6]

And if one looks at the 20 largest public company bankruptcy filings from 1980 to the present time, 17 have happened since 2001, and 8 of those have happened in just the past two years alone.[7]

We could easily retitle Mandel's book today *The Higher-Risk Society*.

Information Technology and the High-Risk Society

Information systems and associated technologies have been major contributors to both the creation of the societal abundance to which Mandel refers, as well as its turmoil. Consider the example of Apple's iPod. Introduced in 2001 in combination with Apple's online iTunes store launched in 2003, the product and service offering together have massively disrupted the business model of the music industry. Apple's iPhone, introduced in 2007, has done the same to major players—both manufacturers and service providers—in the wireless communications industry.

Yes, Apple's ability to create massive industry disruption and generate tens of billions of dollars in revenue doing so (about $9 billion in iPod sales alone in 2008, e.g.) was due not only to savvy corporate strategy, product design, and marketing. These alone would not have resulted in the organization's amazing recent success. Information technology *allowed* Apple to implement its strategy in an inexpensive fashion. For instance, the Internet allowed Apple's iTunes online store to be feasible as well as to flourish; without the Internet, it is highly doubtful that Apple would have had the leverage to impose its two-pronged product and service strategy on the music industry.

When Mandel wrote his book in 1996, there were about 35 million users of the Internet. When Apple introduced the iTunes store in 2003, that figure

---

[5]Jim Collins, *How the Mighty Fall* (New York: HarperCollins, 2009).
[6]Ernst & Young, "Board Members on Risk," 2006.
[7]Source: BankruptcyData.com, New Generation Research, Inc., Boston, MA, www.bankruptcydata.com/Research/Largest_Overall_All-Time.pdf, accessed August 2009.

had grown to some 600 million.[8] Today, the Internet is estimated to have some 1.6 billion users—nearly a quarter of the world's population.

Information technology has radically changed the risk-reward ratios for innovation in the past decade. As pointed out by MIT researchers Erik Brynjolfsson and Michael Schrage in a 2009 *Wall Street Journal* article, "The New, Faster Face of Innovation," information technology allows innovation initiatives that used to take months or years to be developed and tested in weeks or even days, and at the fraction of the cost.[9]

But no technology is risk-free, either.

For instance, the growth of the Internet has also meant new IT security and privacy risks for both businesses and governments. If not managed quickly and well, these can quickly create massive reputational and financial problems.

To get a sense for the magnitude of the IT security issue today, in 2008 there were 90 confirmed security breaches resulting in some 285 million compromised records worldwide, according to a 2009 Verizon Corporation report.[10] Automation increasingly provides greater opportunity to organizations, but at a risk that is rising as well.

Additional Risks Stemming from IT Mismanagement

While IT security and privacy issues may garner headlines, poorly developed IT systems usually more consequentially affect an organization's bottom line and incense company shareholders. For instance, the giant British food retailer J Sainsbury PLC in October 2004 had to write off its $526 million investment in an outsourced automated supply-chain management system, causing it to post its first loss in 135 years. System disruptions caused merchandise to become stuck in depots and warehouses, resulting in a large number of Sainsbury's 460 stores having inadequate or incorrect stock. As a result, Sainsbury had to revert to manual stock-control procedures, requiring some 3,000 additional stock persons to be hired.[11]

It took Sainsbury over six months to gain control of its supply chain again. Sainsbury ended up canceling its outsourcing contract and bringing its IT development and operations back in-house at an additional cost of nearly $300 million. What's more, it took five years before the company

---

[8]Source: Internet World Statistics, www.internetworldstats.com/emarketing.htm, accessed August 2009.
[9]Erik Brynjolfsson and Michael Schrage, "The New, Faster Face of Innovation," *Wall Street Journal*, August 17, 2009, R3.
[10]*2009 Data Breach Investigations Report*, VerizonBusiness, 2009.
[11]Robert Charette, "While Software Fails," *IEEE Spectrum*, September 2005, 42–49.

felt financially and technically secure to undertake the task of completely updating its supply-chain IT systems once more.

While corporate IT foul-ups may affect shareholders' wallets, when a government organization experiences IT problems, they can directly affect the health and welfare of citizens. As shown in Chapter 1, worries over ensuring the security and privacy of patient records have slowed government efforts to create national electronic health record systems in Australia, the United Kingdom, the United States, and other countries.[12] IT security problems in government and private industry are so prevalent and the threats posed to the United States so great that President Barack Obama in May 2009 declared the threat a national security issue.

Volatility, uncertainty, complexity, change, chaos, risk, opportunity—these are the characteristics of the risk spectrum organizations now face, and the primary driver behind enterprise risk management.

Enterprise Risk Management Overview

Enterprise risk management (ERM) is a relatively new discipline, although the ideas behind it have been evolving for the past 30 years. A generic definition of ERM is that it is the disciplined assessment and management of the entirety of an organization's risk spectrum in a continuous, holistic fashion. This is in contrast to the more traditional practice of corporate risk management, which focuses primarily on periodic assessment of two specific risk areas:

1. *Insurable risk.* Risks that are hazards or threats (pure risks) to the corporation that are typically covered by insurance.
2. *Financial risk.* Risks that are created by approaches to the allocation of corporate resources and managing its finances.

Since the late 1980s, a small number of organizations, including the avionics company Rockwell Collins, energy organizations Hydro One and Pacific Gas & Electric (PG&E), the retailer Tesco and food company Danone, the conglomerate Koch Industries, and British American Tobacco, steadily realized not only that managing financial and insurance risks separately and periodically was inefficient but also that many other types of corporate risk were falling through the cracks.

Operational risks—those risks that are created by an organization's dependence on its systems, processes, and staff—were causing measurable losses of shareholder value in corporations, yet organizations were not

---

[12]Robert Charette, "Dying for Data," *IEEE Spectrum*, October 2006, 22–27.

actively managing them. The same was true of cross-business unit risks or gray-space risks where actions taken by one business unit negatively affect another.

Similarly, strategic risks—those risks that can cause a corporation to stagnate or collapse because of a failure to adapt to a changing environment—were also not being managed in any formal manner, or at least not in relation to other organizational risks.

Studies such as one by the Mercer Consulting Group in the late 1990s began indicating that strategic and operational risks together were accounting for nearly 90 percent of significant drops in share price. Gradually, corporations started to realize that they needed a more comprehensive and integrated approach to managing *enterprise* risk—not one focused mainly on insurable and financial risks.[13] The dot-com bubble's implosion and the 9/11 terrorist attack reinforced this notion.[14]

ERM and IT

ERM and IT are closely intertwined for two reasons. First, as mentioned at the beginning of this chapter, IT is a major source of enterprise risk as well as opportunity. Second, IT is needed to support the implementation of ERM. It is virtually impossible to introduce and implement ERM in any organization of size without automation support. Organizations like Thomson Reuters, SAP, Oracle, SAS, IBM, Strategic Thought, and some 400 others claim to provide software support tools that cover all or some aspect of ERM, along with corporate compliance and/or governance.[15] Readers interested in ERM platforms can access periodic assessments by research organizations such as the Gartner Group and Forrester Research, Inc. Forrester, for example, publishes a fee-based quarterly review of enterprise governance, risk, and compliance (GRC) platforms.

IT projects generally fall into the operational risk category, although these risks cross into the strategic and financial domains, as most business risks do. For instance, an IT project can easily fall into the strategic risk category because IT is used as a means for organizations to implement their

---

[13] *Enterprise Risk Management: Implementing New Solutions* (Economist Intelligence Unit, 2001), 8. The aforementioned 2008 IBM study found roughly the same percentage, as did a 2005 Corporate Executive Board study titled "Organizing for Risk Management: Key Decisions Guiding Risk Management Activities."

[14] Two major ERM frameworks currently exist: ISO 31000 and the *COSO Enterprise Risk Management—Integrated Framework*. For more on these, please see http://philsimonsystems.com/nwot_extras.html.

[15] Chartis Research, "Chartis-RiskTech 100 Rankings—2008," 2008.

strategies. Similarly, IT project failure, either in the project's development or during operations, can fall into the financial risk category as well. The earlier Sainsbury automated supply chain management system example was an IT project that crossed into all three risk categories. For more on project failures, see Chapter 18.

Implications for ERM

Sainsbury is not alone in failing with an ambitious IT project. Estimates made about IT project failure rates range from the very conservative 15 percent[16] to over 60 percent.[17] This factor alone shows the necessity to address IT risk in a systemic fashion and for IT project risk management to be integrated into an organization's ERM processes.

Indeed, a 2007 survey of C-level executives indicated that information systems and security ranked fourth on the list of top ten risks agenda items.[18] Another survey taken in 2007 and covering the United Kingdom and Ireland found that the top six IT risks as perceived by senior corporate managers and internal auditors, ranked by their order of importance, were:[19]

- The failure of IT project developments to deliver benefits or stay within budgets.
- Operational systems being insufficiently resilient.
- Lack of alignment of IT investments and business strategy.
- Inadequate data security and privacy.
- Inadequate updating or upgrading of operational IT systems.
- Poor data quality.

These two surveys show that IT project risk management must also be performed continuously. It should start with concept formulation to IT system retirement and include contingency management plans for the inevitable problems that IT systems face.

Adequately maintaining existing IT systems is an area of growing concern. A decade ago, IT maintenance was concerned most about what new features would be added to an existing system or perhaps what needed to be included in a major upgrade.

---

[16]Robert Charette, "While Software Fails," *IEEE Spectrum*, September 2005, 42–49.
[17]http://advice.cio.com/remi/two_reasons_why_it_projects_continue_to_fail.
[18]Protiviti, "2007 US Risk Barometer," 2007.
[19]Institute of Internal Auditors (UK and Ireland), "IT Risk—Closing the Gap," 2007.

Now IT maintenance includes not only those items, but also the following:

- Managing patches—security and bug fixes—from third-party software vendors.
- Operational integrity as IT systems become increasingly integrated not only internally within a company but often with a supplier's IT system.
- Operational resilience as corporate IT systems become globally disbursed and/or outsourced.
- Ensuring licensing agreements with third-party vendors are up to date.

Tying IT maintenance risk management into ERM is vital. Unfortunately, organizations are doing little in this regard in practice, even though IT maintenance consumes about 70 percent of every IT dollar.[20]

IT security has become a major enterprise risk issue for many corporate boards, as well as for senior government managers, as we have mentioned. In addition, the recent phenomenon of social media sites like Twitter and Facebook are presenting new challenges to enterprise managers. Exactly what is appropriate information for employees to disclose on Twitter, Facebook, or blog pages? These are thorny questions without clear answers.

Even email, the Web's first killer app, continues to be a concern. A survey taken in 2009 reportedly found that corporations are so worried about sensitive organizational information being leaked that 38 percent of them have employees on their payroll to monitor communications.[21] If the wrong corporation information is leaked, an operational risk can quickly turn into a strategic, reputational, and possibly financial risk for an organization.

ERM, Innovation, and Entrepreneurship

While we have focused on ERM and the management of risk, ERM is also meant to improve organizational innovation and risk taking.

To be sure, the emerging technologies in this book promise interesting business possibilities to corporations and governments alike. From an ERM perspective, the trick will be whether organizations can manage the spectrum of strategic, operational, financial, and possibly insurable risks that come along with them. It is doubtful that any of the new technologies described in this book will not impact one or more of these risk categories to some degree.

---

[20]Robert Charette et al., "Managing Risk in Software Maintenance," *IEEE Software*, May 1997, 43–50.
[21]ProofPoint, "Outbound Email and Data Loss Prevention in Today's Enterprise," 2009.

For several reasons, ERM enhances innovation. First, good ERM allows an organization to avoid outsized risks that others take as well as to take risks others won't or can't.

Second, ERM increases organizational trust. To be innovative means to challenge the status quo. It is difficult for an organization to foster an innovation if it cannot openly and honestly discuss the risks to its current course and speed or its current cash cows.

Third, all profit ultimately stems from (reducing) risk. In other words, profit is payment for risk taking and/or problem solving.

It is an obvious but often forgotten fact that business transactions are really an exchange of goods or services that reduce a customer's risk. For example, customers typically buy from your company because it provides a product or service at a lower risk than your customers could provide the same product or services themselves. If the customers could manage the risk themselves, they wouldn't need to buy anything from your company.

The customer also buys from your company instead of the Acme Company because you are better at reducing the customer's risk than Acme (or again, the customer) is able to do so.

Profit is the money paid for your company to take on risks that your customers do not want to—or cannot—take on their own. Alternatively, innovation is, at its core, risk reduction; it is the allocation of resources from areas of low return to those of higher return.

It is this constant search for better ways to manage risk that drives innovation—and business opportunities. ERM can help organizations become more risk entrepreneurial, that is, see the management of risk as a competitive weapon.[22]

Who Owns ERM?

Ultimately, a corporate board owns ERM since it has a duty to ensure that not too much risk is taken given opportunities pursued on the behalf of the shareholders. While the board sets the risk-reward tenor and policies for the corporation, the day-to-day ownership responsibility of ERM in organizations usually rests primarily with the chief financial officer (CFO), although some chief executive officers (CEOs) and chief technology officers also are tasked with the responsibility.

In other organizations, the responsibility for ERM rests with the internal audit or risk oversight committees. These oversight committees typically have representatives from the financial, insurance, and planning

---

[22]Robert Charette, "The Competitive Edge of Risk Entrepreneurs," *IT Pro*, July/August 1999, 69–73.

departments who work with different project/product-line managers to examine the risks and opportunities confronting the lines of business (LOBs). The committee then helps the individual units reduce their risks or provides investment or other support for their opportunities.

Some organizations, especially those in the financial industry, have created the organizational position of chief risk officer (CRO), who has the responsibility for implementing and overseeing the ERM process. In these organizations, CROs typically report to the CEO or the CFO and manage the risk oversight committees.

The purpose of the CRO is to provide a focal point for all the risk management efforts and provide the coordination needed to produce a comprehensive view of an enterprise's risks and opportunities. The three general areas of responsibility for the CRO are:

1. Perform enterprise-wide systemic analysis and management.
2. Develop risk/opportunity management policies and procedures.
3. Develop the necessary support elements required to implement ERM across the enterprise.

The CRO also will work with the corporate board, CEO, and CFO to define the risk appetite and/or tolerance for the enterprise as a whole, as well as for the different business units.

The CRO works closely with his or her counterparts in the financial, marketing, planning, and other corporate departments. The main objective is to ensure that the risk-related information required by executive-level decision makers, usually in terms of a corporate risk profile, is provided in a timely fashion. This includes information in situations in which a major crisis hits the enterprise and executives are required to address the public about the situation.

Along with the enterprise CRO, many organizations have business unit or regional CROs who gather and then report a local risk profile up to the enterprise CRO. But even regional CROs depend on getting access to local risk information. As a result, although it sounds trite, everyone in a company is ultimately responsible for ERM, if only to provide the state of risk on their projects.

Chief information officers (CIOs) are now becoming more involved in the ERM process, generally for three reasons. The first, especially for CIOs of public organizations, is Sarbanes-Oxley (SOX). The need to ensure that there are adequate internal controls on a corporation's IT financial systems have placed the CIO on that hot seat.

The second reason, as we have outlined throughout this chapter, is the importance of IT to an organization's health and welfare. The CIO is frequently the most important operational risk manager in corporations.

The final reason is that the CIO is also an important strategic risk management player. Who else has the responsibility for ensuring that business strategy and IT are in fact in alignment?

Who Is Doing ERM?

According to different surveys, about half of organizations today have some formal ERM functions in place, although probably only half of those can actually be said to actually manage risk in an integrated fashion across the enterprise. The 2005 Open Compliance & Ethics Group (OCEG) benchmark on ERM maturity notes that only 15 percent of organizations claim to have a highly integrated approach to managing enterprise risk.[23] My own survey of formal ERM practice for the Cutter Consortium placed it at 30 percent in 2006.[24]

ERM is also taking hold more in government, especially in Australia, Canada, and the United Kingdom. Lately, the United States has also begun to embrace a more government-wide view of risk management. ERM in government, however, is often more difficult than in the private sector because the stakes are usually higher; there are more stakeholders involved in decisions and more people can second-guess those decisions. What's more, the success of a decision isn't easily measured in something like revenue or profit, but more in terms of "value for money," where value is based on some political equation.[25]

ERM typically takes several years to roll out across a company or government organization. However, there are few examples where publicly available lessons learned information is available to look at how it was successfully accomplished. One company that was an early adopter of ERM and is seen as an ERM role model is the avionics company Rockwell Collins. I was intimately involved in this effort. With colleagues from Collins, I have written extensively about it.[26]

---

[23]Open Compliance & Ethics Group, "2007 OCEG GRC Strategy Study," 2007.

[24]Robert Charette, "State of Risk Management Practice—2006 (Parts I and II)," *Cutter Consortium*, 2006.

[25]For more information, see Robert Charette, "On the Lookout," *Government Executive*, March 2009, 28–34.

[26]Robert Charette et al., "Profiting from Risk: A Transformation of One Company's Risk Culture," *Cutter Consortium*, December 2004. This section is based on this report. I have also written several other articles on aspects on ERM at Rockwell Collins in other publications, such as "The Fruits of Frustration," *BI Review*, November 29, 2006. An article in the December 2004 issue of *CIO Magazine* by Scott Berinato called "Risk's Rewards" also has some useful information about ERM at Collins.

Case Study: Rockwell Collins

Collins began its ERM practice in the early 1990s at the behest of Jack Cosgrove, the company CEO. At the time, rapid hardware-to-software changes occurring in the avionics industry were creating new technical and management risks quite unlike the old ones present across the spectrum of Collins's business operations. The organization's senior management realized that if they didn't start dealing with these emerging risks while the company was still successful, Collins's long-term future might be in doubt.

Collins embarked on a multiyear program to increase its ability to assess and manage risk across the full spectrum of its operations. For instance, more than 3,000 managers and technical people were trained in risk management. As risk management has become institutionalized at Collins, the company has found that it could take on larger and more risky projects with a high degree of confidence. For example, much of its government business is based on offering firm fixed-price contracts—something that most organizations shy away from, especially when it comes to software-intensive systems development.

Collins also trained the suppliers in its supply chain about risk management, realizing that it was at risk if its suppliers did not manage their own risks effectively. Risks that turned into major problems with its supply chain have caused major reputational, financial, and technological difficulties for Boeing in the development of its new 787 Dreamliner aircraft.[27]

Collins took an ERM approach to its consolidation of its many financial and ERP systems into one. This was done not only to save money but to give senior management a consolidated view of its financial risks. Collins is one of the few organizations that experienced virtually no major problems when it turned on its new ERP system. The CIO attributed this to the organization's disciplined ERM approach, attitudes, and philosophy. The company makes it a point to recognize the risks and problems involved with any effort, never to hide them, and not to force certainty onto uncertain situations.

When 9/11 hit, Collins lost nearly 20 percent of its projected revenue in the two weeks that followed, as airlines and airline manufacturers canceled contracts. And even more contract cancellations appeared on

(continued)

---

[27]Joseph Weber, "Boeing to Rein in Dreamliner Outsourcing," *BusinessWeek*, January 16, 2009.

the horizon. From a business perspective, 9/11 couldn't have happened at a worse time, because the company had just gone public.

However, Collins's management was able to assess the impact of this radically changed business environment extremely quickly—within fewer than ten days—and take the necessary steps to assure its shareholders that the company could survive. A major reason for the corporation's ability to move so quickly and decisively was the availability of its ERP system, which allowed senior management to understand the full ramifications of the financial impact of the events unfolding. While Collins was forced to lay off employees, the company worked hard to find new markets for its products, all the while looking for ways to increase operational efficiency.

Not only has Rockwell Collins's ERM helped it survive; it has prospered. In 2004 and 2006, *Forbes* magazine named Collins one of the best-managed organizations in the United States. The current CEO, Clay Jones, says that the organization's ability to manage risk is a corporate competitive advantage.

The Limits of ERM

ERM has helped organizations manage their risks better, as well as become more innovative. However, it is no panacea. All one needs to do is look at ERM practices on Wall Street to see that. There, instead of reining in excessive risk taking, ERM helped fueled it.[28] CROs who spoke up about the risks were seen as "wanting to take the punchbowl at the party away." Many times, they were fired for their effort.

Conversely, ERM has also been blamed for making organizations and government organizations too timid.[29] Even former UK Prime Minister Tony Blair, a strong supporter of government-wide approaches to managing risk, began to feel a few years ago that British government and UK society in general had possibly begun to be too risk-averse, which was inhibiting the risk taking needed for economic growth.[30]

---

[28]Joe Nocera, "Risk Mismanagement," *New York Times*, January 2, 2009.
[29]See Benjamin Hunt's *The Timid Corporation: Why Business Is Terrified of Taking Risk* (Hoboken, NJ: John Wiley & Sons, 2003), as well as Michael Power's *The Risk Management of Everything: Rethinking the Politics of Uncertainty* (London: Demos, 2004), see www.demos.co.uk/files/riskmanagementofeverything.pdf.
[30]Tony Blair, "The Compensation Culture," speech at the University College, London, May 26, 2005.

It is useful to remember that ERM will not make the current environment any friendlier, nor automatically turn a bad situation into a good one. ERM will not guarantee success; sometimes good decisions and good risk management result in bad outcomes. It doesn't provide facts where there are none, turn uncertain information into certain information, nor ensure perceived risks are real ones.

ERM, in my view, also requires encouragement to actually take hold in most organizations. Normally this takes place in the form of a material risk (or two) that serves as a major embarrassment to the organization. Very few corporations start ERM initiatives of their own volition because they think ERM is a good idea.

Summary

This chapter has presented a short overview of ERM and its core components. There are a number of books on the subject that a can provide significantly more detailed information.[31]

ERM is a disciplined, systems-oriented approach that identifies and manages risks—and decisions about risk—across the enterprise in a unified way. Its primary purpose is to improve decision making throughout the enterprise. Paraphrasing the late economic historian Peter Bernstein, author of the classic book *Against the Gods: The Remarkable Story of Risk*, ERM is meant to protect the organization from undesirable and unexpected decisions of others, and in so doing, make better decisions than they can.[32]

Change generates choices that, in turn, create risk and opportunity. Tomorrow's business environment is not likely to become any friendlier or less complex than today's. ERM is now starting to be seen as mere table stakes of good corporate governance and management practice by corporate credit rating organizations and increasingly by government regulators as well. Studies are showing that organizations with robust ERM are outperforming those without it. This most of all will increase the slow but steady pressure already building on corporations to at least begin to look at it implementing ERM.

---

[31]See, for instance: "Enterprise Risk Management: Implementing New Solutions" (Economist Intelligence Unit, 2001); Thomas Barton et al., *Making Enterprise Risk Management Pay Off: How Leading Companies Implement Risk Management* (London: Financial Times Press, 2002); James Lam, *Enterprise Risk Management: From Incentives to Controls* (Hoboken, NJ: John Wiley & Sons, 2003); Michel Crouhy et al., *The Essentials of Risk Management* (New York: McGraw-Hill, 2005); Bridget Hutter and Michael Power, *Organizational Encounters with Risk* (London: Cambridge University Press, 2005).

[32]Peter Bernstein, *Against the Gods: The Remarkable Story of Risk* (New York: John Wiley & Sons, 1996).

As W. Edwards Deming once famously said, "Change is not necessary. Survival is optional."

For those wishing to survive, changing to embrace ERM is likely to become a necessity.[33]

Next Steps: Are You Ready for ERM?

We conclude this chapter with seven questions that you can ask yourself to see whether your organization should think about taking on ERM. In conjunction with these, you may wish to consult the Canadian Institute of Chartered Accountants booklet, "20 Questions Directors Should Ask about Risk," which was developed to help company directors assure themselves that risk has been fully considered in the strategic and business planning processes.[34]

Does My Organization Need ERM?

Is your organization regularly surprised by a material event, or does it encounter a predictable material event but is unprepared to handle it? Are there corporate problems that in retrospect could have been reduced in consequences or even eliminated early on, but no one spoke up about them? Are opportunities slipping away because your organization can't manage the spectrum of risks associated with them or, worse, the vast majority of organizational resources are allocated to fighting problems, thereby leaving few to pursue opportunities?

If the answer to any of these is yes, you should consider ERM.

How Will I Know If the Organization Is Ready for ERM?

As mentioned earlier, most organizations need two of what can be called near-death experiences; that is, some events—call them corporate heart attacks—that cause a fundamental rethinking of the organization's current management decision making.

Why two? The first usually only serves to capture the organization's attention; the second tends to keep it.

Machiavelli once said, "Never waste the opportunities offered by a good crisis," and for implementing ERM, this is typically a rule to follow.

---

[33]For additional information on ERM Frameworks, please see http://philsimonsystems.com/nwot_extras.html.
[34]Hugh Lindsay, "20 Questions Directors Should Ask about Risk," Canadian Institute of Chartered Accountants, 2003.

Where Does ERM Start?

Every organization is going to be different, of course, but if you don't want to wait for some surprising material event to appear to convince management that there is a need to manage risk better, then I would suggest taking a look at a strategic opportunity that is being pursued. It is hard to argue that, given the stakes involved, risks on these projects shouldn't be managed extra aggressively.

Large IT projects are perfect candidates since they cross strategic, operational, and financial risk management domains; their size and importance guarantee senior management's attention; the risks are big, as are the likely benefits; and so on.[35] If you have a good IT project risk management process in place already, you can start to leverage that into something that can be used for the enterprise. The ISO/IEEE standard 16085 on systems and software engineering risk management was purposely designed to build a foundation to support ERM from an IT project risk management base.[36]

In the Rockwell Collins case, the implementation of its ERP system showcased to the rest of the organization the effectiveness of the ERM process that had been put into place inside the company. It also solidified an attitude within the company along the lines of "Why would you ever try to do something like this without an enterprise-wide risk management approach?"

In other words, performing ERM became a mark of a professional inside the company.

Another way to implement ERM is to build on the financial compliance efforts that already exist. Many organizations have gone to the Committee of Sponsoring Organizations (COSO) ERM framework because it is relatively straightforward to extend the basic internal control processes to encompass ERM activities.[37] You must, however, be careful not to let it just turn ERM into yet another accounting or audit exercise.

The most successful ERM initiatives, like all successful change process initiatives, try to start in a single business unit, division, and group, and then work out to the rest of the enterprise. The same is true for a government agency and department. ERM is a change management process like any other, and possesses the same requirements and obstacles.

---

[35]Robert Charette, "Large-Scale Project Management Is Risk Management," *IEEE Software*, July 1996, 110–117.
[36]ISO/IEEE standard 16085:2006. "Systems and Software Engineering: Life Cycle Processes; Risk Management," 2006.
[37]COSO, "Enterprise Risk Management—Integrated Framework," 2004.

What Is Needed to Implement ERM?

To implement ERM efficiently and effectively is going to require at the very least some sort of automated support to gather up, analyze, and report the risk information throughout the enterprise. But before selecting an ERM tool, an organization needs to think through what one can call "the three ERM Ps and a B": principles, process, performance, and behavior.

In other words, what enterprise risk management principles should people in the organization follow? At Rockwell Collins, for example, one principle is "no surprises." All aspects of a business opportunity—the good and the bad—are expected to be communicated to all relevant decision makers. Holding back information is not a good way to get ahead in the company. "Communicate all risks" is another principle that is expected— indeed is an obligation—to be followed.

Another principle is that "risk and reward must be commensurate," and it is codified in the question, "Does this activity still make business sense?" This question is asked at every Rockwell Collins program and project review. This keeps people in the organization focused on the fact that what they are doing must create benefits for the organization and company shareholders proportionate with resources allocated and the risks being taken.

Principles are important because they give everyday guidance to people in the organization when faced with questions involving risk.

Process deals with the enterprise risk management process to be used, along with the policies, organization structure, and personnel resources need to support it. Do you want a CRO? Or should the CFO handle ERM? Does the process need to be internationally standard compliant (e.g., with ISO 31000)?[38] How will it play into your current management processes, like budget setting and reviews? Who is responsible and accountable for mitigating risks if they are identified? Who sets the risk appetite and tolerance levels of the organization, and how are these translated into something decision makers at the operational level can understand? How are risks to be communicated and to whom (i.e., what are the risk information needs of the organization)?

Performance involves defining what organization, project, and personal success (or failure) mean. If you can't tell me what success or failure mean, managing risk is meaningless. IT projects that should be canceled often are left to drift on because their success (or failure) criteria are so poorly defined.

Behavior is the final and most important element. What decision behaviors in the face of risk and opportunity do you want your people to take?

For example, the dominant engineering mind-set of many Rockwell Collins managers in the late 1980s and early 1990s frequently led to two

---

[38]ISO/FDIS 31000:2009, "Risk Management—Principles and Guidelines," 2009.

mutually reinforcing and ultimately troublesome behaviors: (1) seeing business risks almost solely in terms of technical (deterministic) risk, and (2) when technical risks created business problems, creating an overdependence on "engineering your way out of (business) trouble" as the preferred solution.

The effect on the enterprise's ability to manage risk effectively was pervasive, as each group of managers who assumed key decision-making roles were also engineering trained. With Collins facing an increasingly uncertain business and technological environment, it was imperative that the company develop internally or hire in a strong cadre of managers who were competent and comfortable operating in both worlds. Those who weren't comfortable saw their careers limited.

In other words, Collins had to say not only what unacceptable decision-making behavior was but, more important, what *was* acceptable. Eliminating dysfunctional behavior doesn't help much if there isn't a functional behavior available to take its place.[39]

Once these four aspects of ERM are thought through and defined (and, it is hoped, crafted in a way to be mutually self-reinforcing), then go out and select an ERM support tool.

How Long Will It Take for ERM to Take Hold?

It will take a few years at a minimum for ERM to take hold. At Rockwell Collins, it took over five years to become fully embedded, even with full management support. It also took several more years to make sure the discipline required stayed embedded, and management today continues to ensure there is no backsliding on its importance because of business or economic pressures.

Even when ERM is successfully rooted, it takes a sustained effort to get it to a point that it becomes second nature to the organization. What happened to several of Jim Collins's great organizations should be a warning that success needs to be earned each and every day.

How Can ERM Fail?

ERM initiatives can fail in several ways. The first is if it doesn't help improve organizational decision making. As a friend of mine says, risk management is interesting and useful only if it helps you make a better decision.

Implementing ERM requires a large effort (remember the *E* stands for enterprise). It often involves exposing the facts that some in the organization

---

[39]Art Gemmer, "Risk Management: Moving Beyond Process," *IEEE Computer*, May 1997, 33–43.

may not want discussed openly. If not managed appropriately, ERM can easily turn into one of the following:

- Operational and program managers blaming each other for suboptimal outcomes.
- Parties second-guessing each other after highlighting risks.
- In the end, parties subsequently having their heads handed back to them.

ERM also requires *real* senior management support. For instance, if senior management doesn't ask for risk information that is fact-based, it isn't going to get it. In addition, if senior management doesn't share its view of risk—for example, what types of decisions are considered to be too risky—expect ERM will fall apart as well.

ERM is a difficult way of thinking about and doing business, and requires a discipline that many organizations find difficult. Author Tim Lister likes to say that IT project risk management is only for adults; ERM is for grandparents who have seen it all and have a lot of patience.[40]

How Will I Know If ERM Is Succeeding?

No one will talk about risk management as a "new" practice very much anymore. It will be an accepted part of the corporate way of doing business and making decisions. Corporate surprises will still occur, but will be fewer and far between. And, finally, everyone will wonder how decisions could have been made before without explicitly taking risk into account.

---

[40]Tim Lister, "Point: Risk Management Is Project Management for Adults," *IEEE Software*, May/June 1997, 20–22.

CHAPTER 16

Implementing Open Source Software

Steve King

A company that does want innovation needs to take risks. Like a surfer riding a big wave, they don't rely on containment or tight control of the environment to maintain their position, but rather, an exquisite balance and an ability to respond to rapidly changing conditions. This kind of responsiveness is hard for a large company to achieve, but not impossible, especially in the presence of the kind of competition that open source brings back to the market.

—Adam Turoff

Introduction

Open source (OS) technologies can be found at the center of some of the most popular and powerful systems on the World Wide Web—systems that are used by billions of people every day. Google, Yahoo!, and NASA are among the most content-rich organizations in the world with complex, mission-critical requirements. These selfsame organizations all have significant investments in initiatives powered by OS technologies.

So what is it that makes these organizations choose free software over the established, proprietary equivalents?

Let's start by shattering one myth: Open source software (OSS) is not necessarily free. However, it does offer a unique flexibility to developers and organizations demanding that their software vendors be as robust in their after-sales support as they are in the development of their product. Nearly all software that is free is open source, and nearly all software that is open source is free.[1] OS vendors will often provide the product license at no cost but charge organizations for support—including service-level agreements (SLAs) and software updates. As a result, organizations have complete flexibility to tailor a support package that meets their requirements.

Open source, as described in Chapter 5, is software that the developers of the product have released back to the community for any of a number of potential reasons, such as:

- To make it better.
- To make it faster.
- To expand its feature set beyond the original conception of the product.

OS technologies offer a safe, low-cost alternative to products delivered by major software vendors that command heavy subscription or license fees and limit the ability to extend the functionality of a product. OS vendors reject that model and promote a paradigm whereby a community of developers can extend a product over a weekend and the extensions can then be included into the main product in the very next release—often within a matter of days. This type of development cycle means that products can be generated by millions of developers from around the world or by a handful in Oakland, California, thus giving the product agility that major commercial vendors are incapable of matching.

The myth that OS software is strictly for the technically competent or development community is quickly dissipating. In its place, there is a growing sentiment that OS can benefit organizations both financially and practically. The replacement of such commercial products as operating systems, office productivity tools, and customer relationship management (CRM) applications with OS equivalents is becoming harder to ignore. Moreover, the divide between the features of each camp is quickly eroding. In fact, in some cases that chasm no longer exists and the overlap is already complete. For example, most major OS projects now offer (either directly or through a network of affiliates) a comprehensive set of professional services and support and a controlled, regular release of application updates.

In this chapter, we explore:

- Differences between OS and commercial software.
- What to take into consideration when choosing between the two.

To do this, I evaluate Microsoft SharePoint, a commercial content management framework, and Alfresco, its OS competitor. Through exploring

---

[1]For a comprehensive definition of categories of free and nonfree software licenses, see www.gnu.org/philosophy/categories.html.

these products, we will see the key strengths and weaknesses of each. We can also easily identify how the different offerings in the OS space can benefit all organizations. Through the realization of faster returns on investment, lower capital costs, and flexible support offerings, we will see that OS technologies are enterprise ready and may well be a logical candidate for your next enterprise software project.

A Different Software Model

Open source is a different way of looking at software development, both for use within the enterprise and for use in the digital presentation of our organization. OS has at times been perceived as an unstable or partially completed project or as free equivalents of commercial offerings. This is clearly not the case. The ideal of free software is not lost; rather, it is replaced with a sustainable model of software development targeted at the improvement of the application. It is for this reason that being an OS software vendor can be a commercially viable business regardless of the fact that your application is being provided at no cost.

Projects released back into the community through the OS initiative are often released to ensure that the application continues to evolve and adapt to the constantly changing environments in which it is used. Releasing the code can ensure that a project continues to be developed well beyond the standard end of life of a one-time development project. Another common reason for project initiators to consider making their projects open source is the economy of scale of a worldwide, low-cost community of contributing developers. Take for example a niche development with very specific requirements. A development project of this nature may require funding well beyond the means of a subject matter expert or small nonprofit organization. As a result, it may have never gotten off the ground. Going OS and calling for contributing developers (on a pro-bono basis) from the community at large with an interest in the subject matter area can make an otherwise commercially unviable project a success. Many organizations the world over have used these niche OS projects to build complex and often highly successful online businesses that make millions of dollars every year.

OS projects tend to have a faster development cycle, with updates and modifications being developed by the community—a community of developers from all over the world. This kind of development approach gives the project a greater flexibility: It enables the core team to focus on defining and developing the core functionality of a project and ensuring its commercial viability. At the same time, it leaves some of the minor features to develop organically.

Traditionally, organizations pay for the cost of the software up front. This fee generally entitles the licensee to a basic level of support. The exact nature of that basic support varies from vendor to vendor but usually consists of access to an online knowledge base on a self-help basis. For a lot of clients, particularly when contemplating mission-critical systems, self-help is not enough, as the risk of the internal support staff not being able to diagnose and rectify the issue in a timely manner is too great. Most clients pay for an enhanced level of support that includes access to telephone or email support on a case basis, guaranteeing that qualified personnel from the vendor will work with the client until the issue is resolved.

Software updates are inclusive generally for the life of the license; however, in some situations the software updates are available well beyond the support period. It's not uncommon for them to last for the life of the product.

It is a common misconception that all software needs to be supported directly by the vendor. Considering that most organizations have now outsourced their technology management to external vendors, they may wind up paying for the same thing twice. This is generally apparent in situations in which organizations pay a per-unit cost for hardware that includes things like the operating system and office productivity tools and related software that includes a support or management component, and then continue to outsource the support of these systems to an external party.

In contrast, OS software will almost always give organizations free product updates for the life of the product at no cost. Support for the product usually comes in the form of organizational support; that is, clients can pay per incident requiring support or for a predefined period of time or number of hours. OS gives us a clear alternative to the traditional way of acquiring software: It allows organizations to control their initial capital spend and be more selective around their support and update requirements.

Organizations that have technical staff on hand can substantially reduce costs by removing the support requirements of each instance of an OS product. As an alternative, the organization can train and develop its technical staff to understand the inner workings of the product. In turn, the organization can perform the first level of support and triage. This is also helped by the ability of the organization to reduce the number of support licenses required from its vendors, as the support is often based on the support contract itself, not on the number of instances of a product that the organization is running.

Digital presence is another concept that is being pushed further with the advent of OS technologies. Many software development companies, including some of the major commercial vendors, are publishing OS libraries that can be included in development projects. This encourages the integration of their services with the developer's product. Many brands are now pushing forward with video marketing, a concept well beyond the reach of many organizations only five years ago, with application programming interfaces (APIs) enabling the immediate broadcast of material through sites like YouTube and Vimeo.

PC magazine defines an API as

> *a language and message format used by an application program to communicate with the operating system or some other control program such as a database management system (DBMS) or communications protocol. APIs are implemented by writing function calls in the program, which provide the linkage to the required subroutine for execution. Thus, an API implies that some program module is available in the computer to perform the operation or that it must be linked into the existing program to perform the tasks.*

Another key area of expansion is the use of commodity hardware and the LAMP stack. LAMP is an open source Web platform consisting of the following technologies: Linux, Apache, and either Perl, Python, or PHP. Collectively, these tools are giving organizations maximum flexibility with regard to deploying enterprise applications. In point of fact, many of the OS business management products now run on the LAMP stack, as they are easily scalable from one to one million users with the addition of inexpensive hardware and the OS LAMP stack.

Getting into Open Source

Despite what the fearmongers suggest, OS is safe and very pervasive. The number of projects and products available is astonishing. Since its inception in the late 1990s, the OS Initiative has been a key driver in a number of projects that are either full-OS projects or make use of alternative technologies, such as the Google Search Appliance, an enterprise search platform developed by Google that extensively uses OS technologies. There are many ways that organizations can benefit from the generosity and dedication of the millions of OS developers from around the world.

So how does it work? OS projects come in a few different flavors. OS projects range from code libraries that enable developers to develop applications rapidly or expand the base functionality of their applications through the use of the code library itself, right through to research and development by the OS project and fully functional business applications. As a business, it is unlikely that you are ever going to use the former. However, it's important to remember that the use of OS technology is not limited to developers. Many organizations can benefit from no-cost to low-cost implementations of OS applications in place of their commercial rivals. The use of OS does not necessitate spending a fortune on developers. Many OS applications are as easy to install, configure, customize, and manage as their commercial rivals.

There are OS products available for just about every area of business operations, as well some more obscure areas. Microsoft Windows is the most commonly used operating system today, with over 89 percent of the market share.[2] It is easy to put this down to the ease of use of the Windows product or its availability from popular hardware vendors like Dell. However, its largely misunderstood OS rival Linux may have you second-guessing installing Windows as the base operating system on your next computer.

Ubuntu Linux, a project that found its roots in another OS product in 2004,[3] is a completely free operating system that was developed to replace Windows as a market leader in the operating system space. Users, organizations, and institutions around the world quickly took up this relatively new alternative. Ubuntu was different from other previous OS operating systems because it was easy to install and came bundled with all of the applications that you would expect in a computer, such as word processing and spreadsheet tools.

Of course, replacing the operating system in an organization is not a common or even advisable first step. There are many other projects that seek to replace the more conventional and often overlooked portions of an organization's day-to-day operations that lend themselves to open source. Many businesses are already taking up the call and deploying OS applications across their organizations. Table 16.1 presents some examples of this.

OS software has changed the way that many organizations look at acquiring software. What's more, OS software is rapidly changing the way organizations present themselves digitally. Recent OS arrivals such as enterprise relationship management, online marketing, business intelligence (BI), and, of course, operating environments have opened the floodgates of choice. Organizations now can choose from a wide variety of platforms to meet their requirements. With all that choice comes a greater responsibility to select the right product: the product that meets the organization's business requirements, provides the greatest opportunity to reduce operating costs, and has the lowest total cost of ownership and therefore the highest return on investment.

OS and Digital Presence

In discussing OS technology, we have been focusing primarily on the use of OS inside the organization. However, there is a growing list of available technologies that are helping organizations manage their digital presence.

---

[2]www.w3schools.com/browsers/browsers_os.asp.
[3]www.ubuntu.com/community/ubuntustory.

TABLE 16.1 Comparison of Commercial and OS Products

Commercial Product	OS Contender
Microsoft Office	Open Office
The Microsoft Office Suite, available for Windows and Mac, provides Word (a word processing application), Excel (a spreadsheet application), Access (a database management and manipulation application), and PowerPoint (a slide show creator and viewer).	The Open Office suite, available for Mac, Windows, UNIX, and Linux, provides Write (a word processor), Calc (a spreadsheet manager), Draw (a graphic design program), Base (a database management and manipulation application), and Impress (a slide show creator and viewer).
Internet Explorer	Mozilla Firefox
Available for free; however, it is a closed source application available from Microsoft. Updates and security fixes are only available once developed by Microsoft.	Available for free, with full source code published on the Mozilla web site. Built on the OS code provided by Netscape, Mozilla has developers working on security, plug-ins, and features from around the world. Updates are centralized through the Mozilla Update site.

Over the past several years and through the advent of Enterprise 2.0, we have seen a paradigm shift from organizations simply having a Web page to having a digital presence. A digital presence is the collection of Web assets and brands operated by the organization to promote itself and its products and services, including the use of sites like Facebook and LinkedIn as marketing tools. A digital presence can also help organizations expand their customer bases through inexpensive and relatively simple processes, a number of which are available as open source.

With the increase in online services offering OS libraries, organizations can more easily develop fully interactive and highly content-rich applications. Never before has it been as simple for organizations to keep customers informed through a stream of updates, news, and other information on public web sites. The engineers who build and operate web sites have a greater flexibility with OS libraries like the Prototype JavaScript Library and other projects that reduce the build time for web sites by weeks and months and enable web sites to be better equipped to provide up-to-date information.

While many organizations continue to publish weekly or monthly updates to their web sites, the new OS technologies have reduced the cost of deploying easily manageable content for web sites with OS content management systems. Organizations can deploy these systems and make content ready for consumption in a matter of minutes. These enterprise-ready OS products enable organizations to tie the content publishing and generation to their internal security systems. Identity management systems can ensure that information published to the web site is auditable and strictly controlled.

Open source continues to make headway into other key areas of our digital presence. OS tools can also manage communications with clients. OS email marketing systems like OpenEMM (www.openemm.org/) are providing organizations with complete email marketing solutions, enabling them to actively communicate with their existing clients and increase return business by increasing customer awareness of the organization's activities.

Enterprise customer relationship management is an important part of digital presence management, providing more than just a repository of client information for internal staff. What's more, it provides an often-overlooked repository of contacts to be leveraged to encourage repeat business from clients. Through OS projects like opentaps (www.opentaps.org), this process becomes not only easier to manage, but also more cost-effective.

As our organizational demand on information systems increases, so do the operating costs of the systems in question. Often these costs can be prohibitive when investigating new technologies or test-driving new systems. OS has responded with a plethora of services, systems, and application platforms to power not only organizations' heavy requirements on internal systems but also outward-facing client-access systems and digital assets. Many of these can easily replace expensive commercial products. While the platforms themselves are open source based, many of the applications that they power are from commercial vendors, such as Atlassian.

Commercial applications, like Jira's issue management and tracking system from Atlassian, run on OS application platforms like Apache's Tomcat Server. A number of commercial content management systems continue to run on the OS LAMP stack. Utilizing OS application servers and server operating systems can work to significantly reduce operational costs. These savings can help organizations reduce their costs related to expanding digital assets and managing digital presence.

OS and Managing Your Business

Consider enterprise document management and content management systems. Both types of applications have commercial and OS alternatives. This section focuses on two products under consideration for internal use at the DMBST Group.

DMSBT is a regional business and technology consulting firm operating across the Asia-Pacific and Southeast Asia regions. It specializes in information management, Enterprise 2.0, and Web 2.0 portal development. DMSBT is also a Google Enterprise Partner specializing in developing applications that use the Google Search Appliance, Google Apps Premier Edition, and Google Maps.

As a business and technology consulting firm, DMSBT retains a large amount of information about its customers and their commercial histories. Its daily dealings with support, integration, and systems designs ensures that it develops and acquires extensive documentation about existing systems, its product range, and custom solutions designed and built by its development and consulting teams. This adds up to an extensive collection of documents previously stored on a network file share to which only the office had access. This approach suffered from a number of drawbacks, predominantly access control and ease of access to the content from outside the business.

Of course, the immediate solution became clear. DMSBT needed a document management system to help collate and control the information that the business dealt with daily. Apart from consolidating information into a simple repository, DMSBT looked at the capabilities of different applications in order to find a product that met not only its business needs but also its budgetary requirements.

DMSBT investigated both Microsoft SharePoint Server and the Alfresco Enterprise Content Management system. On paper the two products looked virtually identical. They offered the features expected of any enterprise content management system. Again, both products met each of DMSBT's business requirements. In other words, the features of each of the applications were not the deciding factor.

Microsoft Office SharePoint Server 2007 is an integrated suite of server capabilities that can help improve organizational effectiveness. SharePoint provides comprehensive content management and enterprise search. This accelerates shared business processes and facilitates information sharing across boundaries for better business insight.[4]

Alfresco is the leading OS enterprise content management system and is built by the most experienced team in the industry, drawn from Documentum, Vignette, and Interwoven.[5]

Of course, the results here show that the OS alternative to the commercial product is virtually identical in terms of features and functionality. Apart from the brand, end users would rarely be able to distinguish what they gain or lose by using either platform. This is largely true across many OS products; the divide between the commercial world and the OS one is slowly disappearing.

---

[4]http://office.microsoft.com/en-us/sharepointserver/HA102063361033.aspx.
[5]www.alfresco.com/products/.

Appearances Can Be Deceiving

Advertising, marketing, packaging, and the general promotion of software have an effect on the software adopted by both consumers and businesses. Major software vendors spend a great deal on advertising. For example, Apple's budget was $486 million for the 2008 financial year.[6] As a result, it should be no surprise that we rarely hear the OS conversation anywhere but in technology blogs, magazines, and the workplace. This raises the following questions:

- How do we find out about open source?
- Where do we go to locate these great free products?
- What are the key ways to filter out the white noise generated by the budgets of these software giants?

You can find OS projects on providers like Sourceforge and Google Code. These sites offer project hosting services and collaborative tools to OS projects. Although not all OS projects use these services, often their products are listed and can be easily found from there. OS directories like these provide great starting points to discover OS technologies. Note, however, that they are far from being a comprehensive guide.

Development costs reflect only a small fraction of an application's price. The cost of most software is a function of vendors' large advertising budgets. OS products are quite different in this regard. OS "vendors" do not actively promote or advertise their products by traditional means. While this makes it more difficult to find OS products, it does not limit organizations' abilities to locate them. Many of the OS products are discovered simply via word-of-mouth advertising. OS products need to rely on the strength of the product and its features in order to attract new business. A great example of this method being successful in OS is the Mozilla Firefox browser. A campaign called "Spread Firefox" encourages Firefox users to tell other users about the product. This earns them points on the Spread Firefox web site (www.spreadfirefox.com). The web site then awards top promoters with iPods, gift certificates, and other products.

One of the easiest ways to locate OS software is to use search engines like Google. Targeted searches for products like "OS Enterprise Relationship" reveal a number of potentially useful products available to the end user. A few searches on the product names provide access to reviews and comparisons. Do not be surprised if you find yourself doing the investigatory legwork when it comes to reviews and comparisons. Major review web sites such as www.cnet.com that rely on commercial software advertising revenue

---

[6]http://edgar.sec.gov/Archives/edgar/data/320193/000119312508224958/d10k.htm.

rarely, if ever, provide extensive and well-documented comparisons of OS and products.

Web sites such as Osdir (http://osdir.com) and relatively new player EOS Directory (www.eosdirectory.com) specialize in the enterprise OS products. These are also popular destinations for those looking for OS solutions. These web sites provide feedback, ratings, and reviews of the products and can be great starting points in discovering what OS has to offer you and your organization.

Product Development Agility

In a world of rapidly changing environments and constantly evolving standards, the products we acquire for our business can sometimes become out of date before we've even finished integrating them into our operations. In response to this, OS delivers a product agility that even some of the major software vendors have difficulty keeping up with. As discussed previously in this chapter, this comes down to the immense communities that some of the OS projects command as well as the initiative of businesses that take up the software.

Concepts and requirements in OS projects are needs driven, resulting in a more refined product in a shorter period of time; and with OS projects being built by developers from disparate geographical locations with varied experience and abilities, the result is a truly dynamic and often highly agile development environment. With traditional software, feature requests can take many months or even years to implement, and some features never make it at all. This can mean that features that your business requires may never make it to production. The OS model changes this by enabling the end users of the software to post feature requests that are viewed by the entire development community. Development on these features can take place over a weekend and can often be included in the very next update of the software; your company benefits from the developer community that the project enjoys, which means that product improvements and expansion do not come solely from the project itself but from the end users of the products.

Projects are also more complete in their functionality, and you as a consumer are rarely required to purchase additional plug-ins (modules that are optional extras not included in the base package). While this can sometimes mean that your software contains more features than you require, many of the features can be disabled or removed in your specific installation with little or no fuss.

Minor customization of the products can also be relatively easy to implement. While as an organization you are unlikely to ever customize or redevelop the underlying code of an application, it's important to know that if the need arises, your product is built on a highly extensible base that is well documented and tested by organizations all across the world. Your application comes with the support of not only the OS company but also the community that drives its development, and this often results in a highly extensible application that is module driven so that new features and services offered by the OS product can improve drastically between releases.

Support

When things go wrong, businesses want to know that someone is going to make them right. This is where support and training come into play. Any product you implement in your organization is going to require a support strategy and often a training strategy to train existing staff on how to use the services that you provide. OS products generally have comprehensive support plans that are available on a subscription basis, and this is almost always where the OS company becomes commercially viable.

OS projects have a number of different options when it comes to support. With an emphasis being placed on flexibility, most will provide you with a number of options that enable to you to choose the plan that suits your business requirements. Support plans vary from a per-issue basis to full subscription plans with service-level agreements, and all OS projects provide documentation and access to the development notes.

Occasionally an OS project will require the end user to subscribe to the support program in order to receive the latest program updates or access to the developer community; although this is not standard practice, it does occur. When this situation arises, it is of course ideal to ensure that the support program has guarantees around the response times of issue management and a published release schedule.

As with major commercial projects, OS projects follow a basic model of support that is optional. Support extends for the life of the agreement and provides assistance with all issues relating to the product, from installation and evaluation through to upgrades application updates and security fixes. Many OS vendors will actively contact their support subscribers in the event of an issue affecting them and assist in the process of correcting the problem.

You can expect the same level of support from your OS product vendor as you would from any commercial vendor, including full telephone support, global coverage, access to technical staff, and in some cases access to the development team. Choosing OS does not reduce the quality of service provided by the company when it comes to support. While the community as a whole may conduct the development of the product, the vendor itself manages the support, with employees working to service-level agreements and key performance indicators.

Open source companies provide many avenues of acquiring support, including advanced telephony systems with interactive fault reporting through OS products like Asterisk. These programs allow developers and end users to create and log issues online by utilizing a coordinated tracking system. Alternatively, more traditional means such as calling a help desk operator or emailing in a support request are also available.

In addition, OS communities exhaustively document their systems and processes for their developers and customers alike, which can often give the solutions to problems without requiring the intervention of a support operator at all. Communities run knowledge-base repositories with typical scenarios, frequently asked questions, and known issues, as well as providing access to collaborative community systems, such as wikis, discussion groups, and email lists.

Whether your organization chooses a periodical support plan, prepaid support, or on-demand support, the quality of service and level of support will rival that of the commercial vendors. While your application benefits from the support of developers globally, your organization will benefit from the security of a dedicated support team with intimate knowledge and understanding of the product.

Product Types

Open source software provides the community with an edge that enables it to rapidly publish applications to the market and often produces complex applications in a substantially reduced time frame compared to traditional software development. Whether the product is a fully functional application, an extension to an existing system, or a product add-on, OS enables users, businesses, and developers to be more flexible with their projects and products, allowing them complete access to the source code that powers it.

Whether you are looking at OS from an enterprise systems point of view with products such as Alfresco, in desktop environments with products like Mozilla Firefox, or at a core application level with development libraries, OS has something to offer your business. When we take a closer look at the various types of products available through OS, the clarity of that benefit becomes quite clear.

Enterprise systems that are available via OS systems such as Alfresco, Apache Web Server, and opentaps are providing businesses with significantly reduced costs in managing their enterprise relationships both with customers and also with their own staffs or internal processes. OS enterprise applications are generally also deployed onto commodity hardware using other OS products as the basis for their core systems, such as Apache Tomcat and Java.

The reason for this is the extensive scalability of the server products and the ease of installation that the platforms offer. While the Internet will have you convinced that all OS applications for the Internet are PHP driven, the reality is that a substantial portion of the applications are built on Java technology (another OS project), which can be freely downloaded and installed on virtually any server system. This essentially means that your newly acquired OS enterprise application can run on your existing hardware if required.

Organizations are continuing to adopt OS desktop applications. Perhaps the most prevalent example is organizations' relatively widespread adoption of the Mozilla Firefox Web browser. Mozilla is very rapidly encroaching upon Microsoft Internet Explorer in general consumption as the browser of choice with a near 48 percent market share in July 2009.[7] Considered to be a major hurdle, the adoption of products like Mozilla Firefox into the standard operating environment is demonstrating that organizations are increasing their awareness of both the OS products and their viability and security inside the organization.

As with all OS projects, Mozilla Firefox provides the end user with a developer community that is truly global, operating 24 hours a day, seven days a week, ensuring that the application is packed with the latest features, that it meets the highest levels of product compliance, and that security issues and application errors are fixed within hours or days of being identified, compared to the weeks and months of development required by a single organization performing the updates.

A key contributor to the reduction in development times and costs can be attributed to the exhaustive availability of development libraries or code to the OS community, as well as partial or complete applications that are available for the community to modify or extend to meet its requirements. Development libraries are one of the more common uses of OS licensing, with code libraries available from a number of web sites on the Internet. The libraries enable developers to extend their own applications with functionality that would normally take weeks or even months to develop on their own.

Often, development libraries not only reduce the time it takes to include functionality into an application or service, but can mean the core team can focus on the key areas of their application that leverage their business or domain subject matter expertise. Wheels have been round for millennia and there is no real need to reinvent them. Likewise, OS development libraries provide significant predeveloped, pretested functionality that can be rolled

---

[7] www.w3schools.com/browsers/browsers_stats.asp.

into your development project. The time it takes to stay cross-skilled in all areas can create a significant deficit on the overall project or business as a whole, particularly if the involvement of technical staff includes training or additional certifications in a technology. It makes it easy to see the substantial time savings that OS development libraries and code classes provide to businesses and developers alike.

Development libraries in combination with the openness of the application itself often result in the rapid development of product extensions, customization, and add-ons that enable the applications to support additional services and functionality, or even enhance the look and feel of the application itself, by replacing the user interface with a completely new or customized skin, as discussed earlier in the chapter. These changes can be community driven or initiated by the organization acquiring the software.

These extensions or modifications to the software do not need to be drastic. Often organizations do not want to make extensive changes to the application itself but would rather make minor modifications to meet additional requirements.

Whatever the selection made by the organization, the choice of an OS technology or product has its distinct benefits at many levels. All of the positive and negative elements of each should be weighed against the organization's requirements and operating structure to ensure that the product is a good fit. Attention should be paid also to the extensibility of the product to insulate against future change in the business requirements. While many commercial applications do offer a certain level of flexibility, OS provides true control over the entire solution.

Crowdsourcing

Crowdsourcing is a relatively new concept that places the task of development or consultancy in the hands of the general public while enabling the initiating company to retain control over the overall direction of the project. While uniquely different from traditional open source, it gives greater flexibility to and management over problems that a company may face that would usually involve the engagement of an entire workforce to complete. Crowdsourcing not only provides an immeasurable workforce at the click of a button, but it also enables the initiating company to retain full ownership of the solutions it acquires and, in most cases, the complete intellectual property.

Although the concept is not strictly related to OS methodologies, crowdsourcing is an evolution of the more traditional outsourcing of development or process to an external agency or consultant. The key difference is that crowdsourcing releases the idea to a wider audience that may form groups to solve your problem collaboratively, thus expanding the reach of the project well beyond the borders of your organization. (See Chapter 17, Global Engineering.)

Crowdsourcing adopts the principles of transparency that OS invokes with the initiating company publishing its requirements in an open and public forum, describing both the requirements of the project and the underlying technologies that are being adapted. Communities and developers from around the world identify the development requirements and propose solutions based on the published requirements. Once the initiator has reviewed the solutions, it may award the project to the best solution.

With the flexibility of setting budgets, or bounties, organizations can make requests for functionality and features that the existing product may not contain. It can be used to extensively modify the original project to meet the business requirements or to make simple changes or improvements that are a better fit for the business requirements or internal process management. Many crowdsourcing initiatives can have you up and running in only minutes, and once you have posted the bounty, you are free to review and reject as many responses as you feel.

In our example of Microsoft SharePoint and Alfresco, the utilization of crowdsourcing may have benefited us by enabling us to post requirements of a migration from one product to the other on a crowdsourcing service. This would have reduced the need for external contractors or integrators to come on board to perform the work. While still achieving our project goals, our core team would be responsible for the actual migration while the technology could be sourced from the collaborative crowd, substantially reducing the deployment time.

Crowdsourcing is not to be considered a complete replacement of contract labor. However, it is a viable option for ad-hoc projects or complex tasks that would require highly skilled, short-term staff to be involved. Crowdsourcing resources become like a disposable workforce that can be employed for a day, a week, or a month depending on the project requirements and can be managed and directed by the internal project leader or technical staff.

Niche Markets

Proprietary software applications are built with two main objectives in mind: first, to meet the needs of the end user the software is developed for, and, second, to earn money. With this in mind, it's obvious why many niche markets often go for long periods without adequate software to meet their operational needs or why they adopt more expensive software in order to utilize a small fraction of the overall functionality of the application. They are in effect forgotten in the overall scheme of things. As a result, OS has made huge headway into market share of software for niche markets.

A prime example of this is small to medium-sized not-for-profit organizations that are generally run by volunteer staff. Such organizations generally lack the large budgets necessary to utilize traditional software acquisition practices. In these scenarios, too, the requirements of the organizations differ from their commercial counterparts, and therefore the requirements they have for the software that operates the business are largely different. However, the need for effective software in the organization is still as important as it is in any other group.

Open source solutions provide these organizations with the tools they require and the support they need at a fraction of the commercial cost. In many situations OS vendors give substantial discounts on their support packages for not-for-profit organizations that take up their software. This marriage has proven to be highly effective at both the reduction in operational costs by the organization and the promotion of the OS product for the vendor.

Niche markets and requirements are not limited to not-for-profit organizations, as even large-scale businesses often face challenges with software requirements versus the solutions that are available to them. The situation is the same; the niche requirements of the organization have not previously been explored by major software vendors, or, in most situations, it has been deemed to be unprofitable to have a dedicated product in the space.

Organizations facing these situations are embracing a combination of methodologies to meet their needs, such as acquiring OS software and modifying the software itself to meet their requirements. Achieving this is a matter of employing technical staff with the acumen to make modifications to the software and release it to the business. However, this is not always possible, as an animal rescue group would hardly be expected to employ a team of applications developers in order to fulfill its requirements. In these situations the organization can turn to crowdsourcing.

Summary

As the OS conversation continues around the world and organizations become more aware of the opportunities OS can create inside an enterprise, the list of products available continues to grow. While we can largely continue with the commercial model of software acquisition, the benefits and features of the OS model cannot be ignored.

The challenge continues to be recognizing the OS counterparts to the commercial products our organizations consume. Although investigating these options can become a time-consuming process, the avenues of exploration continue to grow as the OS model receives more recognition.

Many consulting organizations now offer services to help organizations understand what OS technologies can do and identify areas where substantial cost savings can be made. These consulting firms and freelance consultants will provide you the information you need to make informed decisions in regard to going open source. They will also provide you with information on how to acquire the software and support that your organization needs.

Traditional investigation into open source, through online directories and search engines, is an easy and effective way to begin understanding the availability of products, and business analysts are increasingly being educated in the potential for OS inside the enterprise. Although we should not expect to see significant advertising and glossy reviews in magazines on open source, many of our colleagues and business associates are already making the move, and information can be obtained from these sources.

While we investigate the large-scale implications of OS inside our enterprise, attention can be paid to the management of our digital presence and the benefits that many of the projects available can contribute. As an entry into the OS model, digital presence management, such as Web content management systems, is often a great starting point for investigating the technologies and becoming familiar with them.

Security, product updates, and responsiveness of the product vendors will always be a key deciding factor in the process, and OS offers a unique product agility that commercial vendors cannot compete with. The abilities, experience, and dedication of potentially thousands of developers worldwide provide a solid base and rapid response to product issues and vulnerabilities well beyond that of the commercial counterparts, and this translates into a stronger, more viable product for your organization.

When things do go wrong, the support plans and management of the support process provided by the OS vendor are as flexible, reliable, and liable as those of the commercial vendors. Service-level agreements and appropriate support channels contribute to organizations feeling more comfortable with making the switch to open source.[8]

Next Steps

Open source is here; it is not going away. Begin investigating the potential that OS has not only in your enterprise but also for your digital experience in general; and with this, I would like to leave you with these final suggestions:

---

[8]For additional information on open source product types, please see http://philsimonsystems.com/nwot_extras.html.

- Download Firefox; see what all the fuss is about.
- Explore Sourceforge and many OS applications available right now.
- Talk to geeks—ask them what is in their OS armada.
- Talk to other leaders who have experimented with OS applications in their organizations. What has worked for them? What hasn't? Why?
- Be open.

CHAPTER 17

Global Engineering
Jason Horowitz

Great teamwork is the only way we create the breakthroughs that define our careers.

—Pat Riley

Introduction

For many years now, globalization has garnered particular attention in high-tech fields for a number of valid reasons. First of all, the high-tech workforce in the United States is particularly diverse in its international origins and has been since the 1960s. Second, the nature of technology projects lends itself more easily to remote or distributed collaboration. For example, a software development project is better suited to this type of work arrangement than many other kinds of endeavors ranging from manufacturing to provision of services that require an on-site presence. These two factors helped lead the IT industry to become a kind of standard-bearer for outsourced and or offshore business models.

Distributed Teams: An Integral Part of Enterprise 2.0

Sun Microsystems was not unlike many organizations in its adoption of a globalized product development model. Founded in the early 1980s by a quartet that included an Indian and a German, it employed a cosmopolitan engineering force in California for its first ten years before initiating product localization in Japan. During the talent shortages occasioned by the dot-com boom in the late 1990s, the emphasis moved to accessing hidden talent in places like India and China, well before doing so was chic. After the subsequent dot-bomb crash, cost savings that could theoretically be realized by employing engineers at roughly one-fourth of the Silicon Valley rate became a major motivation. Recently, Sun—like many organizations—has embraced the idea of developing products in emerging economies, particularly in the BRIC nations (Brazil, Russia, India, China). The rationale for such a move is that organizations would enjoy greater success accessing those markets.

I have been surprised at the degree to which the smaller businesses, nonprofit organizations, and political movements are also globalized. Ever wider availability of low-cost and free software tools has made it easier for entrepreneurs and small businesses to give a professional and very big impression. In just a couple of years, we have moved from free email to telephone and video conferences, project management and customer relationship management (CRM) tools, custom Web domains, blogs, and wikis. Small organizations are now just as able to access remote talent and work with specialized vendors (outsourcers) as large organizations are.

These technologies have enabled very positive trends. They allow (and even require) a degree of agility greater than any before. Organizations and social movements are able to get off the ground in a matter of days. The technology also enables collaboration among individuals and groups in different countries that, in the long run, makes nations themselves more amenable to collaboration and diplomacy than to more hostile interaction.

Room for Improvement

Yet, as widespread as these technologies and work practices are becoming, organizations do not completely think through the reasons for deploying them and often fail to consider all of the potential pitfalls:

- They almost always exaggerate the cost savings, as lower salaries are offset by communications, travel, and other expenses.
- They almost always overlook the need for implementing different (and usually more robust) project management methodologies.
- They tend to overlook the human dynamics of working in a distributed fashion (i.e., are people in one area disadvantaged in terms of effectiveness, visibility, enjoyment of work, career advancement, etc.?).

For these reasons, among others, globalized projects often fail to achieve their business objectives. This chapter reviews the major reasons driving organizations to distribute information technology (IT) projects and/or to send them offshore. It then discusses both the positive consequences of this trend and the reason that such projects often fail to meet their goals. Some of the emerging Web and Enterprise 2.0 technologies are specifically aimed at enabling distance collaboration. As such, we will look at how these are changing the game. Finally, I will recommend best practices that will enable chief information officers and other technology executives to maximize their chances for successful projects and turn their globalized workforces into sources of competitive advantage.

Preconditions and Reasons for Distributing Technology Projects

There are a number of necessary preconditions for the distribution of IT projects. Many or these are noted by journalist Thomas Friedman in his 2005 best seller, *The World Is Flat*. Certainly some multinational corporations such as General Electric created research and development (R&D) centers in locations such as India prior to the rise of the Internet. However, these required tremendous foresight on the part of visionary leaders such as then chief executive Jack Welch.[1] Though Friedman speaks about ten "flatteners," these factors can be divided into three general categories:[2]

1. Geopolitical factors
2. Economics
3. Technology

Geopolitical Factors

One cannot overstate the importance of the fall of the Soviet empire, the widespread acceptance of free trade, and the subsequent promulgation of different free trade agreements. The end of the Cold War enabled organizations to think beyond the timeworn categories of East-West relations. The pro–free trade mentality that took hold in the 1990s helped lead to a rise in global commerce flows.

Economics

Economic growth and the rise of large, educated middle classes in the largest emerging economies were also critical. As a result, the United States was not the only country with a workforce capable of performing technological services. Aside from the expansion of the IT labor market, the demand for new IT products and services was no longer confined to the United States.

---

[1]Jack Welch with John A. Byrne, *Jack: Straight from the Gut* (New York: Warner Business Books, 2001), 30–31, 307–310.
[2]Thomas Friedman, *The World Is Flat* (New York: Farrar, Straus & Giroux, 2005), 48–173.

Technology

Technological preconditions have also allowed for the internationalization of work. Perhaps the most important has been the explosion of the Internet and the widespread use of related forms of electronic communication such as email. Subsequent technological enablers include development of what Friedman calls "workflow software" enabling projects to be broken up into smaller pieces, assigned to different groups, and then reassembled. As a result, we have seen the widespread adoption of de facto and de jure standards. Microsoft Word is an example of the former and XML is an example of the latter: They are important because both enable collaboration of different types.

One example from my personal experience demonstrates how quickly things have progressed over the past 15 years. When Sun Microsystems began collaborating with Russian scientists in 1993, people inside of the corporation had email accounts, but the Russians engineers did not all have them. Bandwidth in Russia was also extremely limited. In those days, taped backups of the respective source bases were flown back and forth with all of the complications related to international shipping and customs compliance. Each project team of about ten people was required to send an engineer to California to synchronize the team's contribution and test it for any defects. By the late 1990s, corporations, including both Sun and its overseas partners, had decent Internet connectivity (T1 lines or equivalents). Data transfers were done over the network. More multinational corporations started to locate IT operations outside the United States—most notably in India and, to a lesser extent, in China and Eastern Europe.

Drivers of Global IT

High-level preconditions are one thing, but one should ask, "What are the primary operational reasons driving the distribution of global IT?" I would argue that they are the following three reasons:

1. Cost savings
2. Availability of talent
3. Access to key emerging markets

Cost Savings

During the late 1980s and throughout the 1990s, corporations were rapidly growing existing IT operations and creating new operations from scratch. Adding head count is very expensive. From an organization's perspective, salaries in emerging economies have been—and still remain—a source of costs savings, especially in comparison with the developed world. In the 1990s, organizations could hire engineers in developing countries for one-tenth the cost of their equivalents in the United States. Even now, after a decade of competition and economic growth, salaries in places like Russia and India are one-quarter to one-third the typical U.S. or European Union levels.

In larger corporations, the official or strategic reasons for growing off-shore operations emphasized other considerations (to be discussed next), particularly talent availability and expansion of new markets. However, middle- and lower-level management had to live with flat or, in many cases, shrinking budgets. This predisposed them toward the approach with the lowest apparent costs. Corporations are much better at counting hard costs like salary and real estate leases than harder-to-quantify things such as the relative productivity of a colocated versus distributed team. As a result, many organizations were predisposed to grow teams offshore.

Technology entrepreneurs have always valued the small, colocated team, knowing that the combination of tacit knowledge and the ability to meet extemporaneously can enable a relatively tiny group to create what a larger company would need a 100-person team to develop. However, a breed of entrepreneurs has evolved that recognizes that the offshore development can be a source of competitive advantage.[3] Many of these entrepreneurs were born outside of the United States but are familiar with the technology start-up and venture capital cycle. From a cost-benefit analysis standpoint, developing a product offshore is often one of the major reasons for starting a business outside the United States. This is doubly true if the start-up is a bootstrapped operation at first. Ultimately, these entrepreneurs are intimately familiar with the technology talent available in their home countries, not to mention languages spoken. This brings us to the next major operational reason to develop in globally distributed teams.

Availability of Talent

U.S. technology organizations have always been in the market for global talent. Traditionally, however, they have been able to find it domestically. U.S. universities, particularly those with graduate programs in science and technology, have been a magnet for international students since World War II. While the majority of foreign graduate students did eventually return to their

---

[3]Examples of Web/Enterprise 2.0 start-ups where the product is globally developed include business intelligence provider Good Data (developed in the Czech Republic), knowledge management tool Evernote (developed in Russia), and project management tool Wrike (developed in Russia).

home countries, a percentage of them remained in the United States to live and work. A remarkable number of founders of iconic Silicon Valley organizations were born outside of the United States and originally came to this country to study. In fact, according to Vivek Wadha, a scholar cited in the *New York Times* in April 2009, over half the organizations started in Silicon Valley between the mid-1990s and mid-2000s had foreign-born founders.[4]

The sufficiency of U.S.-based sources of talent came into question in the 1980s and 1990s. As corporations increased their IT investments, they required a much larger cadre of IT workers to deploy and manage those investments. Graduates from U.S. universities met only a small portion of the demand. As a result, organizations started to look abroad both because of perceived cost savings and due to the current and projected need for qualified specialists.

The situation changed drastically after September 11, 2001. Not only was it objectively more difficult for foreign students and workers to obtain visas after 9/11, but the perception of immigrant communities is that the United States suddenly became much a much less open and welcoming place to work. September 11 also coincided with the first U.S. recession in over a decade, a downturn that hit the high-tech sector particularly hard. The dot-com crash coincided with the end of a period of corporate overinvestment in IT. For the first time in memory, IT workers were losing their jobs. Some lost their residence visas as well and headed back to their home countries, leaving the United States with fewer highly skilled IT workers. Many organizations complained about restrictions in H1-B visas.

Access to Key Emerging Markets

Access to developing markets is the third reason driving the adoption of a globalized approach to software development. First cited in the expansionary 1990s, it was rarely heard during the 2001 recession or for a while afterward. It was around this time that Goldman Sachs coined the phrase "BRIC countries" (Brazil, Russia, India, China) to signify the largest, fastest-growing emerging economies.[5] Perhaps coincidentally, these countries are all IT powerhouses with large, well-educated populations with sources of competitive IT advantage. Global technology giants such as Google, Microsoft, Cisco Systems, and Hewlett-Packard quickly recognized that attracting an ecosystem of developers, system administrators, and small organizations building on their platforms would help to eventually capture the most end users. The organizations invested serious money in providing

---

[4]Matt Richtel, "Tech Recruiting Clashes with Immigration Rules," *New York Times*, April 11, 2009.
[5]www2.goldmansachs.com/ideas/brics/book/99-dreaming.pdf.

equipment and software to schools. They evangelize their technologies in universities. They also realized that developing technology in the local markets would enhance their bona fides.

Why International Distributed Projects Sometimes Fail

Notwithstanding the presence of these three strong drivers—cost savings, talent availability, and market access—many international software development projects fail. Organizations rarely publicize these failures, because doing so would demoralize their workforces, offend customers, and damage reputations of executive champions of offshore development. How do these projects fail?

- By not delivering products or projects of sufficient functionality and quality.
- Because promised cost savings fail to materialize.
- By causing distress within a global organization in the general workforce and, in particular, among managers responsible for deliverables by a global team.

Let's look at the major challenges presented by managing a distributed engineering workforce.

Time Zones

One of the most obvious challenges is the difficulty of collaborating when different members of the same product/project team are located in different parts of the globe. Extreme examples of this are the common scenarios of team members located in California collaborating with folks located in India (12.5 hours) or New York teams working with ones in China (12 hours). Even with smaller time-zone gaps, it is very difficult to find time for one-on-one meetings, let alone project team or staff meetings. It is advisable in such cases to rely more heavily on other tools, including instant messaging (IM), forums, discussion groups, wikis, blogs, or even social media sites. However, very few organizations have embraced specific products to use for such nontraditional interactions. What is more, few managers are adept at leading through their use.

Language

English is the lingua franca of the technology world, but this does not imply the absence of a language barrier within distributed technology teams.

Project leaders soon discover that an engineer who is capable of writing lucid emails or participating wittily in IM discussions may not be able to follow even slow, well-enunciated discussion in a conference call. Even among native speakers, it is very difficult to follow a fast discussion in a remote conference room. As a result, engineers may miss direct instructions, feedback may be misunderstood as criticism, and team camaraderie can quickly devolve into "us versus them."

Culture

Workplace cultural expectations vary greatly across the globe. Silicon Valley prides itself on flat management structures, open-door policies, and employees addressing executives by first name. In India, team members are reluctant to be openly critical of others in meetings. In Russia, relationships among employees and managers are much more hierarchical: Many managers expect to be addressed politely and treated deferentially; employees expect to be told what to do. These differences, of course, are not insurmountable; they are often what make working in a distributed environment fascinating and delightful. In the high-tech world, the development of a Silicon Valley–type corporate culture is a great attraction to developers and other IT workers. However, from the leadership perspective, it is essential to recognize that these cultural differences require time, effort, and money to overcome and turn into a source of potential strength.

Travel

Management often makes the following mistakes with regard to projects requiring distributed teams. First, they assume that the electronic tools available to IT workers mean that the project requires no travel budget. Second, they erroneously assume that face-to-face meetings and collaboration are superfluous. Quite often, the financial calculations that lead to the decision to send IT projects offshore leave travel out of their cost scenarios.

In reality, the opposite is true. To meet the lofty goals of these projects, regular face-to-face meetings between managers, between managers and technical teams, and even among key technical players are essential. These meetings foster strong relationships that enable successful remote teams. Conversely, without the face-to-face exposure, teams flounder because miscommunications multiply and people who have never met each other grow suspicious of the unknown.

As mentioned previously, these failures are all too common. The following case study describes an example of a dysfunctional global team suffering from many of the issues just described.

Case Study: An International Project Gone Awry

The following case study involves an engineering team doing some work for an IT products start-up. The chief technology officer (CTO) leading the technical development effort was based in Boston, Massachusetts. Several key software architects and product marketing personnel were based in New York City. The majority of the team—the rest of development engineering, the user interface (UI) group, the entire quality organization—was based in St. Petersburg, Russia. The overall size of the team was approximately 50 people.

The key driver, though not the only reason, for locating the team in St. Petersburg was cost savings. The founder of the company was originally from Russia, so he understood the talent available on the labor market. Clearly, for him there was no language barrier. His previous company also maintained a Russian presence, which, in turn, allowed him to tap into some managers he respected. To be sure, other things factored into the decision to develop the product in a distributed fashion. However, at the end of the day, the decisive factor was money: The organization could support the engineering team for 25 to 33 percent of the cost of having the same team in the United States.

The product under development was something that any office worker would use on a daily basis. There were a number of competitive products on the market. This product's key innovations were twofold:

1. To bundle specific functions together in a way that would help office workers work more productively.
2. To enable business owners to save money on software purchases and telecommunications costs.

Problems

Communication issues plagued the project from the beginning. Native English speakers in product marketing did not communicate well with the native Russian speakers on the engineering team. This resulted from a combination of language and cultural issues combined with differing management styles. Since the young Russian developers had very little experience with office work, they did not clearly grasp many of the key end-user requirements.

Largely because of the communication issues, spending on travel was much higher than anticipated. First, the U.S.-based team had to

(continued)

(continued)

decamp to Russia for relatively long periods in order to help the development team to understand the customer requirements and then later to ensure that the first couple of releases would happen on time. Later, in the release cycle, Russian-based engineers traveled to the United States in order to better understand market requirements and work directly with potential customers.

Outcomes

So, how did the project go? Not well....

- For starters, development of the first prototype product took more than twice as long as expected. With the CTO and chief architects in the United States, each feature took twice as long to specify, code, test, and iterate.
- Usability of key functions was substandard. In large part, this was a function of the aforementioned cultural and communication issues.

Because of the cost overruns, the company burned through its cash at a much higher than expected rate. This is a terrible thing for a cash-strapped start-up. Even worse, however, was the additional year required to develop the first working prototype. By the time the project was released in beta, a number of powerful corporations had moved into the space by extending the functionality of their existing products. Some market opportunity remained to become a niche product for small businesses, but the chance to become a mass-market product had passed this company by.

Global Engineering 2.0

International, distributed technology teams are here to stay. For one thing, the world economy has become so globalized that many organizations are distributed by their very nature. This may mean a few colleagues working from home or from another city, collaborating closely with a vendor or strategic partner in another country, or a multinational corporation dealing with the full implications of getting projects done using distributed teams. The three-headed monster of low cost, access to scarce talent, and development of emerging markets produces powerful incentives to distribute work.

Fortunately for the business executive operating in this environment, many of the Enterprise 2.0 technologies enable people to work together over the network without necessarily having any face-to-face contact. Think about some of the best-known brand names of the past five years: Skype, Gmail, Amazon Web Services (AWS), Twitter, WordPress, Craigslist, LinkedIn, and Facebook. Consider also that the cost of setting up an online presence is rapidly converging to zero. Need to set up a branded email domain and provide accounts to employees? Google lets you do it for free. Want to provide a consumer-facing Web service, but don't have the cash to set up a server farm? Create a virtualized service using Amazon Elastic Compute Cloud (EC2) and scale your service up according to usage.

Unlike his colleague in the IT start-up, the enterprise executive does not have to worry about the cost of setting up email or whether there is a data center available to host an app. However, the same considerations of providing up-to-date software and services and reducing hardware and energy costs apply to the largest corporate environments as well. The following are the major IT trends with short descriptions, including their relevance to distributed project teams.

Cloud Computing

Consider the XaaSs of infrastructure, platform, and, software as a service (IaaS, PaaS, SaaS). SaaS, for example, allows continuous versioning of software without the need for an update cycle for physical machines. Additionally, many of the applications that have been developed as SaaS are designed as collaborative platforms themselves: Salesforce.com is one example out in the broader marketplace. Another instance is Google Docs. Forget for a moment its weak document editing capabilities. Consider that many people use it as a broadly available platform that allows for sharing and version control of group documents. In Silicon Valley, managers have their hands constantly slapped for sharing proprietary or confidential information on Google Docs; the security concerns were valid, but corporate IT had not provided a convenient equivalent.

Virtualization

Often provided in the context of cloud computing, this technology allows for the provision of virtual machines (computing resources) throughout an organization. Further, this provision takes place without respect to the physical location of computing resources. Virtualization enables employees of all types to work in different functions wherever they are located.

Collaborative Software and the Interactive Web

Use of knowledge-sharing platforms is hardly a new event in the enterprise. Lotus Notes was an early example of so-called teamware. However, there have been many changes, including the quality and availability of the offerings and their penetration into the public consciousness. Wikipedia has helped people understand the concepts that make wikis work. As discussed in this book, organizations are using wikis both as a way to collaborate on internal projects and, in some cases, as a platform to communicate with customers. Wikis are an outstanding way to work remotely. They allow individuals to make changes to documents on their schedule while building on the work of colleagues in other locations. Since changes can be rolled back to prior versions if necessary, there is little risk that valuable information will be deleted or lost. Blogs are another way to collaborate. Through their comments, really simple syndication (RSS) feeds, and other notifications, the best blogs become virtual discussion boards around which communities develop.

Search

The proliferation of high-quality search engine technology deployed either on the Web or internally in a corporate environment (i.e., enterprise search and retrieval—ESR) allows for easy collection and aggregation of useful data. This is generally useful and particularly so for teams that collaborate remotely.

Increasing Importance of Project Management

One additional requirement for successful global technology development is adoption of a formal technology development method and its adaptation for distributed teams. Gallons of ink have been spilled discussing the merits of traditional waterfall software development life cycle (SDLC) methodologies versus the various agile methodologies.[6] Traditional SDLC, such as the capability maturity model (CMM) framework, is more focused on specifications and longer-term planning. As discussed in Chapter 14, agile software development is more focused on iterative communication and developing a working prototype as quickly as possible. The methodologies are each developed in different customer environments and in response to different stimuli. Each is probably better suited to certain development

---

[6]"CMM vs. Agile: Methodology Wars in Software Development," Harvard Business School Case Study 9-607-804, updated September 10, 2008.

scenarios in different industries. However, these two methodologies have at least one thing in common: They spell out the ways in which project plans are documented and issues or defects are flagged, tracked, and resolved.

This predictability and repeatability around information are even more critical to distributed teams than to colocated teams. Some organizations eschew this formality and the associated time and expense. The lack of a formal project planning or management process can work in very specific circumstances. Consider a project involving a small team based out of one office (in one single room to boot). Everyone works the same schedule. Each is in a position to answer each other's questions repetitively.

That rarely happens these days. For a distributed team, even within a small company such as the start-up discussed earlier, a set of repeatable procedures is critical. Ironically, project management methodologies such as agile were developed with colocated teams in mind. This means that the distributed organization must improvise ways to use them for distributed teams. Nevertheless, recently collected data shows that distributed teams benefit from the use of agile methods.[7]

Summary

The rise of global technology teams has been enabled by geopolitical, economic, and technological preconditions. It has become a phenomenon driven by:

- The promise of significant cost savings.
- Inexhaustible demand for technical talent.
- Access to key emerging markets (e.g., India, China, etc.).

However, successfully implementing projects globally is even more difficult than doing so within the traditional enterprise. Organizations tend to underestimate formidable challenges ranging from travel costs to the tax on managerial bandwidth. Fortunately, recent trends in IT are helping to bridge the gap between distributed teams. Executives need to be proactive—rather than reactive—to ensure the success of distributed projects.

---

[7]James Kile, "An Investigation into the Effectiveness of Agile Software Development with a Highly Distributed Workforce" (dissertation submitted in partial fulfillment for degree of doctor of computer science, Pace University, 2007).

Next Steps

Management should take the following steps to increase the chances that the global projects will be successful.

- If a company is not yet distributed geographically, then make sure that you are analyzing the drivers behind your decisions. Are promised cost savings leading the way? How real are they? Or is it access to a key market or to hard-to-find talent? At the executive level, make sure that an honest discussion about this and about trade-offs is happening. Set expectations correctly at the outset.
- Once you have made the decision to proceed with global engineering (or if you already are distributed), ask yourself whether managers and executives are sufficiently experienced with leading global teams. If not, then consider mandating assignments in which your leaders must work from a remote geography for a fixed period (not less than six months).
- Allocate sufficient travel budget to ensure that each member of your engineering team is visiting another site at least once per year. This is a rule of thumb: Not everyone will be able to travel, and some people will benefit from more extended work visits. The important thing is to build the higher level of travel into your cost models. If you are working with lower-cost locations such as India or China, there will still be cost savings.
- Examine how your organization gets its daily work done. Meetings are important, but is your organization too dependent on staff meetings, all-hands meetings, and so on? Make those meetings regular but infrequent, and instead make sure that your staff is proficient in the use of wikis, blogs, and other tools that allow asynchronous sharing of information. Using new tools does not happen overnight, so make sure that you assign owners to specific aspects of this program and provide sufficient training.
- Implement a formal project management methodology if you don't have one already. Make sure to use it in a form well adapted to distributed teams rather than colocated teams. Agile development is one methodology that has been shown to help global engineering teams work together effectively. Formal methodologies institutionalize some of the key communications that are vital to the success of international teams.

CHAPTER 18

Enterprise 2.0 IT Project Failure
Michael Krigsman

Knowledge is more than equivalent to force.

—Samuel Johnson

Introduction

Information technology (IT) failure remains a serious problem for many organizations. Despite years of study and millions of dollars invested to prevent failure, the problem remains. This chapter attempts to explain why projects fail and suggests methods to achieve success.

The techniques presented here apply to both traditional project failure and failure of Enterprise 2.0 projects. The main message of this chapter: Failure is a human concept and the solution therefore lies in human, rather than technical, realms.

The perspective on failure described in this chapter goes far beyond that of project management alone. Although project management techniques are valuable, too many books and articles focus on checklists rather than organizational dynamics. Static requirement lists alone do not interrupt cycles of project failure. Instead, we should view failure as a dynamic system involving interactions among stakeholders and participants across an organization. In fact, a complete view of failure must also consider stakeholders in the entire project ecosystem, which includes external vendors.

This chapter concludes by describing straightforward techniques to measure and analyze potential project vulnerabilities. These methods go far beyond simple risk analysis and reflect a comprehensive and broad view of what is required to combat failure.

Enterprise 2.0: An Evolving Concept

For many people, the term *Enterprise 2.0* has a vague meaning and nebulous definition, something addressed in Chapters 1 and 2. Nonetheless, this concept represents a philosophy of grassroots, decentralized organizational empowerment. The Enterprise 2.0 concept is pregnant with the potential to redefine organizational work relationships and information flows by leveraging software that facilitates knowledge sharing and collaboration, even across organizational boundaries.

Enterprise 2.0 suggests a network of organizational activities involving collaboration, cooperation, and engagement as part of a broader ethos of social interaction in business.

This perspective of management and organizational behavior is inspired by interactions online that developed organically among the community of Enterprise 2.0 early adopters. In a sense, the view embodied in this description serves as an archetype for a more humanistic form of consensus-based management than typically exists inside large organizations today.[1]

On the surface, Enterprise 2.0 appears like a technology application area covering domains such as content management and Internet-based social media. While blogs, wikis, Twitter, and Facebook are useful tools that support collaboration, understanding the true meaning of Enterprise 2.0 requires deeper analysis.

To understand Enterprise 2.0, it is helpful to look first at a common enterprise organizational model. Most companies and bureaucracies employ command-and-control hierarchies based on clearly defined chains of communication and responsibility. This model creates operational efficiencies and allows organizations to scale in size without replicating corporate functions unnecessarily. For example, large companies have a clear management reporting structure, which is essential to coordinating the entire organization around shared goals and strategies.

At the same time, command-and-control bureaucracies create their own inefficiencies that interfere with information and communication flows. Anyone who has registered a car or applied for a passport knows that rigid bureaucracies can be inefficient and difficult to navigate. These inefficiencies arise when organizational hierarchies and functional departments value internally focused goals over serving customer needs. In extreme cases, customer needs and requirements become almost meaningless in the organization's quest to remain efficient and follow the rules.

If information silos and rigidity characterize traditional organizational systems, then flexibility and collaboration are hallmarks of the Enterprise

---

[1]Michael Krigsman, "Enterprise 2.0: The Kumbaya Irony," ZDNet, June 29, 2009, http://blogs.zdnet.com/projectfailures/?p=4370.

TABLE 18.1 CRM Failure Statistics (2001–2009)

Year	CRM Failure Rate
2001	50%
2002	70
2005	18
2006	31
2007	56
2009	47

2.0 philosophy. This chapter examines Enterprise 2.0 projects to understand where they differ from traditional organizational technology initiatives. In particular, our focus is comparing Enterprise 2.0 failure to conventional IT project meltdowns.

To place Enterprise 2.0 into proper context, we begin with a discussion of failure on traditional enterprise system deployments.

Understanding Traditional IT Failure

Studies tell us that 30 to 70 percent of information technology projects fail: They are late, are over budget, or do not achieve planned goals or expectations.

The truth is that failure is a big problem with IT projects, and it has been for quite a while. For example, Table 18.1 shows customer relationship management (CRM) failure statistics for selected years in the period from 2001 to 2009.[2]

Let us use CRM as an example. Depending on how you define failure and who is doing the counting, the most conservative failure rate is around 18 percent, and a broader definition will give a rate of maybe 70 percent. If we split the difference and call the failure rate 30 to 40 percent, that is still pretty terrible.

When looking at failure statistics, it is important to bear in mind that different studies often measure different things. For example, they may define failure differently, or measure degree of satisfaction rather than failure itself. The term *failure* doesn't always have a precise meaning, so be careful when comparing numbers from year to year. Even so, there is clearly a great deal of unhappiness with IT out there.

---

[2]Michael Krigsman, "CRM Failure Rates: 2001–2009," ZDNet, August 3, 2009, http://blogs.zdnet.com/projectfailures/?p=4967.

Why do these failures happen? Well, the conventional wisdom is that software vendors produce buggy products. I won't argue that technology is flawless, but this theory just does not match the facts. In most cases of failure, we are looking at off-the-shelf systems that have been installed successfully at hundreds and sometimes thousands of customers. Product defects may cause an occasional delay, but it would be hard to find a case where an out-of-the-box system caused real damage.

Another theory is that bad project management is to blame. This gets closer to the truth, but we still see surprisingly large-scale failures even when customers have adopted popular project management methodologies.

The best methodologies describe a reasonable, logical road map for deploying complex software. In theory, these road maps should ensure success by establishing a shared process and common expectations among all project participants. In practice, however, distortions interfere with success: Personal agendas, politics, and organizational and information silos all conspire to drive projects to fail. So, the great process gets sidetracked by lack of consensus and other problems that arise when people attempt collaborative work in organizations.

In extreme cases, the IT department may consider a completed project to be successful, while business users find the implemented software to be useless and a complete waste of money. In a sense, that scenario is process run amok beyond reason. Such cases result from misaligned expectations and are surprisingly common.

Collaborative distortions, information hoarding, and silos play significant roles in virtually every IT failure. However, we need to look further to fully understand IT failures.

The Devil's Triangle

Three parties participate in virtually every major software deployment:

1. Software vendors
2. System integrators or consultants
3. Customers

Each of these groups has its own view of success, leading to overlapping and interlocking agendas and conflicts of interest.

As referenced in Chapter 2, the Devil's Triangle arises because the three groups each define success differently.

SOFTWARE VENDORS Software vendors primarily want to sell product licenses, but where do their loyalties actually lie? Ostensibly with the customer, but what about the system integrator who influences many deals?

When the software vendor becomes torn between customer interests and system integrator interests, who wins? It's an interesting question, and the answer is not always clear.

Software vendors also maximize revenue by attempting to charge full list price on software licenses, while trying to lock buyers into long-term support and maintenance contracts. Often, software vendors will reduce license fees for the initial product sale, knowing that real profit lies in years of recurring maintenance revenue. Technology sourcing expert Vinnie Mirchandani has called these fees "empty calories" that provide little benefit to customers. Mirchandani goes on to write that "along with printer ink at $5,000+ a gallon, mobile overseas roaming at $3 per minute, outsourced storage at $3 per GB each month, software maintenance with its 95% gross margins is one of the most 'empty calories' in tech spend."[3]

SYSTEM INTEGRATORS Of course, system integrators ostensibly have the customer's best interests at heart. However, consider what happens when a project goes over budget. The customer pays much of that extra cost to the system integrator in the form of additional services fees, creating a form of so-called annuity consulting that is detrimental to the customer.

The system integrator therefore often has a dual incentive: building a long-lasting customer relationship while racking up change order fees if the project runs late.

The IT Project Failures blog described this conflict in a post:[4] "In private moments, many third-party consultants dream of long projects, where billable hours and customer purchase orders flow like water. This kind of 'annuity consulting' is *never* good for the ERP buyer." On the blog, I wrote that "almost by definition, when projects exceed their schedule and budget, the extra dollars go into the consultant's pocket. Some forward-thinking consulting companies now offer so-called packaged services to help alleviate this conflict of interest."[5]

TECHNOLOGY BUYERS The customer's role in many failed projects is also significant. Despite presenting a unified appearance to vendors, many organizations have internal conflicts and disagreements that surface during the implementation process.

---

[3]Vinnie Mirchandani, "SAP to Kill TomorrowNow," *Deal Architect*, July 21, 2008, http://dealarchitect.typepad.com/deal_architect/2008/07/sap-to-kill-tomorrownow.html.

[4]Michael Krigsman, "The ERP Devil's Triangle," ZDNet, October 9, 2007, http://blogs.zdnet.com/projectfailures/?p=433.

[5]Michael Krigsman, "Packaged Services in ERP," ZDNet, October 25, 2006, http://blogs.zdnet.com/projectfailures/?p=260.

For example, the accounting department may specify business requirements that are not practical from a technology perspective. At the same time, the IT department may not completely understand the accounting department's business goals. As a result, the customer gives the system integrator conflicting instructions, which pushes rework and changes of scope back to the integrator. When the integrator complains, the customer calls the software vendor, who must then play peacemaker.

Although the software vendor and integrator are contractually bound to serve the customer, practical loyalties and conflicts of interest interfere. These are some of the distortions discussed earlier.

How project participants manage the fundamental tensions among these groups can determine whether a project succeeds or fails. Success arises when the three groups align expectations, working together in a spirit of cooperation and mutual benefit. Conversely, implementations fail when greed, inexperience, or arrogance surface and one party attempts to gain unreasonable advantage over another.

Diagnosing Failure

IT projects are complex, which partially explains why success rates are typically low. However, there is also another reason that many projects do not achieve expected results.

Accurately analyzing and diagnosing causes of failed IT projects are difficult because most IT failures experience problems rooted in organizational, political, or cultural challenges. Projects rarely fail for technical reasons alone.

A study by the British Computer Society reported 20 management reasons that cause organizations to cancel IT projects:[6]

1. Inability to adapt to new resource combinations
2. Differences between management and client
3. Insufficient risk management
4. Insufficient end-user management
5. Insufficient domain knowledge
6. Insufficient software metrics
7. Insufficient training of users
8. Inappropriate procedures and routines
9. Lack of management judgment
10. Lack of software development metrics

---

[6]Dr. John McManus, "A Study in Project Failure," British Computer Society, June 2008, www.bcs.org/server.php?show=ConWebDoc.19584.

11. Loss of key personnel
12. Managing legacy replacement
13. Poor vendor management
14. Poor software productivity
15. Poor communication between stakeholders
16. Poor contract management
17. Poor financial management
18. Project management capability
19. Poor delegation and decision making
20. Unfilled promises to users and other stakeholders

The same study reported an additional 15 nontechnical reasons projects fail.[7]

Understanding the Hidden Causes of Failure

Failure becomes a strong likelihood when project stakeholders do not clearly understand the primary determinants of project success. The nontechnical, management causes of failure often come down to misplaced expectations among Devil's Triangle participants in a project. Fundamentally, problems in human communication lie at the root of most failures.

These expectation and communication mismatches are difficult to detect systematically, precisely because they are not quantitative or technical in nature. Projects fail due to hidden issues that the team does not discuss or analyze. Analytical techniques that reveal the presence of these issues can prevent failure.

Traditional project management methodologies have not improved project success rates adequately, because they do not isolate and address the hidden causes of failure. These hidden causes of failure are the bedrock on which all successful projects are established. Without understanding the root causes that determine IT success, projects are doomed to fail repeatedly.

Achieving project success depends on understanding, and objectively examining, all the elements in the complex chain of successful project delivery.

These elements represent seven pillars of project success. They cover a range of business, context, planning, and management matters that are all crucial to avoiding failed IT.

Taken together, these seven pillars provide an analytical framework for examining major components of successful IT projects. They address

---

[7]Michael Krigsman, "15 Non-Technical Reasons IT Projects Fail," ZDNet, June 18, 2008, http://blogs.zdnet.com/projectfailures/?p=837.

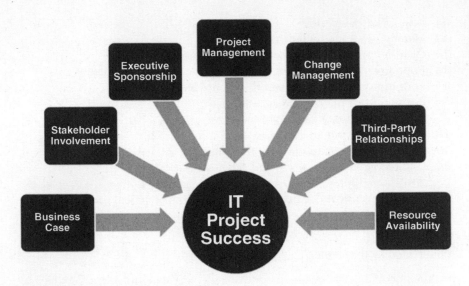

FIGURE 18.1 Key Vulnerabilities
© Copyright 2009 Asuret Inc. All rights reserved.

conflicting agendas, multiple perspectives, and a broad range of business-oriented conditions that drive projects to succeed or fail.[8]

1. Business case
2. Stakeholder and user engagement
3. Executive sponsorship
4. Third-party relationships
5. Project management
6. Change management
7. Resource availability

Figure 18.1 summarizes these key issues.[9]

Enterprise 2.0 Failure

Enterprise 2.0 projects differ from traditional IT in several important ways. Most significantly, Enterprise 2.0 draws on communication, collaboration, and knowledge sharing to improve organizational and operating efficiency.

---

[8]"Seven Fundamentals of IT Success," Asuret, Inc., 2009, http://asuret.com.
[9]Michael Krigsman, "CRM Failure: An Ounce of Prevention," ZDNet, August 27, 2009, http://blogs.zdnet.com/projectfailures/?p=5610. Diagram copyright Asuret Inc.

In contrast, traditional IT projects generally deploy functional automation systems, such as accounting, across multiple departments or an entire organization. Enterprise 2.0 systems do not automate core organizational backbone functions such as finance or manufacturing. Instead, Enterprise 2.0 applications work beside these core functions, facilitating communication and making the supporting human interactions more efficient.

Because Enterprise 2.0 deployments are relatively new at the time of this writing, cases of substantial success or failure remain somewhat theoretical. Nonetheless, we can create a model of Enterprise 2.0 based on lessons drawn from traditional IT projects.

Despite the differences between traditional and Enterprise 2.0 projects, key similarities remain. Most important, Enterprise 2.0 deployments, like all other projects, are rooted in the efforts of a team working together. This *social* dynamic drives success or failure on every type of corporate initiative, from IT to real estate, and includes Enterprise 2.0 efforts.

Reasons Enterprise 2.0 Projects Fail

While the importance of Enterprise 2.0 projects goes beyond technology, most often these initiatives do involve software. When organizations implement Enterprise 2.0 systems and applications poorly, users will not adopt the new software or processes, causing the project to fail. Conversely, well-implemented Enterprise 2.0 initiatives encourage end-user adoption and give the organization genuine and sustainable benefit.

There are four major pitfalls that plague many enterprise initiatives. While not a comprehensive inventory of potential problems, many projects succumb to the following four common causes of failure:[10]

1. Installing technology without a business strategy
2. Paying insufficient attention to user needs and benefits
3. Using ambiguous (or nonexistent) measures of project completion and success
4. The Kumbaya Zone

Failure 1: Installing Technology without a Business Strategy

Many organizations fall into the trap of deploying tools and technology without creating a proper Enterprise 2.0–related business strategy.

---

[10]Michael Krigsman, adapted from "Three Big Reasons CRM Initiatives Fail," ZDNet, August 11, 2009, http://blogs.zdnet.com/projectfailures/?p=5143.

For most organizations, collaborative relationships involve a range of interactions that together achieve (it is hoped) positive results. Creating and executing a business strategy are difficult because Enterprise 2.0 initiatives typically involve numerous components and moving parts.

A Nielsen Norman Group research document describes the importance of strategy, stating that "we can't put too fine a point on this. The only reason to take on the challenge of E2.0 is to fulfill a business need. Period. Creating collaboration or community with these tools, just for the sake of it, will not yield satisfactory results for most companies. Nor will merely adding new 'tools' to a knowledge worker's toolset increase productivity or encourage adoption. The question one should ask when considering this type of project is: what problem are you trying to solve, not what tool should you use."[11]

A unified strategy is absolutely critical to Enterprise 2.0 success, but developing and implementing such a strategy can be a complex, difficult, and intensely political process. In other words, successful Enterprise 2.0 initiatives focus on business objectives and use technology as a support to help reach those goals.

Think about Enterprise 2.0 as a business strategy to help you organize plans and activities around better serving customers; although technology can help, it's not the goal. Forget this lesson at your peril.

Failure 2: Paying Insufficient Attention to User Needs and Benefits

Engaging users is critical to the success of any software deployment, but particularly so in the case of Enterprise 2.0, where users can often sidestep the technology entirely and still accomplish their job function.

A research note from AMR Research explains why this aspect of CRM is different from other enterprise software categories. The message is applicable even more strongly to Enterprise 2.0. "In applications such as ERP, supply chain, or financial management applications, the users have much less flexibility or choice in whether or not to adopt an enterprise application standard. And when was the last time you heard someone question why financials were implemented?"[12]

In my view, poor end-user adoption is not the direct cause of Enterprise 2.0 project failure. Rather, it's a symptom that the organization has not anticipated obstacles that may interfere with users embracing the new system.

---

[11]Jakob Nielsen, "Enterprise 2.0: Social Software on Intranets," Nielsen Norman Group, 2009, www.nngroup.com/reports/intranet/social/.

[12]Chris Fletcher, "Ending CRM Failures: Get in the Loop," AMR Research, September 28, 2007, www.amrresearch.com/Content/View.aspx?pmillid=20784.

Adoption may lag for many reasons, including:

- Software that is complicated or difficult to use.
- Salespeople who don't see adequate value in the new system.
- Poor communication of benefits to users.

One anonymous banker involved said, "Frontline users, particularly the most effective 'top producers,' will adopt the system only on the basis of real or perceived value."

Engage users early and often during the system planning and implementation phases, so they understand what's in it for them. When users do not adopt a system as planned, seek their honest feedback on how to make it more usable, helpful, and valuable.

Failure 3: Using Ambiguous (or Nonexistent) Measures of Project Completion and Success

Successful Enterprise 2.0 projects are rooted in a clear trajectory aimed at achieving specific goals and objectives. Projects without concrete goals *and* a plan to measure both progress and results are distinct candidates for failure.

To solve the problem, articulate specific goals and create a targeted measurement plan designed around your organization's business objectives. Paying attention to the right metrics can help ensure that your project produces the results you seek.

Forrester CRM and customer service analyst Natalie Petouhoff is an expert on using metrics to align technology initiatives with business goals. She commented, "You get what you measure. Without measuring, how can you know whether the business case used to sell the value proposition actually achieves results? This obvious point has somehow eluded most companies. Organizations should measure changes in business results arising from software deployments. Use metrics to drive results that support your business goals. In the absence of metrics, expensive initiatives can drift into failure without ever delivering meaningful benefit."[13]

Failure 4: The Kumbaya Zone

The first three Enterprise 2.0 risks derive from experience studying IT projects across a range of organizations, environments, and situations. However, the Kumbaya Zone is unique to Enterprise 2.0 and related social tools.

---

[13]Natalie Petouhoff, private email correspondence, August 2009. Described in relation to CRM in Michael Krigsman, adapted from "Three Big Reasons CRM Initiatives Fail."

Enterprise 2.0 intersects people, business processes, and technologies in new ways. Change leads to disruption, which is exciting and confusing all at the same time. Enterprise 2.0 cannot credibly show market maturity unless adherents move beyond good feelings to demonstrate how the new methods of work and leadership create clear business value.

Kumbaya feelings, no matter how enthusiastic, are insufficient to build a successful business case. Enterprise 2.0 adoption will grow to mainstream levels only when realistic, data-driven return on investment (ROI) frameworks are broadly established and used.

Responding to this point, independent analyst Jonathan Yarmis advises clients to stay away from the Kumbaya Zone.

Jonathan explained that "the Kumbaya Zone is where we all sit around the campfire, singing odes to social media, and how important it is to 'engage in the conversation.' If I hear that phrase one more time, I think I'll go crazy. Instead, we need to apply social media strategies with a sound business strategy in mind. Why should I do this? Which conversations do I want to engage in? What outcomes do I hope to achieve from engaging in those conversations?"[14]

To help place Kumabaya Zone risks into a business context, Jonathan created the diagram shown in Figure 18.2 when he worked as an analyst at AMR Research.[15]

Case Study: Social CRM

Enterprise 2.0 philosophy promises the opportunity for workers to pool and share knowledge in exciting new ways.[16] Similarly, Web-based software such as YouTube and Twitter let consumers band together, sometimes quite unexpectedly, to form massive, ad hoc influence groups.

These changes hold profound implications for the expression of IT-related problems, which become something quite different from the failure in the traditional enterprise software world.

Let's examine social CRM as an example.

---

[14]Krigsman, "Enterprise 2.0: The Kumbaya Irony."

[15]Jonathan Yarmis, "First Steps in Social Media and Networking: Avoiding the Kumbaya Zone," AMR Research, September 13, 2008, www.amrresearch.com/Content/View.aspx?compURI=tcm%3a7-38542&title=First+Steps+in+Social+Media+and+Networking%3a+Avoiding+the+Kumbaya+Zone.

[16]Michael Krigsman, "Social CRM: Shifting Power and Rapid Burn," ZDNet, August 19, 2009, http://blogs.zdnet.com/projectfailures/?p=5367.

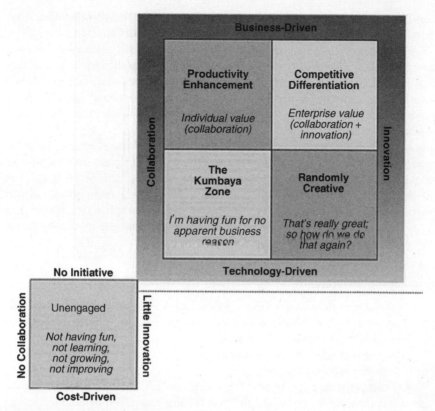

FIGURE 18.2 The Kumbaya Zone
© AMR Research, 2008.

Acknowledging Customer Power

The mere fact of customers sharing information among themselves is nothing new, but the Web lets positive or negative viral consumer crusades arise faster than ever before.

Social CRM is a powerful tool for quickly tracking and understanding customer sentiment. Such formal programs symbolize that an organization cares for its customers. After all, if you don't believe customer sentiment matters, there's no reason to implement social CRM and track opinions.

Bob Warfield, chief executive officer (CEO) of Helpstream, which helps companies build customer service communities, described the shift from traditional, top-down marketing to building social relationships with customers. Warfield says, "Companies still need command and control, and hence CRM. But it's hard to be control-focused in an era where the customer has regained control. Companies need to embrace and engage with customers more now than ever to succeed. That's what social CRM is all about."[17]

Vinay Iyer, vice president of CRM global marketing at enterprise software company SAP, emphatically agreed regarding the implications. Iyer states that "companies can no longer control how customers interact and share information about their products and services. This fundamental shift of power to the customer has profound implications for sales, marketing, and customer service."[18]

Enterprise 2.0 strategist Dion Hinchcliffe placed the shift into broader context, saying that "social CRM is not the technology, not the tools, and certainly not the customer. It's changing the mind-set about what CRM is all about. It's not about managing or riding herd over customers. It's about forming a close partnership, where the organization still has a leadership role, and where intelligent use of social environments can result in vibrant customer community relationships."[19]

Examples of Social Failure

Since consumer-oriented influence groups can rapidly go viral for, or against, any organization or government, extreme reputation failure sometimes occurs with almost astonishing speed.

Wise organizations respond quickly when customers assert a leadership position over marketing messages.

On the positive side, forward-thinking companies talk back to happy and vocal customers. For example, Sonos sent me a T-shirt after I praised the company's iPhone application on Twitter.[20] Sure, it's only a tweet, but Sonos listened and responded fast.

Not all companies handle the social world with such aplomb:

- United Airlines ignored pleas from an unhappy customer and ended up experiencing the butt end of a YouTube video called "United Breaks Guitars."[21] That highly critical video has received over five million page views to date.
- Amazon.com also faced large-scale social failure[22] but, unlike United, handled the aftermath fairly well. After selling Kindle copies of George

---

[17]Ibid.
[18]Ibid.
[19]Ibid.
[20]Michael Krigsman, from Twitter: http://twitter.com/mkrigsman/status/2304121181.
[21]Sonsofmaxwell, "United Breaks Guitars," YouTube, www.youtube.com/watch?v=5YGc4zOqozo.
[22]Brad Stone, "Amazon Erases Orwell Books from Kindle," *New York Times*, July 17, 2009, www.nytimes.com/2009/07/18/technology/companies/18amazon.html?_r=3.

Orwell's book *1984*, the company discovered it didn't have proper rights from the publisher and so remotely deleted copies from customers' Kindle devices. The Web got angry and CEO Jeff Bezos apologized.[23]

As United and Amazon can attest, risk of failure is present in the brave new social world. However, empowered social groups do not need permission to congregate and act, leaving little choice for organizations regarding participation in this world.

The risk associated with nonparticipation means an organization can completely lose control of social Web conversations, often without recourse, if trouble arises. In today's social environment, the greatest threat of failure comes from standing aloof and not becoming engaged.

Preventing Failure through Measurement

Preventing failure and achieving successful projects are the primary reasons for studying and analyzing projects that do not succeed. This section describes a method for systematically examining projects to determine likely vulnerabilities that might cause failure. These techniques use methods quite different from those employed in traditional risk assessments.

The seven fundamentals of success described earlier in this chapter represent a grouping of important organizational, political, and cultural factors that present obstacles to many projects. Since the basis of all project failure in both the traditional and Enterprise 2.0 worlds is the human element, much of the framework holds true in both cases.

To convert the general framework into a useful analytical device and early warning system requires techniques to gather data rapidly from the project at key times. The crowdsourcing method is ideally suited for this purpose.

Wisdom of Crowds

Academics refer to crowdsourcing as "collective intelligence." The phrase *wisdom of crowds*[24] is also applied frequently. This chapter uses all three terms interchangeably.

In the context of IT project implementations, wisdom of crowds is just the notion that you can derive insight into success and failure simply by collecting opinions from stakeholders knowledgeable about the project.

---

[23]Brad Stone, "Amazon Faces a Fight over Its E-Books," *New York Times*, July 26, 2009, www.nytimes.com/2009/07/27/technology/companies/27amazon.html.

[24]James Surowiecki, *The Wisdom of Crowds* (New York: Random House, 2005).

Applications typically involve large numbers of participants—for example, predicting the future of financial markets—by harnessing their collective intelligence.

Since poor communication across organizational boundaries is a key cause of project failures, attempts to improve the likelihood of success by systematically gathering data must operate across silos.

For example, the perspective of the IT department often focuses on technical or nonbusiness issues, such as server capacity and network availability. However, we need to look at the finance department to learn that the chief financial officer will put a halt to a project if it goes over budget, which could be significant project vulnerability. Further, IT may not be aware that end users have a serious morale problem and require special training far beyond that specified in the project plan.

The simplest way to gather wisdom and intelligence from the group is to go around and talk with people—everyone. Ask them about the project, the implementation process, and how they think it's likely to proceed. Ask them about prior projects, and why those succeeded or failed. Get group discussions going. It's probably a lot of work, but a well-rounded understanding of vulnerabilities that are likely to affect the project—and that can easily cost the company millions of dollars if a new system fails—will emerge, or more if the failure impacts basic relationships with customers.

In the second quarter of 2009, net income of clothing retailer Levi Strauss dropped 98 percent due to failure on a technology project.[25] Certainly, rescuing a whole quarter's worth of profits would have justified the investment of time needed to gather information from a few dozen stakeholders.

Although interviewing project stakeholders to discern potential issues is a great idea, there are several limits to the effectiveness of this approach:

- The interview process is time-consuming and expensive.
- Interviewers can project their own bias, coloring results.
- Lack of anonymity inhibits respondents.

Overcoming these issues requires systematic, data-driven tools and approaches. The goal is capturing sufficient data from across the project so subsequent analysis can reveal weakness and potential points of vulnerability to failure.

For Enterprise 2.0 projects, points of failure to measure must include issues that could inhibit users from adopting the software once the project is complete. Respected Enterprise 2.0 analyst Dion Hinchcliffe said, "Enterprise

---

[25]Michael Krigsman, "Levi Strauss: SAP Rollout 'Substantially' Hurt Quarter," ZDNet, July 18, 2009, http://blogs.zdnet.com/projectfailures/?p=917.

2.0 success is about adoption, not technology. Successful initiatives combine grassroots action with top-down executive support."[26]

Wisdom of crowds measurement must target a variety of indicators that reflect known drivers of project success and failure. This technique can prioritize vulnerabilities and raise awareness of likely problems, interrupting the cycle of potential failure and driving toward success.

Nontechnical issues are a primary driver of failure on business initiatives. These issues cause misinterpretation, poor communication, and misplaced expectations among project participants. The best way to interrupt the cycle of failure is implementing standardized and systematic measurement techniques to surface these unspoken goals and expectations and make them explicit. Having done that, project stakeholders can discuss their goals and plans with efficiency and clarity. In many organizations, this in itself can turn the tide of failure and push a project toward success.

Measuring Sentiment to Gauge Vulnerability

The hidden causes of failure disrupt projects in proportion to the extent these conditions exert influence, which varies from one project to another. Therefore, a key measurement challenge is determining which of these factors have a strong impact on any given project.

The nature of nontechnical drivers of failure, such as insufficient executive sponsorship or lack of a business case, suggests they cannot be measured directly without introducing substantial bias. Analytical techniques must therefore gather data indirectly.

COLLECTING DATA Since direct techniques, such as asking stakeholders whether they have sufficient executive sponsorship, for example, are not reliable, indirect measurement is required. In the case of executive sponsorship, one can ask stakeholders to state observations about simple organizational conditions known to influence whether sponsorship is likely to arise.

Executive sponsorship, continuing with the example, is often a highly charged issue, so we must break it down into simpler, more neutral components. For example, examining whether management is stable and whether the project champion has made a public commitment to support the initiative can help determine whether the conditions exist for executive sponsorship to arise. If management is stable and has a long history of cooperation, the likelihood of executive sponsorship arising is higher than the case where high executive turnover is the norm.

---

[26]Dion Hinchcliffe, personal conversation, August 13, 2009.

Management Stability
Senior management is stable and has a long history of cooperation.
Senior management is stable, but there is competition for resources.
The company is growing rapidly, and management roles are changing.
Management turnover is likely as a result of a merger, declining revenues, or a change in company strategy.

FIGURE 18.3 Management Stability
© Copyright 2009 Asuret Inc. All rights reserved. Used with permission.

Asking stakeholders to evaluate straightforward situations of fact inside their organization sidesteps and reduces bias in collecting data. To understand project dynamics across silos, departments, and vendors, the participants must be selected carefully. In general, participants should be drawn from all relevant stakeholder groups, including IT, the line of business, the software vendor, and the system integrator.

By gathering data across sufficient stakeholders—generally, ten is the minimum required—one can obtain a broad view of the project. Achieving statistical prediction is not the goal; rather, the point is achieving rapid and accurate diagnosis: collecting sufficient data against a benchmark framework to rank key project vulnerabilities. While statistically reliable prediction is always desirable, it is not necessary in this case to gain confidence that key vulnerabilities have been surfaced.

Figure 18.3[27] shows the range of responses used to measure the management stability indicator. Participants respond with their perception, or sentiment, toward this particular issue.

ANALYZING RESULTS Data collected in this manner yields a broad organizational view of stakeholder sentiment toward key project issues. Consultants then analyze the data, comparing results across organizational silos and even among participants themselves.

Figure 18.4 shows how indicators such as management stability and project champion roll up to form a composite view of stakeholder sentiment about executive sponsorship.[28] Measuring participant consensus is also necessary to help understand the degree of difference and alignment among stakeholders.

---

[27]Krigsman, "CRM Failure."
[28]Ibid.

Item	Vulnerability	Consensus	Importance	Consensus
+ Business Case	2.01	★ ★	★ ★ ★	★ ★
+ Stakeholder Attitudes	2.21	★ ★	★ ★	★ ★
− Executive Sponsorship	1.95	0.40	2.26	0.46
+ Management Commitment	1.73	★ ★	★ ★ ★	★ ★
+ Management Role	1.98	★	★ ★	★ ★
+ Project Champion	2.05	★ ★	★ ★ ★	★ ★
+ Management Stability	2.03	★ ★	★ ★	★ ★
+ Project Management	2.17	★ ★	★ ★	★ ★
+ Change Management	2.35	★ ★	★ ★	★ ★
+ Third-Party Relationships	2.4?	★ ★	★ ★	★ ★

FIGURE 18.4 Results of Project Failures Analysis

Rolling up this data into a composite view of executive sponsorship helps identify, with a surprising degree of precision, which project vulnerabilities are most dangerous and likely to cause problems downstream. Using the comparison data, one can analyze and understand alignment gaps, highlighting variances in perception and sentiment from one department to another.

The same sentiment analysis techniques apply to analyzing individual responses. Just as internal groups may not agree with the system integrator, for example, so individual perceptions toward the indicators can vary. Various anonymous charting techniques bring these perception gaps to light, creating a neutral and relatively unbiased framework for viewing stakeholder sentiment toward the project.

Summary

Project failures are a serious drain on corporate resources, morale, efficiency, and ability to accomplish strategic goals. The underlying causes of failure are frequently misunderstood, leading to continued high rates of project dissatisfaction.

While Enterprise 2.0 failures have unique attributes, such as the focus on end-user adoption, primary causes of failure remain clearly in the human domain. For this reason, efforts to improve Enterprise 2.0 projects can learn much from the traditional project failure world. At the same time, measurement techniques must adapt their model to reflect the specific attributes of Enterprise 2.0. The basic techniques of wisdom of crowds and sentiment analysis, leading to organizational and individual alignment segmentation, continue to be effective.

Failure arises from negative organizational dynamics that occur when groups work together collaboratively. The techniques described in this chapter uncover these issues, so stakeholders can prioritize and discuss them objectively. That is the surest way to interrupt the cycle of failure and ensure success.

Next Steps

- *Prevention is all-important.* There's always time to fix project problems but rarely time to prevent them. Work with stakeholders before your project starts to ensure that everyone is definitely on the same page about important issues. This is the best, and cheapest, investment you can make to ensure success.
- *Be your own critic.* Use the seven pillars of success described in this chapter to be certain you have sufficient executive sponsorship, a solid business case, and so on.
- *Take a systematic view.* Look carefully across all project stakeholder groups to surface underlying concerns, tensions, or issues. Impartiality leads to success.
- *Gain consensus.* Every complex project involves differences of opinion. Invite representatives from key stakeholder groups to respectfully discuss difficult or contentious issues.
- *Track alignment gaps in addition to project status.* Project management tools, such as Gantt charts, are important but do not manage unspoken expectations. The key to success is making expectations explicit through the entire project.
- *Remain flexible.* Business needs do change over time, and projects must adjust accordingly. However, be sure every major change offers a legitimate business benefit. Don't go late or over budget without clear reasons for doing so.

CHAPTER 19

Readying the Troops for Battle
Phil Simon

He who fears being conquered is sure of defeat.
—Napoleon Bonaparte

Introduction

Today's dizzying array of technological options has left many senior executives justifiably confused. The overriding objective of this book is to reduce that confusion.

Few chief information officers (CIOs) or chief technology officers (CTOs) have articulated a clear and cohesive Enterprise 2.0 strategy. If the CIO is the organization's information technology (IT) commander-in-chief, then confusion at the highest level can only cascade down through the ranks. Even if CIOs "got Enterprise 2.0 religion," there may be legitimate obstacles preventing their organizations (such as those mentioned in Chapter 3) from taking the plunge.

Let's be clear here. Relatively low penetration rates of Enterprise 2.0 technologies does *not* mean zero. Some organizations have already figured out how to swim and have jumped into the pond. A technological divide is growing between the haves and have-nots—that is, those that have effectively implemented such a vision and those that have not. Some organizations are carefully determining how to best use emerging technologies. They understand that their technological advantage is fleeting, as we saw in Chapter 1 with upstart LinkedIn challenging Monster.com. They are anything but complacent.

CXOs cannot expect their organizations to survive, must less sustain a competitive advantage, by simply purchasing and haphazardly implementing the most current technologies, equipped with the latest bells and whistles. Doing so is tantamount to giving Tiger Woods's driver to Charles

Barkley.[1] Sure, Sir Charles might find the fairway on any given hole. More likely, however, a loud "Fore!" and a couple of choice profanities will come soon after his creative swing. Having the right tools is a necessary but not sufficient cause for success; you have to know how to use them.

With that in mind, consider the following seven realities:

1. All IT projects face different challenges, many of which are rooted in effectively managing and communicating with different types of people.
2. The emerging technologies discussed in this book cannot be viewed in a vacuum; they do not implement themselves—at least not yet, anyway. People of all sorts and from all places contribute in a wide variety of capacities on IT projects.
3. This trend will only intensify.
4. Many—if not most—organizations have struggled implementing new technologies.
5. This struggle continues.
6. The importance of human resources has only become more pronounced, given the collaborative nature of Enterprise 2.0 projects.
7. Organizations that optimize their contributions from individuals and teams stand a much better chance of successfully deploying these new technologies than those that do not.

If we accept the previous seven statements as true, then the following stands to reason: The folks in corner offices need to ensure that the skills of their employees meet the needs of their organizations and the marketplace. Organizations cannot expect Enterprise 2.0 projects to be successful if employees lack the requisite people, technical, project management, and management skills. Having these skills present will help them find ever-elusive opportunities admidst the technological chaos presented by Enterprise 2.0.

But how? What specifically does senior management need to do? The fundamental question driving this chapter is: "How can senior management utilize internal and external human resources to deploy new technologies better than they have over the past 25 years?" To this query, I offer seven answers.

1. Know your organization's limitations from the get-go.
2. Insist on maximum collaboration with external parties.
3. Blur the traditional technical/functional distinction.
4. Prepare for sudden, unexpected growth.

---

[1] Formerly a respectable golfer, Charles Barkley now has one of the oddest swings in the sport. Barkley can no longer break 100 and was recently the subject of a reality show designed to fix his horrific swing.

5. Recommit to employee training.
6. Embrace uncertainty to foster innovation.
7. Flip the switch: reverse mentoring.

This chapter provides the organizations' generals (CIOs) with recommended techniques for better preparing their troops for battle.

Know Your Organization's Limitations from the Get-Go

For organizations to realize the benefits of the emerging technologies discussed in this book, C-level executives need to embrace the unknown and avail themselves of many traditional beliefs.

Certainly not every organization needs to adopt each technology in this book. On the contrary, CXOs should consider utilizing each emerging technology with respect to many factors, shown in Table 19.1.

Ultimately, there is no one right answer to extremely broad but critical questions such as:

- Which technologies should we use?
- When and how should we use them?
- What are the risks if we use them?
- What are the risks if we don't use them?

In fact, there is no single correct answer to any of these questions when applied to any one individual technology or any one industry. Translation:

TABLE 19.1 Organizational Considerations for Enterprise 2.0 Projects

Internal	External	Technological
Culture	Industry	Maturity of the specific technology
Size (revenue, number of employees)	Competitive pressures	Alternatives to the technology
Financial situation	Regulatory environment	Other IT projects
Time, budget, and other organizational constraints	Labor market for employees with desired skills	
Current workload of key staff		
Other major projects that could interfere with project		
Current in-house expertise		
Current state of systems and data		

What has worked for one organization may well not work for another—even similar—organization. CXOs need to use their judgment in balancing many internal, external, and organizational factors.

Consider four scenarios in which CIOs are considering implementing a few of the different technologies discussed in this book:

1. To realize the benefits of software as a service (SaaS), an organization needs to let go of its Enterprise 1.0 mind-set of owning and controlling all of its data. If security concerns are sufficiently strong, then the organization should pass on SaaS and stick with its on-premises applications.
2. Organizations will not see the benefits of agile software development if they continue to approach all projects with a waterfall mentality, crucifying IT staff for rolling out applications with known issues. It's foolish for the organization to expect to see rapid rollouts if errors are not going to be tolerated.
3. The company unwilling to ask fundamental questions about its patchwork of systems has no business going to service-oriented architecture (SOA).
4. If a firm's senior leadership is unable to define key data elements consistently throughout the organization, then it should pass on a master data management (MDM) effort.

Let us analyze the first scenario in a bit more detail. Assume that the company that spends $200,000 in total annual costs on its on-premises applications. Costs include annual support fees to the vendor, IT salaries, and occasional consulting. The same company uses roughly 20 percent of the application's functionality. Based on the number of transactions, the organization can expect to pay $50,000 per annum under an SaaS arrangement. Yet the security concerns of senior management persist.

The fundamental questions now become:

- Are the alleged security risks associated with SaaS applications worth $150,000 per annum?
- Are there alternatives that would allow the firm to concurrently save money and address these concerns, such as a private cloud, as described in Chapter 4?

CXOs will save their organizations a great deal of time, money, and effort if they understand the following: A particular emerging technology may not make sense at a particular time. By the same token, however, CXOs should not consistently make excuses to justify the continued maintenance of antiquated applications, systems, architectures, technologies, and modes of thought that collectively hold the organization back.

In short, if you are going to take the plunge into the sea of Enterprise 2.0, make sure that the water is deep enough, you don't see any sharks, and you know how to swim. Don't assume that you will be able to figure everything out while you're in the water.

Metaphors aside, the rest of this chapter provides technology-agnostic advice and guidance for folks in the corner office to maximize their organizations' chances of effectively implementing—and utilizing—emerging technologies.

Insist on Maximum Collaboration with External Parties

As stated in Chapter 2, consultants on many Enterprise 1.0 projects were often able to work autonomously much of the time. To be sure, client input was imperative for basic questions, such as:

- Who should have security to view key enterprise information?
- Which employees are eligible for different benefit plans?
- Which vendors need to be set up in the system?
- Can you provide the item master?

Absent answers to these questions, consultants could not proceed beyond a certain point. However, if system integrators and individual consultants understood the effects of not having these questions answered and could plan accordingly, these limitations could be definitively articulated. What is more, in many cases, consultants could complete other tasks while clients gathered the required information.

On Enterprise 2.0 projects, organizations still need to utilize consultants in a variety of capacities, depending on the specific project. This has not changed. For instance, it is hard to imagine a large pharmaceutical company such as Merck getting SOA religion and single-handedly changing its systems' architecture without the help of experts who have done this before. However, as a general rule, client-consultant interaction on Enterprise 2.0 projects is more critical for several reasons:

- The objectives of Enterprise 2.0 projects are often more open-ended.
- The metrics of Enterprise 2.0 projects are often more nebulous, especially at the beginning.
- Enterprise 2.0 technologies are more flexible and can be configured in multiple ways; there may not be one best solution.

Insisting on increased collaboration among end users, consultants, and vendors not only makes for more valuable employees, it makes for more

TABLE 19.2 Traditional Vendor Selection versus Speed Sourcing

Traditional Vendor Selection	Speed Sourcing
Customer conducts an exhaustive review of the vendor marketplace.	Customer limits its search to Tier 1 providers, existing partners, or industry-specific specialists.
Customer develops a comprehensive request for proposal.	Customer puts together a streamlined "request for services." For example, "We're a financial institution in ten countries with seven data centers in need of an outsourcing solution to reduce costs and capital expenditures."
Customer receives detailed responses from vendors.	Providers return high-level pitches (e.g., "We can consolidate your IT operations over a period of two years for an estimated savings of 30 to 40 percent").
Customer selects a provider.	Customer selects a provider.

valuable consultants and vendors. Collaboration promotes knowledge transfer in both directions.

Speed Sourcing

Organizations need to do more than merely collaborate with external consultants implementing a commercial, off-the-shelf (COTS) application. A few forms of collaboration involve organizations and their software vendors, or speed sourcing. This process sacrifices the drawn-out request for proposal (RFP) and full-blown vendor selection processes for high-level objectives fulfilled by a predetermined number of vendors. To this end, it flies in the face of traditional software development and application deployment. In a way, speed sourcing resembles agile software development, the antithesis of the traditional waterfall method.

In a recent article,[2] award-winning reporter Stephanie Overby delineates between traditional vendor selection and speed sourcing, as shown in Table 19.2.

Needless to say, for organizations this is an enormous change fraught with potential risks.

---

[2]See www.cio.com/article/492917/Speed_Sourcing_The_New_Outsourcing_Trend_.

Risks and Opportunities

Prior to undertaking an Enterprise 2.0 initiative, organizations tend to benefit a great deal from going through a business needs assessment (BNA), requirements gathering, and discovery. Whatever the terminology, the very process of clients asking themselves what they do, how they do it, and whether there's a better way can pay enormous dividends. Organizations have traditionally not done this process well or comprehensively enough to ensure that projects get off to good starts. Poor requirements gathering is one of the main reasons that many IT projects have historically failed.

In the end, organizations need to clearly understand both the pros and cons of speed sourcing if they expect to benefit. For example, consider an organization replacing its antiquated customer relationship management (CRM) system. Focusing on improving customer retention by 40 percent is clearly a paramount objective that is superior to creating every report in the old CRM application. Organizations that cling to antiquated processes are likely to butt heads with providers trumpeting new and ostensibly better methods that will yield significant results.

Bridge the Gap between Functional and Technical End Users

Since Enterprise 2.0 projects are in many ways different from their predecessors, they require different skills from consultants, employees, and even management. Organizations need to bridge the traditional chasm between functional and technical folks.

Most Enterprise 1.0 IT projects consisted of individuals classified as either one of two things: functional or technical. Add senior management to the mix, and most Enterprise 2.0 projects consisted of three groups.

Many of each group's skills and interests did not overlap with the others, leading to problems throughout many projects. On the worst-conceived projects, senior management made decisions almost independent of both the business and the technical audiences. Functional and technical end users were left holding the bag, attempting to make management's bad decisions operational.

CXOs can no longer afford to make technological decisions in a vacuum. They need to involve key end users early and often, regardless of title. Conceiving of a new architecture and expecting IT midlevel employees to make it happen has a proven track record of resulting in failure, as detailed extensively in my first book, *Why New Systems Fail* and in Chapter 18.

Organizations should seek to hire and grow employee hybrids: end users who understand the front end of an application as well as the corresponding back end of tables, data structures, and fields. Hybrids are often able to solve functional and technical problems with equal aplomb.

Technical End Users

To contribute in an optimal manner, IT end users need to go beyond their historical roles of system administration and knowing the workings of the back end. In an article written by Jennifer Kavur of *ComputerWorld Canada*, Jennifer Perrier-Knox, senior research analyst at Info-Tech Research Group Inc., says that "knowledge of business operations and processes is 'hands down' the most important soft skill. IT people that know about business issues, financial issues, they're the ones that are going to rise to the top. That's been the case for the past couple years now because IT has a reputation of not knowing about the business."[3]

There are simply fewer and fewer projects for traditional, stereotypical techies. Increased collaboration means that nearly every job today is client-facing. There is less and less room for the brilliant technical end user who lacks basic communication and business skills.

Functional End Users

For their part, functional end users need to avail themselves of the notion that IT will continue to handle traditional tasks, such as basic data extraction, report writing, and system testing. There is less and less room for the friendly but technically challenged end user who lacks basic computing and business skills. IT cannot be expected to continually hold the hands of people unwilling or unable to learn how to use technologies that have become increasingly user-friendly over the past ten years.

Prepare for Sudden, Unexpected Growth

Sudden growth may take several forms:

- Employees or customers may adopt a new technology much faster than expected.
- On a related note, the number of transactions may increase, creating much more data than originally projected. (Collectively, these first two bullets refer to Metcalfe's law, which states that the value of a telecommunications network is proportional to the square of the number of connected users of the system.)

---

[3]www.networkworld.com/news/2009/070209-soft-skills-are.html?page=4.

- The importance of a new technology may make it indispensable within the organization much more quickly than anticipated. Newer technologies penetrated markets much faster than their predecessors. It took years for the telephone to catch on, less time for televisions, and much less time for cell phones.

This does *not* mean that senior management should purchase millions of dollars' worth of hardware upon rolling out a social networking tool that may or may not catch on. However, nor should a 50,000-person company use as its back end a very limited database that can handle only 1,000 users. Having to dismantle the application's architecture after a successful launch will only stifle its momentum at a time when end users are warming up to it.

Recommit to Employee Training

Based on economic circumstances, many organizations have recently reassessed their staffing levels (read: laid off employees). The end result: The remaining employees have been asked to do more with less. Aside from reducing head count, many organizations have chopped employee-related expenses, including training and travel to user groups in which employees can network and exchange best practices.

While understandable and often imperative for the continued survival of an organization, the aforementioned cutbacks can promote a vicious cycle of increased organizational risk:

- Organizations reduce or eliminate formal training and informal opportunities for end users to learn how to better utilize existing technologies.
- This solidifies many end users' bad habits and suboptimal processing methods.
- At the same time, organizations trim staff, resulting in more work among fewer employees. This means even less time for cross-pollination where employees are trained in multiple jobs.
- This also increases the risk of key employee attrition.

Risk is compounded if key employees leave the organization and, as is often the case, user documentation is lacking. For example, incumbents may scramble to figure out how Alex ran regular interfaces, Neil matched invoices, Julian filed tax reports with the government, and Nancy created database backups. If Alex, Neil, Julian, and Nancy are no longer with their organizations, then they will probably be unable or unwilling to assist their former employers in the event that their help is needed.

Often, the best-case scenario is that jobs performed by ex-employees are partially understood by their replacements. Nonetheless, this may very well result in increased risk of error, financial irregularities, expensive engagements with external consultants, or some other highly undesirable outcome. In the extreme, a single employee's departure may result in a missed payroll, an eventual government audit, or security breaches.

Training as a Means to Increase Organizational Bench Strength

There is a fundamental tension between lean staffing levels and organizational bench strength. The recent economic meltdown has caused many organizations to opt for the former at the expense of the latter. While understandable, the risks of being lean cannot be understated. Lack of widespread end-user application, programming, or technical knowledge is dangerous in the event that a key employee exits. Remember that not all exits are forced or foreseeable; even in harsh economic times, some employees voluntarily leave their jobs for whatever reason.

To this end, senior management needs to recommit to employee training, despite the incentives to cut back. Whether employees are being cross-trained in different functions or learning new technologies altogether, the benefits of training can more than offset their costs for several reasons.

First and foremost, training can mitigate the risk of key employee turnover and the resultant costs associated with finding a suitable replacement. Estimates for the costs of replacing employees vary a great deal, depending on the economy, field, skills required, and the like. One ostensibly plausible estimate is roughly one-third of the incumbent's salary, including benefits and other perks. (This number is typically much higher for CXOs and directors and less for entry-level employees.) The theory here is that employees will recognize the commitment that their organizations are making to them. While hardly tantamount to quelling all fears from nervous employees about their employment futures, training can send a strong message to attendees: "The organization wants employees to develop their skills; despite current economic challenges, we are committed to growing our employees' skills and abilities." This attitude may reduce the likelihood of voluntary employee attrition.

Second, the mid- or long-term savings of training may more than pay for itself. Two super end users with substantial skills and a global perspective may be able to do the work of three or four limited end users, especially if they are skilled in different automation methods.

Considerations and Caveats

Training for training's sake is fruitless. Organizations would do well to ensure that their training investments will result in tangible benefits. End users may learn a robust new technology over the course of a three-day class. However, this certainly does not equate to mastering it or effectively deploying it in the organization, even for highly motivated and skilled attendees.

Consider two examples. Boris attends a class on Cognos PowerPlay, a robust business intelligence (BI) tool. Patty attends a class on Crystal Reports, a powerful reporting application. (Much like in Chapter 2, the use of these examples is in no way meant as an endorsement. While I have used both of them and found them to be very useful and powerful, I cannot claim that they are appreciably better than comparable applications—Business Objects, Hyperion, and so on.) Boris and Patty are both highly skilled end users who have long expressed to their managers a desire to learn more about each application. During and after their classes, they are excited about the new features and possibilities now available to them. Both are eager to begin using their new toys in their jobs.

This is where the similarities end. Boris simply has no time to use PowerPlay. Building cubes of data takes time, and he is simply swamped with his daily responsibilities. While he finds half-hour increments every two weeks or so to play around, the phone invariably rings and he forgets much of what he has learned. His excitement for—and knowledge of—the product wanes, and PowerPlay never gains traction in the organization.

In contrast, Patty immediately begins writing Crystal Reports and distributing them to others throughout the organization. She builds on the knowledge and excitement from class and joins online discussion groups promoting best practices. She is able to "kick the tires" on new reports and experiment with different ways of extracting, manipulating, and presenting her organization's data to her internal clients. As a result of her efforts, many end users have freed up additional bandwidth; they no longer have to manually compile reports from disparate sources of information. Now reports arrive via email as attachments with no further manipulation of the data required. Patty's employer saves thousands of dollars in overtime and now has access to accurate and actionable business information. In this case everybody wins: Patty gains valuable skills that will help her be more productive. For its part, the organization will recognize a significant return on investment (ROI) on the course and might even unearth new knowledge through data mining.

The benefits of employee training cannot be viewed in isolation or in a vacuum; they must be considered within the context of the real world. The organization that sends an overworked, overwhelmed end user to class is wasting its money. Forget the fact that the attendee's mind may be back at work throughout the class. Knowing what an application can do but ultimately not having the time to play around with it at work will result in attendees not utilizing their newly acquired skills and knowledge. Ultimately, neither the end user nor the organization will reap the benefits from the class.

Even if the end user returns to the application six months or a year later, it is highly unlikely that she or he will remember the material covered beyond broad strokes; that end user will have to essentially relearn the concepts.

While there are no guarantees that an employee will use a new technology in his or her job after class (much less effectively), organizations can take the following steps to maximize the chances of this happening:

- Ensure that employees have the time to play around with these new technologies.
- Hold employees accountable to deploying them via annual objectives and performance reviews, which can also ensure that employers actually benefit from their training investment.

Along with potentially reduced risk from key employee turnover and greater internal system knowledge, application training can be a wise investment for an organization even in a tough economic environment.

Embrace Uncertainty to Foster Innovation

Organizations need to be more tolerant of issues related to premature releases of applications. This is not to say that all mistakes, sloppy programming, and a carefree attitude should permeate the organization. However, crucifying employees for not catching everything undermines the central tenets of agile software development. Remember that Enterprise 2.0 technologies will probably not be perfect when released. Organizations will learn a great deal by throwing things on a wall to see what sticks, especially through pilot programs. Encouraging innovation and risk taking means that the organization has to tolerate failure.

Because Enterprise 2.0 projects will differ from their predecessors (see Chapters 2 and 14), it stands to reason that project management (PM) will differ as well. Unlike their predecessors, Enterprise 2.0 projects are less likely to culminate in one massive event in which an entire system is activated. Rather, discrete functionality will be gradually introduced throughout the life cycle of a system. As such, PM will take on more of a cyclical form.

Wouter Baars, project controller at University Medical Hospital Utrecht in the Netherlands, writes on the PMHut blog that

> *in cyclical project management, the project goal is pursued in several short, successive consecutive cycles. Each cycle is relatively short, preferably lasting less than one month. Within each cycle, a portion of the project is carried out. Analysis, design, implementation, and testing occur within each cycle. This is fundamentally different from the*

waterfall method, in which these activities all take place within their own separate phases. In addition, the waterfall method prescribes only single moments for definition, design, implementation and testing. In the cyclical method, this occurs many times in sequence.[4]

In *The Art of War*, Sun Tzu wrote, "Treat your men as you would your own beloved sons. And they will follow you into the deepest valley." Folks in the corner office should take heed.

Flip the Switch: Reverse Mentoring

It is simply foolish for CXOs to assume that knowledge transfer is a one-way street. Yes, to ascend to the corner office, one typically needs years of experience, assignments of increased responsibility, and the managerial chops to handle uncertain business situations. (We're not in the dot-com era anymore.) Technology is changing so quickly, though, that it's virtually impossible for upper-level management to keep abreast of key recent developments that may well benefit organizations. Generation Y employees, in particular, have grown up with the Internet and bring a great deal of expertise to the table. Executives should harness that expertise as much as possible.

One way to do so is through reverse mentoring, a concept popularized by former General Electric head Jack Welch. In her article "How 'Reverse Mentoring' Can Make Your Organization More Effective," Diane Piktialis explains how Welch forced senior managers at GE to listen to younger workers on a number of important issues.

Senior employees can learn from younger coworkers. It's common knowledge that younger people can benefit from older mentors who can transfer their accumulated knowledge and expertise. What can an experienced employee learn from a younger coworker? The answer is: quite a bit. Piktialis lists a number of areas in which CXOs can learn from newbies:

- *Technology. The youngest generation in the workforce today, known as Millennials or Generation Y, is the first group of "digital natives." Having grown up with technology and the Internet their entire lives, they are tech-savvy multitaskers who easily master the latest tech gadget or tool. Baby Boomers and older workers, on the other hand, often need to upgrade their technology skills—and for many who plan to remain in the workforce tech competence is a must.*
- *Subject matter advances. With the recent explosion of information, even the most accomplished professional has difficulty keeping up*

---

[4]See www.pmhut.com/cyclical-methods-of-project-management.

with the latest developments in his or her field. Employees who are fresh out of school can share the latest thinking in a specific field (e.g., health care delivery, education, or the environment), thereby helping later-stage careerists remain current and enhancing their own capabilities and contributions.

- *Risk taking. Younger employees who grew up with technology developed a trial-and-error style of learning in which they are comfortable jumping into a situation to figure things out. Such risk taking can free up old habits and drive workplace innovation.*
- *Global perspective. The Internet has expanded younger workers' geographic perspective. On social networking sites like Facebook and MySpace, young adults learn about global social issues such as world hunger, genocide in Darfur, or endangered beluga whales off Alaska. Their day-to-day social networks often include friends from all over the world. Even if a friend moves back to Paris or Taiwan (as was the case with two of my daughters' friends), they are just a click away. "Think global, act local" is second nature.*[5]

Whether via a formal program or just culturally encouraged interaction, organizations should ensure that the upper echelon and worker bees commingle.

Summary

The promise of emerging technologies can be realized only through the intelligent management of people. CXOs need to understand that the new technological world that they have entered (or will soon enter) is hardly the same as its predecessor. Traditional employee roles and skills are changing; very defined roles and responsibilities, too, have started to blur among employees, consultants, and vendors. Rather than fight these changes, senior management needs to embrace them and find ways to capitalize on the opportunities that they present. Over the long term, an organization cannot expect the following imbalance to sustain itself: successful technologies run by employees lacking the sufficient skills to utilize, maintain, or enhance them. CXOs can expect to maximize their investments in technology only with corresponding investments in their human resources.

However, equipping people with the right skills is a necessary but not sufficient condition for a successful Enterprise 2.0 project. The organization's culture and priorities have to support an endeavor for it to be successful. Old-school tricks such as "throwing more consultants at the problem"

---

[5]www.encore.org/find/advice/how-reverse-mentoring-ca.

are unlikely to produce desired results—for example, real improvement, progress on key issues, and knowledge transfer to otherwise-occupied end users. At a core level, senior management need to understand the requisite trade-offs that each of Enterprise 2.0 technology poses to all concerned. Those unwilling or unable to accept these trade-offs are better off waiting until the time is right. Remember that smaller IT budgets mean that organizations will only get one bite of the apple.

Next Steps

- What skills are your employees lacking with respect to technical knowledge, management, and communication?
- What are the most effective means of developing these skills? On-the-job training? Formal classes? Mentoring?
- Are your employees trainable? Do they have enough time or skills to improve in these areas with existing staffing levels?
- Does it make more sense to bring in external talent, rather than hoping that incumbents grow into the roles that the organization requires?

CHAPTER 20

Sustainability and Green IT
Charlie Bess

When the winds of change blow, some build walls while others build windmills.

—Chinese proverb

Introduction

Sustainability is about striking the balance between economics and ecology, making the most of the consumption required. Green information technology (IT) is the current name for applying these techniques to IT in business. It is about efficiency—not just efficiency in the use of IT resources, but also using IT to shift the efficiency for the whole enterprise. All the sensors and edge computing techniques that are available can be applied to more deeply understand and improve the processes and resource consumption across the entire ecosystem of an organization.

Sustainability is not limited to just business. Frugality in energy consumption is becoming a matter of pride for individuals as well. "Hyper-milers practice such unorthodox techniques as coasting for blocks with their car's engine turned off, driving far below speed limits on the freeway, pumping up tire pressure far beyond car and tire makers' recommendations and carefully manipulating the gas pedal to avoid fuel-burning excess."[1]

Many individuals are personally focused on sustainability. Consider those who try to maximize their own power generation and efficiency, taking pride in moving their consumption off the grid by generating power via solar or other sustainable techniques.

---

[1] www.usatoday.com/money/autos/2008-06-23-hypermilers-saving-gas_N.htm?loc= interstitialskip.

As this trend begins to enter the core of our psyche and becomes part of the purchasing decision-making process, organizations will not only need to be more energy and resource efficient, but also be known for that efficiency.

Growing Impact on Organizations

Real pressures exist for organizations to change their resource consumption behavior. These pressures can come from the following sources:

- Within their customer bases.
- Via legislation.
- From their own personnel.

Although these pressures act on the organization in different ways (see Figure 20.1), the additive effect will cause them to do more than maintain a so-called green sheen. Rather, they will have to take real action that shows up in their annual reports.

Political and Legal Pressures

Organizations are taking the green movement to heart at nearly the same rate as consumers. This is taking place at two levels:

1. Internally in their use of our planet's resources.
2. Externally in the products released into the marketplace.

Australia leads most of Europe, and both are ahead of the United States in public and government demand for corporate adoption of green policies. This demand can be broken into three categories:

1. More efficient products.
2. More visibility into information concerning the organization's efforts to improve its use of resources.
3. Transparency of the relationships and resources consumed in building and assembling products.

This demand for transparency and visibility of an enterprise's activities will require IT departments to gather and present information in new ways.

Google "green regulation" and you will receive more than 29 million hits. During the most recent U.S. presidential election, both John McCain and Barack Obama committed to some form of carbon cap and trade. In other words, this is not a one-party issue or a concern of only fringe groups.

Economic Pressures
- Increased costs for power and cooling
- Increased risk from changing weather events
- Corporate responsibility reporting requirements
- Competitive advantage for companies perceived as green
- Carbon trading
- E-waste penalties

Social and Environmental Pressures
- Lifestyle impacts from global warming, pollution, and waste
- Increased concern for the environment
- Lobbyist and other direct-action groups
- Green investment portfolios
- Customers' willingness to pay for green premium products

Being Green

Political and Legal Pressures
- Environmental Protection Agency (EPA) standards
- Political green agenda
- Globalization driving government environmental policies
- Carbon-cap legislation and other compliance requirements
- Government procurements standards
- Local versus national laws and enforcement

Technical Pressures
- E-waste
- IT contributions to CO_2 emissions
- Consumerization and the explosion of devices applied to business
- Increasingly powerful devices providing greater capabilities at a lower operating cost

FIGURE 20.1 Organizational Pressures to Become Green

To be sure, additional environmental impact laws will have a negative effect on the productivity and profitability of many organizations.

Why have organizations waited when legislation has been imminent for some time? In part, facing so much uncertainty, few organizations want to be first. As a result, organizations have until now made relatively little investment in addressing the new level of productivity required. This will change for one simple reason: Constituents are demanding a shift in corporate perception and behavior. Expect to see more legislation on controlling the production of greenhouse gases, the level of which is currently rampant. This will require new technology for governments to monitor conformance, as well as organizations becoming efficient from within.

In addition to new legislation concerning carbon dioxide (CO_2) production, discussions are under way to place environmental information on product labels. This will be implemented similar to the way in which governments have required consumer product organizations to place nutritional information on packaging. Environmental impact information will likely include:

- The effect of production on the environment.
- The resource consumption of moving the product to the location where it is being sold.

This type of labeling will need to include more information than the static information in nutritional labeling. The labels will need to be more dynamic, depending on whether the product was shipped by rail or truck. Two cans sitting on a shelf that contain the same product but were delivered via different routes would need to have different labels. This will enable customers to make decisions and vote with their wallets on the products they support. Organizations would be wise to understand the different carbon implications of different shipping methods as well as the implications of this trend on buying behavior. In other words, there can be "gold in that green."

The impact on the IT department in gathering and analyzing this information can be profound and may require the use of radically different labeling techniques than those applied today.

For centuries, national governments have used regulation to attempt to change public behavior. Regulations are being mandated at the local level as well, with municipalities declaring themselves nuclear-free[2] or noise-free, or enforcing local ordinances based on ecological impact.

Unless the regulatory confusion is clarified, consider the following possibilities:

---

[2]www.gzcenter.org/campaign/resolution.htmA.

- An airplane taking off over several different subdivisions could receive fines from some but not others due to the exhaust and noise from the jet engines.
- Large retailers could require your address in order to sell you a product that might be all right on one side of the street but not on the other.
- A gasoline station could be in violation for having a certain fuel formulation on one corner of the property but not on another.
- Medicinal radioactive materials may not be available in certain hospitals.

This area is simply ripe for court action. Poorly written laws with areas of confusion and judicial overlap will doubtless invite litigation. Naturally, taxpayers will have to support and fund the enactment of new legislation as well as resolve confusion. Businesses will be at the heart of the conflict because they are most likely to be the targets of violation lawsuits.

Economic Pressures

Although many people may think of becoming green as an end in itself, for organizations it is not. For-profit organization need to make money and generate returns for their stockholders. They can achieve this by charging what the market will bear for their products. They can also increase their margins by becoming more efficient, something that yields a nice side effect: a reduction in waste and by-products of production. In turn, this can allow one organization to be greener than another, due to fewer costs for materials and less waste to clean up. These benefits are part of the economic pressures that both make the company stronger and improve its sustainability.

E-waste is becoming a significant concern everywhere in the world. Historically, consumers and organizations have thrown away electronics and other indirect materials once they have reached the end of their useful lives. These are not just small consumables such as ink cartridges and compact disks (CDs), but large items such as computers and monitors. Many organizations do not plan for specific action as the life span of devices draws to an end. They have not given much consideration to their options or responsibilities for efficient and effective disposal. This luxury is over. Organizations are already starting to develop well-understood and consistently executed policies. To this end, organizations can become part of the solution and not the problem.

Laws concerning the disposal of obsolete electronics are changing. In many locations, it is now illegal to throw hardware devices in the trash; recycling has become compulsory (or will be soon in most of the rest of the country). Product organizations are now accepting trade-ins of obsolete electronics either by choice or by law.[3]

An organization's environmental reputation often hinges on what it does with obsolete hardware. Many organizations are looking to minimize their e-waste by using products with longer life spans. For example, consider thin client terminals connected to a cloud instead of dedicated personal computers. The rationale here is that their longer life spans will have significant environmental benefits.

Consider the following statistics from the consumer side of electronics:

- Nine out of ten U.S. consumers own a computer that they use.
- Three in ten U.S. consumers replaced their computers last year.
- Two in ten U.S. consumers have either a desktop or a laptop that they own but aren't using.
- Twenty-one percent of those who disposed of a desktop computer or monitor threw it in the trash.
- Fourteen percent of those who disposed of a laptop computer last year threw it in the trash.

These statistics roughly apply to businesses.[4]

According to the Silicon Valley Toxics Coalition, with the current hardware replacement rate, "some 300 million to 600 million personal computers in the U.S. could be headed to dumps in the next few years."[5]

In addition to just the computer itself:[6]

- Each cathode ray tube (CRT) computer display contains an average of four to eight pounds of lead.
- Polyvinyl chloride (PVC) coated on copper cables and in plastic computer casings releases highly toxic dioxins and furans when burned.

The disposal of products at end of life can have a long-term effect. We all know about the dangers of lead paint, but recently a new cause for concern has developed. "Lead poisoning is the number one environmental disease among children in developing countries. The full impact of lead poisoning on the health of children and adults is becoming clearer to most countries, and many governments have begun to take action."[7]

---

[3]http://h71036.www7.hp.com/hho/cache/505112-0-0-225-121.html?jumpid=reg_R1002_USEN.
[4]www.greenerchoices.org/electronicsrecycling/el_ewaste.cfm.
[5]http://svtc.svtc.org/site/PageServer?pagename=svtc_washtimes_1_14_2004.
[6]http://svtc.svtc.org/site/DocServer/ppcttv2004.pdf?docID=301.
[7]www.tgfworld.org/lead.html.

Once everyone realizes that electronic devices have significant environmental impact, we can expect that the severity and breadth of the laws will increase, so understanding your options now will produce economic dividends for the organization down the line.

Make no mistake: The problem of obsolete electronics is not limited to just personal computers and CRTs. Gartner Research states that "about half the world's data centers will be functionally obsolete due to insufficient power and cooling capacity to meet the demands of high-density equipment."[8] Organizations will be disposing of whole data centers in the coming years as they shift to use more leveraged and cloudlike computing techniques. Fortunately, new data centers are significantly more efficient—both in their use of power as well as in their supporting infrastructure. As a result, their ongoing environmental impact will be lower, but the disposal costs will be high.

Social and Environmental Pressures

So far most of the pressures being discussed have been quantitative in nature. There are clear measures that can be performed, and organizations should get the same result every time. Social pressures, however, are based on the perception of how environmentally concerned and proactive the organizations appear.

Organizations' reputations are being put on the line as Wall Street analysts rate their ecological focus. Stocks are being packaged into mutual funds that focus on green organizations and targeted at environmentally concerned investors. The previously mentioned environmental labeling will enable consumers to vote with their pocketbooks, deciding whether to reinforce a green effort through purchase or to rebuff a nongreen effort by passing on products.

To be sure, the standards of what is green (and related levels of greenness) are still evolving. However, they will be worked out in the marketplace and then applied ruthlessly. The current rebranding of a product as green may cause a short-term spike in demand, but the market is smart and will figure out those who are "greenwashing" their product to boost sales.

In today's Web-enabled world, don't underestimate the power of one consumer to negatively impact an organization's brand through YouTube, Twitter, or other social networks. In turn, this means that organizations must be green—or defend themselves in the court of public opinion. They will be forced to communicate with customers—and the public at large—via web

---

[8]http://vmblog.com/archive/2007/06/16/gartner-predicts-data-center-power-and-cooling-crisis.aspx.

sites, social media, and blogs. Organizations will need to understand the following:

- Their market.
- Their market's expectations of ecological responsibility.
- How they compare to (or are perceived against) their competitors.

Organizations leading and committed to addressing sustainability issues can use that information to shape the market and create demand.

Organizations can also affect their environmental reputation via the diversity of employees available to them. Great organizations usually want to have access to the widest range of employees. Some potential and even current employees are using ecological information to select employers.

Fifty-nine percent of 2,000 workers surveyed by Adecco USA, a Melville, New York–based human resources (HR) firm, said they felt that their employers should be taking more steps to reduce or recycle. While this may not be a big issue during an economic downturn, a weak environmental reputation costs an organization not only customers but potential employees.

It's not just Generation Y who is interested in these environmental issues. Remember there are quite a few baby boomers left in organizations who were part of the ecological movement in the 1960s.

Organizations that want to hire and retain the best workers (or at least have the choice among the widest audience of workers) will need to have public and positive environmental reputations, because people are interested in working for more than just one type of green.

Technological Pressures

The final pressure to cover are the technical pressures—today's technology may deliver significantly greater computational capability than in the past, but it can also break the bank (either through the cost of cooling and power or through the fact that you do not have enough capacity and floor space to do what you need to get done). According to an EPA report in August 2007:[9]

> It is estimated that this sector consumed about 61 billion kilowatt-hours (kWh) in 2006 (1.5 percent of total U.S. electricity consumption) for a total electricity cost of about $4.5 billion USD. This estimated level of electricity consumption is more than the electricity consumed by the nation's color televisions and similar to the amount of electricity consumed by

---

[9]www.energystar.gov/ia/partners/prod_development/downloads/EPA_Datacenter_Report_Congress_Final1.pdf.

approximately 5.8 million average U.S. households (or about five percent of the total U.S. housing stock). Federal servers and data centers alone account for approximately 6 billion kWh (ten percent) of this electricity use, for a total electricity cost of about $450 million USD annually. The energy use of the nation's servers and data centers in 2006 is estimated to be more than double the electricity that was consumed for this purpose in 2000.

The report goes on to state that

under current efficiency trends, national energy consumption by servers and data centers could nearly double again in another five years (i.e., by 2011) to more than 100 billion kWh . . . , representing a $7.4 billion annual electricity cost. The peak load on the power grid from these servers and data centers is currently estimated to be approximately 7 gigawatts (GW), equivalent to the output of about 15 base-load power plants. If current trends continue, this demand would rise to 12 GW by 2011, which would require an additional 10 power plants.

Clearly this ever-increasing demand for computational resources will become significant for organizations as well as the world.

There are numerous ways to address the demand for computing. Unfortunately, one of the side effects of an organization's success using IT is that there will be a buildup of layer upon layer of applications, each successful in its own right. These consume power as well as HR to maintain and keep them operational. One way to cut power consumption is within an organization's IT team. The elements that make up an organization's application portfolio need to be assessed on a "value per watt consumed" basis. The infrastructure also needs to be addressed through virtualization and be evaluated based on an applied MIPS/watt basis, as well.

In addition to the standard buildup of applications through success, as organizations undergo mergers and acquisitions, redundant technologies need to be filtered out. After a few mergers, organizations can end up with multiple HR or financial systems, for example, that individually do not add much business value. Each of these resides on hardware that typically is not used efficiently. Whittling the portfolio applications down to just a few core highly valued systems or, better yet, leveraged services where an organization can pay for only what it consumes will have a tremendous effect for the company, focusing scarce resources on areas that return results.

For each 100 watts of power that is dug out of the ground in the form of coal, a significant portion (as much as 60 percent) is consumed in the power plant itself. Another 10 percent is lost in the transmission process to get the power to the data center. This is one of the reasons many organizations are moving their data centers close to power plants. They are usually given power at lower rates, because they do not have to pay the transmission line penalty.

Once the power arrives at the traditional data center, another 13 percent of the original energy is consumed by cooling, lighting, and power conditioning; this is approximately half of what comes into the data center. New techniques in lighting and data center design are being applied to address this area. A technique that is being investigated in many organizations to cut down the loss in power conditioning is the direct current (DC)–only data center, but this requires special approaches to both powering the equipment as well as the power supplies in the equipment itself.

Now that the electricity has finally reached the servers, the power supplies and fans consume another 8 percent of the original power. This leaves approximately 9 of the original 100 watts available to do work. Most computers run at 15 percent efficiency or less, so that leaves approximately 1 watt to apply to applications. If we take out held-over, obsolete applications that do not add value and inefficient processes that are in most businesses, hardly any real business value comes out of that initial 100 watts of power.

Understanding the portfolio of hardware and software and weeding out the deadwood can radically improve the carbon footprint of an organization's IT investment. If you were able to kill off a parasitic application that has stopped generating value and save 1 watt's worth of power at the server, it actually can save 100 watts' worth of power being pulled out of the ground.

The Green Fad

No matter how admirable the sustainability movement is in its own right, there is a market push behind it. Many green products are coming on the scene, with many more to come in the future. Google "green product" and you will find more than 160 million hits. People have talked about ecology and efficiency since nearly the start of the industrial age. This time it appears to be entering the consciousness of everyone, everywhere, and will be lodged in our actions as well as our thought processes for the foreseeable future.

Unfortunately, with the massive push for sustainability, the ecological movement is taking on some of the tendencies of a fad, with special terminology and consulting. We are hearing about it from all sides. It can be confusing about what is real and what products are being "greenwashed" to capture market share.

Many products are being presented as green without any real change in their characteristics. We do not really know if they are better or worse for what is needed. Some examples are:

- *Climate Change Chocolate.* Claims that "Reducing your carbon footprint just got a whole lot tastier." It includes 133 pounds of verified TerraPass carbon offsets with every bar of chocolate and has 15 tips for reducing your carbon footprint on the wrapper.
- *Waterless Car Wash.* Owned by Eco Touch, which is committed to "providing vehicle owners everywhere with a superior line of car care products that do not harm the planet or the user. We strive to conserve water, eliminate contaminated runoff, and save you time when cleaning your car. Through our marketing, we aim to educate consumers that it is possible to enjoy a clean car, boat or RV without using petro-based chemicals—and to save enormous amounts of water at the same time. We're committed to clean cars and a non-contaminated environment."
- *PO-ZU Edible Shoe Cream.* "The newly launched 'edible shoe cream' made from 100% coconut not only cleans and polishes shoes when they need it, it's also a delicious 'all-in-one' beauty product that can be used as a lip balm, skin moisturizer, hair conditioner, massage oil and even as an alternative cooking oil. You can even spread it on your toast! Ideal for anyone who won't put anything on their skin or clothes that isn't safe to eat."

There does not seem to be a clear definition of what it means to be green. There are real products out there like a variety of pure electric and hybrid cars that definitely use less fossil fuel, but their costs and environmental impact from manufacturing, use, and disposal are still under dispute. It is clear that consumers and businesses are aware of a perceived need to address these issues, and the marketing organizations are seizing the opportunity.

Organizational Response to Sustainability

An organization's response to sustainability needs to be multifaceted. The resources being consumed need to be taken into account as well as the impact of the actual product over its life span. The toxicity of the products as well as the by-products created during manufacturing need to be understood and their impact minimized.

Our previous behavior of viewing energy resources as abundant will need to change. Our actions—consuming resources that appeared inexpensive, inexhaustible, and easy—are causing side effects that are expensive, scarce, and difficult to produce or clean up. Fortunately, a wide range of actions can be performed to improve the green performance of your organization.

Understanding Consumption

Even though the demand for our IT resources is increasing, there is fundamental inconsistency in how they are used. In nearly every industry, we expect business assets to be utilized efficiently. For example, in manufacturing, a 90 percent utilization rate is not unusual. Or consider call centers. Representatives should be busy over 90 percent of the time during the business day. Yet for IT, the average utilization for the servers of most organizations is under 15 percent.[10] When those servers are idle, they still consume a significant percentage of the power they need when they are fully occupied. This dormant resource's consumption is costing organizations dearly.

Even for highly used resources, their consumption of energy can be overlooked. The network (the global Internet) consumes more than 100 billion kilowatts of electricity and costs organizations over $7.2 billion annually. The amount of data transferred has doubled in the past five years[11] and should double again by the end of 2012.

Power consumption doubled for computer use between 2000 and 2005 and is on track to double again by 2010. Even if we were to keep our consumption the same, the cost of power is on the increase.

The way electricity is delivered is under tremendous demand-based pressure. The power utility grids are not keeping up with demand although they are trying to gain control through the use of Smart Grid technologies. Most metropolitan areas cannot easily take on a new world-class data center. Four out of five large European organizations are planning data center expansions within the next two years. Organizations are projecting a 21 percent increase compared to a 2008 survey in average power capacity per rack (4.7kW versus 5.7kW), which is a significant metric for data center power requirements.

In 2008, the annual cost of electricity exceeded the annual cost of the server (assuming a three-year server life span). The average 25,000-square-foot data center spent $2.6 million a year on power in 2007. That amount is projected to increase by 400 percent in five years. This total cost perspective is critical to investing and consuming computing resources.

---

[10]www.transitionaldata.com/insights/EPA_Datacenter_Report_Congress_Final.pdf.
[11]www.internetworldstats.com/emarketing.htm.

Fortunately, organizations do not need to address this issue on their own. More than 60 percent of organizations plan to use a partner to expand rather than taking a do-it-yourself approach to these large data center projects.[12] Many organizations are focused to deliver leveraged computing. Like most IT services, they divide into those that focus on a market niche like small businesses versus large business versus multinational enterprises. However, cloud computing and software as a service (SaaS) are fundamentally different from previous leveraged computing approaches in the following manner: With clouds and SaaS, even small business can take advantage of the scaling capabilities of these leveraged computer centers. This was not the case with previous new products in corporate computing. In fact, small businesses are adopting cloud techniques at least as rapidly as their big brothers, if not more so.

Even within an organization's existing systems, a technique being used to maximize the business value of its existing investment is virtualizing servers and turning off any that are not used. This is an obvious way to save money. If you have six servers running at 15 percent utilization and can combine them into one server, you will have saved significant energy and hardware costs, resulting in a machine that is fully utilized and five that can be applied elsewhere or sold. Unfortunately, with today's virtualization technology, much of the management costs to maintain the operating system image will remain, since there is nearly as much work as before to maintain the operating systems. Automation and operating system design techniques to address this are being developed all the time. In the process of performing the consolidation, the applications will also need to be rigorously tested to ensure they can still meet the required service levels.

This type of consolidation is possible because many applications are overserved by Moore's law.[13] As hardware upgrades take place, the same applications will use less and less of the available hardware, unless they are central processing unit (CPU) bound. Sun (now owned by Oracle) has a discussion of this phenomenon that it calls "red shifting." Organizations can understand the extent of their underutilization and application design in their current environment by performing enterprise application and infrastructure portfolio assessments, thus quantifying the software maintenance costs, energy consumption, and business value by application and the servers on which they run. This technique will bring areas requiring action to light. It

---

[12]www.datacenterdynamics.com/ME2/Audiences/dirmod.asp?sid=&nm=&type=news &mod=News&mid=9A02E3B96F2A415ABC72CB5F516B4C10&AudID=E5BD2FF22AF 74DF3A0D5F4E519A61511&tier=3&nid=7FB207E2402241588B0DBA05E6BAD054.
[13]www.informationweek.com/shared/printableArticle.jhtml;jsessionid=MWVZKQTD WKHGBQE1GHPSKH4ATMY32JVN?articleID=201800873.

will expose bloated, redundant, and obsolete applications that can be tuned or eliminated to reduce their energy consumption and help to actively weed out the underperformers. Addressing this low-hanging fruit should free up funds of which a portion can be' reinvested in further improvements. Eventually, organizations can focus their enterprise architecture by using a business-value-generated per-watt perspective, maximizing the use of corporate resources while still making IT be a differential factor for the business.

Another near-term activity for IT departments is to ensure that the hardware is performing at optimum efficiency and does not have any poorly performing fans, power supplies, or an overallocation of storage for the business needs. A review of the entire hardware inventory and a hardware portfolio assessment looking at power consumed versus the business value generated from a hardware perspective should also be performed.

This concept of negawatts—watts saved by not being consumed—is focused on increasing the value generated by removing low-value and wasteful systems.

When we are done with systems, we do not always effectively turn them off. For example, a large financial firm was going through a data center consolidation. One of the first things it did was create an initiative to identify the owners of all the systems currently being operated in the data center. An owner could not be found for 15 percent of the systems, so the firm started shutting them down. Owners came forward willing to support and fund only two of the systems that were shut down, bringing them back on line. This reduction in support costs and power utilization for the rest of the systems went straight to bottom-line savings.

Organizations are moving toward a holistic understanding of operating costs. An easy starting point for many organizations is to force their data center managers to be aware of their power usage. Many organizations pay for their data center power consumption out of their overall facilities budgets. This artificial separation of costs from the IT budget needs to be stopped. The folks who run the data center should have clear visibility into the value and power consumption of every box under their control and be part of the team driving an increase in business performance.

Organizations need to evaluate IT costs from an all-inclusive, business-value-generation perspective.

Distributing Bits, Not Atoms

Other virtualization opportunities for organizations exist beyond just the use of operating system virtualization. We can focus on moving bits, not atoms. In other words, we can maximize the movement of data and not physical objects, whether they are paper or personnel.

Most organizations are moving to electronic documents, billing, and payment. This is a radical shift from using paper and relying on digital archiving for storage. There are significant environmental implications of this move.

The marketplace has quickly embraced online access of books, newspapers, and content. Case in point: Amazon's Kindle sold out when it premiered. For me personally, three out of every four books I read in the past year, I have read on my phone. The form factor is a bit small, but it is always with me. I find myself reading whenever I am waiting for longer than a few minutes. If I am forced to queue up to address bureaucratic issues, I just pull out my phone and start reading.

The amount of content in the world continues to increase, doubling every 18 months.[14] For most organizations, their digital content increases at an even faster rate as they begin to deploy sensors and collaboration tools. This material is a mix of structured (database) data as well as unstructured data, with unstructured data growing the fastest. Moving to electronic content management and workflow allows for greater access and less rework and process control, improving organizational efficiency.

The traditional content creators and networks recognize this shift. More magazines and information sources are providing their content in electronic forms, and whole new business models have cropped up to take advantage of the shift.

IT departments can also address environmental concerns for an enterprise via the use of a virtual presence. This entails moving beyond the normal teleconference call to provide personalized services for consumers at kiosks and at individuals' desks. This reduces the amount of travel required as well as improving the availability of scarce personnel.

Efficiency through IT

We are in the process of shifting from thinking about computers as devices to thinking about them *in* devices. The average car has many computers and hundreds of sensors that collectively improve overall performance and efficiency.

Contextualizing content is another powerful technique to reduce energy consumption and improve the value generated. People make decisions based on context, not on content. Using sensors in the organization can provide a much more granular and complete understanding of what is actually going on. Sensor data is one of the main reasons that digital content is growing so fast.

---

[14]www.infoniac.com/hi-tech/digital-content-today-to-double-every-18-months.html.

Case Study: Great Duck Island

Great Duck Island is an example of a new use of sensors. On this island there is a species of bird being studied by some scientists from the College of the Atlantic, in collaboration with the University of California–Berkeley and Intel Corporation. Since the birds (petrels) nest underground, scientists had great difficulty studying them and acquiring the detailed information needed. To counter this issue, scientists began dropping into the birds' nests sensors (motes) that included a self-organizing (mesh) network capability. As a result, scientists were able to gather the information without disrupting the environment. Over a three-month period during the summer of 2002, the sensor network delivered approximately 1.8 million measurement packets to the base station, with individual motes delivering up to 50,000 packets. Each mote was programmed to measure several environmental variables, including temperature, humidity, barometric pressure, and light level.

Just like in the Great Duck Island study, the increasing use of sensors is providing the kind of information needed to manage IT environments. Green IT can be as much about how we use the available computational capability to have greater effect, understanding and tuning the enterprise environment.

Organizations can use the same type of automation within data centers and facilities. These projects do not have to be all-encompassing in scope. EDS has been working with a company called Fifth-Light that has created a way to manage and dim florescent lighting, with each fixture being individually addressable over TCP/IP. In addition, these fixtures can sense movement and ambient lighting change, dimming themselves when their output is no longer needed. The minimum lighting energy saving using this technology has been 70 percent, and it improves from there based on the situation where the fixtures are used. Something as ubiquitous as lighting can use computer monitoring and automation techniques to improve efficiency, so there are numerous possibilities for almost any organization.

Greater Visibility through IT

To be sure, at a minimum IT can help organizations save costs via helping end users find information. For more on this, see Chapter 10, Enterprise Search and Retrieval. New display and interface techniques are being developed every year. Pattern recognition and simulation approaches can reduce the latency in decision-making processes. While each of these techniques may consume greater energy in the data center, the benefits of aggregate reduction in waste and improved performance more than offset their costs.

For their part, IT departments can also help by consuming better energy. For example, consider the data centers going into the Olympic River valley in Washington or even being powered by Niagara Falls.[15] These approaches are using available power sources in new ways and reducing the costs of computing resources (although in the case of Washington State, the local tax laws are currently having a dampening effect).[16] Renewable solar and wind installations are springing up across the globe as well. Geothermal opportunities are making remote locations like Iceland appear to be ideal for zero-carbon-footprint installations.[17] Organizations can both reduce costs and improve their reputations by understanding their sources of power and sharing that knowledge with others.

The Future of Green IT

Expect green IT to continue to blossom. In August 2009, Claire Cain Miller wrote a *New York Times* article about venture capitalist money pouring into green start-ups. Miller stated that:

> *Vinod Khosla, the prominent venture capitalist who has been investing hundreds of millions of his own dollars in green technology companies for the last several years, will now invest other people's money, too. Khosla Ventures, the firm he founded in 2004 after leaving Kleiner Perkins Caufield & Byers, is announcing on Tuesday that it has raised $1.1 billion in two funds that will invest in green technology and information technology start-ups. This is the largest amount raised by a venture capital firm since 2007 and the largest first-time fund raised since 1999, according to the National Venture Capital Association.*[18]

Raising over $1 billion during a terrible economic climate is further testament to the long-term commercial viability of many start-ups and green IT in general. Stay tuned. Green IT isn't going anywhere.

---

[15]http://green.yahoo.com/blog/ecogeek/1125/yahoo-data-center-will-be-powered-by-niagara-falls.html.

[16]http://gigaom.com/2009/08/07/washington-vs-washington-the-cloud-computing-edition/.

[17]www.greentelecomlive.com/2008/04/22/the-first-green-data-haven-iceland/.

[18]www.nytimes.com/2009/09/01/business/01khosla.html?partner=rss&emc=rss.

Summary

Sustainability is an issue that we are going to be living with for the foreseeable future. It will change both how and why organizations consume every level of IT resources.

To maximize the benefits of sustainability, IT teams need to plan for that future and provide innovative solutions for their organizations. Doing so will enable them to improve organizational performance and perception in the marketplace.

Next Steps

- Look for the metrics critical to understanding efficiency and performance, and develop a plan to gather and track them.
- Define goals for consumption, visibility, and transparency. Create a plan that can be executed and tracked.
- Support the organization's public commitments with the information required to shift the public perception.
- Work with the business teams to understand their objectives and suggest ways to innovatively use IT to meet those goals.
- Look for ways to increase capability while still reducing power consumption.
- Define new sources for power.
- Ensure that your hardware and software portfolios are used and delivering value.

PART V

Conclusion

CHAPTER 21

Finding Opportunity in Chaos
Phil Simon

It's clear there's a lot of room for improvement; there's no inherent ceiling we're hitting up on.

—Sergey Brin

Introduction

To be sure, this book has covered a great deal of ground. I hope that you have found the content interesting, whether you have read only a few chapters or the entire book. Two things should be painfully clear: There's more than a little chaos in the information technology (IT) universe right now, and that very chaos begets opportunity.

However, a few words of caution are in order before readers attempt to uproot the current applications, systems, and IT architecture in their organizations. Yes, Enterprise 2.0 technologies are very powerful and can yield tremendous benefits. However, technology endeavors of all sorts should be handled carefully, whether they fall under the umbrella of Enterprise 1.0, 2.0, or 15.0. Different organizations—even within the same industry—often face different technology, business, financial, people, and data challenges.

Even heeding all of the advice in this book cannot guarantee the successful adoption of a new technology, much less its continued success. No book, consulting company, management guru, or software vendor can promise that an organization will coast along, free from the daily—and often harsh—realities of technology and business. Both change far too often and far too dramatically for any organization to sit on its laurels years—or even months—after introducing a new technology.

The best-managed project may fail, while a horribly managed project may come in under budget and ahead of schedule and do everything that a software vendor or systems integrator promised at the outset. In reality, however, organizations are very unlikely to find themselves in one of these extreme scenarios. On a fundamental level, successfully activating and utilizing an emerging technology is about minimizing risk from day one until the end of the project and beyond, as explained in Chapter 15. The organization that can do this stands the best chance of averting failure and realizing the potential gains available through these exciting technologies.

This final chapter provides a summary of the book, identifies the drivers of Enterprise 2.0 adoption, and looks at both where we are now and where we are going.

Summary of Book

Part I of the book established the basic framework for different Enterprise 2.0 projects, with particular attention regarding the differences in relation to their predecessors. What's more, technologies then and now need to be viewed against the backdrops of individual organizations and their IT departments.

The book then focused on enterprise architecture—the building blocks available to organizations to create a set of connected, intelligent, adaptable systems and technologies. Overviews of open source (OS), mobile technologies, service-oriented architecture (SOA), software as a service (SaaS), cloud computing, and social networking provided insights into some of the new ways of building applications. The reader learned about the different tools, materials, and options for building different IT architectures and the pros and cons of each. Equipped with them, each organization can build what meets its needs.

Next, the book concentrated on data, information, and knowledge. Organizations should not lose sight of the fact that a system or technology is only as good as the data that it stores and creates. Tools such as master data management (MDM), business intelligence (BI), enterprise search and retrieval (ESR), and procure-to-pay (P2P) automation can make organizational data more meaningful, contextual, and apt to produce bottom-line results.

Part IV discussed implications of these emerging technologies—and the data that they create, store, and provide—within a managerial context. Even the best-conceived technologies, applications, and architectures with pristine, secure, and accessible data need to be managed properly. Failure to do so increases risk for project failure, organizational decline, security breaches, and other suboptimal outcomes. Green IT, SaaS, open source applications, enterprise risk management (ERM), global engineering, and additional management techniques should assist organizations in optimizing their technologies and the data that they store.

This book concludes with a brief look toward the future.

Where Are We Now?

To be sure, most organizations have not completely embraced Enterprise 2.0. In other words, I know of no organization that has done all of the following:

- Replaced all of its on-premises software with SaaS equivalents.
- Replaced its old IT architecture with contemporary SOA alternatives.
- Purchased, implemented, and effectively used BI and ESR applications, enabling end users to easily locate information and make better business decisions.
- Introduced effective internal collaboration tools that increase employee productivity and communication.

The list could continue, but the fundamental point remains: Most organizations are at a technological crossroads. They may have dipped their feet into some of these pools. Few, if any, are completely ensconced in the Enterprise 2.0 world.

Note that not all organizations will equally embrace each Enterprise 2.0 technology. Nor should they; not every organization needs every conceivable tool. For example, the company that manages its exceptionally data well can probably skip MDM altogether. Still, the different Enterprise 2.0 technologies discussed in this book will have much different penetration rates, especially across different industries.

Enterprise 2.0 Drivers

Many factors will drive each technology's penetration rate, eventual success, and long-term viability. In a similar vein, these technologies are not completely independent of each other. For example, consider open source software. If the vast majority of organizations struggles with OS or views its risks as excessive, then one would expect to see a bump in alternatives such as SaaS. The following factors will drive the adoption of Enterprise 2.0 technologies:

- The economy
- The regulatory environment
- Security concerns
- Technology maturity
- Organizational size and culture

- Reasonable expectation of results
- Business imperatives
- Risks and rewards

The Economy

With IT budgets in limbo, many organizations are unwilling to undertake a major technology initiative, especially when the other uncertainties are considered. Again, many have a subpar track record introducing new technologies. Many CXOs rightly believe that, if their organizations lack the funds or personnel to start a project with proper financial and human resources, then they might as well wait. The status quo may be inefficient but it does work, at least for now. As they say, the devil you know is better than they devil you don't.

Three things militate against normal organizational risk aversion:

1. These technologies offer tremendous cost savings.
2. These technologies offer other benefits unmatched by the organization's current systems and applications.
3. The chronic need to do more with less forces even conservative organizations to take IT-related risks.

In other words, the risks of Enterprise 2.0 technologies may be more than worth their rewards, especially as other organizations iron out the kinks. For example, ESR offers the promise of more accessible and accurate information. Social networking can improve organizational communication among employees and between customers.

The Regulatory Environment

The economy aside, eventually organizations will no longer have a choice to continue with old methods. Green IT is a perfect case in point. Regardless of the economic benefits of using IT in a more environmentally friendly fashion, government regulation will soon prohibit inefficient, pollution-generating techniques—or make continuing these processes prohibitively expensive. In the latter case, adoption of Enterprise 2.0 technologies is the lesser of two evils.

Security Concerns

Because of its historically prominent role in the functioning of businesses, security concerns are at the forefront of IT. As described in the book, Enterprise 2.0 technologies offer tremendous benefits, but those benefits have to be considered against any breaches in corporate data or networks. Threats have multiplied, but so have organizations' tools to combat those threats. Rest assured, the only way to make data, networks, and individual personal computers and mobile devices *completely* secure is isolation. That's just not a realistic consideration in an increasingly interconnected world.

Technology Maturity

Many experienced IT professionals and chief information officers (CIOs) have seen new technologies come and go. As such, they do not want to commit their organizations to technologically untenable paths when the future is so nebulous. The benefits of any one technology may be too disruptive for an organization to stomach.

Clearly, as each technology matures, more examples and case studies become available. The number of experienced personnel also increases, creating a larger pool of expertise. Given changes in the global workforce and increased collaboration discussed in Chapters 14 and 17, expect the project orientation of many teams to only increase. Organizations may be more willing to take technological risks if they know that they can contract hired guns and experts who have shown a clear ability to demonstrate concrete business results. Until that time, many CIOs and chief technology officers (CTOs) will stand on the sidelines, afraid of wasting enormous sums of money on IT projects.

Organizational Size and Culture

Larger, successful organizations with strong cultures spread out across the globe tend to be less agile than smaller start-ups. As such, one would expect Goliath-sized organizations to view these technologies skeptically. Even the biggest organizations have gotten Enterprise 2.0 religion, though, as evidenced by IBM's forays into both social networking and open source.

Of course, there's no substitute for size. A small organization unencumbered by a stifling bureaucracy will have a much easier time moving to an SOA compared to a multinational corporation with layers and layers of patchwork architecture.

Reasonable Expectation of Results

While many Enterprise 2.0 technologies may be new, one thing has not changed: Most organizations will not adopt them unless they can expect to see concrete results. Of course, the carrot may not be enough. Organizations that fear the stick may also go down this road, although it's hard to imagine a scenario in which a government agency mandates that all organizations adopt SOA or open source. Some of these results include:

- Reduced costs.
- A reasonable return on investment (ROI).
- Increased revenue.

What's more, depending on the technology, other benefits will make certain technologies too tempting to resist, even if their results are difficult to quantify. For example, it may be difficult for a company to prove that the adoption of a social networking application has resulted in:

- Increased access to information.
- Increased customer retention.
- Improved employee productivity and communication.

Ironically, Enterprise 2.0 technologies can be used to track these very measures, as described in Chapter 11.

Ultimately, this might not matter. To continue with the example, an organization may not be willing to pony up $1 million for a social networking application with uncertain benefits. However, if that same organization can test-drive the application for $2,000 per month and has a reasonable level of success after only a few months, then the uncertain upside is more than justified by the relatively minimal up-front cost.

Business Imperative

An Enterprise 2.0 technology may become a differentiator. As mentioned in Chapter 20, for example, environmentally friendly organizations might have a competitive advantage over others, resulting in better access to qualified job applicants and more employees. In other words, an organization may have to keep up with the Joneses in order to stay competitive.

Also consider organizations' need to minimize costs. Remember that many clients of on-premises software vendors pay for shelfware—software owned by the organization but not used in a production environment. To trim costs, the organization may replace its vendor with an SaaS alternative, figuring that the pay-per-transaction or pay-per-use model simply makes more sense.

Risks and Rewards

Despite the enormous amount of information available to them, it's unlikely that CXOs will ever have complete or perfect information to make decisions.

Most would settle for having the *right* information at the *right* time. At some point, the perceived rewards of Enterprise 2.0 technologies will outweigh the risks. Each organization will have its own tipping point, with some deciding earlier than others to take the plunge. Lessons learned will only increase, and the gap between rewards and risks will only increase. Organizations now that effectively use ESR, for example, may be the exception to the rule. In five years, faced with undeniable benefits of being able to Google enterprise data, organizations *without* ESR (or some equivalent) will stand out just as much.

From an ERM standpoint, many shareholders will insist that organizations minimize risk, using Enterprise 2.0 technologies to proactively address problems before they become crises.

Where Are We Going?

Yes, greenfield start-ups have innate advantages over larger organizations in adopting Enterprise 2.0 technologies. This is not to say, however, that large organizations are standing idly by as the world passes them by. This book has listed many examples of old-school organizations that have used technology in very unusual ways to produce amazing results. IBM and Wal-Mart are only two cases in point.

More examples and case studies become available every day. Enterprise software behemoth SAP has been reworking its complicated—and some would say unwieldy—applications to make them more Enterprise 2.0 friendly. In August 2009 at the organization's third annual Academic Research Conference, SAP chief executive Hasso Plattner demonstrated future functionality designed to enable its customers to analyze unstructured, contextual data.

Enterprise 2.0 expert Oliver Marks writes on his blog that SAP's new tools will offer

> *increased transaction speed (stuff happens on screen quicker) combined with broader surfacing of contextual data (more valuable information appears around the subject you are looking at). Plattner envisages a future world where executives sit in a business 'cockpit' combining the human-to-human communication strengths of Cisco's Telepresence with sophisticated contextual data dialed up on the fly in a much more agile future SAP enterprise infrastructure. To achieve this Plattner's institute has been investigating stripping down the complexity of the dozens of database tables to two columnar constructs.*[1]

---

[1]http://blogs.zdnet.com/collaboration/?p=846&alertspromo=&tag=nl.rSINGLE.

You read right: SAP is embracing collaboration, BI, cloud computing, agile software development, and other emerging technologies. For those familiar with the company, its shift in mind-set is a far cry from its historically conservative stance regarding embracing newer technologies. Translation: Even technological stalwarts are embracing Enterprise 2.0.

A System of Systems

While many of the technologies in this book address different aspects of organizations and offer different benefits, all have several things in common. First, they generally allow for greater automation and integration of formerly disparate and isolated systems, business processes, and networks. Second, they allow organizations and end users to create, generate, store, retrieve, and analyze data more effectively than their predecessors. Finally, Enterprise 2.0 technologies are built to maximize speed and power. Collectively, these technologies are hastening the path toward a system of systems.

In a 2004 white paper entitled "A System of Systems: Perspective for Decision-Support," the authors define a system of systems as "a collection of task-oriented or dedicated systems that pool their resources and capabilities together to obtain a new, more complex 'meta-system' which offers more functionality and performance than simply the sum of the constituent systems." The authors go on to note that "systems of systems is a critical research discipline for which frames of reference, thought processes, quantitative analysis, tools, and design methods are incomplete." In other words, while technology is allowing systems, applications, and data to become increasingly interconnected, we currently lack a comprehensive framework for understanding each technology, the totality of technologies, and their implications.

Final Thoughts

In *Technopoly: The Surrender of Culture to Technology*, Neil Postman tells an amazing story about the advent of the mechanical clock in the twelfth and thirteenth centuries. Postman writes that "the impetus behind the invention was to provide a more or less precise regularity of the routines of monasteries, which required, among other things, seven periods of devotion during the course of the day." Of course, the mechanical clock was used for a great deal more than that, allowing for standardized production methods and the very notion of a regular workday. In a nutshell, the clock ultimately enabled modern-day capitalism.

Postman continues, writing that "the paradox, the surprise, and the wonder are that the clock was invented by men who wanted to devote themselves more rigorously to God; it ended as the technology of greatest use to men who wished to devote themselves to the accumulation of money. In the eternal struggle between God and Mammon,[2] the clock quite unpredictably favored the latter."

Postman's fable resonates today. In the end, no one has a crystal ball predicting how any technology will ultimately be used and by whom. Even the experts in this very book cannot foresee with any degree of certainty where we are going, much less how we are going to get there.[3] In five years, any one of the Enterprise 2.0 technologies discussed in this book may have already fizzled. We may look back at any one of them and say, "What were we thinking?"

For instance, while clouds may be all the rage today, something may happen that obviates the need for that very technology. Something else may come along making its predecessor seem dated, bulky, less secure, expensive, or simply impractical. Perhaps there will be a high-profile IT project failure with social networking, and many organizations will subsequently retreat. One thing is certain, however: It will be a bumpy but exciting ride with magnificent rewards at the end for those able to find opportunity in chaos.

---

[2]The *Oxford Advanced Learner's Dictionary* defines Mammon as a god of wealth, regarded as evil or immoral.
[3]Indeed, a few of the contributors had to revise their contributions toward the end of the writing process precisely because events took place that changed the landscape of a technology, such as Apple's deal in late August 2009 to sell its iPhone in China.

Bibliography

Adam, C., and V. Katos. "The Ubiquitous Mobile and Location-Awareness Time Bomb." *Cutter IT Journal* 18, no. 6 (June 2005): 20–26.

Akcayli, E., D. Brooks, J. Laszlo, and S. McAteer. "Location-Aware Applications—Improving End-User Value Despite Carrier Hesitation." *Jupiter Research* 3 (November 20, 2001).

Aldeman, Sid, Larissa Moss, and Majid Abai. *Data Strategy*. Upper Saddle River, NJ: Pearson Education, 2005.

Anderson, Chris. *Free: The Future of a Radical Price*. New York: Hyperion, 2009.

Anderson, Chris. *The Long Tail*. Rev. ed. New York: Hyperion, 2009.

Arunatileka, D., and B. Unhelkar. "Mobile Technologies, Providing New Possibilities in Customer Relationship Management." Proceedings of 5th International Information Technology Conference, Colombo, Sri Lanka, December 2003.

Augustine, Sanjiv. *Managing Agile Projects*. Upper Saddle River, NJ: Prentice Hall, 2005.

Beinat, E. "Privacy and Location-Based Service." *Geo Informatics* (September 2001).

Berkun, Scott. *Making Things Happen: Mastering Project Management* (Theory in Practice). Sebastopol, CA: O'Reilly, 2008.

Berry, John. "A Democratic Revolution in Business Intelligence?" *Cutter Executive Update* (2006).

Brans, P. *Mobilize Your Enterprise: Achieving Competitive Advantage through Wireless Technology*. Upper Saddle River, NJ: Hewlett-Packard, Pearson Education as Prentice Hall PTR, 2003.

Butler, David. "MDM as a Foundation for SOA: An Oracle White Paper." Oracle, 2007.

Butler, David, and Stackowiak. "Master Data Management: An Oracle White Paper." Oracle, 2007.

Butler, Maureen. "Building the Business Case (Parts 1, 2, 3 and 4)." Hub Designs Blog, 2008.

Carr, Nicholas. *Does IT Matter? Information Technology and the Corrosion of Competitive Advantage*. Boston: Harvard Business School Press, 2004.

Carrol, Paul B., and Chunda Mui. *Billion-Dollar Lessons: What You Can Learn from the Most Inexcusable Business Failures of the Last 25 Years*. New York: Portfolio Hardcover, 2008.

Cohen, Adam. *The Perfect Store: Inside eBay*. New York: Back Bay Books, 2003.

Collins, Jim. *How the Mighty Fall: And Why Some Companies Never Give In*. Np: Author, 2009.

Constantine, L. L., and L. A. D. Lockwood. *Software for Use: A Practical Guide to Models and Methods of Usage-Centered Design*. Boston: Addison-Wesley, 1999. Also see www.foruse.com.

Deshpande, Y., S. Murugesan, B. Unhelkar, and D. Arunatileka.Workshop on "Device Independent Web Engineering: Methodological Considerations and Challenges in Moving Web Applications from Desk-Top to Diverse Mobile Devices." Proceedings of the Device Independent Web Engineering Workshop, Munich, 2004.

Devereaus, M., and R. Johansen. *Global Work: Bridging Distance, Culture and Time*. San Francisco: Jossey-Bass, 1994, 38–39.

Dyché, Jill, and Evan Levy. *Customer Data Integration*. Hoboken, NJ: John Wiley & Sons, 2006.

Elliott, G., and N. Phillips. *Mobile Commerce and Wireless Computing Systems*. Harlow, England: Pearson/Addison-Wesley, 2004.

English, Larry P. *Improving Data Warehouse and Business Information Quality: Methods for Reducing Costs and Increasing Profits*. New York: John Wiley & Sons, 1999.

Evans, Nicholas D. *Business Innovation and Disruptive Technology: Harnessing the Power of Breakthrough Technology for Competitive Advantage*. Upper Saddle River, NJ: FT Press, 2002.

Ferguson, Mike. "Getting Started with Master Data Management." Intelligent Business Strategies, 2008.

Fink, S. "The Fine Line between Location-Based Services and Privacy: Public Safety Report." *Radio Resource* 17, no. 7 (August 2002).

Fisher, Tony. *The Data Asset: How Smart Organizations Govern Their Data for Business Success*. Hoboken, NJ: John Wiley & Sons, 2009.

Frappaolo, Carl, and Dan Keldsen. *What Is Web 2.0?* Association for Information and Image Management, 2008.

Ginige, A., S. Murugesan, and P. Kazanis. "A Road Map for Successfully Transforming SMEs into e-Businesses." *Cutter IT Journal* 14 (2001).

Godbole, N. "Mobile Computing: Security Issues in Hand-Held Devices." Paper presented at the National Seminar on Networking and e-Security by the Computer Society of India, 2003.

Godbole, N., and B. Unhelkar. "Enhancing Quality of Mobile Applications through Modeling." Proceedings of the Computer Society of India's 35th Convention, Indian Institute of Technology, Delhi, India, December 2003.

Gray, Patrick. *Breakthrough IT: Supercharging Organizational Value through Technology.* Hoboken, NJ: John Wiley & Sons, 2007.

Griffin, Jane. "Overcoming Challenges to Master Data Management Implementation." *Information Strategy* (2006).

Hamel, Gary, and Bill Breen. *The Future of Management.* Boston: Harvard Business Press, 2007.

Hammer, Michael. *The Agenda.* New York: Random House, 2001.

Hansen, Dain. "Demystifying Data Federation for SOA." *SOA Magazine* (2008).

Harmon, R. R., and G. Laird. "Linking Marketing Strategy to Customer Value: Implications for Technology Marketers." In *Innovation in Technology Management: The Key to Global Leadership*, edited by D. F. Kocaoglu et al., 896–900. Portland International Conference on Management and Technology July 27–31, 1997.

Hazra, Tushar K. "Smart Sourcing: Myths, Truths, and Realities." *Cutter IT Journal* 19, no. 12 (December 2006).

Hazra, Tushar K. "SOA Governance: Building on the Old, Embracing the New." *Cutter IT Journal* 20, no. 6 (June 2007).

Hentzen, Whil. *The Software Developer's Guide.* 3rd ed. Milwaukee, WI: Hentzenwerke Publishing, 2002.

Ho, S. Y., and S. H. Kwok. "The Attraction of Personalized Service for Users in Mobile Commerce: An Empirical Study." *ACMSI Gecom Exchanges* 3, no. 4 (2003): 10–18.

Hsu, H. Y. S., G. C. Burner, and S. Kulviwat. "Personalization in Mobile Commerce." Proceedings of the IRMA Conference 2005, San Diego, California, 2005.

Hurwitz, Judith, Carol Baroudi, Robin Bloor, and Marcia Kaufman. *Service Oriented Architecture for Dummies.* 2nd ed. Hoboken, NJ: John Wiley & Sons, 2009.

Kanter, T. "Going Wireless, Enabling an Adaptive and Extensible Environment." *Mobile Networks and Applications* 8, issue 1 (February 2003): 37–50.

Kelly, Jeff. "Data Federation Technology Complements Fragmented Data Warehouses." SearchDataManagement.com, 2009.

Kimball, Bruce, and Margy, Ross. *The Data Warehouse Toolkit: The Complete Guide to Dimensional Modeling (Second Edition).* 2nd ed. Hoboken, NJ: John Wiley & Sons, 2002.

Lan, Y., and B. Unhelkar. *Global Enterprise Transitions.* IDEAS Group Publication. Hershey, PA: IGI Press, 2005.

Lazzaro, Joseph J. *Adaptive Technologies for Learning & Work Environments.* 2nd ed. Washington, DC: American Library Association, 2001.

Liker, Jeffrey K. *The Toyota Way: 14 Management Principles from the World's Greatest Manufacturer.* New York: McGraw-Hill Professional, 2004.

Lipták, Béla G. *Instrument Engineers' Handbook: Process Control and Optimization.* Boca Raton, FL: CRC Press, 2006.

Loshin, David. *Master Data Management.* Burlington, MA: Morgan Kaufmann, 2008.

MacIver, Kenny. "Driving Value from Data—Survey Results." *Information Age,* May 19, 2009.

Marlin, Steven. "What's in Capital One's Wallet?" *InformationWeek,* September 19, 2005.

Marmaridis, Ioakim (Makis), and B. Unhelkar. "Challenges in Mobile Transformations: A Requirements Modeling Perspective for Small and Medium Enterprises." Proceedings of International Conference on Mobile Business, Sydney, Australia, 2005.

McAfee, Andrew P. "Enterprise 2.0: The Dawn of Emergent Collaboration." *Sloan Management Review* 47, no. 3 (2006): 21–28.

McKnight, L., and James Howison. "Wireless Grids: Distributed Resource Sharing by Mobile, Nomadic, and Fixed Devices." *IEEE Internet Computing* (July/August 2004), http://dsonline.computer.org/0407/f/w4gei.htm (last accessed July 19, 2004).

McKnight, William. "Justifying and Implementing Master Data Management." Information Management, Lucidity Consulting Group, February 2009.

Meeker, Heather. *The Open Source Alternative: Understanding Risks and Leveraging Opportunities.* Hoboken, NJ: John Wiley & Sons, 2008.

Moeller, Robert R. *Sarbanes-Oxley and the New Internal Auditing Rules.* Hoboken, NJ: John Wiley & Sons, 2004.

Murugesan, S., ed. *Handbook of Research in Web 2.0, Web 3.0 and Beyond.* Hershey, PA: IGI Global Publications.

Murugesan, S., Y. Deshpande, S. Hansen, and A. Ginige. "Web Engineering: A New Discipline for Development of Web-Based Systems." In *Web Engineering: Managing Diversity and Complexity of Web Application Development,* edited by S. Murugesan and Y. Deshpande. Berlin, Germany: Springer-Verlag, 2001.

Papows, Jeff. *Enterprise.com: Market Leadership in the Information Age.* New York: Perseus Books, 1999.

Piktialis, Diane. "How 'Reverse Mentoring' Can Make Your Organization More Effective." Encore Careers, January 26, 2009.

Poppendieck, Mary, and Tom Poppendieck. *Lean Software Development.* Boston: Addison-Wesley, 2003.

Popper, S., S. Bankes, R. Callaway, and D. DeLaurentis. *System-of-Systems Symposium: Report on a Summer Conversation.* July 21–22, 2004, Potomac Institute for Policy Studies, Arlington, VA.

Postman, Neil. *Technopoly: The Surrender of Culture to Technology.* New York: Vintage, 1993.

Prem, E. "Innovative Mobile Services and Revenue Models." *EUTEMA Report*, February 2002.

Ranjbar, M., and B. Unhelkar. "Globalisation and Its Impact on Telecommuting: An Australian Perspective." Presented at International Business Information Management Conference (www.ibima.org), Cairo, Egypt, 2003.

Ranzal & Associates. "Avoiding Pitfalls in Designing a Master Data Management (MDM) Architecture." http://ranzal.wordpress.com/2008/12/08/avoiding-pitfalls-in-designing-a-master-data-management-mdm-architecture/.

Rao, B., and L. Minakakis. "Evolution of Mobile Location-Based Services." *Communications of the ACM* 46, no. 12 (2003): 61–65.

Ravn, Thomas, and Martin Høedholt. "How to Measure and Monitor the Data Quality of Master Data." *Information Management*, 2009.

Reinertsen, Donald. *Managing the Design Factory.* New York: Free Press, 1997.

Rico, D. F., H. H. Sayani, and S. Sone. *The Business Value of Agile Software Methods.* Ft. Lauderdale, FL: J. Ross Publishing, 2009.

Robinson, J. J. "The Integration Imperative." *Information Age*, February 13, 2009.

Robinson, J. J. "Master Data Management Shows Dramatic Growth." *Information Age*, December 11, 2008.

Schumpeter, Joseph A. *Capitalism, Socialism, and Democracy.* New York: Harper Perennial Modern Classics, 2008.

Schwaber, Ken, and Mike Beedle. *Agile Software Development with Scrum.* Upper Saddle River, NJ: Prentice Hall, 2002.

S'duk, R., and B. Unhelkar. "Web Services Extending BPR to Industrial Process Reengineering." Proceedings of International Resource Management Association (IRMA) Conference (www.irma-international.org), San Diego, May 15-18, 2005.

Smalltree, Hannah. "Gartner and Forrester Refute Master Data Management System Claims." SearchDataManagement.com, 2006.

Smalltree, Hannah. "How to Build a Business Case for Master Data Management." SearchDataManagement.com, 2005.

Subramanian, C., A. Kuppuswami, and B. Unhelkar. "Relevance of State, Nature, Scale and Location of Business e-Transformation in Web Services." Proceedings of the 2004 International Symposium on Web Services and Applications, Las Vegas, Nevada, June 21–24, 2004, www.world-academy-of-science.org.

Takeuchi, Hirotaka, and Ikujiro Nonaka. "The New New Product Development Game." *Harvard Business Review*, January 1, 1984.

Tapscott, Don. *Wikinomics: How Mass Collaboration Changes Everything.* New York: Portfolio Hardcover, 2008.

Unhelkar, B."Globalization with Mobility." Presented at 12th International Conference on Advanced Computing and Communications, Ahmedabad, India, 2004.

Unhelkar, B. "Mobile Enterprise Architecture: Models and Applications." *Cutter IT Executive Report* (April 2008).

Unhelkar, B. *Mobile Enterprise Transition and Management.* Boca Raton, FL: Taylor and Francis Auerbach Publications, 2009.

Unhelkar, B. "Paradigm Shift in the Process of Electronic Globalisation of Businesses Resulting from the Impact of Web Services Based Technologies." Paper presented at the IRMA, 2004.

Unhelkar, B. *Process Quality Assurance for UML-Based Projects.* Boston: Addison-Wesley, 2003.

Unhelkar, B. "Transitioning to a Mobile Enterprise: A Three-Dimensional Framework." *Cutter IT Journal* 18, no. 8 (2005).

Unhelkar, B. "Understanding Collaborations and Clusters in the e-Business World." We-B Conference (www.we-bcenter.com; with Edith Cowan University), Perth, Australia, November 23–24, 2003.

Unhelkar, B., and A. Dickens. "Lessons in Implementing 'Green' Business Strategies with ICT." *Cutter IT Journal* (February 2008).

Unni, R., and R. R. Harmon. "Location-based services: Opportunities and challenges." In *Handbook of Research in Mobile Business: Technical, Methodological and Social Perspectives*, edited by Bhuvan Unhelkar. Hershey, PA: Idea Group Publishing, 18–34.

Ward, Patricia, and George Dafoulas. *Database Management Systems.* London: Thomson Learning, 2006.

Williams, D. H. "It's the (LBS) Applications, Stupid!" White paper, 2003, www.e911-lbs.com.

Wohl, Amy. *Succeeding at SaaS: Computing in the Cloud.* Np: Wohl Associates, 2008.

Wolter, Roger, and Kirk Haselden. "The What, Why, and How of Master Data Management." Seattle: Microsoft Corporation, 2006.

Younessi, H. "Strategic View on Creating Business Value through Mobile Technologies." Chapter 1 in *Handbook of Research in Mobile Business: Technical, Methodological and Social Perspectives*, 2nd ed., edited by B. Unhelkar. Hershey, PA: IGI Global, 2008.

Zeid, Aiman."Your BI Competency Center: A Blueprint for Successful Deployment," www.tdwi.org/Publications/BIJournal/display.aspx?ID=8131.

About the Author

Phil Simon is the author of the acclaimed book *Why New Systems Fail* (Cengage, 2010). He began independent software consulting in 2002 after six years of related corporate experience. He has cultivated over 30 clients from a wide variety of industries, including health care, manufacturing, retail, and the public sector. His consulting focuses on helping organizations optimize their use of different technologies.

While not consulting, Phil speaks about how organizations can more effectively deploy technologies. He also writes for a number of technology-oriented media outlets.

He received a BS in policy and management from Carnegie Mellon University and a master's in industrial and labor relations from Cornell University.

An avid but poor golfer and respectable tennis player, Phil lives in northern New Jersey.

To find out more about Phil or read his blog, visit his web site: www .philsimonsystems.com.

Index